World Hunger

World Hunger

A Guide to the Economic and Political Dimensions

Nicole Ball

ABC-Clio

Santa Barbara, California Oxford, England

Library of Congress Cataloging in Publication Data

Ball, Nicole.
World hunger.

(War/peace bibliography series; 15)
Includes index.
1. Underdeveloped areas—Food supply—Bibliography. I. Title.
Z7164.F7B34 [HD9000.5] 016.3381'9'1724 80–22504
ISBN 0–87436–308–X

ABC-Clio, Inc.
Riviera Campus
2040 Alameda Padre Serra, Box 4397
Santa Barbara, California 93103

Clio Press Ltd.
Woodside House, Hinksey Hill
Oxford, OX1 5BE, England

1 2 3 4 5 6 7 8 9 0

Manufactured in the United States of America

The War/Peace Bibliography Series

RICHARD DEAN BURNS, EDITOR

#1 *Songs of Protest, War & Peace*
A Bibliography & Discography
R. SERGE DENISOFF

#2 *Warfare in Primitive Societies*
A Bibliography
WILLIAM TULIO DIVALE

#3 *Guide to the Vietnam Conflict, 2 ed.*
Its Geographical Dimensions, Political Traumas & Military Developments
MILTON LEITENBERG & RICHARD DEAN BURNS

#4 *The Arab-Israeli Conflict*
A Historical, Political, Social & Military Bibliography
RONALD M. DEVORE

#5 *Modern Revolutions and Revolutionists*
A Bibliography
ROBERT BLACKEY

#6 *Arms Control & Disarmament*
A Bibliography
RICHARD DEAN BURNS

#7 *The United States in World War I*
A Selected Bibliography
RONALD SCHAFFER

#8 *Uncertain Judgment*
A Bibliography of War Crimes Trials
JOHN R. LEWIS

#9 *The Soviet Navy, 1941–1978*
A Guide to Sources in English
MYRON J. SMITH, JR.

#10 *The Soviet Air and Strategic Rocket Forces, 1939–1980*
A Guide to Sources in English
MYRON J. SMITH, JR.

#11 *The Soviet Army* (tentative title)
A Guide to Sources in English
MYRON J. SMITH, JR.

#12 *The Secret Wars*
A Guide to Sources in English
Volume I: Intelligence, Propaganda and Psychological Warfare, Resistance Movements, and Secret Operations, 1939–1945
MYRON J. SMITH, JR.

#13 *The Secret Wars*
A Guide to Sources in English
Volume II: Intelligence, Propaganda and Psychological Warfare, Covert Operations, 1945–1980
MYRON J. SMITH, JR.

#14 *The Secret Wars*
A Guide to Sources in English
Volume III: International Terrorism, 1968–1980
MYRON J. SMITH, JR.

#15 *World Hunger*
A Guide to the Economic and Political Dimensions
NICOLE BALL

#16 *Peace and War*
A Guide to Bibliographies
BERENICE A. CARROLL, CLINTON F. FINK & JANE E. MOHRAZ

About the War/Peace Bibliography Series

With this bibliographical series, the Center for the Study of Armament and Disarmament, California State University, Los Angeles, seeks to promote a wider understanding of martial violence and the alternatives to its employment. The Center, which was formed by concerned faculty and students in 1962–63, has as its primary objective the stimulation of intelligent discussion of war/peace issues. More precisely, the Center has undertaken two essential functions: (1) to collect and catalogue materials bearing on war/peace issues; and (2) to aid faculty, students, and the public in their individual and collective probing of the historical, political, economic, philosophical, technical, and psychological facts of these fundamental problems.

This bibliographical series is, obviously, one tool with which we may more effectively approach our task. Each issue in this series is intended to provide a comprehensive "working," rather than definitive, bibliography on a relatively narrow theme within the spectrum of war/peace studies. While we hope this series will prove to be a useful tool, we also solicit your comments regarding its format, contents, and topics.

RICHARD DEAN BURNS
SERIES EDITOR

List of Abbreviations

ACAST	The Advisory Committee on the Application of Science and Technology to Development
ADB	Asian Development Bank
CADU	Chilalo Agricultural Development Unit
ECA	Economic Commission for Africa
ECAFE	Economic Commission for Asia and the Far East
ECLA	Economic Commission for Latin America
EEC	European Economic Community
FAO	Food and Agriculture Organization
HYC	High-yielding variety (grain)
ICP	Industry Cooperative Programme
ICP	Integrated Commodity Program
ILO	International Labour Office
ILR	International Labour Review
IMF	International Monetary Fund
IRRI	International Rice Research Institute
LAAD	Latin American Agribusiness Development Corporation
MSA	Most Seriously Affected (Nations)
NIEO	New International Economic Order
OECD	Organization for Economic Cooperation and Development
OPEC	Organization of Petroleum Exporting Countries
OPIC	Overseas Private Investment Corporation, a quasi-governmental agency of U. S. government
P.L. 480	Public Law-480

SFDA	Small Farmers' Development Agency (India)
UN	United Nations
UNEP	United Nations Environment Programme
UNICEF	United Nation's Children's Fund
UNCTAD	United Nations Conference on Trade and Development
UNIDO	United Nations Industrial Development Organization
UNRISD	United Nations Research Institute for Social Development
UNDP	United Nations Development Programme
US	United States
USAID	United States Agency for International Development
WEP	World Employment Programme

Acknowledgments

I would like to thank Richard Dean Burns who first suggested I prepare this bibliography, the many research librarians—particularly those at Cornell University—who have patiently answered my questions over the last two years, and Milton Leitenberg who has provided me with much appreciated support.

Contents

Foreword

INCLUSION OF THIS BIBLIOGRAPHY on world hunger in the War/Peace Bibliography Series published by ABC-Clio is a clear recognition that hunger and underdevelopment are forms of violence and sources of conflict. Nicole Ball, who prepared this outstanding instrument for researchers, the first of its kind, subtitled her work *A Guide to the Economic and Political Dimensions.* This in itself is a step forward for scholarship. Indeed, until recently, hunger was generally regarded as a technical problem, amenable to technical solutions, or at most as the temporary malfunctioning of an essentially viable world economic system. Ball, both in her general introduction and her headings for subsections, correctly guides the reader toward those studies which examine hunger as a function of poverty and poverty as a function of fundamentally inequitable power structures both within and between nations. She has done this as competently as she has collected the source materials—which is saying a great deal—and this foreword need not restate her fully justified conclusions.

Ball has also given us an important tool for examining how the allocation of power influences scholarship itself. A bibliography is not merely a convenience to the general reader and a time-saver for academics in libraries. It is also, particularly in the present case, a contribution to the sociology of knowledge—a documentary record of the ways in which scholars and institutions have viewed one of the great issues of their time. If we try to analyze this bibliography as an object in itself—concentrating not, as most of the following entries do, on poverty and hunger, but on what has been said about them—we may ask a few basic questions conducive to healthy critical thinking.[1]

First question: Who is doing the talking? Which is to say, who is in a position to publish books, monographs, and scholarly articles on various aspects of world hunger and underdevelopment? Despite Ball's careful inclusion of many third world sources and authors (a rarity in

[1]This is the approach taken by Pierre Spitz, to whom I am much indebted, in "Silent Violence: Famine and Inequality" (entry 1924), a study of the significance of the views on inequality within and between nations, especially the views of those in a position to institutionalize violence against the poor and to deprive them of their right to food.

the bibliographical genre), she herself would be the first to admit that those who publish are mostly Westerners. In other words, certain groups have the power to make their views known. Whatever their personal hardships may have been, chronic hunger has surely not been among them. Just as there were no third world peasant representatives at the 1974 World Food Conference or at the 1979 World Conference on Agrarian Reform and Rural Development, so there are no hungry people speaking from direct and painful experience in these pages. Although it is perhaps not necessary to have known physical or social deprivation to write about them, one should still note that the works listed here proceed from a particular kind of external knowledge and that a collection of people with university educations, frequently PhDs, are, by any standards, part of a privileged minority. This does not, of course, predestine them to adopt the point of view characteristic of the group to which they belong, but statistically speaking, they are likely to share common intellectual or class biases and to ignore certain problems, not out of personal malice but because these problems may appear unworthy of notice or remain wholly invisible. Non-Western authors are not exempt from such tendencies, particularly when they have received their education under Western auspices.

These observations may become more persuasive when we ask a second question: What—and whom—are these authors talking about? The subject matter of most "development" writing is more circumscribed than such a copious bibliography suggests. The disregard for the specific problems of third world women in the male-dominated literature is one striking example (see, however, entries 776 to 830); the absence of consideration for peasants' specific agricultural knowledge as opposed to that of "scientific experts" is another. Cause for even more serious concern is the proportion of research devoted to the study of poor and powerless groups. This choice of subject is generally accompanied by a lack of interest in the doings of the rich and powerful in the same society. Research directed exclusively toward the victims of hunger, rather than toward their relationships with the powerful (locally, nationally, and internationally), helps to mask the basic reasons for the poor's lack of access to food. Such a focus may help to explain the success of the "overpopulation-is-the-cause-of-hunger" school. (Here, had Ball wished to provide an exhaustive bibliography, she might have needed roughly a third of the pages of this volume.) By placing the hunger problem squarely in the laps, figuratively and literally, of the people having the babies, scholarship has deflected attention from the responsibilities of the "haves" to the plight of the "have-nots," thus obviating the need for any changes in present power arrangements.

The sheer weight of the literature devoted to topics that are at best marginal in explaining, much less attacking, the root causes of poverty also stifles academic and public debate and creates confusion in the minds of the general public. And yet, in spite of such obvious cases of scholarly bias or blindspots, a significant portion of the academic establishment would still have us believe that the social sciences are objective, or in the jargon of the trade, "value-free"; that the social scientist is an impartial, politically neutral expert. Here a paraphrase of Orwell seems called for: All social scientists are neutral, but they are more neutral toward some social groups than toward others.

Third question: What goals does research serve, and whose goals are they? At one level, not so trivial as it might first appear, it serves the interests of the people publishing. All of us listed in these pages must live with the uncomfortable truth that at least a part of our own livelihood derives from the existence of the suffering of others. Our published works and inclusion in catalogs like this one may help us gain income or prestige and a higher rung on the career ladder. This in itself should cause us to feel in some way accountable to the third world countries and people who provided raw material for our research, or at least to our colleagues on the three poor continents. This, unfortunately, is not often the case. As of 1979, a massive publication on the Sahelian countries, compiled by a prestigious US university team, was unavailable to scholars in Upper Volta. This is not merely a lack of academic courtesy, but a demonstration of the social and political priorities and loyalties of mainstream scholarship.

What of the goals of research and the accountability of intellectuals at a more general level? Just as most work done in the physical and natural sciences ultimately serves production, so much social science eventually contributes to social control.

Research is intellectual production, and like other kinds of production, must be paid for. The government or international agencies and large foundations that fund scholarship have their own economic and political vision of what constitutes the desirable society. Viewed in this light, it is doubtful that (as Ball states in her introduction) "foundations sponsoring the HYV research and the plant scientists whom they employed *could have chosen* to address the question of developing 'peasant-biased' high-yielding varieties of seeds rather than the 'landlord-biased' varieties which ultimately became the basis of the 'seed-fertilizer [green] revolution'" (emphasis added). This revolution was, in fact, an alternative to agrarian reform, which implies redistribution of power; it was a means of increasing food production without upsetting entrenched interests (as well as a means of providing increased revenues to the Western firms supplying industrial inputs). The choices made by research sponsors were, from their point of view, altogether logical ones; the alternative of peasant-biased varieties was probably not even imagined, much less given serious consideration. Academic defenders of the green revolution—and they were legion—rarely bothered to ask "Production by whom? and for whom?"; questions which have now been answered, for example, in the case of India where substantial grain reserves exist partly because half the population is too poor to buy them.

Knowledge costs money, and money is not thrown away by those who dispose of it. It is no accident that our libraries are filled with studies on the hungry and poverty-stricken of the third world. Cynically but realistically put, the more one knows about those who may, in desperation, become restive and dangerous, the better tools one possesses for keeping them in check. Scholarship may also, wittingly or unwittingly, serve purely commercial interests. One fears, for instance, that the current vogue for studying "appropriate technology" may become a vehicle for introducing new dependency-creating products in societies where incomes are inadequate for the purchase of expensive high-technology goods, but which can contribute to Western corporate interests at their own level.

Finally, social scientists can also function as promoters of particular ideologies and help to create a climate in which development strategies devised by the powerful may be pursued without hindrance or criticism (entry 47 will do as an example). Intellectuals, as Noam Chomsky has put it, are "experts in legitimation" and in packaging concepts so that they will sell, even if the wrappings conceal shoddy and adulterated merchandise.

There are basically three paradigms or models in the literature of development and hunger alleviation. The first is the "growth/trickle-down" model, more fully described by Ball, which seeks the increase of gross national product through industrialization and by concentrating on those elements of society supposedly most "modern" or "entrepreneurial" (poor peasants, in contrast, are "backward" or "traditional," although it is no longer considered fashionable to say so). The accumulated wealth of these "modernizing elites" will, eventually, also benefit the worse-off. This model encourages the import of foreign capital and technology (as well as the implantation of multinational corporations) and assumes that the development process in the third world should be imitative of the one that occurred in the now industrialized Western countries. Economic and social control is concentrated in the hands of the classes which act as motors of growth. This paradigm presupposes harmony: harmony at the national level (the elites will somehow want to share their advantages with their poorer compatriots, toward whom their attitude is essentially benevolent); harmony at the international level, also called "interdependence" (the present world system is beneficial to all nations which should trade according to the principles of "comparative advantage"). Due to its generally recognized failure, this first model has lately been perceived as badly in need of a facelift. This has been undertaken but is largely rhetorical. New keywords are *basic needs* and *participation,* but as defined by experts, mostly from developed countries. Deprived people are neither to be consulted as to their needs nor allowed to participate to the degree that they might demand fundamental changes in existing patterns of income or power distribution.

The second model is based on "dependency theory" which holds that there is a center (the rich countries, with the US as the center of the center) and a periphery (the third world); and that the former has consistently exploited the latter since colonial times. The goal of development is thus to correct this historic and ongoing imbalance through the use of measures summed up in the New International Economic Order (NIEO) strategy: fair and stable prices for third world raw materials, free access to Northern markets for industrial goods, state control over multinational corporations' practices, alleviation of debt, etc. This model also rests on an assumption of global interdependence, but stresses that serious adjustments will have to be made in the world system so that all nations can benefit and achieve that mutuality of interests which does not yet exist. This is the stance from which nearly all third world governments (the so-called Group of 77) argue in international negotiations.

The third model does not deny the need for an NIEO, but tries to enrich this concept with a class analysis. The world is not merely divided into rich/powerful and poor/relatively powerless nations: all countries, including the rich ones, are characterized by a dominating and a dominated class (each, of course, with its own subdivisions). The NIEO is an incomplete solution to the problems of hunger and underdevelopment because nothing guarantees that increased national revenues will benefit the poor more than marginally. In the third model, the goal of development is not merely greater equality between states, but the decent livelihood and dignity of all human beings. Unlike the first model, this approach assumes not harmony but conflict. Third world elites will not give up their privileges without a struggle and will meanwhile prevent any substantial advantages from trickling down. Rich nations will continue to exploit poor ones, but industrialized country elites will also support their third world counterparts so that this exploitation may more conveniently continue.

People who work and write from the third model are convinced (frequently from field experience in underdeveloped countries) of the logic of the following propositions:

(1) Development (strategies, projects, innovations, etc.) which benefits the least favored classes or nations will not be acceptable to the dominant classes or nations unless their interests are also adequately served.
(2) Development (. . .) which benefits *only* the poor will be ignored, sabotaged, or otherwise suppressed by the powerful.
(3) Development (. . .) which serves the interests of the elites while doing positive harm to the poor will still be put into practice and if necessary maintained by violence so long as no basic change in the balance of social and political forces takes place.[2]

Advocates of the third model (to whom Nicole Ball frequently directs the reader's attention) see hope for the third world not in the greater integration of the less developed countries into the world system but in their greater independence from it. They call for self-reliance—the full use of all local material and human resources—before asking for outside help, and for a fundamental redistribution of power as the only way to end hunger and misery. *Basic needs,* yes, but as defined by the communities concerned; not so much *participation* as *empowerment*—the capacity to control those decisions which most affect one's life.

Has scholarship anything to contribute to the emergence and the enforcement of the third model (for which my own bias will be obvious)? Development students, researchers, and writers must address the needs of the most deprived and must be accountable for the work they produce. Students who see such accountability as an intellectual and moral imperative can begin by approaching the material listed here with their critical faculties on full alert and by asking the kinds of questions we have sketched here: Is the study part of the "conventional wisdom," or does it try to take an opposing or unpopular point of view? Where does it stand in relation to the above three models, i.e., to power? Does it presume harmony and proceed in a social and political vacuum? Could the work contribute to increasing the knowledge—and thus the manipulative capacity—of national or international elites?

The reader, and especially the writer, should not forget that researchers, too, stand somewhere in the power structure. Their work can be used by the rich against the poor, but one may also hope, vice versa. Why not turn our sights toward those who hold control, with a view to giving a clearer understanding of their activities to those whose lives

---

[2]Cf. a similar analysis in Barbara Chasin and Richard Franke, "Science vs. Ethics," *Science for the People,* July 1975.

they affect? This is often a difficult task, for the well-endowed are less vulnerable to scholarly scrutiny than those who have no choice but to let themselves be studied; we should accept this as a challenge.

The mass of scholarship listed here represents an incalculable number of man/woman hours devoted to examining various aspects of world hunger, and while all of us have been writing, the relative and absolute numbers of hungry and destitute people have vastly increased. It is time we ask ourselves why, as scholars, we are still discussing poverty and want, and apply ourselves to transforming the contents of future bibliographies into explosive devices and instruments of liberation.

SUSAN GEORGE
Transnational Institute
Paris, France

Introduction

HUNGER IN THE third world is a phenomenon familiar to any reasonably well informed citizen of the industrialized countries. For the past 30 years, organizations such as CARE and UNICEF have urged the affluent of the West to "give generously" to feed the starving children of Asia, Africa, and Latin America. Development agencies like the World Bank and USAID have pledged themselves time and again to eradicate poverty and hunger in the less-developed areas of the world. Yet, according to UN figures, per capita food production in all areas of the third world has been virtually stagnant since the mid-1950s.

As with many statistics relating to the third world, food production figures vary in reliability. For one thing, some countries are better equipped administratively to collect statistical information. For another, the most reliable figures are those for major food crops. Other foods form an important part of third world diets but are largely omitted from food statistics because they are unfamiliar to many agricultural experts and are gathered by women from a variety of places such as woods, the edges of fields, or small garden plots. An additional problem as far as per capita production figures are concerned is that the population estimates used in their calculation may also be inaccurate or out-of-date. Even if they were reasonably reliable, neither overall production figures nor per capita ones give any indication of the actual *distribution* of food stuffs, and statistics on distribution are scarce.

There are thus many problems involved in quantifying hunger. Nonetheless, the statistics do give an indication of the trends and it is clear from these that large segments of the population in most third world countries are malnourished. The 1970s have been particularly difficult in terms of third world hunger. In the early 1970s, production shortfalls in the USSR, China, India, and in West and East Africa caused world grain reserves, already at a very low level, to decline by approximately 30 percent. As a result, prices rose substantially and food aid was curtailed. For people whose cash income was low and who were unable, for one reason or another, to grow enough food for their own needs, the situation was grave. In order to prevent a repetition, or even a worsening, of this situation, the World Food Conference of 1974 called for the replenishment of grain reserves and increased emphasis on third world agricultural production. However, at the end of the 1970s, considerable pessimism about the global food situation was expressed by Maurice Williams, executive director of the World Food Council (an outgrowth of the 1974 World Food Conference).

> It is not possible to be optimistic or complacent in the face of evidence which indicates that there are probably more hungry and malnourished people in 1979 than the 450 million to whom the 1974 conference directed its attention.[1]

In 1976, the UN Department of Economic and Social Affairs surveyed the progress made by some 100 developing countries (with a combined population of about 1.8 billion) in fulfilling the goals of the Second Development Decade (entry 53). While the findings of this survey are subject to the same qualifications noted above concerning third world food production statistics, they do serve to give an idea of the magnitude of the problem.

It was found that between 1970 and 1975 only 27 percent of the countries surveyed were estimated to have reached or exceeded the target growth rate for the agricultural sector of 4 percent per year. More important, just under 10 percent of the combined population lived in these countries. In addition, it was the poorest countries which were found to have the lowest agricultural growth rates. About one-third of the countries surveyed were estimated to have both per capita incomes of less than $250 per year *and* agricultural growth rates of less than 2 percent per year. Fifty-three percent of the combined population lived in these low-income, low-productivity countries (Table 1).

The per capita figures were, if anything, less encouraging. Between 1971 and 1975, per capita agricultural production in 87 of the countries surveyed (accounting for 97 percent of the combined population, or 1.75 billion people) was estimated to have grown at less than 2.5 percent per year. That was less than the average annual rate of population growth in the same period. If one looks separately at the 45 Most Seriously Affected (MSA) nations, the situation was even more discouraging. In three-quarters of the MSA nations (with 93 percent of the MSA population), per capita agricultural production was estimated to have *decreased* in the years 1971-1975 (Table 2).

Overall agricultural output rose in the second half of the 1970s and some countries, notably India, had sufficient reserves to see them through at least one bad harvest. However, at the end of 1979, FAO officials expressed concern that the failure to replenish global food

[1] Henry Giniger, "Food Council Warned of Rising Hunger," *International Herald Tribune*, 6 September 1979, p. 5. (Reprinted from the *New York Times*.)

TABLE 1

Distribution of Gross Agricultural Growth Rates and Per Capita Income, 1970–1975

Rate of Growth in Agricultural Production, 1971–1975 (% per annum)	All Developing Countries[a]				Countries with 1970 per capita gross domestic product of									
					$100		$100-249		$250-499		$500-749		$750+	
	Number	Population (millions)[b]	% Total Population	Cumulative %	Number	Population[b] (millions)	Number	Population[b] (millions)	Number	Population[b] (millions)	Number	Population[b] (millions)	Number	Population[b] (millions)
<0	25	246	13.6	13.6	9	129	8	92	3	7	2	9	3	8
0.0-0.99	8	99	5.5	19.1	1	24	1	13	3	27	—	—	3	35
1.00-1.99	19	771	42.8	61.9	7	629	7	82	3	57	2	3	—	—
2.00-2.99	9	160	8.9	70.8	2	22	2	68	3	12	2	58	1	1
3.00-3.99	10	359	19.9	90.7	—	—	2	169	5	80	3	111	—	—
4.00-4.99	11	103	5.7	96.4	2	19	3	58	4	15	—	—	1	11
5.00+	16	64	3.6	100.0	1	6	3	10	7	37	2	4	3	8
Total	98	1,802	100.0	100.0	22	829	26	492	28	235	11	185	11	63

a = for which relevant data available
b = mid-1973 estimates

Source: Adapted from United Nations, Department of Economic and Social Affairs, *Economic and Social Progress in the Second Development Decade*, Report of the Secretary-General, E/5981. ST/ESA/68. New York: 1977, Table 7, p. 71.

TABLE 2

Distribution of Per Capita Agricultural Growth Rates, 1971–1975

Rate of growth of gross agricultural production, per capita (% per annum)	All Developing Countries[a]				Most Seriously Affected Countries	
	Number	Population[b]	% Total Population[b]	Cumulative %	% Countries[c]	% Population[b,c]
<0	58	1,260	69.9	69.9	74.0	93.0
0.0-0.4	9	117	6.5	76.4	5.0	1.0
0.5-0.9	9	275	15.3	91.7	5.0	2.0
1.0-1.4	5	75	4.2	95.9	5.0	2.0
1.5-1.9	3	15	0.8	96.7	2.0	<1.0
2.0-2.4	3	8	0.5	97.2	—	—
2.5-2.9	2	15	0.8	98.0	—	—
3.0-3.4	5	9	0.5	98.5	5.0	<1.0
3.5-3.9	2	9	0.5	99.0	—	—
4.0+	4	18	1.0	100.0	5.0	1.0
Total	100	1,801	100.0	100.0	101.0	101.0

a = for which relevant information available
b = mid-1973 estimates
c = totals do not equal 100 due to rounding.

Source: Adapted from United Nations, Department of Economic and Social Affairs, *Economic and Social Progress in the Second Development Decade,* Report of the Secretary-General, E/5981. ST/ESA/68. New York: 1977, Table 8, p. 72.

reserves would lead to a serious crisis if bad harvests occurred in two, or more, consecutive years.[2]

However, as a report on rural poverty produced by the International Labour Office has stressed, the food problem in the third world is by no means exclusively, or even largely, a production problem.

> Where the poor starve, it is not mainly because there is no food but because they do not have the wherewithal to acquire food. . . . The solution requires better distribution and more productive employment both to increase incentives to expand output and create effective demand for greater food output. (entry 1399, p. 17)

Within the limits imposed by the availability of data, this study documents a decline in the share of national income accruing to the lowest income groups in several South and Southeast Asian countries. Corresponding to this is a decline in the ability of the poor to purchase food, a problem that can only increase in severity as the number of rural landless grows.

According to the Economic Commission for Latin America (ECLA),

[2]"Bad Harvest Threatens Hungry Millions," *Observer,* 22 July 1979.

some 40 percent of all households in Latin America were living in "conditions of poverty" in 1970, with 50 percent of these being unable to purchase or produce enough food to ensure "a minimum adequate diet."

Considering the amount of resources—financial, human, and material—that have been devoted to economic development since the end of World War II, it may be surprising that the world food situation appears so bleak. One explanation of this apparent paradox lies in the nature of the development strategies followed by most third world countries during the last three decades. These development strategies grew out of the international economic system that evolved over the last 200 to 300 years. During the pre-colonial and colonial periods, Africa, Asia, and Latin America increasingly came to be seen as suppliers of primary products (raw materials and food crops) and as markets for finished goods from the industrializing "mother countries." Often indigenous "industries" such as weaving or ironsmithing were destroyed by this international division of labor. The emergence of nationalist movements during the 20th century in most of what is now called the third world did not alter this relationship appreciably. Where the bourgeoisie led these movements (and that was in most third world areas), they tended to be more interested in obtaining their share of the benefits to be derived from the prevailing economic system than in changing that system. As a result, once independence was won, these leaders followed development strategies that led their countries to be tied even more closely to the economies of the industrialized nations. Self-sustaining, self-reliant economic development was thus not sought, and its attainment in the future was made more difficult. (Entry 100 is recommended as an introduction to this topic.)

Until recently, conventional wisdom decreed that development strategies were to be "growth-oriented" and that reliance was to be placed on "modernizing elites" (i.e., the wealthy and powerful) in both the agricultural and the urban-industrial sectors. The idea behind this approach was that the "modernizing elites" were best placed to make efficient use of resources channeled into the economy as a whole. The emphasis was on the attainment of high growth rates because it was thought that the faster an economy grew, the more rapidly the benefits, originally given to only a small number of "progressive" farmers and businessmen, would "trickle down" to the poorer segments of society.

In addition, the conventional approach to development gave preference to the industrial sector in the allocation of resources because it was believed that the rich countries had "developed" by concentrating on industrial expansion and modernization. This emphasis on industry meant that the agricultural sector was relatively neglected. The expectation that economic development in the third world would follow the same pattern as it had in the now-industrialized nations led to the assumption that agriculture would progressively employ fewer and fewer people. The larger, wealthier landowners were thought to operate more efficiently than smallholders. Because of this and because large farms were the norm in the industrialized countries, such resources as were made available to the agricultural sector tended to be directed towards the larger, "progressive" farmers. World Bank President Robert McNamara has admitted that

> . . . very little has been done over the past two decades specifically designed to increase the productivity of subsistence agriculture. Neither political programs, nor economic plans, nor international assistance — bilateral or multilateral—have given the problem serious and sustained attention. The World Bank is no exception. In our more than a quarter century of operations, less than $1 billion out of our $25 billion of lending has been devoted directly to this problem. (entry 1253, p. 44)

Nevertheless, the agricultural sector was expected to play an important role in the development process. According to the FAO, a dynamic agricultural sector was required because

> . . . agricultural exports must provide the bulk of the foreign exchange earnings for the import of capital goods required for industrialization. Agriculture releases labor and often finance to industry. The agricultural population provides a market for industrial products, not only for consumer goods but also for a wide range of equipment and materials used in agricultural production. (entry 522, p. 3)

Thus, the conventional development strategy of the 1950s and 1960s did not alter the colonial-era pattern of third world countries providing raw materials and labor power for the industrialized countries while remaining dependent on the latter for a wide range of manufactures.

Not surprisingly, given the need for agriculture to earn foreign exchange, there has been considerable emphasis on the cultivation of export crops. Multinational corporations have become increasingly involved in this activity. Aid agencies have also promoted export crop production, often by directly aiding agribusiness firms. Not only is the cultivation of "traditional" cash crops (tea, coffee, jute, cotton, oilseeds, and so on) stressed, but multinationals have increasingly become involved in the production of meat, fresh and processed fruits and vegetables, seafood, dried and fresh flowers, and other luxury items. In some cases, the land on which these export crops are grown had been lying fallow. More often, however, land is withdrawn from food production for domestic, third world consumption in order to provide people in the developed countries with food that they do not really need.

In some instances, foreign companies own land in less-developed countries and produce export commodities on them as they choose. The well-known involvement of fruit companies such as Del Monte and United Brands in Central America is an excellent example of this alienation of land. Increasingly, however, corporations are opting for the "satellite farm" approach to producing crops for export. Contracts are signed with third world producers whereby the farmer agrees to produce a crop of a certain standard at a fixed price while the company provides the inputs and markets the produce. Farmers involved in this sort of scheme can be large landholders or people cultivating a relatively few acres. In either case, land that could and should be used for producing food to feed the millions of hungry people in the third world is used to feed the much smaller number of the world's food elites—the wealthy in developing countries and just about everyone in the developed world. (Entries 1887 and 1890 are recommended as introductions to this topic.)

The domestic food requirements of the third world have not been completely ignored. A good deal of the investment in food production for domestic, third world consumption has focused on the development and dissemination of high-yielding varieties (HYVs) of grain—initially wheat, rice, and maize—originally promoted by the Rockefeller Foundation and then jointly with the Ford Foundation. There was great hope that HYV technology would enable third world farmers to raise the productivity of their land significantly and thus help to eliminate hunger in the developing countries. Those who believed that the HYVs were the answer to the problem of hunger were buoyed by the initial success of the new seeds in India, Pakistan, Mexico, and the Philippines. They began to talk, in the late 1960s, of a "Green Revolution" and to predict that the next agricultural problem to confront the third world would be how to dispose of the surpluses generated by Green Revolution technology.

By the end of the 1960s, however, it began to be evident that the traditional development strategy was not working in a number of ways for most of the third world. Although some countries had managed to attain quite high rates of growth of their gross national product, poverty and hunger were widespread. Unemployment and underemployment were problems of considerable magnitude and were exacerbated by fairly rapid rates of population growth. Overpopulation was, in turn, recognized to be at least in part a result of poverty. The "trickle-down" approach simply had not worked for the most part. The concentration of development resources on "progressive" farmers and industrialists had all too often ended by increasing the wealth and power of those individuals at the expense of most of the rest of the people in the third world. ECLA reports, for example, that between the early 1960s and the early 1970s, 60 percent of the growth in incomes which occurred in Latin America accrued to the wealthiest 20 percent of the population while the income share of the poorest 40 percent declined from 10 percent to 9 percent.[3]

The failure of the industrial sector to become the "engine of growth" as once anticipated can be traced to the following problem: the wrong goods were produced by the wrong methods. As has been stressed by Ewing and Koch (among others),

> ... development rests on *two* pillars of production: (i) the goods and services needed for mass consumption, and (ii) the "muscle" required to make them, *viz.* the necessary intermediate and capital goods. (entry 78, pp. 459–460)

However, in many countries, industries producing luxury goods and light manufactures for export have obtained more of the investment resources than either of the "two pillars." What is more, because the capacity of third world economies to produce capital goods has been limited, developing countries have remained largely dependent on the industrialized countries for the machinery to run their industries. In part, this limited industrial capacity is a legacy of the colonial period. Perhaps even more important, it is also a result of the decision on the part of third world manufacturers and government officials to give preference to luxury items and export production and not to attempt to break out of the export-oriented development pattern.

A further complication has been that most of the machinery imported from the industrialized countries has been designed to be labor-saving and capital-intensive in accordance with the factor endowments (land, labor, and capital) of the industrialized countries. But whenever possible, developing countries need to use technologies with a relatively high labor content and relatively low capital intensity, in accordance with *their* factor endowments. As a result of all this, third world industrial sectors have not generated the amount of employment that development officials once thought they would, even under conditions of fairly rapid growth. Industrial sectors in many third world countries are now producing goods that the mass of the population is too poor to buy or which are designed for export, using too much capital and too little labor.

It is, however, in the rural areas of the third world that poverty is most severe. As UNRISD has pointed out (entry 54, p. 3), the statistical basis for assessing third-world income distribution, employment, and access to services is weak and it is difficult, in empirical terms, to prove

---

[3]"Latin American Economy in 1978," *Economic and Political Weekly* 15 (3 March 1979): 507–509, 511.

the continued existence of social injustice. Even so, UNRISD estimates that as much as half of the world's population may be negatively affected by the decline in the ability of small farmers to maintain self-sufficient farming systems and by the expansion of commercial farming systems. These two processes have led to the impoverishment of much of the peasantry in the third world and its incorporation—on unfavorable terms—into societies which are increasingly focusing on industrialization and production for the market (rather than for personal consumption).

By the early 1970s, it became increasingly evident that there were serious social problems associated with the Green Revolution. While some regions within developing countries were producing more food, large segments of the populations in those countries remained malnourished. The new seeds could be used only in certain areas, where irrigation was available, because of their heavy dependence on water. The requirements for the HYVs to produce up to expectations (primarily water, chemical fertilizers, pesticides) were expensive. This meant that it was easier for wealthier farmers with larger holdings to adopt the new seeds successfully. All too often, the larger landholders began to mechanize production, thereby expanding the number of landless laborers. Sometimes governmental policies exacerbated these shortcomings, for example by encouraging mechanization in order to have a fully "modern" agricultural sector.

It can be argued, as Lester Brown has done, that the growing economic disparities that appeared to come along with the Green Revolution were not the fault of the technology itself:

> The new seeds can be used with equal success by both large- and small-owners *if* the farmers have equal access to the requisite inputs and supporting services. [emphasis added] (entry 2006)

The agricultural technology that the Chinese have devised is similar in many ways to Green Revolution technology. Yet, the recent history of agricultural development in China has been different from that of India or Mexico, for example. The Chinese recognize technology's social component. They have attempted to implement *their* Green Revolution technology with the social goals they seek to attain firmly in mind. And despite problems, they have had more success than many other countries in distributing food produced equitably.

The trouble with Brown's analysis, and those of other Green Revolution proponents, is that they seem to forget that the "if" exists and is a formidable obstacle to the attainment of their objectives. Rather, they assume that because governments *ought* to behave in a certain way to obtain the greatest benefits for the greatest number of their citizens, governments *will* act in that way. History has shown otherwise. One of the major obstacles to the greater production of food and its more equitable distribution in the third world is inequitable land tenure arrangements. The second Asian agricultural survey (entry 2262) concluded that land ownership patterns act as an obstacle to development because they promote the *status quo* and lead the wealthier landowners to attempt to control or to take "active resistance to productive land or capital-saving innovation, even when these would be mutually beneficial to all economic or status groups" (entry 2262, p. 233).

However, most third world governments avoid the implementation of genuine land reform because they are politically dependent upon the large landowning classes for their political positions. The proponents of land reform who are often the proponents of less foreign intervention in the economies of the third world are not trusted by the foundations and aid agencies to run their countries according to the needs of the industrialized nations and, therefore, are not helped into positions of power. Only when the socio-economic imbalances are blatantly excessive—as in the case of Nicaragua—is opposition to change muted.

It should also be remembered that the foundations sponsoring the HYV research and the plant scientists whom they employed could have chosen to address the question of developing "peasant-biased" high-yielding varieties of seeds rather than the "landlord-biased" varieties which ultimately became the basis of the "seed-fertilizer revolution." Such seeds would have required minimum inputs and have been designed to make the most of the natural milieu in which they were grown. "Peasant-biased" seeds would not have eliminated all of the problems confronting small farmers but they might have minimized them to some degree. At the very least, it is unlikely that they would have exacerbated peasants' problems to the extent that the "landlord-biased" seeds did.

It is nonetheless not entirely surprising that the possibility of developing "peasant-biased" seeds was not pursued by scientists or foundations. Researchers would have had to familiarize themselves with a multitude of local crops and ecological and social conditions. It was clearly much easier to work on crops familiar to North Americans and to assume a social setting similar to the one in the United States or Canada. This aspect of the Green Revolution raises serious questions about the extent to which technology transfer from the industrialized countries to the third world can actually benefit the latter, particularly the poorest individuals in the developing world.

When the International Development Strategy for the UN's Second Development Decade was formulated in 1970, it contained many fine words about the need for reducing inequality:

> It is essential to bring about a more equitable distribution of income and wealth for promoting both social justice and efficiency of production to raise substantially the level of employment, to achieve a greater degree of income security, to expand and improve facilities for education, health, nutrition, housing and social welfare, and to safeguard the environment. Thus, qualitative and structural changes in the society must go hand in hand with rapid economic growth, and existing disparities—regional, sectoral, and social—should be substantially reduced. (cited in entry 54, p. 2)

However, as the ILO found in its mid-term review of the International Development Strategy in 1975 (entry 34) and UNRISD found in its end-of-the-decade review (entry 54), these were not much more than fine words:

> Although the Strategy represents an undoubted advance over earlier statements of development objectives and policies . . . its implicit conceptual framework resembles the conventional development approach which has been the mainstay of economic development thinking since the end of the Second World War. . . . it is economic growth which turns out to be given the primary or even exclusive emphasis. (entry 34, p. 72)

Evidence is now mounting for the precise ways in which the "conventional development approach" has failed to produce development. A number of its tenets have been discredited. Consider, for example, the findings of the Second Asian Agricultural Survey in relation to the notion of the "progressive" farmer:

> Although large inequitable landholdings have been justified on the grounds that they promote agricultural output, the survey argued otherwise. Marginal savings behaviour [proportion of an increase in income which will be saved] is identical between large and small landholders, so that there is no greater mobilization of savings by the rich landowners. In addition, more equitably sized, though small, farms in South Korea and Taiwan have boosted productivity. (entry 2276, pp. 49–50)

Or the findings of the World Employment Programme in relation to the notion that economic growth can be best generated by concentrating on "modernizing elites":

> The question is not so much whether to sacrifice growth for employment or vice versa, as to choose among a number of paths towards growth which combine in various ways products different both in volume and in composition, with variable structural and temporal employment conditions. It is quite possible (as has been pointed out by the WEP country missions) that the choice of growth path oriented towards the creation of employment and the elimination of poverty may in fact result in a higher rather than a lower rate of economic growth. (entry 34, p. 75)

Furthermore, the export-oriented development strategy has not produced all the benefits ascribed to it. Despite the attainment of relatively high rates of growth by some developing countries at various points over the last two or three decades, nearly two-thirds of the 87 countries surveyed in Table 3 recorded either virtually no change or a decline in the average annual rate of growth of their per capita incomes between 1961/70 and 1971/75.

At least part of the problem can be traced to the fact that since the early 1950s the terms of trade have consistently favored the industrialized countries (Graph 1). This problem has been exacerbated by the oil price rises which have occurred since 1973. Not only have third world energy bills increased substantially, but the prices of goods imported from the industrialized countries also reflect the rising cost of fuel.

The failure of conventional development strategies to overcome the problem of poverty and rural stagnation in developing countries led many of the international lending agencies, notably the World Bank and USAID, to direct more of their resources towards third world rural sectors. They began to speak of focusing on "the poorest of the poor," "the forgotten 40 percent" of the world's population. For the Bank, the turning point came in 1973 when, in an address to the Board of Governors of the World Bank, McNamara stated,

> The data suggest that the decade of rapid growth has been accompanied by greater maldistribution of income in many developing countries, and that the problem is most severe in the countryside. . . .
>
> . . .In my view, therefore, there is no viable alternative to increase the productivity of small-scale agriculture if any significant advance is to be made in solving the problems of absolute poverty in rural areas. (entry 1253, pp. 10, 14)

While it cannot be denied that more resources should be concentrated in the rural sectors, it is open to debate whether an expansion of the activities of international aid agencies in the third world rural areas will help or hinder "the poorest of the poor."

The objectives of foreign aid have often been described in humanitarian terms, particularly in the last decade. Although there is no reason to believe that aid agency officials actively seek to harm the poor, post-World War II aid to the third world can be viewed as having served to perpetuate the economic and political imbalances both between the industrialized West and the third world and within third world countries themselves. One way in which this has occurred is through the support that projects sponsored by aid agencies have provided for the activities of multinational corporations.

Private business always invests with an eye toward profit, whether it operates in an already industrialized or in a less-developed country. In the third world, it has sought to obtain raw materials and labor power at the lowest possible prices. Frequently, however, private business has felt

TABLE 3

Distribution According to Changes in Rates of Growth in Per Capita Income Between 1961–1970 and 1971–1975

Countries in which, relative to the rate of increase in the 1960s, the average annual rate of increase 1971–1975 represents	Per capita gross domestic product 1970 (US dollars)	Average annual percentage rate of increase 1961–1970	1971–1975
Acceleration of >2%			
Gabon	671	6.6	15.9
Brazil	513	3.1	6.5
Fiji	424	2.4	4.8
Iraq	384	2.7	7.0
Dominican Republic	342	1.7	6.1
Algeria	320	1.1	3.4
Tunisia	281	2.4	7.5
Syrian Arab Republic	270	3.1	9.2
Ecuador	259	1.9	6.3
Mauritius	229	1.2	3.6
Botswana	135	3.5	15.1
Sudan	117	−0.4	2.3
Haiti	97	−0.8	2.0
Bangladesh	94	−1.1	1.3
Indonesia	86	1.0	3.7
Guinea	82	−1.4	1.0
Malawi	75	2.6	6.3
Burundi	67	−3.3	—
Acceleration of 0.6–2.0%			
Singapore	914	7.2	7.9
Trinidad & Tobago	912	2.3	3.4
Saudi Arabia	500	6.4	8.1
Iran	412	6.7	7.4
Malaysia	368	3.0	4.0
Colombia	350	1.9	3.0
Southern Rhodesia (Zimbabwe)	283	1.5	3.3
Republic of Korea	265	6.8	8.0
Paraguay	261	2.1	3.2
Senegal	217	−1.4	−0.7
Bolivia	213	2.8	3.3
Nigeria	145	2.9	4.2
Central African Empire	127	0.3	1.3
Somalia	90	−0.2	0.4
Zaire	88	−0.6	1.1
Chad	74	−1.7	−1.0
Mali	54	−1.7	−0.7

Countries in which, relative to the rate of increase in the 1960s, the average annual rate of increase 1971–1975 represents	Per capita gross domestic product 1970 (US dollars)	Average annual percentage rate of increase 1961–1970	1971–1975
More or Less Unchanged			
Argentina	1,071	2.9	2.6
Lebanon	640	1.9	1.9
Costa Rica	567	3.2	3.3
Peru	469	2.5	2.5
Guatemala	359	2.6	2.6
El Salvador	293	2.1	1.8
Angola	290	2.5	2.9
Ghana	257	0.7	0.7
Morocco	222	1.3	1.5
Philippines	182	2.2	2.6
Thailand	181	4.5	4.1
Kenya	143	1.7	2.2
Nepal	80	0.9	0.5
Afghanistan	56	0.1	0.6
Decline of 0.6–1.9%			
Venezuela	1,094	2.5	1.7
Uruguay	831	0.4	−0.7
Mexico	666	3.6	2.3
Nicaragua	422	3.6	1.8
Guyana	376	1.1	—
Ivory Coast	347	5.5	4.5
Swaziland	277	6.2	4.4
Sri Lanka	179	3.0	2.4
Mauritania	164	3.4	2.9
Comoros	109	2.9	1.5
India	99	1.4	0.9
United Republic of Tanzania	97	2.7	1.2
Benin	82	0.8	−0.2
Burma	78	2.2	0.6
Ethiopia	72	1.9	0.8
Lesotho	66	3.6	1.8
Rwanda	60	1.6	0.1
Decline of >1.9%			
Kuwait	3,544	−4.0	−8.0
Libyan Arab Jamahiriya	1,021	15.9	−5.2
Chile	887	2.3	−2.9
Surinam	833	4.8	−0.8
Réunion	830	7.6	1.9
Hong Kong	782	7.1	3.5
Panama	717	4.9	2.3

Countries in which, relative to the rate of increase in the 1960s, the average annual rate of increase 1971–1975 represents	Per capita gross domestic product 1970 (US dollars)	Average annual percentage rate of increase 1961–1970	1971–1975
Barbados	697	6.3	−0.9
Jamaica	681	3.6	−0.2
Namibia	565	6.0	1.9
(Decline of >1.9%)			
Zambia	410	3.8	−1.1
Papua New Guinea	289	5.1	2.0
Honduras	280	1.5	−1.0
Liberia	268	3.6	1.2
Equatorial Guinea	266	2.0	−4.3
Guinea-Bissau	262	4.7	0.1
Jordan	258	2.6	−0.4
Congo	238	6.0	2.5
Mozambique	222	3.1	−3.1
Cape Verde	220	6.0	−2.1
Egypt	217	3.1	−0.4
United Republic of Cameroon	187	3.7	1.3
Pakistan	175	3.7	0.3
Sierra Leone	161	3.5	−0.3
Togo	135	5.1	1.4
Uganda	135	2.4	−3.0
Madagascar	130	0.5	−2.1
Democratic Kampuchea	107	−0.8	—
Gambia	100	2.8	−0.3
Niger	91	−0.7	−5.8
Upper Volta	64	1.9	−0.7

Source: United Nations, Department of Economic and Social Affairs, *Economic and Social Progress in the Second Development Decade,* Report of the Secretary-General. E/5981. ST/ESA/68. New York: 1977, Table 5, pp. 66–68.

that it needed help in expanding into developing regions. Foreign aid has provided the necessary assistance.

Prabhat Patnaik, an Indian economist, has pointed out that,

> From its very infancy, capital has needed the support and protection of a nation state. Aid was a means by which the metropolitan State, by putting pressures on the underdeveloped State, supported the operations of its own national capital—be these trade or investment—in the latter's territory. (entry 100, p. 204)

In many instances during the last 30 years, this "support and protection" has come from bilateral (national) aid agencies such as USAID. In

GRAPH 1
Terms of Trade, 1938–1971
(1950 = 100)

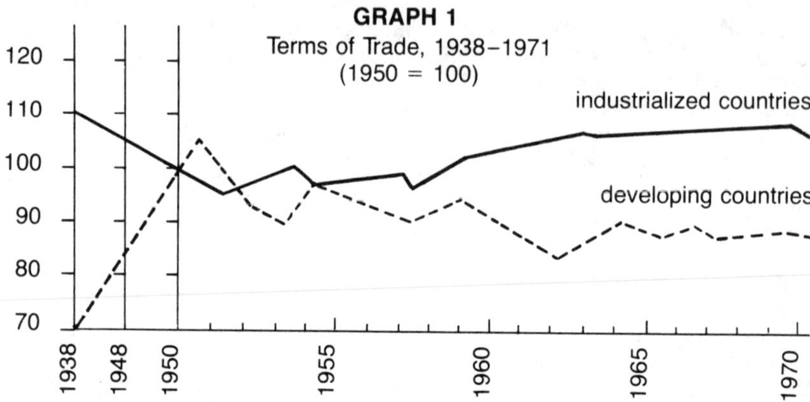

Source: *IBRD Trends, 1973,* as presented in Swedish International Development Authority, *Kort och Lätt om Sveriges Samarbete med U-Länderna,* Stockholm: 1977, p. 20.

the mid-1960s, for example, an AID official testified before a Congressional committee that,

> The fostering of a vigorous and expanding private sector in the less developed countries is one of our most important responsibilities. . . . We can and do endeavor to influence relevant attitudes directly. . . . Already we can see evidence of such ideological evolution in some key countries. For instance, Colombia, Venezuela, Ethiopia, the Philippines, India and Pakistan have taken practical measures to improve the climate for private foreign enterprise. (entry 1887, pp. 72–73, Penguin ed.)

Multinational agencies such as the World Bank, the FAO, or UNDP provide similar "support and protection." The Bank, for example, has tended to concentrate on projects that strengthen the infrastructure of a poor country (transportation and communications, power, irrigation, flood control, etc.). Without such improvements, foreign corporations can be slow to invest in third world economies: their operations will be more difficult; they might have to provide some of the infrastructure themselves; and, as a result, their profit margins could be reduced.

Multilateral agencies have also assisted multinational corporations directly. Until 1978, there was a bureau within the FAO called the Industry Cooperative Programme (ICP). This was, in essence, the voice of agribusiness in the UN as well as the means by which specific agribusiness firms became involved in FAO-sponsored projects. Ejected from the FAO following accusations that the investments it supported failed to benefit local people, the ICP began to seek a new home for itself within the UN system. By mid-1979, it had convinced the United Nations Development Programme to grant it affiliate status under the name of Industrial Cooperation for Development. A similar unit, called the International Finance Corporation, has been part of the World Bank since 1964.

As for USAID,

> . . . the chief administrator of AID serves at the same time as the chairperson of OPIC, an insurance and lending agency that puts the U.S. government squarely behind investments by multinational corporations in underdeveloped countries.
>
> AID directly aids some of the world's largest corporations. One case in point is the Latin American Agribusiness Development Corporation (LAAD), a holding company that numbers among its fifteen shareholders a Chase Manhattan agribusiness subsidiary, the Bank of America, Borden, Cargill, CPC International, John Deere, Gerber, Goodyear, Castle and Cook, Ralston Purina, and ADELA. . . . (entry 1607, p. 45)

Although aid agencies are now increasingly talking in terms of "redistribution from growth" rather than of "growth-for-its-own-sake" and Bank President McNamara has called for the adoption of "a socially oriented measure of economic performance" to replace gross national product, it remains to be seen if these changes are more than cosmetic. Aid agencies have not yet shown themselves willing to pressure third world governments into making the sort of structural changes necessary if the agricultural sector is to increase productivity substantially. Indeed, Robert McNamara insists that aid agencies find their hands pretty well tied:

> The need to reorient development policies in order to provide a more equitable distribution of the benefits of economic growth is beginning to be widely discussed. But very few countries have actually made serious moves in this direction. And I should stress that unless national governments redirect their policies toward better distribution, there is very little that international agencies such as the World Bank can do to accomplish this objective. (entry 1253, p. 11)

> . . . the potential for using Bank influence to press or even force the issue of structural reform on member countries is severely circumscribed. (cited in entry 1887, p. 259, Penguin ed.)

However, we have seen that USAID believed not only that it was capable of exerting such pressure, but also that it was its duty to do so. Nor should anyone be fooled by McNamara's disclaimers. The Bank can and has influenced the economic policy decisions of third world governments. What McNamara means is that *the World Bank is unwilling to "force the issue of structural reform."* The implications are serious. World hunger is a political problem. It can only be solved by political means. The history of post-World War II aid, particularly aid to the rural sector, has been one of attempting to resolve political and social problems by technical means. Most experts agree that low productivity in the agricultural sector is linked to the maldistribution of land. Yet, the "answer" to this problem offered by the foundations and aid agencies and largely accepted by third world governments was the Green Revolution. If each acre of land could be made to grow more food than previously, then it would be unnecessary to press for land reform. The question of what to do for those people who were too poor to purchase the anticipated surplus was seemingly not considered.

The Green Revolution may also have been seen as a "solution" to the cash crop versus food crop dilemma. The need to import a wide variety of items from industrialized countries that is implicit in the export-oriented development strategy and the fact that the terms of trade are almost always against the developing countries has meant that the temptation to increase the amount of land devoted to cash crops is great. It is no less great when the land has been used for food crops. However, if Green Revolution technology allowed more grain to be grown on each acre of land, then it would become possible *both* to increase the proportion of a country's land devoted to cash crops *and* to overcome the hunger problem. Unfortunately the Green Revolution has not eradicated hunger but cash crop production has expanded. Without an agricultural sector that is capable of fulfilling at least the minimum needs of a country's population, it is simply not possible to create or sustain self-reliant economic development.

The developing countries have had their own ideas of how to deal with the failure of conventional development strategies. In the early 1970s, one began to hear about the need for "self-reliant" economic development for individual countries and "collective self-reliance" for the third world as a whole. An important element in this broad schema was the establishment of a new international economic order (NIEO) under which developing countries would be able to gain more control over their own resources and would obtain more equitable treatment in the world market. There was concern on the part of some third world analysts that the new strategy might end up as no more than a "new unequal division of labor." (See entry 149 for an introduction to this line of thinking.) In any event, by the end of the 1970s one heard less and less about "self-reliance" and NIEO negotiations had been largely sidetracked.

The industrialized countries never were enthusiastic about third world NIEO demands. The recession of the mid- and late-1970s enabled them to argue that times were bad for everyone and that the third world should not expect too much from them, and certainly not before the economic situation improved. Furthermore, the industrialized countries argued that most of the problems confronting the third world were internal in nature and that they could not justify using the tax money of their own poor to finance third world elites.

We have seen that a good deal of the socio-economic and political inequity in third world countries has its roots in domestic power structures. But we have also seen that industrialized countries have given considerable support to those same domestic power structures. There is clearly substantial scope for reform on the part of all nations. What is more, arguing as the rich countries did at the end of the 1970s that it was too much to expect them to finance a $6 billion Common Fund for commodities, for example, when their military expenditures during the same recession period were running at about $300 billion *annually,* shows exactly where the priorities of the industrialized world lie.

Rather than seeing a new, more equitable international economic framework erected, third world countries have been faced with growing protectionism on the part of the industrialized trading partners. In addition, as international economic problems have increased, the industrialized countries have shown themselves to be much more concerned with their relations with each other than with their relations with developing countries. The limits of the conventional, export-led development strategy have thus been amply demonstrated over the last decade. Nonetheless, it seems unlikely that the awareness of these limits will lead developing countries to move toward a more self-reliant form of development. Most third world leaders seem prepared to accept—if grudgingly—the little that is offered by the industrialized world rather than face the difficult task of formulating genuinely new approaches to the development problem. Their reaction to the failure of NIEO suggests that their earlier espousal of "self-reliance" did not extend much beyond the level of rhetoric.

It is, however, in the direction of greater self-reliance that third world countries must move if they are to have any hope of eradicating poverty and hunger within their borders. The success of foreign aid in promoting development has been, at best, uneven. All too many foreign assistance schemes have failed to take into account the social component of self-reliant, self-sustaining development. The current concern with "the poorest of the poor" does not mean that aid agencies will promote the significant structural changes required in most of the third world.

Furthermore, the entire notion of constant growth as the foundation on which socio-economic and political progress rests must be reconsidered, by third world *and* by industrialized countries be they capitalist, socialist, or communist. It simply is not possible, given the finite nature of the world's resources, to believe that the standard of living now prevalent in the West can be sustained indefinitely, let alone extended to four or six or eight billion people. Poverty in the third world causes a good deal of ecological damage. Too many people and animals attempt to use too little land too intensively. The result is the destruction of forests, the creation of deserts, flooding and famine. The search for affluence has also taken its toll of global resources. Apart from pollution and resource depletion in industrialized nations, a considerable portion of the West's standard of living has been created at the expense not only of the people of the third world but of their natural environment as well. Yet the need to find a new framework which will institutionalize a more rational use of our resources is nowhere given enough thought, particularly—but by no means exclusively—in governmental circles.

It is time for less-developed countries to assess their resources and needs and to begin to address their problems in their own way. They must come to see that the kind of "assistance" proffered by the industrialized countries over the last 30 years—in terms of development strategies and the finance with which to implement them—has not been, on balance, as beneficial as the industrialized countries would have them believe. The rich countries, for their part, must develop methods of providing for their own populations that are not dependent on the exploitation of the people or the resources of the third world. Once that happens, we will see the beginning of international development and the end of hunger.

Part I: Economic Development

The Political Economy of Underdevelopment

Books and Monographs

Not only did the conventional development theories of the 1950s and 1960s have economic growth as their major objective, but they also envisaged development occurring in stages. One of the most controversial statements of this concept is found in Rostow. Rostow identified five stages through which all economies were said to pass: traditional society, preconditions for take-off, take-off, drive to maturity, and the age of mass consumption. By the end of the 1960s, however, it was clear that, while many countries did achieve high rates of economic growth at least for short periods of time, poverty and inequality were not declining in the third world (see, for example, Morowetz, ILO, pp. 72–74). According to the Commission on International Development (commonly called the Pearson Commission after its chairman, Lester Pearson), the problem lay in the low growth of exports and the inadequacy of development financing.

However, a growing number of analysts have come to believe that it is precisely this outward orientation of third world economies which has been the root of their problems. Marxists have long argued, of course, that underdevelopment is a result of the process of capitalist development. But many Marxist writings on underdevelopment have been Eurocentric and rather simplistic in their analysis of this process. A somewhat more sophisticated view is offered by Baran in his widely read study *The Political Economy of Growth.*

The classical Marxist view on imperialism and underdevelopment has been given somewhat more depth in the last decade or so by the *dependencia* school in Latin America. *Dependencia* was originally an outgrowth of the failure of import-substitution-oriented development strategies (strategies that promote the domestic production of goods otherwise imported) to fulfill a number of goals for Latin American countries, such as reducing the degree of dependence on foreign trade or equalizing income distribution. There are now at least three separate branches of the *dependencia* school. The first has a structuralist orientation and includes people such as Osvaldo Sunkel and Celso

Furtado. The second has a Marxist orientation and includes people such as Ruy Mauro Marini, Theotonio Dos Santos and André Gunder Frank. The third group includes people like F. H. Cardoso who combine the two approaches. Three of the classic *dependencia* studies are Marini, Sunkel and Paz, and Cardoso and Faletto.

While the *dependencia* school was formed by conditions specific to Latin America, by the early 1970s "dependency theory" was used to analyze problems of development and underdevelopment throughout the world. More recently, the validity of dependency theory has been questioned. Amin, in entry 4, discusses and analyzes Marxist dependence theories. Hettne describes the evolution of what he prefers to call the "dependence paradigm" (arguing that *dependencia* was "a new point of departure rather than a new theory") and summarizes some of the criticisms of *dependencia*. In his contribution to Oxaal, Barnett, and Booth, O'Brien surveys the writings of major Latin American *dependencia* adherents. While he finds that the theory has many merits, the failure to "enumerate and analyse the essential characteristics of dependency" is identified as one of its major shortcomings. Others find that the emphasis on the external nature of dominance allows the crucial issue of the domestic origins of exploitation to be side-stepped.

Theorists may not be in agreement concerning the genesis of underdevelopment, but at the end of the 1970s large numbers of people in third world countries continued to live in extreme poverty. According to the review of the International Development Strategy by the UN Centre for Economic and Social Information, three years after its adoption that strategy remained "much more a wish than a policy." The studies by the UN Department of Economic and Social Affairs and by the ILO discuss the economic and social progress recorded in the first half of the Second Development Decade. The latter focuses on progress in expanding employment opportunities and concludes, "With respect to the adoption and actual implementation of employment-oriented strategies as opposed to their formal incorporation in planning documents, the progress made is much less impressive" (entry 34, p. 69). The best that the Department of Economic and Social Affairs can report is that "... if the developing countries are considered as a whole—as they are for the targets set in the International Development Strategy—the outcome, though a serious disappointment, was not as disastrous as at one stage was widely feared" (entry 53, p. 1). Yet, once one begins to break down these aggregate figures, it is clear that "there was a sharp contrast between the achievements of the petroleum-exporting countries and those of other developing countries" (entry 53, p. 2).

This section includes several books composed of articles covering a wide variety of topics that are recommended as introductions to the subject of development and underdevelopment: Copans et al., and the volumes edited by Rhodes, Bernstein, and Oxaal, Barnett and Booth. Beckford is recommended as an introduction to underdevelopment in plantation economies, while Rodney is a useful introduction to the impact of colonialism on Africa.

A topic that is receiving increasing examination is the relationship between military activities in third world countries and development/underdevelopment. The study by Benoit concludes that military expenditure may have a positive effect on third world growth and is widely quoted by academics and government officials. However, the Benoit study is open to serious methodological and definitional criticisms and it is by no means clear that Benoit's main conclusion is valid. Furthermore, if one looks at more than purely economic growth, as does the study by Albrecht, Ernst, Lock and Wulf, the impact of military activities on development/underdevelopment is not at all clear-cut. The volume edited by Kaldor and Eide assesses some of the effects military technology has on third world countries.

Abbott discusses debt structures, the international economic order and developing countries, international investment and capital flows, and the tendency of industrialized countries to use international investment to extract capital from developing countries to finance economic growth in the industrialized countries. Amoa and Braun discuss the relationship between the EEC and Africa in terms of the ways in which this relationship has contributed to African underdevelopment. Caldwell identifies food and energy supplies as important ingredients of third world development and discusses why the third world suffers from chronic food and energy shortages.

Cortés Conde examines the growth of Latin America's export economy in relation to the world economy from about 1850 to the 1920s. Furtado argues in entry 26 that the notion that all countries can follow the development path of the industrialized countries and attain a standard of living equivalent to that now prevailing in those countries is simply a myth. The structure of the existing capitalist economic system is said to prevent such an outcome. Sine offers a critique of development sociology.

Hayter looks at the work of the World Bank in Latin America. This book received considerable attention in the early 1970s because of the World Bank's attempt to prevent its publication. Payer offers a critique of IMF policies in the Philippines, Indonesia, Indochina, Brazil, India, Chile, Ghana, and North Korea. Tendler argues that organizational factors have been most important in shaping US aid policies. The volume edited by Ward, d'Anjou, and Runnals is composed of papers presented at a conference to discuss the Pearson Report. The collection edited by Agarwala and Singh runs the gamut of major development theorists of the 1950s and includes articles by Baran, Furtado, Chenery, and Rostow, among others.

Wall concludes that countries give aid out of a combination of self-interest (desire to retain or obtain rights to raw materials, food, markets, and the like) and fear (of war, of loss of supply of raw materials or markets). Aid may neither lead nor be meant to lead to social and economic development or political stability in developing countries. The volume edited by Widstrand contains ten case studies of multinational corporations in Africa that focus on how the development of each region has been stunted by corporate activities. It also includes three chapters that offer suggestions on how countries can attain independence from multinational corporations. The study edited by Wilber includes case studies of Taiwan, South Korea, Brazil, and China and gives some attention to alternative forms of development.

1. Abbott, George. *International Indebtedness and Developing Countries.* London: Croom-Helm, 1979.

2. Agarwala, A. N., and Singh, S. P., eds. *The Economics of Underdevelopment.* London and New York: Oxford University Press, 1958.

3. Albrecht, Ulrich; Ernst, D.; Lock, P.; and Wulf, H. *Rüstung und Unterentwicklung. Iran, Indien, Griechenland/Türkei: Die Verscharfte Militarisierung.* Hamburg: Rororo Aktuell, 1976. (English translation forthcoming.)

4. Amin, Samir. *Accumulation on a World Scale: A Critique of the Theory of Underdevelopment.* 2 vols. New York: Monthly Review Press, 1974.

5. ______. *Imperialism and Unequal Development.* New York and London: Monthly Review, 1979.

6. ______. *Neo-Colonialism in West Africa.* Trans. Francis McDonagh. New York and London: Monthly Review, 1973.

7. Amin, Samir, and Vergopoulos, Kostas. *La Question Paysanne et le Capitalisme.* Paris: Editions Anthropos-IDEP, c. 1975.

8. Amoa, Ga-Kwame, and Braun, Oscar. *Echanges Internationaux et Sous-Développement.* Paris: Editions Anthropos-IDEP, 1974. (The section by Amoa is particularly relevant.)

9. Angelopoulos, Angelos. *Le Tiers-Monde Face aux Pays Riches. Perspectives pour l'An 2000.* Preface by Josué de Castro. Paris: Presses Universitaires de France, 1972.

10. Balogh, Thomas. *The Economics of Poverty.* London: Weidenfeld and Nicolson, 1966.

11. Baran, Paul A. *The Political Economy of Growth.* 2nd ed. New York: Prometheus Paperbacks/Marzani & Munsell, 1960. (Also available from Penguin, Harmondsworth, UK, 1973.)

12. Barnet, Richard J. *Can the United States Promote Foreign Development?* Development Paper 6. Washington, D. C.: Overseas Development Council, 1971.

13. Bauer, Peter Tamàs. *Dissent on Development: Studies and Debates in Developing Economics.* rev. ed. Cambridge, Mass.: Harvard University Press, 1976.

14. Beckford, George L. *Persistent Poverty: Underdevelopment in Plantation Economies of the Third World.* New York: Oxford University Press, 1972.

15. Benoit, Emile. *Defense and Economic Growth in Developing Countries.* Lexington, Mass.: Lexington, 1974. (A summary of the argument can be found in Emile Benoit, "Growth and Defense in Developing Countries," *Economic Development & Cultural Change* 26 [January 1978]: 271–280.)

16. Bernstein, Henry, ed. *Underdevelopment and Development.* Harmondsworth, UK: Penguin, 1973.

17. Caldwell, Malcolm. *The Wealth of Some Nations: An Introduction to Political Economy.* London: Zed Press, distributed by Monthly Review Press, c. 1978.

18. Cardoso, F. H., and Faletto, Enso. *Dependencia y la Desarrollo en America Latina.* Mexico: Siglo XXI Editores, 1969.

19. Chenery, Hollis, et al. *Redistribution with Growth.* London: Oxford University Press, 1974.

20. Cockcroft, James D.; Frank, André Gunder; and Johnson, Dale L. *Dependence and Underdevelopment: Latin America's Political Economy.* Garden City, N.Y.: Anchor/Doubleday, 1972.

21. Commission on International Development. *Partners in Development.* New York: Praeger, 1969.

22. Copans, Jean, et al. *Qui est Responsable du Sous-Développement?* Paris: Maspero, 1975.

23. Cornelius, Wayne, and Trueblood, Felicity M., eds. *Urbanization and Inequality: The Political Economy of Urban and Rural Development in Latin America.* Beverly Hills, Calif.: Sage, 1975.

24. Cortés Conde, Roberto. *The First Stages of Modernization in Spanish America.* Trans. Toby Talbot. New York: Harper & Row, 1974. (Chapters 1, 3, 6, and 7 are relevant.)

25. Frank, André Gunder. *Latin America: Underdevelopment or Revolution.* New York and London: Monthly Review, 1970.

26. Furtado, Celso. *The Myth of Economic Development and the Future of the Third World.* Working Paper no. 16. Cambridge, UK: Centre of Latin American Studies, Cambridge University, 1974.

27. ———. *Obstacles to Development in Latin America.* Trans. Charles Ekker. Garden City, N.Y.: Anchor, 1970.

28. ———. *Underdevelopment and Dependence: The Fundamental Connections.* Working Paper no. 17. Cambridge, UK: Centre of Latin American Studies, Cambridge University, 1973.

29. Griffin, Keith. *Underdevelopment in Spanish America: An Interpretation.* Cambridge, Mass.: The MIT Press, 1969.

30. Hayter, Teresa. *Aid as Imperialism.* Harmondsworth, UK: Penguin/Pelican, 1971.

31. Heeger, Gerald A. *The Politics of Underdevelopment.* New York: St. Martin's, 1974.

32. Hettne, Björn. *Current Issues in Development Theory.* Sarec Report R5:1978. Stockholm: Swedish Agency for Research Cooperation with Developing Countries, 1978.

33. Hettne, Björn, and Wallensteen, Peter. *Emerging Trends in Development Theory.* Sarec Report R3:1978. Stockholm: Swedish Agency for Research Cooperation with Developing Countries, 1978.

34. International Labour Office. *Time for Transition: A Mid-Term Review of the Second United Nations Development Decade.* Geneva: 1975.

35. Jalée, Pierre. *Imperialism in the Seventies.* Trans. Raymond and Margaret Sokolov. New York: Third Press, 1972.

36. ———. *The Pillage of the Third World.* Trans. Mary Klopper. New York: Monthly Review, 1968.

37. ———. *The Third World in World Economy.* Trans. Mary Klopper. New York: Monthly Review, 1969.

38. Kaldor, Mary, and Eide, Asbjørn, eds. *The World Military Order.* New York: Praeger, 1979.

39. Kautsky, John H. *The Political Consequences of Modernization.* New York: Wiley, 1972.

40. Leys, Colin. *Underdevelopment in Kenya: The Political Economy of Neo-Colonialism, 1964–1971.* London: Heinemann, 1975.

41. Marini, Ruy Mauro. *Dialectica de la Dependencia.* Mexico: Era, 1973.

42. Morowetz, David. *Twenty-Five Years of Economic Development—1950 to 1975.* Washington, D. C.: World Bank, 1977.

43. Oxaal, Ivar; Barnett, Tony; and Booth, David, eds. *Beyond the Sociology of Development: Economy and Society in Latin America and Africa.* Lawrence, Mass.: Routledge and Kegan Paul, 1975.

44. Payer, Cheryl. *The Debt Trap.* Harmondsworth, UK: Penguin, 1974.

45. Rhodes, Robert, ed. *Imperialism and Underdevelopment: A Reader.* New York: Monthly Review, 1970.

46. Rodney, Walter. *How Europe Underdeveloped Africa.* London: Bogle-l'Ouverture Publications and Dar-es-Salaam: Tanzania Publishing House, 1972.

47. Rostow, W. W. *The Stages of Economic Growth: A Non-Communist Manifesto.* Cambridge, UK: Cambridge University Press, 1960.

48. Sau, Ranjit. *Unequal Exchange, Imperialism and Underdevelopment.* Calcutta: Oxford University Press, 1978.

49. Sine, Babakar. *Impérialisme et Théories Sociologiques du Développement.* Paris: Editions Anthropos-IDEP, 1975.

50. Sunkel, Osvaldo, and Paz, Pedro. *El Subdesarrollo Latinoamericano y la Teoria del Desarrollo.* Mexico: Siglo XXI Editores, 1970.

51. Tendler, Judith. *Inside Foreign Aid.* Baltimore, Md.: Johns Hopkins University Press, 1975.

52. United Nations, Centre for Economic and Social Information. *First Biennial Over-All Review and Appraisal of Progress in the Implementation of the International Development Strategy for the Second United Nations Development Decade.* CESI/OPI. New York: 1974.

53. United Nations, Department of Economic and Social Affairs. *Economic and Social Progress in the Second Development Decade.* E/5981. ST/ESA/68. Sales No. E.77.II.A.11. New York: 1977.

54. United Nations, Research Institute for Social Development. *Social Development and the International Development Strategy.* Geneva: UNRISD, 1979.

55. Vaitsos, Constantine V. *Policies on Foreign Direct Investments and Economic Development in Latin America.* IDS Communication 106. Brighton, UK: Institute of Development Studies, University of Sussex, 1973.

56. Veliz, Claudio, ed. *Obstacles to Change in Latin America.* New York: Oxford University Press, 1965.

57. ______. *Politics of Conformity in Latin America.* London: Oxford University Press, 1967.

58. Wachtel, Howard M. *The New Gnomes: Multinational Banks in the Third World.* Washington, D. C.: Transnational Institute, 1977.

59. Wall, David. *The Charity of Nations: The Political Economy of Foreign Aid.* New York: Basic Books, 1973.

60. Wallerstein, Immanuel M., ed. *World Inequality: Origins and Perspectives on the World System.* Montreal: Black Rose, 1975.

61. Ward, Barbara; d'Anjou, Lenore; and Runnals, J. David, eds. *The Widening Gap.* New York: Columbia University Press, 1971.

62. White, John. *The Politics of Foreign Aid.* New York: St. Martin's, 1974.

63. Widstrand, Carl Gösta, ed. *Multinational Firms in Africa.* Dakar: Africa Institute for Economic Development and Planning, 1975; and Uppsala: Scandinavian Institute of African Studies, 1975.

64. Wilber, Charles K., ed. *The Political Economy of Development and Underdevelopment.* 2nd ed. New York: Random House, 1979.

Articles

Together the articles by Ewing and by Ewing and Koch survey much of the important literature on economic development which appeared between the early 1950s and the mid-1970s. Kaldor (entry 87) surveys the literature on the role of the military in development. The article by Patnaik is an excellent introduction to the political economy of underdevelopment written from a Marxist perspective. The second article by Kaldor (entry 88) outlines some of the most important effects third world militaries and military activities have on social development and social formation. Ball and Leitenberg examine the relationship between disarmament and development and conclude that, if one is speaking only of disarmament for the rich countries and development for the poor countries, the two topics may not be linked at all. It is suggested that a more fruitful topic for study is the relationship between armament and underdevelopment.

The article by Dos Santos in the *American Economic Review* (entry 76) is a useful short introduction to the topic of dependence. In entry 75, Dos Santos replies to critics who argue that dependency theory ignores very real domestic obstacles to development through its emphasis on the external origins of dependence. Dos Santos stresses that the accumulation process in dependent countries is *conditioned* by their position in the international economy but is *determined* by their own laws of internal development.

The articles by Leys, Lall, Leaver, and Laclau offer critiques of dependency theory. The latter two discuss Frank and should be read together. Laclau focuses his criticism on Frank's *Capitalism and Underdevelopment in Latin America* (entry 1298). Lall argues that the elements identified as creating "dependence" are really only elements that are present due to the development of capitalism. Thus, what one should be discussing are the costs and benefits of capitalist development. Because many of the conclusions concerning the effect of dependence on development cannot be generalized, Lall judges that the concept of "dependence" is not a useful analytic tool for development theorists. Leys believes that mainstream dependency theory is based on radical structuralism. As such, it gives insufficient attention to the analysis of class relations. Furthermore, according to Leys, mainstream dependency theorists describe the current situation in developing countries but not how or why that situation evolved.

The articles by Payer, Rothschild, and Fishlow, and those in the issue of *World Development* edited by Wionczek, discuss the debt problems of the developing countries. The articles by Gustafsson and Fishlow offer critiques of Rostow's *The Stages of Economic Growth* (entry 47). Fishlow summarizes a meeting of the International Economic Association that was highly critical of the Rostow thesis because it was concluded that this thesis was not based upon historic reality. Amin (entry 66) offers a critique of the Pearson Report (entry 21). Amin finds that the kind of analysis on which the Pearson Report is based ignores the structural changes that are required in third world countries and between rich and poor countries if development is to occur. It also does not take into account the ways in which integration into the world market hinders rather than promotes development.

Kurien examines the Indian Sixth Draft Plan 1978–83 which recognizes that the most important objectives of past plans have not yet been met. Kurien discusses why this failure has occurred (primarily because the effective demand of the wealthy, not the planners, has determined what will be produced in India) and why the Sixth Plan will not alter that situation. Marsden argues that, if third world countries are to close the gap between their "advanced" and "backward" sectors, they must promote growth from the "bottom upward." What is more, he believes it can be shown empirically that this "bottom upward" approach was the one followed by most industrialized countries. Santa Cruz argues that external development assistance should be of less importance to developing countries than the mobilization of domestic surpluses which are presently often used in unproductive ways.

The article by McHenry has a somewhat different focus than most of the others in this section. McHenry argues that there is no evidence that colonial or neocolonial countries encouraged foreign investment in Tanzania which resulted in the siphoning off of that country's economic surplus. Furthermore, he finds little support for the argument that colonial or neocolonial countries encouraged the development of an indigenous class which acts in the interests of foreign countries to perpetuate the conditions of underdevelopment. This analysis is based on the relationship between Tanzania and Britain in the exploitation of *dagaa,* a minnow-like fish, and cannot be considered typical of all interactions between colonial powers and indigenous populations.

The article by Subrahmanian and Pillai is also recommended.

65. Alavi, Hamza. "Rural Bases of Political Power in South Asia." *Journal of Contemporary Asia* (UK) 4 (1974): 413–422.

66. Amin, Samir. "En Partant du 'Rapport Pearson': Développement et Transformations Structurelles. L'Expérience de l'Afrique (1950–1970)." *Revue Tiers-Monde* 13 (July–September 1972): 467–490.

67. ______. "Underdevelopment and Dependence in Black Africa, Origins and Contemporary Forms." *Journal of Modern African Studies* 10:4 (1972): 503–524.

68. Bagchi, A. K. "Notes Toward a Theory of Underdevelopment (In Memorium: Michael Kalecki)." *Economic and Political Weekly* 6 (Annual Number 1971): 351–366.

69. ______. "Some International Foundations of Capitalist Growth and Underdevelopment." *Economic and Political Weekly* 7:31–33 (Special Number 1972): 1559–1570.

70. Ball, Nicole, and Leitenberg, Milton. "Disarmament and Development: Their Interrelationship," pp. 102–130. In *Disarmament and Development: Thought and Action to Date; Towards a Conceptual Framework.* Dick A. Leurdijk and Elisabeth Mann Borgese. Rotterdam: Foundation Reshaping the International Order, 1979. (Also available in "Disarmament and Development" (Issue Title). *Bulletin of Peace Proposals* (Oslo) no. 3 (1979): 247–259.)

71. "Capitalism in Africa" (Issue Title). *Review of African Political Economy* no. 8 (January–April 1977): 1–98.

72. Chandra, N. K. "Western Imperialism and India Today—I." *Economic and Political Weekly* 8:4–6 (Annual Number 1973): 221–244.

73. Chilcote, Ronald H. "Ruling Classes and Dependency in Two Backland Communities of Northeast Brazil." *Studies in Comparative International Development* 11 (Summer 1976): 35–50.

74. Cunningham, G. L. "Peasants and Rural Development in Tanzania." *Africa Today* 20 (Fall 1973): 3–18.

75. Dos Santos, Theotonio. "Dependence Relations and Political Development in Latin America: Some Considerations." *Ibero America* 7:1 (1977).

76. ______. "The Structure of Dependence." *American Economic Review, Papers and Proceedings* 60 (May 1970): 231–236.

77. Ewing, Arthur. "Some Recent Contributions to the Literature on Economic Development." *Journal of Modern African Studies* 4 (September 1966): 335–348.

78. Ewing, Arthur, and Koch, Gloria-Veronica. "Some Recent Literature on Development." *Journal of Modern African Studies* 15:3 (1977): 457–480.

79. Fishlow, Albert. "Debt Remains a Problem." *Foreign Affairs* no. 30 (Spring 1978): 133–143.

80. ———. "Empty Economic Stages?" *The Economic Journal* 75 (March 1965).

81. Girvan, Norman, ed. "Dependence and Underdevelopment in the New World and the Old" (Special Issue). *Social and Economic Studies* 22 (March 1973): 1–202.

82. Griffin, Keith. "The Role of Foreign Capital," pp. 225–244. In *Financing Development in Latin America.* Ed. Keith Griffin. London: Macmillan, 1971.

83. "Growth and Development" (Editorial). *Civilisations* 22:2 (1972): 183–197.

84. Gustafsson, Bo G. "Rostow, Marx and the Theory of Economic Growth." *Science & Society* (New York) 25:3 (1961): 229–244.

85. Ikonicoff, Moises, ed. "Le Capitalisme Périphérique" (Special Issue). *Revue Tiers-Monde* 13 (October–December 1972): 691–862.

86. Joseph, Richard. "The Gaullist Legacy: Patterns of French Neo-Colonialism." *Review of African Political Economy* no. 6 (May–August 1976): 4–13.

87. Kaldor, Mary. "The Military in Development." *World Development* 4:6 (1976): 459–482. (Reprinted as "The Military in the Third World," pp. 57–82, 161–170. In *Disarmament and World Development.* Ed. Richard Jolly. Oxford: Pergamon Press, 1978.)

88. ———. "The Arms Trade and Society." *Economic and Political Weekly* 11:5–7 (Annual Number 1976): 293–301.

89. Kurien, C. T. "The New Development Strategy: An Appraisal." *Economic and Political Weekly* 13:31–33 (Special Number 1978): 1257–1264.

90. Laclau, Ernesto. "Feudalism and Capitalism in Latin America." *New Left Review* no. 67 (1971): 19–38.

91. Lall, Sanjaya. "Is 'Dependence' a Useful Concept in Analysing Underdevelopment?" *World Development* 3 (November–December 1975): 799–810.

92. Leaver, Richard. "The Debate on Underdevelopment. 'On Situating Gunder Frank.' " *Journal of Contemporary Asia* 7:1 (1977): 108–115.

93. Leys, Colin. "Underdevelopment and Dependency: Critical Notes." *Journal of Contemporary Asia* 7:1 (1977): 92–107.

94. McHenry, Dean E., Jr. "The Underdevelopment Theory: A Case-Study from Tanzania." *Journal of Modern African Studies* 14:4 (1976): 621–636.

95. Marsden, Keith. "Toward a Synthesis of Economic Growth and Social Justice." *International Labour Review* 100 (November 1969): 389–418.

96. Morgan, T. "Trends in Terms of Trade and Their Repercussions on Primary Producers," pp. 52–95. In *International Trade Theory in a Developing World.* Eds. Roy Harrod and Douglas Hague. New York: St. Martin's; London: Macmillan, 1963.

97. Müller, Ronald. "Poverty is the Product." *Foreign Policy* no. 13 (Winter 1973/74): 71–103.

98. Odle, Maurice. "Guyana—Caught in an IMF Trap." *Caribbean Contact* (October 1978): 10–11.

99. Patel, Surendra J. "Collective Self-Reliance of Developing Countries." *Journal of Modern African Studies* 13:4 (1975): 569–583.

100. Patnaik, Prabhat. "On the Political Economy of Underdevelopment." *Economic and Political Weekly* 8:4–6 (Annual Number 1973): 197–212.

101. Payer, Cheryl. "Third World Debt Problems: The New Wave of Defaults." *Monthly Review* 28 (September 1976): 1–19.

102. Petras, James F. "Sociologie du Développement ou Sociologie de l'Exploitation?" *Revue Tiers-Monde* 17 (July–September 1976): 587–613.

103. Rao, G. V. "Neocolonialist Aid and Trade." *Social Scientist* 4 (January 1976): 57–61.

104. Rothschild, Emma. "Banks: The Coming Crisis." *New York Review of Books* (27 May 1976): 16–22.

105. Santa Cruz, Hernán. "Comments on the RIO Project." *Development Dialogue* 2 (1976): 104–111.

106. Sau, Ranjit. "Indian Economic Growth: Constraints and Prospects." *Economic and Political Weekly* 7:5–7 (Annual Number 1972): 361–378.

107. Shaw, Timothy M. "Zambia: Dependence and Underdevelopment." *Canadian Journal of African Studies* 10:1 (1976): 3–22.

108. Subrahmanian, K. K., and Pillai, P. Mohanan. "Multinational Firms and Export Processing Zones." *Economic and Political Weekly* 13 (26 August 1978): 1473–1477.

109. Sunkel, Osvaldo. "National Development Policy and External Dependence in Latin America." *Journal of Development Studies* 6 (October 1969): 23–48.

110. United Nations, Department International Economic and Social Affairs, Center for Development Planning, Projections and Policies. "Development Trends Since 1960 and Their Implications for a New International Development Strategy." *Journal of Development Planning* no. 13 (1978): 123–192.

111. United Nations, Economic Commission for Latin America. "The Terms of Trade in Latin America," pp. 267–297. In *Economic Survey of Latin America, 1969*. New York: UNECLA, 1970.

112. Wallerstein, Immanuel. "Dependence in an Interdependent World: The Limited Possibilities of Transformation within the Capitalist World Economy." *African Studies Review* 17 (April 1974): 1–26.

113. Ward, Barbara. "Survival and Development." *Stanford Journal of International Studies* 6 (Spring 1971): 4–18.

114. Weaving, Rachel. "The World Development Report: Main Themes." *Finance & Development* 15 (September 1978): 30–33.

115. Wionczek, Miguel S., ed. "International Indebtedness and World Economic Stagnation." *World Development* 7 (February 1979): 91–223.

The New International Economic Order and Basic Needs

In the mid-1970s, encouraged by the success of OPEC and by rising prices for non-oil commodities, third world countries set forward a series of demands for a more equitable distribution of global wealth, for a new international economic order (NIEO). These demands were first made at the Sixth Special Session of the United Nations in 1974 and were elaborated at UNCTAD IV in Nairobi in 1976. They included the alleviation of debts, better terms for the transfer of technology and an acceleration of such transfers, increased aid, expansion of manufacturing capacity and of sales of manufactures to industrialized countries, as well as stable commodity prices and mechanisms for promoting the diversification of commodity production. For a year or two, a good deal of attention was focused on these demands. However, as the world economy entered a period of recession, conflicts between the rich countries came to dominate international economic relations and the demands for NIEO lost much of their momentum. The bargaining power of third world countries declined severely as commodity prices dropped sharply and third world debt problems mounted. By the end of the 1970s, the program set out at UNCTAD IV had been reduced to negotiations on a common fund to support a series of commodity price stabilization agreements. (See also the section entitled "Commodities," pages 224–233.)

Furthermore, the rich countries managed to neutralize much of the force behind the demands for NIEO by arguing that they could not be expected to negotiate a redistribution of global wealth until third world countries made some progress in redistributing domestic wealth. This is the context in which much of the debate concerning "basic human needs" and "the forgotten 40 percent" must be placed. As Geoffrey Barraclough has pointed out, the basic needs concept has been "used both as a stick with which to beat corrupt and greedy Third World elites and as an excuse for the West to drag its feet" (entry 154, p. 52).

Books and Monographs

The UN General Assembly Resolutions cited here are two of the basic documents outlining what the third world hoped to attain from a new international economic order. For an introduction to the background and some of the results of NIEO, readers can consult Minault; Letelier and Moffitt; and *Towards a New International Order* (entry 138). The three entries by the ILO and the studies by Ghai, Khan, Lee and Alfthan and by Hopkins and Norbye all discuss various aspects of the basic human needs concept as formulated by the United Nations. In particular, the UN-sanctioned "Basic Needs Strategy" is outlined in entry 127.

The UNIDO entry discusses how to reach the Lima Target of having 25 percent of world industrial capacity located in the third world by the year 2000. It should be pointed out, however, that not only do many analysts consider this target far too optimistic, but it has been estimated that even if 25 percent of industrial capacity were located in the third world, employment would be provided for only 5 to 10 percent of third world populations (entry 191).

The study coordinated by Tinbergen is essentially a liberal argument for NIEO, as viewed from the perspective of a number of "problem areas" such as food, population, human environment, natural resources, aid and trade, and the arms race. The books by Fishlow, Diaz-Alejandro, Fagen, and Hansen; and Wriggens and Adler-Karlsson are part of the Council on Foreign Relations' 1980s series. In the former, the chapter by Fagen is particularly recommended. In the latter, Wriggens examines various strategies for effecting changes in North-South relations. Adler-Karlsson points out that even if the international economic and political power of third world countries were increased, the lives of the majority of third world populations would not necessarily be improved. He sees a need for grass-roots development strategies which emphasize village-level economic self-reliance and political decentralization.

The volume edited by Frank and Webb discusses a variety of topics related to income distribution in developing countries including industrial policies, population policies, wages policies, educational policies, fiscal policies, and the promotion of more equitable rural income distribution. It is concluded that despite rising gross incomes, income disparities have increased in many instances. The simultaneous expansion of gross national product *and* poverty in seven Asian countries is also discussed in entry 1399.

116. Bhagwati, Jagdish N., ed. *The New International Economic Order: The North-South Debate.* Cambridge, Mass.: The MIT Press, 1977.

117. Erb, Guy F., and Kallab, Valeriana, eds. *Beyond Dependency.* New York: Praeger, 1975.

118. Fishlow, Albert; Diaz-Alejandro, C.; Fagen, R. R.; and Hansen, R. D. *Rich and Poor Nations in the World Economy.* New York: McGraw-Hill for the Council on Foreign Relations, 1978.

119. Frank, Charles R., Jr., and Webb, Richard C., eds. *Income Distribution and Growth in the Less Developed Countries.* Washington, D. C.: The Brookings Institution, 1977.

120. Ghai, D. P.; Khan, A. R.; Lee, E. L. H.; and Alfthan, T. *The Basic-Needs Approach to Development.* Geneva: International Labour Office, 1978.

121. Grant, James P. *Growth from Below: A People-Oriented Development Strategy.* Development Paper 16. Washington, D. C.: Overseas Development Council, December 1973.

122. Hansen, Roger D. *A "New International Economic Order"? An Outline for a Constructive US Response.* Development Paper 19. Washington, D. C.: Overseas Development Council, July 1975.

123. Haq, Khadija, ed. *Equality of Opportunity Within and Between Nations.* New York and London: Praeger, 1977.

124. Haq, Mahbub ul. *The Third World and the International Economic Order.* Development Paper 22. Washington, D. C.: Overseas Development Council, 1976.

125. Hopkins, M., and Norbye, O. D. *Meeting Basic Needs: Some Global Estimates.* World Employment Programme, Working Paper. Geneva: ILO, 1978.

126. International Labour Office. *The Basic-Needs Approach to Development: Some Issues Regarding Concepts and Methodology.* Geneva: 1977.

127. ———. *Employment, Growth and Basic Needs: A One-World Problem.* New York: Praeger, 1977.

128. International Labour Organization. *Meeting Basic Needs: Strategies for Eradicating Mass Poverty and Unemployment.* Geneva: 1977.

129. Kuitenbrouwer, Joost B. W. *Towards Self-Reliant Integrated Development.* ISS Occasional Paper no. 55. The Hague: Institute for Social Studies, 1975.

130. Letelier, Orlando, and Moffitt, Michael. *The International Economic Order.* TNI Pamphlet no. 2. Washington, D. C.: Transnational Institute, 1977.

131. McHale, J., and McHale, M. C. *Basic Human Needs. A Framework for Action.* New Brunswick, N. J.: Transaction, 1978.

132. McLaughlin, Martin M., and Staff of the Overseas Development Council. *The United States and World Development. Agenda 1979.* New York: Praeger, 1979.

133. Minault, Sylvain. *The New International Economic Order: The Promise and the Reality.* London: Friends World Committee for Consultation, 1977.

134. Sauvant, Karl P., and Hasenpflug, Hajo, eds. *The New International Economic Order: Confrontation or Cooperation Between North and South?* Boulder, Colo.: Westview, 1977.

135. Singh, Jyoti Shankar. *A New International Economic Order: Toward a Fair Redistribution of the World's Resources.* New York: Praeger, 1977.

136. Stokes, Bruce. *Local Responses to Global Problems: A Key To Meeting Basic Human Needs.* Worldwatch Paper 17. Washington, D. C.: Worldwatch Institute, 1978.

137. Tinbergen, Jan. *RIO: Reshaping the International Order.* New York: Dutton, 1976.

138. *Towards a New International Order: An Appraisal of Prospects.* Report on the Joint Meeting of the Club of Rome and of the International Ocean Institute, Algiers, 25–28 October 1976. Algiers: 1977.

139. United Nations, General Assembly. *Charter of Economic Rights and Duties of States.* General Assembly Resolution 3281 (XXIX). New York: December 1974.

140. ———. *Programme of Action on the Establishment of a New International Economic Order.* General Assembly Resolution 3202 (S–VI). New York: 1974.

141. United Nations, Industrial Development Organization. *Industrialisation for the Year 2000: New Dimensions.* Joint Study on International Industrial Cooperation. UNIDO/IOD. 268. Vienna: 28 May 1979.

142. Worm, Kirsten, ed. *Industrialization, Development and the Demands for a New International Economic Order.* Copenhagen: Samfundsvidenskabeligt Forlag, 1978.

143. Wriggens, W. Howard, and Adler-Karlsson, Gunnar. *Reducing Global Inequities.* Introduction by Catherine Gwin. New York: McGraw-Hill for the Council on Foreign Relations, 1978.

Articles

For an excellent summary of the state of NIEO and of relations between rich and poor nations at the end of the 1970s, "Waiting for the New Order" (entry 154) and "The Struggle for the Third World" (entry 155) by Barraclough are recommended. An outline of NIEO-related negotiations is found on pages 47–58 of entry 53.

While industrialized nations attacked the demands for NIEO as asking "too much," NIEO has also been criticized, mainly from the left, as asking for the wrong things. Examples of this sort of criticism are found in Atta-Mills and Amin (especially entries 149 and 150). A similar argument is made by Braun, but here the reader must be willing to brave a good deal of rhetoric. Atta-Mills says that most NIEO proposals would lead only to continued dependence on the part of third world countries. The only possible exception is the demands for increased third world sovereignty over natural resources which, if achieved, could lay the groundwork for separating poor countries from the capitalist system, according to Atta-Mills. In entry 150, Amin says that he suspects that NIEO has been emptied of all substance and that, in any case, demands for NIEO should not lead people to ignore the need for dealing with domestic development problems. According to Amin, development is first and foremost a matter of transforming domestic economic, political, and social structures. Foreign relations are said to reflect internal structures, but they can be used either to reinforce the negative aspects of these structures or to induce positive change. Amin calls on developing countries to give priority to self-reliant development and to promote collective self-reliance. In entry 149, Amin examines NIEO proposals in relation to the theory of peripheral capitalism. He asks if NIEO could lead to autonomous capitalist development for third world countries and concludes that it is likely to result only in a new international division of labor in which the dependent condition of third world countries will remain essentially unaltered.

The article by Bergsten sets out some of the policy options available to the US in view of the desire on the part of third world countries for greater independence, especially in the economic sphere. The articles by Fried and by Cooper both call for greater access to industrialized-country markets for manufactures from developing countries. Neither article deals with the problems associated with export-oriented growth and the way in which the dependence on industrialized countries for technology can be enhanced by an export-led strategy. Cotter argues that USAID's stress on basic human needs and on channeling assistance to "the poorest of the poor" had led to a decreased emphasis on building strong local training and research facilities in third world countries and on producing a well-trained indigenous work force.

The special issue of *Industry and Development* (entry 175) is composed of articles discussing various aspects of strategies designed to implement the Lima Declaration and Plan of Action which includes the Lima Target of increasing the third world's share of industrial capacity to 25 percent by 2000.

The article by de Alcantara is an excellent summary of conditions in Mexico in the twentieth century and of that country's "structural inability" to satisfy the most basic needs of the majority of the Mexican population in the post-World War II period. The working of the free market, more than population growth, is considered the main cause of inequalities in Mexico in this period. Other recommended articles include Furtado, Retzlaff, and the three remaining Barraclough articles (entries 152, 153, and 156).

144. Addo, Herbert. "The New International Economic Order," pp. 194–215. In *Peace, Development, and New International Economic Order. Proceedings of the 7th IPRA General Conference.* Eds. Luis Herrera and Raimo Väyrynen. Tampere, Finland: International Peace Research Institute, 1979.

145. Alcantara, Cynthia Hewitt de. "Mexico: A Commentary on the Satisfaction of Basic Needs," pp. 152–207. In *Another Development: Approaches and Strategies.* Ed. Marc Nerfin. Uppsala: Dag Hammarskjöld Foundation, 1977.

146. Amin, Samir. "After Nairobi: An Appraisal of UNCTAD IV." *Africa Development* 1 (September 1976):58–61.

147. ______. "Développement Autocentre, Autonomie Collective et Ordre Economique International Nouveau." *Africa Development* 3:2 (1978): 5–23.

148. ______. "New International Economic Order: How to Put Third World Surpluses to Effective Use." *Third World Quarterly* 1:1 (1978): 65–72.

149. ______. "Self-Reliance and the New International Economic Order." *Monthly Review* 29 (July–August 1977): 1–21.

150. ______. "UNCTAD IV and the New International Economic Order." *Africa Development* 1 (May 1976): 5–11.

151. Atta-Mills, Cadman. "Africa and the New International Economic Order." *Africa Development* 1 (May 1976): 22–27.

152. Barraclough, Geoffrey. "The Great World Crisis I." *New York Review of Books* (23 January 1975): 21–29.

153. ______. "The Haves and the Have Nots." *New York Review of Books* (13 May 1976): 31–41.

154. ______. "Waiting for the New Order." *New York Review of Books* (26 October 1978): 45–53.

155. ______. "The Struggle for the Third World." *New York Review of Books* (9 November 1978): 47–58.

156. ______. "Wealth and Power: The Politics of Food and Oil." *New York Review of Books* (7 August 1975): 23–30.

157. Bergsten, C. Fred. "The Threat from the Third World." *Foreign Policy* no. 11 (Summer 1973): 102–124.

158. Bowring, Philip. "Some Home Truths for the World's Poor." *Far Eastern Economic Review* (22 October 1976): 45, 46, 51–53.

159. Braun, Oscar. "The New International Economic Order and the Theory of Dependency." *Africa Development* 1 (May 1976): 12–21.

160. Brown, Richard Harvey. "Appropriate Technology and the Grass Roots: Towards a Development Strategy from the Bottom Up." *The Developing Economies* 15 (June 1977): 253–279.

161. Choate, Roger. "Sweden Wants 'Marshall-Plan' for Third World." *Report from SIDA* (Special Issue 1978): 6–8.

162. Cooper, Richard N. "Third World Tariff Tangle." *Foreign Policy* no. 4 (Fall 1971): 35–50.

163. Cotter, William R. "How Aid Fails to Aid Africa." *Foreign Policy* no. 34 (Spring 1979): 107–119.

164. Farvar, Mohammed Taghi, and Razavi-Farvar, Catherine. "The Lessons of Lorestan." *Ceres* no. 50 (March–April 1976): 44–47.

165. Fried, Jerome. "How Trade Can Aid." *Foreign Policy* no. 4 (Fall 1971): 51–61.

166. Friedman, Irving S. "The New Foundation for Relations in Development Assistance." *Cooperation Canada* (November–December 1973): 4–11.

167. Furtado, Celso. "Le Nouvel Ordre Economique Mondial. Un Point de Vue du Tiers-Monde." *Revue Tiers-Monde* 17 (July–September 1976): 571–582.

168. Galtung, Johan. "Trade or Development: Some Reflections on Self-Reliance." *Economic and Political Weekly* 11:5–7 (Annual Number 1976): 207–218.

169. Kreinin, M. E., and Finger, J. M. "A Critical Survey of the New International Economic Order." *Journal of World Trade Law* 10 (November–December 1976): 493–512.

170. "A New Economic Order" (Issue Title). *Ceres* no. 49 (January–February 1976).

171. Retzlaff, Ralph H. "Structural Change: An Approach to Poverty in Asian Rural Development." *Economic and Political Weekly* 13 (23–30 December 1978): A105–A112.

172. Sheehan, G., and Hopkins, M. "Meeting Basic Needs: An Examination of the World Situation in 1970." *International Labour Review* 117 (May 1978).

173. Singer, Hans W. "The New International Economic Order: An Overview." *Journal of Modern African Studies* 16 (December 1978): 539–548.

174. Singh, Ajit. "The 'Basic Needs' Approach to Development vs the New International Economic Order: The Significance of Third World Industrialization." *World Development* 7 (June 1979): 585–606.

175. "Special Issue for the Third General Conference of UNIDO" (Issue Title). *Industry and Development* no. 3 (1979): 1–86.

176. Srinivasan, T. N. "Development, Poverty, and Basic Human Needs: Some Issues." *Food Research Institute Studies* 16:2 (1977): 13–28.

177. Streeten, Paul. "The Distinctive Features of a Basic Needs Approach to Development." *International Development Review* 19:3 (1977): 8–16.

178. Streeten, Paul, and Burki, Shahid Javed. "Basic Needs: Some Issues." *World Development* 6:3 (1978): 411–421. (Reprinted in World Bank Reprint Series, no. 53.)

179. "Towards a New International Economic and Social Order" (Issue Title). *International Social Science Journal* 28:4 (1976): 639–830.

180. United Nations, Economic Commission for Latin America. "Latin America and the Transition to a New International Economic Order," pp. 39–48. In *Economic Survey of Latin America, 1975*. Santiago, Chile: ECLA, 1976.

181. "What Now? The 1975 Dag Hammarskjöld Report" (Special Issue). *Development Dialogue* nos. 1–2 (1975).

182. Wignaraja, Ponna. "From the Village to the Global Order: Elements of a Conceptual Framework for 'Another Development.'" *Development Dialogue* no. 1 (1977): 35–48.

The Technology Debate

Although there was some debate at the beginning of the 1950s about the wisdom of adopting the UN position that development strategies should focus on industrialization, by the end of the 1950s, the "industrialization first" approach was widely accepted. Those who argued in favor of this strategy essentially believed "Historical experience shows that a structural transformation mainly based on industry is a *sine qua non* of genuine development" (entry 77, p. 341). Since the third world was to follow in the footsteps of the industrialized, capitalist countries, it stood to reason that the technology necessary for implementing the "industrialization first" strategy would have to be supplied, in one way or another, by the industrialized countries. The recent rethinking of the conventional approach to development—due to its failure to provide many people in the third world with adequate food, employment, shelter, health care, and so on—has been reflected in the debate over the nature and uses of technology for development.

For many critics of third world reliance on technology imported from the advanced industrial countries, the problem lies in the technology itself. Because labor is relatively abundant in developing nations while capital is relatively scarce, it is increasingly argued that the technology employed by third world countries must be adapted to the particular factor endowments and labor-force composition of each importing country (see, for example, Onyemelukwe, Ruttan and Hayami, Baranson, and Chandra). Others have argued that technology must suit not only a country's economic environment, but its social and ecological environments as well (Marsden, and Bunting). Hence the term "appropriate technology."

To a certain degree, "appropriate technology" has come to be considered synonymous with "labor-intensive technology." For example, Jackson summarizes some of the main arguments put forward by people who favor capital-intensive technology and by those who favor labor-intensive, "appropriate" technology. This linking of "labor-intensive" and "appropriate" leads to a restricted understanding of the problem of technological dependence. It may be prohibitively inefficient, for example, to produce certain goods — such as iron or steel — by any other than relatively capital-intensive methods. But it should not be considered "bad" to produce such goods simply because the technology required to produce them is not labor-intensive. Without an indigenous capability of producing items such as iron, steel, or machine tools, a developing country will always be dependent on more industrialized ones for the provision of such basic requirements.

The most important aspects of the question of technology-for-development are social and political (see for example, Edquist and Edqvist, and Stewart in entry 203). Edquist and Edqvist argue that one must analyze these social and political elements in two ways: first, from the perspective of the socio-political properties of the techniques themselves; second, from the perspective of the socio-political biases of the social organism and/or individual who chooses which techniques shall be implemented. The questions of who has the power to implement the choice of technologies and what the effect of that choice is for society as a whole are crucial.

A number of interesting case studies have been produced that consider some of the side-effects of the transfer of technology. Glantz, Omo-Fadaka, and Thomas discuss the ways in which the transfer of deep wells, superdams, and tubewell irrigation, respectively, have negatively affected the social, economic, ecological, and health environments into which they were introduced. Chishti considers trends in the post-independence import of technology into India and how technology transfers have influenced the direction and pattern of economic development in that country. A case of particular interest, also from India, is that of the obstacles confronting the development of the Swaraj tractor—a machine designed indigenously for use in northern India (see Aurora and Moorhouse and, especially, entry 1784).

The US experience in applying science and technology to development both domestically and in third world countries is discussed in the paper by the US Department of State. The relevance to other countries of the Chinese approach to science and technology is examined by Rifkin.

General

Books and Monographs

Recommended studies include Edquist and Edqvist, Stewart, Timmer, Thomas, Wells, and Morawetz, and the volume edited by Cooper (particularly the chapters by Cooper, Herrera, Stewart and Ishikawa).

183. Appropriate Technology Development Group. *Appropriate Technology for Rural and Small Industries.* New Delhi: 1970.

184. Bhattasali, B. N. *Transfer of Technology Among the Developing Countries.* Tokyo: Asian Productivity Organization, 1972.

185. Biggs, Stephen D. *Science and Agricultural Technology for Bangladesh: A Framework for Policy Analysis.* Report no. 43. Dacca: Ford Foundation, July 1976.

186. Canadian Hunger Foundation. *A Handbook on Appropriate Technology.* Ottawa: April 1976.

187. Contreras, Carlos, et al. *Technological Transformation of Developing Countries.* Discussion Paper no. 115. Lund: Research Policy Program, University of Lund, February 1978.

188. Cooper, Charles, ed. *Science, Technology and Development: The Political Economy of Technical Advance in Underdeveloped Countries.* London: Cass, 1973.

189. Darrow, Ken, and Pam, Rick. *Appropriate Technology Sourcebook.* Stanford, Calif.: Appropriate Technology Project, Volunteers in Asia, November 1977.

190. Eckhaus, Richard S. *Appropriate Technologies for Developing Countries.* Washington, D. C.: National Academy of Science, 1977.

191. Edquist, Charles, and Edqvist, Olle. *Social Carriers of Techniques for Development.* Sarec Report R3:1979. Stockholm: Swedish Agency for Research Cooperation with Developing Countries, 1979.

192. Goulet, Denis. *The Uncertain Promise: Value Conflicts in Technology Transfer.* New York: IDOC/North America, 1977.

193. Hayami, Yujiro. *Conditions for the Diffusion of Agricultural Technology: An Asian Perspective.* UMEDC 74–2. St. Paul and Minneapolis, Minn.: Economic Development Center, University of Minnesota, 1974. (Also available in *Journal of Economic History* 34 (March 1974): 131–148.)

194. Jackson, Sarah. *Economically Appropriate Technologies for Developing Countries: A Survey.* Occasional Paper Series, no. 3. Washington, D. C.: Overseas Development Council, 1972.

195. Kuitenbrouwer, Joost B. W. *Science and Technology: For or Against the People.* ISS Occasional Paper no. 49. The Hague: Institute of Social Studies, 1975.

196. McInerney, John P. *The Technology of Rural Development.* Staff Working Paper no. 295. Washington, D. C.: World Bank, October 1978.

197. National Research Council. *U.S. Science and Technology for Development: A Contribution to the 1979 U.N. Conference.* Background Study on Suggested US Initiatives for the UN Conference on Science and Technology for Development, Vienna, 1979. Washington, D. C.: US Printing Office, 1978.

198. Onyemelukwe, Clement C. *Economic Underdevelopment.* London: Longman Group, 1974.

199. Organization for Economic Cooperation and Development. *Choice and Adaptation of Technology in Developing Countries—An Overview of Major Policy Issues.* Paris: Development Centre, OECD, 1974.

200. Ruttan, V. W., and Hayami, Yujiro. *Technology Transfer and Agricultural Development.* UMEDC 73–2. St. Paul and Minneapolis, Minn.: Economic Development Center, University of Minnesota, 1973. (Also available in *Technology and Culture* 14 (April 1973, Part I): 119–151.)

201. Solo, Robert A. *Organizing Science for Technology Transfer in Economic Development.* East Lansing: Michigan State University Press, 1975.

202. Stewart, Frances. *Technology and Employment in Less Developed Countries.* Prepared for the Ford Foundation Seminar on Technology and Employment, New Delhi, 21–24 March 1973. Oxford: Institute of Commonwealth Studies, 1973.

203. ———. *Technology and Underdevelopment.* London: Macmillan, 1977.

204. Timmer, C. Peter; Thomas, J. W.; Wells, L. T.; and Morawetz, D. *The Choice of Technology in Developing Countries, Some Cautionary Tales.* Harvard Studies in International Affairs no. 32. Cambridge, Mass.: Center for International Affairs, Harvard University, 1975.

205. United Nations. *Science and Technology for Development. Report on the United Nations Conference on the Application of Science and Technology for the Benefit of the Less Developed Areas. Vol I: World of Opportunity,* and *Vol. III: Agriculture.* New York: 1963.

206. United Nations, The Advisory Committee on the Application of Science and Technology to Development (ACAST). *Report of the Ad Hoc Working Group on Appropriate Technology.* E/AC.52/XXIII/CRP.2. July 1977.

207. United Nations, Conference on Trade and Development. *Guide-lines for the Study of the Transfer of Technology.* Geneva: 1972.

208. ———. *Technological Dependence, Its Nature, Consequences, and Policy Implications.* Geneva: 1975.

209. United Nations, Economic and Social Council. *World Plan of Action for the Application of Science and Technology to Development. Report of the Advisory Committee on the Application of Science and Technology to Development. Addendum. Vol. II.* E/4962/Add. 1 (Part III). New York: 20 April 1971.

210. ———. *World Plan of Action for the Application of Science and Technology to Development. Addendum. Vol. II: IV. Food and Agriculture.* E/4962/Add. 1 (Part IV). New York: 20 April 1971.

211. United Nations, Economic Commission for Africa. *African Regional Plan for the Application of Science and Technology to Development.* E/CN.14/579. Sales no. E.73.II.K.3. New York: 1973.

212. United Nations, Educational, Scientific, and Cultural Organization. *International Aspects of Technological Innovation.* Proceedings of a Science Policy Symposium, Paris, 7–9 September 1970. Paris: 1971.

213. United States, Agency for International Development. *Appropriate Technologies for International Development. Preliminary Survey of Research Activities.* TA/OST 72–11. Washington, D. C.: Office of Science and Technology, USAID, September 1972.

214. ______. *Technology and Economics in International Development. Report of a Seminar.* TA/OST 72–9. Washington, D. C.: Office of Science and Technology, USAID, May 1972.

215. United States, Department of State. *Science and Technology for Development.* US National Paper, Department of State Publication 8966. Washington, D. C.: Office of the Coordinator for the 1979 UN Conference on Science and Technology for Development, January 1979.

Articles

The article by Diwan should be read with the report by Eckhaus (entry 190). The latter is a typical neoclassical analysis in which there is only one possible means of developing a country and which places great importance on economic growth and efficiency. Recommended articles include Chishti, Cooper, Dos Santos, Rifkin, Thomas, The Sussex Group, and Stewart. Entry 1784 is also of interest here.

216. "Appropriate Technology" (Issue Title). *Impact of Science on Society* 23 (October–December 1973): 251–352.

217. Atta-Mills, Cadman, and Girvan, Norman, eds. "Technology and Development in Africa" (Issue Title). *Africa Development* 2 (April–June 1977).

218. Aurora, G. S., and Moorhouse, Ward. "Dilemma of Technological Choice: The Case of the Small Tractor." *Economic and Political Weekly* 7:31–33 (Special Number 1972): 1633–1644.

219. Baranson, Jack. "Economic and Social Considerations in Adapting Technologies for Developing Nations." *Technology and Culture* 4 (Winter 1963): 22–29.

220. Bedrani, S. "La Technologie Agricole en Algérie." *Africa Development* 3 (April–June 1978): 21–38.

221. Chambers, Robert, ed. "Indigenous Technical Knowledge" (Issue Title). *IDS Bulletin* 10 (January 1979).

222. Chandra, N. K. "Western Imperialism and India Today — II." *Economic and Political Weekly* 8 (17 February 1973): 403–408.

223. Chishti, Sumitra. "Monitoring Import of Technology into India." *Economic and Political Weekly* 10 (31 May 1975).

224. Clawson, Marion; Landsberg, H. H.; and Alexander, L. T. "Desalted Sea Water for Agriculture: Is It Economic?" *Science* 164 (6 June 1969): 1141–1148.

225. Cooper, Charles. "Choice of Techniques and Technological Change as Problems in Political Economy." *International Social Science Journal* 25:3 (1973): 293–304.

226. Diwan, Romesh. "How Appropriate is Inappropriate?" *Economic and Political Weekly* 13 (22 July 1978): 1181–1182.

227. Dos Santos, Theotonio. "Transfert Technologique et Dépendence Economique." *Revue Tiers-Monde* 19 (April–June 1978): 397–413.

228. Eckhaus, Richard S. "Notes on Invention and Innovation in Less Developed Countries." *American Economic Review* 56 (1966): 98–117.

229. Evenson, Robert. "International Transmission of Technology in the Production of Sugar Cane." *Journal of Development Studies* 12:2 (1976): 208–231.

230. Garmany, J. W. "Technology and Employment in Developing Countries." *Journal of Modern African Studies* 16:4 (1978): 549–564.

231. Germides, Dimitri, ed. "Le Transfert de Technologies" (Issue Title). *Revue Tiers-Monde* 17 (January–March 1976): 5–220.

232. Girling, R. K. "Technology and Dependent Development in Jamaica: A Case Study." *Social and Economic Studies* 26 (June 1977): 169–189.

233. Glantz, Michael H. "Water and Inappropriate Technology: Deep Wells in the Sahel." *Journal of International Law and Policy* 6 (1976): 527–540.

234. "Integrated Technology Transfer — 1" (Issue Title). *Impact of Science on Society* 28 (April–June 1978): 95–197.

235. "Integrated Technology Transfer — 2" (Issue Title). *Impact of Science on Society* 28 (October–December 1978): 303–367.

236. Islam, Rizwanul. "Some Constraints on the Choice of Technology." *The Bangladesh Development Studies* 5 (July 1977): 255–279.

237. Lance, Larry M., and McKenna, Edward E. "Analysis of Cases Pertaining to the Impact of Western Technology on the Non-Western World." *Human Organization* 34:1 (1975): 87–94.

238. Marsden, Keith. "Progressive Technologies for Developing Countries." *International Labour Reivew* 101 (May 1970): 475–502.

239. Omo-Fadaka, Jimoh. "Superdams: The Dream That Failed." *PHP*, August 1978, pp. 10–20.

240. Reddy, Amulya Kumar N. "The Nature of Western Technology: Why Does It Inevitably Produce Alienation, Unemployment and Environmental Damage?" *Mazingira* no. 5 (1978): 20–26.

241. ______. "The Trojan Horse." *Ceres* no. 50 (March–April 1976): 40–43.

242. Rifkin, Susan B. "The Chinese Model for Science and Technology: Its Relevance for Other Developing Countries." *Development and Change* 6 (January 1975): 23–40.

243. Sachs, Ignacy. "Transfer of Technology and Strategy of Industrialisation." *Economic and Political Weekly* 5:29–31 (Special Number 1970): 1267–1270.

244. Schumacher, E. F. "The Work of the Intermediate Technology Development Group in Africa." *International Labour Review* 106 (July 1972): 3–20.

245. Stewart, Frances. "Capital Goods in Developing Countries." In *Employment, Income Distribution and Development Stategy: Problems of Development Strategy.* Eds. Alexander K. Cairncross and Mohinder Puri. London: Macmillan, 1976.

246. ______. "Too Dear to Work." *Mazingira* no. 5 (1978): 32–37.

247. ______. "Trade and Technology," pp. 231–263. In *Trade Strategies for Development.* Ed. Paul Streeten. New York: John Wiley and Sons, 1973.

248. Stewart, Frances, ed. "Special Issue on Technology." *World Development* 2 (March 1974): 1–85.

249. Streeten, Paul. "Technology Gaps Between Rich and Poor Countries." *Scottish Journal of Political Economy* 19 (November 1972): 213–230.

250. The Sussex Group. "Science, Technology and Underdevelopment: The Case for Reform." Prepared for the Meeting of the UN Advisory Committee on the Application of Science and Technology to Development, Addis Ababa, November 1969. Brighton, UK: Science Policy Research Unit, University of Sussex, January 1970.

251. Thomas, John W. "The Choice of Technology in Developing Countries: The Case of Irrigation Tubewells in East Pakistan." *LTC Newsletter* no. 41 (July–September 1973): 2–5.

252. "Transferts de Technologie" (Issue Title). *Options Méditerranéennes* no. 27 (New Series) (1975).

253. Westphal, Larry E. "Research on Appropriate Technology." *Industry and Development* no. 2 (1978): 28–46.

254. Wijewardene, Ray. "Appropriate Technology in Tropical Farming Systems." *World Crops* 30 (May–June 1978): 128–129, 132, 134.

Technology for Basic Human Needs

Edquist and Edqvist (entry 191) argue that it is extremely unlikely that basic needs can be fulfilled through the expansion of employment due to the introduction of labor-intensive techniques—as is suggested, for example, by Singer—if a country remains within the framework of the capitalist market economy. A somewhat similar conclusion is reached in the study by Bhalla; that is, the fulfillment of the "core" of basic needs can only marginally be achieved through price and market mechanisms alone. Institutional reforms that increase social equity are necessary.

Appu and Dommer discuss the bamboo tube well, an indigenously designed, low-technology device which is attractive to small and medium farmers, but not large ones. These articles might be contrasted with Thomas's findings (entry 251). Other recommended studies are the article by Bunting and the issue of *Development Dialogue* devoted to science and technology for development (entry 269).

255. Appu, P. S. "The Bamboo Tubewell: A Low Cost Device for Exploiting Ground Water." *Economic and Political Weekly* 9 (29 June 1974): A63–A64.

256. Bhalla, Ajit S. *Technologies Appropriate for a Basic Needs Strategy.* Geneva: ILO, December 1977.

257. Bunting, A. H. "Science and Technology for Human Needs, Rural Development and the Relief of Poverty." *IADS Occasional Paper.* New York: International Agricultural Development Service, 1979.

258. DeWalt, Billie R. "Appropriate Technology in Rural Mexico: Antecedents and Consequences of an Indigenous Peasant Innovation." *Technology and Culture* 19 (January 1978): 32–52.

259. Dommer, Arthur J. "The Bamboo Tube Well: A Note on an Example of Indigenous Technology." *Economic Development and Cultural Change* 23 (April 1975): 483–489.

260. Gotsch, Carl H. "Technical Change and the Distribution of Income in Rural Areas." *The American Journal of Agricultural Economics* 54 (May 1972): 326–341.

261. Jéquier, Nicolas. "Intermediate Technology: A New Approach to Development Problems." *The OECD Observer* no. 75 (May–June 1975): 26–28.

262. Jéquier, Nicolas, ed. *Appropriate Technology: Problems and Promises.* Paris: OECD, 1976.

263. Lipton, Michael. "The International Diffusion of Technology," pp. 45–63. In *Development in a Divided World.* Ed. Dudley Seers and Leonard Joy. Harmondsworth, UK: Penguin Books, 1971.

264. Lund, M. A. *Identifying, Developing, and Adopting Technologies Appropriate for Rural Development with Applications to Huari Province in Peru.* PN–AAC–317. Washington, D. C.: US Agency for International Development, 1975.

265. MacPherson, George, and Jackson, Dudley. "Village Technology for Rural Development: Agricultural Innovation in Tanzania." *International Labour Review* 112 (February 1975): 102–112.

266. Moyes, Adrian. *Good Servant, Bad Master: Technology and the Very Poor.* Oxford: Public Affairs Unit, Oxfam, c. 1979.

267. Rattner, Henrique. "Développement et Emploi: La Viabilité d'une Technologie Intermédiaire." *Revue Tiers-Monde* 16 (April–June 1975): 295–310.

268. Singer, Hans. *Technologies for Basic Needs.* Geneva: ILO, 1977.

269. "Towards Another Development in Science and Technology" (Issue Title). *Development Dialogue* no. 1 (1979): 1–80.

Multinational Corporations and Technology Transfer

Recommended studies include Helleiner, Pillai, Subrahmanian, and Pillai and Subrahmanian.

270. Clark, Norman. "The Multi-National Corporation: The Transfer of Technology and Dependence." *Development and Change* 6 (January 1975): 5–21.

271. Constantino, Renato. "Global Enterprises and the Transfer of Technology." *Journal of Contemporary Asia* 7:1 (1977): 44–55.

272. Driscoll, Robert E., and Wallender, Harvey W., III, eds. *Technology Transfer and Development: An Historical and Geographic Perspective.* New York: Fund for Multinational Management Education, in cooperation with the Council of the Americas, c. 1974. (Concentrates on Latin America)

273. Germidis, Dimitri. *Transfer of Technology by Multinational Corporations.* 2 vols. Paris: Development Centre, OECD, 1977.

274. Helleiner, Gerald K. "The Role of Multinational Corporations in the Less Developed Countries' Trade in Technology." *World Development* 3 (April 1975): 161–189.

275. Pillai, P. Mohanan. "Foreign Collaboration in Public Sector." *Economic and Political Weekly* 13 (27 May 1978): M48–M55.

276. Pillai, P. Mohanan, and Subrahmanian, K. K. "Rhetoric and Reality of Technology Transfer." *Social Scientist* 5 (January–February 1977): 73–92.

277. Singer, Hans. "Multinational Corporations and Technology Transfer: Some Problems and Suggestions," pp. 208–233. In *The Strategy of International Development.* Eds. Sir Alec Cairncross and Mohinder Puri. White Plains, N. Y.: International Arts and Sciences Press, Inc., 1975.

278. Subrahmanian, K. K. *Import of Capital and Technology: A Study of Foreign Collaboration in Indian Industry.* New Delhi: People's, 1972.

Rural Employment

Until the beginning of the 1970s, the problems of low labor utilization and low earnings were not given much attention by development planners in aid agencies or governments. However, one of the major failures of the development strategy followed by most third world countries in the 1950s and 1960s was the inability to utilize adequately the available work force. The high rates of unemployment and underemployment which have been estimated for all third world areas have resulted from low rates of growth in the productivity of agriculture and from the emphasis on setting up "modern," capital-intensive industries. High rates of population growth have compounded the problem.

It is now evident that simply increasing the rate of economic growth in developing countries will not by itself lead to the fuller utilization of third world labor. Attention must be given to making all sectors productive and to spreading the benefits of growth (past as well as future) more evenly throughout society. In the 1970s, there has been increasing recognition that programs that have as their central goal the reduction of unemployment and underemployment can also lead to economic growth. More and more, the focus has been on increasing employment opportunities in rural areas, both in agriculture and in industries designed to serve the needs of rural populations. In 1969, the ILO launched its World Employment Programme which has concentrated on devising development strategies to increase adequately remunerative employment and particularly rural employment in developing countries. Readers interested in rural employment issues should regularly survey the *International Labour Review,* put out by the International Labour Office, and ILO reports related to the World Employment Programme.

General

Books and Monographs

The monograph by Scott is recommended as an introduction to agricultural employment issues in Asia. Scott argues that the two primary constraints on expanding rural employment opportunities are the greater access to services on the part of the rural rich as compared to the rural poor and on the part of urban dwellers as compared to rural dwellers. The monograph by Turnham and Jaeger looks at labor-force structure, unemployment, income distribution, nutrition, and trends in and prospects for expanding employment opportunities in third world countries. Turnham and Jaeger stress the importance of greater development in the agricultural sector if employment opportunities are to improve for the majority of the people in the third world.

The book by Harbison is not uniquely concerned with rural employment, but one of its themes is the need to find ways to employ rural manpower adequately. Harbison says the purpose of development must be to increase the "opportunity-generating capacity" of rural areas, because it is simply not possible to find urban employment for the millions of rural poor, at least in the short-run. Falcon discusses the agricultural employment issue in terms of population growth and the failure of GNPs to expand sufficiently to generate enough employment opportunities to absorb the growing labor force.

Thorbecke and Stoutjesdijk attempt to devise a methodology for determining the number of underemployed in a particular economy. Rawski reviews the current understanding of the employment situation in China and surveys Chinese policies designed to increase labor use throughout the economy. While there was considerable unemployment in the 1950s, it is now believed that China has gone a long way toward achieving a fully, productively employed labor force. Increased labor utilization in rural areas is identified as the key to this success.

Entries 290–293, 295, and 296 are all products of the ILO World Employment Programme. The latter is the first in-depth pilot study of employment and underemployment problems in a developing country and of the possible solutions to these problems. Entry 34 should be consulted as well, particularly pages 21–32 which deal with the rural sector.

The study by Dasgupta et al. is also recommended.

279. Chambers, Robert. *Towards Rural Futures: An Approach Through the Planning of Technologies.* IDS Discussion Paper D–134. Brighton, UK: Institute of Development Studies, University of Sussex, 1978.

280. Chawdhari, T. P. S.; Tripathy, R. N.; Rao, T. V.; and Sharma, J. N. *Resource Use and Productivity on Farms: A Comparative Study of Intensive and Non-Intensive Agricultural Areas.* Hyderabad: National Institute of Community Development, 1969.

281. Cohn, Edwin J., and Eriksson, John R. *Employment and Income Distribution Objectives for A.I.D. Programs and Policies.* Policy Background Paper. Washington, D. C.: Bureau for Program and Policy Coordination, US Agency for International Development, October 1972.

282. Connell, John, and Lipton, Michael. *Assessing Village Labor Structures in Developing Countries.* New Delhi: Oxford University Press, 1977.

283. Dasgupta, Biplab, et al. *Village Society and Labor Use.* New Delhi: Oxford University Press, 1977.

284. Eicher, Carl K.; Zalla, T.; Kocher, J. E.; and Winch, F. *Employment Generation in African Agriculture.* Research Report No. 9. East Lansing: Institute on International Agriculture, Michigan State University, July 1970.

285. Falcon, Walter P. *Agricultural Employment in Less Developed Countries: General Situation, Research Approaches, and Policy Palliatives.* Economic Staff Working Paper 113. Washington, D. C.: World Bank, April 1971.

286. Food and Agriculture Organization. *Agricultural Development and Employment Performance: A Comparative Analysis.* Agricultural Planning Studies no. 18. Rome: 1974.

287. Ghosh, B. N. *Disguised Unemployment in Underdeveloped Countries (With Special Reference to India).* New Delhi: Heritage, 1977.

288. Harbison, Frederick H. *Human Resources as the Wealth of Nations.* New York: Oxford University Press, 1973.

289. Harvey, Charles; Jacobs, J.; Lamb, G.; and Schaffer, B. *Rural Employment and Administration in the Third World.* Farnsborough, UK: Gower Publishing Co., in association with the International Labour Office, 1979.

290. International Labour Office. *Employment in Africa: Some Critical Issues.* Geneva: 1973.

291. ______. *Employment, Incomes and Equality: A Strategy for Increasing Productive Employment in Kenya.* Geneva: 1972.

292. ______. *Growth, Employment and Equity: A Comprehensive Strategy for the Sudan.* Geneva: 1976.

293. ______. *Matching Employment Opportunities and Expectations: A Programme of Action for Ceylon.* 2 vols. Geneva: 1971.

294. ______. *Rural Employment Problems in the United Arab Republic.* Employment Research Papers. Geneva: 1969.

295. ______. *Sharing in Development: A Programme of Employment, Equity, and Growth for the Philippines.* Geneva: 1974. (Chapter 3 and Special Papers 5–8 deal specifically with the agricultural sector.)

296. ———. *Towards Full Employment. A Programme for Colombia.* Geneva: 1970.

297. Ramanujam, M. S.; Sharma, R. K.; Raghavan, K.; and Arora, S. L. *Manpower Development in Rural India: A Case Study.* Institute of Applied Manpower Research Report, no. 1. New Delhi: Allied, 1977.

298. Rawski, Thomas G. *Industrialization, Technology and Employment in the People's Republic of China.* Working Paper no. 291. Washington, D. C.: World Bank, August 1978.

299. Richards, P. J. *Employment and Unemployment in Ceylon.* Development Centre Studies, Employment Series: no. 3. Paris: OECD, 1971. (Chapter 4, "Land and Labour in Agriculture," is of particular relevance here.)

300. Scott, Henry G. *Aspects of Agricultural Employment and Productivity in Some Developing Asian Countries.* Occasional Paper no. 16. Birmingham, UK: Faculty of Commerce and Social Science, University of Birmingham, 1972.

301. Singh, Inderjit, and Choong Yong Ahn. *Employment and Capital-Labour Substitution in South Brazilian Agriculture.* Economics and Sociology Occasional Paper no. 72. Columbus: Department of Agricultural Economics and Rural Sociology, Ohio State University, March 1972.

302. Singh, Inderjit, and Day, Richard H. *Capital-Labour Utilization and Substitution in Punjab Agriculture.* Economics and Sociology Occasional Paper no. 70. Columbus: Department of Agricultural Economics and Rural Sociology, Ohio State University, March 1972.

303. Suriyakumaran, Canaganayam. *The Economics of Full Employment in Agricultural Countries, With Special Reference to India and Ceylon.* Colombo: De Silva, 1957.

304. Thorbecke, Erik, and Stoutjesdijk, E. *Employment and Output—A Methodology Applied to Peru and Guatemala.* Paris: Development Centre, OECD, 1971.

305. Turnham, David with the assistance of Ingelies Jaeger. *The Employment Problem in Less Developed Countries.* Development Centre Studies, Employment Series: no. 1. Paris: OECD, 1971.

306. Ward, William A. *Incorporating Employment into Agricultural Project Appraisal: A Preliminary Report.* Working Paper no. 6. East Lansing: African Rural Economy Program, Michigan State University, February 1975.

Articles

Islam discusses agricultural development strategies which absorb rather than displace labor. Based on his survey of several African countries, de Wilde concludes that the agricultural sector will have to absorb most of the available labor force in developing countries for some time to come. Owens looks at the expansion of rural employment through agricultural development from the perspective of the difference between this approach and the US-Western Europe farming strategy which has been promoted as a model for third world countries since the 1950s.

Thiesenhusen argues that Latin American development strategies must include programs designed to promote labor-absorbing agricultural development. Roussel finds that despite a labor shortage in rural areas of the Ivory Coast and labor surpluses in urban areas, migration from countryside to town continues. He argues that the government must concentrate on making rural employment more attractive and outlines a number of proposed government programs in this area. Mueller and Zevering suggest that rather than create new jobs in rural areas, the Nigerian government would be well advised to increase the productivity of those farmers and craftsmen already employed. They estimate that the increase in incomes generated by this greater productivity would serve to expand overall employment opportunities in the long run. The articles by Clayton and Faaland discuss some of the results of the ILO Employment Missions to Kenya and Sudan, respectively. (These missions are discussed in entries 291 and 292.)

Bardhan provides quantitative dimensions for some of the employment and unemployment characteristics of Indian rural women which differentiate the rural female labor market from the rural male labor market. Dantwala surveys the literature on the relationship between the level of agricultural output and employment in India and discusses the prospects of increasing employment in the agricultural sector. The ECAFE Secretariat finds that low labor utilization in Asian agriculture is related to low agricultural productivity. This in turn is related to the maldistribution of resources both within the rural sector and between the rural and the urban sectors. Sinha argues that strategies designed to increase rural employment should be composed of a "judicious mix" of rural works programs, development measures to stimulate agro-industries, and programs to provide the poor with their minimum needs in food, shelter, clothing, health care, and so on. These strategies should also be concerned with raising productivity *and* generating income. The article by Nadkarni reviews the book on disguised unemployment by Ghosh (entry 287).

The articles by Dorner, Tiano, Bartsch and Richter, and Lorenzo are also recommended.

307. Abercrombie, K. C. "Rural Employment—A Primary Objective." *Ceres* no. 31 (January–February 1973): 45–49.

308. "Agricultural Development and Employment." *Economic Survey of Asia and the Far East, 1971.* E/CN.11/1047. Bangkok: UN Economic Commission for Asia and the Far East, 1972, pp. 35–40.

309. Ahmed, Iqbal. "Unemployment and Underemployment in Bangladesh Agriculture." *World Development* 6 (November–December 1978): 1281–1296.

310. Bardhan, Pranab. "Some Employment and Unemployment Characteristics of Rural Women: An Analysis of NSS Data for West Bengal, 1972–73." *Economic and Political Weekly* 13 (25 March 1978): A21–A26.

311. Bartsch, William H., and Richter, Lothar E. "An Outline of Rural Manpower Assessment and Planning in Developing Countries: I." *International Labour Review* 103 (January 1971): 65–76; "II," 103 (February 1971): 179–194; and "III," 103 (March 1971): 269–285.

312. Byerlee, Derek; Eicher, C. K.; Liedholm, C.; Spencer, D. S. C. "Rural Employment in Tropical Africa." Working Paper no. 20. East Lansing: African Rural Economics Program, Michigan State University, February 1977.

313. Clayton, Eric S. "Kenya's Agriculture and the I. L. O. Employment Mission—Six Years After." *Journal of Modern African Studies* 16:2 (1978): 311–318.

314. Dantwala, M. L. "Rural Employment: Facts and Issues." *Economic and Political Weekly* 14 (23 June 1979): 1048–1057.

315. Dasgupta, Biplab. "Labour Utilisation in Poor Country Agriculture." *Institute of Development Studies Bulletin* 5 (May 1974): 8–12.

316. Davies, William J. "Politics, Perception and Development Strategy in Tropical Africa." *Journal of Modern African Studies* 13:1 (1975): 35–53.

317. Dorner, Peter P. "Needed Redirections in Economic Analysis for Agricultural Development Policy." *American Journal of Agricultural Economics* 53 (February 1971): 8–16.

318. ECAFE Secretariat, Research and Planning Division. "Agricultural Employment and Productivity." *Economic Bulletin for Asia and the Far East* 23 (December 1972): 45–62.

319. "Education et Développement. Etudes sur la Formation, l'Enseignement et la Planification des Ressources Humaines" (Issue Title). *Revue Tiers-Monde* 11 (January–March 1970): 7–218.

320. "Employment in Agriculture" (Section Title). *Development Digest* 9 (January 1971): 77–124.

321. Faaland, Just. "Growth, Employment and Equity: Lessons of the Employment Strategy Mission to the Sudan." *International Labour Review* 114 (July–August 1976).

322. Fredericks, L. J., and Wells, R. J. G. "Patterns of Labor Utilization and Income Distribution in Rice Double Cropping Systems: Policy Implications." *The Developing Economies* 16 (March 1978): 54–73.

323. Islam, Nurul. "Output and Employment Objectives in Agricultural Development." *Teaching Forum* no. 40. New York: The Agricultural Development Council, May 1974.

324. Karcher, Martin. "Unemployment and Underemployment in the People's Republic of China." *China Report* 11 (September–December 1975): 22–49.

325. Lobstein, P. "Prerequisites for a Rural Employment Policy in French-Speaking Black Africa." *International Labour Review* 102 (August 1970): 171–189.

326. Lorenzo, A. "Employment Effects of Rural and Community Development in the Philippines." *International Labour Review* 100 (November 1969): 419–444.

327. Mueller, P., and Zevering, K. H. "Employment Promotion Through Rural Development: A Pilot Project in Western Nigeria." *International Labour Review* 100 (August 1969): 111–130.

328. Nadkarni, M. V. "Fresh Look at Underemployment." *Economic and Political Weekly* 13 (18 March 1978): 521–522.

329. Owens, Edgar. "Rural Development and Employment," pp. 20–35. In *Manpower: Promoting Employment and Reducing Poverty.* International Manpower Institute, Manpower Administration, US Department of Labor. Washington, D. C.: 1972.

330. Rao, S. K. "Measurement of Unemployment in Rural India." *Economic and Political Weekly* 8 (29 September 1973): A78–A90.

331. Reutlinger, Shlomo; Donaldson, G. F.; Duane, P.; Egbert, A. C.; and Husain, T. "Agricultural Development in Relation to the Employment Problem." Economic Staff Working Paper 112. Washington, D. C.: World Bank, May 1971.

332. Rourke, B. E. "Rural Employment and Labour Productivity." *Ghana Journal of Sociology* 8:1 (1974): 108–123.

333. Roussel, Louis. "Employment Problems and Policies in the Ivory Coast." *International Labour Review* 104 (December 1971): 505–525.

334. "Rural Development and Agricultural Employment," pp. 57–75. In *Manpower: Employment Growth and Economic Development.* Proceedings of the Executive Seminar on Employment Growth, 1–20 November 1971. Washington, D. C.: Office of Labor Affairs, Agency for International Development, c. 1972.

335. Sethi, Harsh. "Alternative Development Strategies. A Look at Some Micro Experiments." *Economic and Political Weekly* 13:31–33 (Special Number 1978): 1307–1316.

336. Shaw, Robert d'A. "Jobs and Agricultural Development," pp. 285–376. In *Assisting Developing Countries. Problems of Debts, Burden-Sharing, Jobs and Trade.* Charles R. Frank, Jr.; Jagdish N. Bhagwati; Robert d'A. Shaw; and Harald B. Malmgren. New York: Praeger in Cooperation with the Overseas Development Council, 1972.

337. Shivamaggi, H. B. "The Agricultural Labour Problem: Past Misconceptions and New Guidelines." *Economic and Political Weekly* 4 (29 March 1969).

338. Silberfein, Marilyn, ed. "Agricultural Development and Employment." *Rural Africana* no. 19 (Winter 1973).

339. Sinha, J. N. "Rural Employment Planning: Dimensions and Constraints." *Economic and Political Weekly* 13:6–7 (Annual Number 1978): 295–313.

340. Thiesenhusen, William C. "Population Growth and Agricultural Employment. In *Population Policies and Growth in Latin America.* Ed. David Chaplin. Lexington, Mass.: D. C. Heath and Co., 1971.

341. Tiano, André. "Human Resources Investment and Employment Policy in the Maghreb." *International Labour Review* 105 (February 1972): 109–133.

342. Visaria, Pravin, and Visaria, Leela. "Employment Planning for the Weaker Sections in Rural India." *Economic and Political Weekly* 8:4–6 (Annual Number 1973): 269–276.

343. White, Benjamin. "Population, Involution and Employment in Rural Java." *Development and Change* 7 (July 1976): 267–290.

344. Wilde, John C. de "The Manpower and Employment Aspects of Selected Experiences of Agricultural Development in Tropical Africa." *International Labour Review* 104 (November 1971): 367–385.

Impact of the Green Revolution and Mechanization

One of the reasons why the adoption of Green Revolution technology has been disappointing for third world countries is that it reduced employment opportunities in some rural areas. Where this negative impact on employment has occurred, it has frequently resulted from the eviction of tenants to enable landlords to plant large areas under high-yielding varieties (HYVs) and from the replacement of human labor power with machinery by profit-maximizing HYV users. However, the introduction of HYVs and farm machinery need not create or exacerbate rural unemployment and underemployment. The prevailing distribution of power within societies and the kind of mechanization pursued are two variables which can profoundly affect the impact of Green Revolution technology and mechanization on rural labor utilization.

The study by the International Labour Office is a good introduction to the topic. It contains chapters on East Africa, Latin America, the Philippines, India, Sri Lanka, and Pakistan. The book by Bartsch is also an important contribution, although it only draws upon Asian experiences. Bartsch discusses labor requirements per hectare and per unit of output for nine possible combinations of technology (from HYV packages through traditional seed varieties) and techniques (from mechanized through labor-intensive agriculture). He concludes that the most socially profitable method of promoting agricultural development is to combine biological-chemical innovations with intermediate techniques. This approach is most effective, Bartsch argues, when land reform is also implemented.

Staub finds that the increased use of "modern" inputs is positively related to increased labor use in two districts in India. The positive effects are most marked where labor is abundant and cheap and where rice is the major crop. They are less evident where labor is more expensive and wheat the main crop. Even so, in the second case, farmers with tractors are found to have employed more labor than farmers without tractors, primarily because this form of mechanization permits multiple cropping to be introduced.

Mandal also looks at the relationship between the introduction of tractors, multiple cropping, and labor use. Ahmed (entry 347) discusses some of the employment-related problems that arise out of increased tractor use in third world countries. He cites evidence from Pakistan and Sri Lanka that demonstrates that land polarization and tenant evictions result from "tractorization." In both India and Sri Lanka, tractor ownership is skewed in favor of the larger farmers. In Sri Lanka, where merchants and middlemen own and rent out many tractors, tractor-hire charges increased twofold during the period under study. Ahmed (entry 346) argues that to maximize both employment and output, HYVs should be used with bullocks, rather than tractors or power tillers. Mehra argues that because large farmers who use HYVs also tend to introduce mechanization or to increase their labor substitution, farm sizes should be kept small to obtain the greatest employment-related benefits from the use of HYVs.

The articles by Aggarwal, Wills (entry 365), and Bieri, de Janvry, and Schmitz discuss the ways in which the introduction of Green Revolution technology and mechanization can increase or maintain unequal income distribution in rural sectors. Hall discusses the need for "meaningful mechanization"—which can be the introduction of an improved hoe, a large machine, or something in the middle. Hamid argues in favor of the adoption of two-wheeled tractors which displace animal labor but not human labor. He also discusses the possibility of manufacturing such tractors locally. The OECD study by Yudelman, Butler, and Banerji looks at ways of increasing the capacity of the agricultural sector to absorb more labor *productively.* The authors say that if technology is to contribute to this process, innovations will have to be made available to smallholders, as well as larger farmers. Institutional changes are also important, particularly land reform and the creation of cooperatives. "Complementary research"—the adaptation of imported technology to local conditions—is identified as a necessary concomitant of technology transfer.

A number of entries in the section entitled "Mechanization" on pages 150–155 are relevant here.

345. Aggarwal, Partap C. "Impact of Green Revolution on Landless Labour: A Note." *Economic and Political Weekly* 6 (20 November 1971): 2363, 2365.

346. Ahmed, Iftikhar. "Technical Change and Labour Utilization in Rice Cultivation: Bangladesh." *The Bangladesh Development Studies* 5 (July 1977): 359–366.

347. ______. *Technology and Employment Project: The Green Revolution, Mechanisation and Employment.* WEP2–22. Geneva: International Labour Office, January 1975. (Studies Pakistan, India, Bangladesh, Philippines, and Sri Lanka.)

348. Bartsch, William H. *Employment and Technology Choice in Asian Agriculture.* New York: Praeger, 1977.

349. Bieri, Jurg; de Janvry, Alain; and Schmitz, Andrew. "Agricultural Technology and the Distribution of Welfare Gains." *American Journal of Agricultural Economics* 54:5 (1972): 801–808.

350. Billings, M., and Singh, Arjan. "Mechanisation and Rural Employment: With Some Implications for Rural Income Distribution." *Economic and Political Weekly* 5 (27 June 1970): A61–A72.

351. Collier, William L., et al. "Agricultural Technology and Institutional Change in Java." *Food Research Institute Studies* 13:2 (1974): 169–194.

352. Gwyer, G. D. "Trends in Kenyan Agriculture in Relation to Employment." *Journal of Modern African Studies* 11:3 (1973).

353. Hall, Carl W. "Agricultural Technology and Related Manpower Problems," pp. 189–195. In *Manpower: Employment Strategies for*

Economic Development. Washington, D. C.: International Manpower Institute, US Department of Labor, 1969.

354. Hamid, Javed. "Agricultural Mechanization: A Case for Fractional Technology." *Teaching Forum* no. 33. New York: The Agricultural Development Council, September 1973.

355. Hanumantha Rao, C. H. "Factor Endowments, Technology and Farm Employment: Comparison of East Uttar Pradesh with West Uttar Pradesh and Punjab." *Economic and Political Weekly* 11 (25 September 1976).

356. International Labour Office. *Mechanization and Employment in Agriculture: Case Studies from Four Continents.* Geneva: 1973.

357. Johnston, Bruce F., and Cownie, John. "The Seed-Fertilizer Revolution and Labor Force Absorption." *American Economic Review* 59 (September 1969): 569–582.

358. Lele, Uma, and Mellor, John W. "Jobs, Poverty, and the 'Green Revolution.'" *International Affairs* (UK), January 1972, 20–32.

359. Mandal, G. C. "Observations on Agricultural Technology in a Developing Economy." *Economic and Political Weekly* 7 (24 June 1972): A79–A82.

360. Mehra, Shakuntla. "Some Aspects of Labour Use in Indian Agriculture." *Indian Journal of Agricultural Economics* 31 (October–December 1976): 94–121.

361. Muqtada, M. "The Seed-Fertiliser Technology and Surplus Labour in Bangladesh Agriculture." *The Bangladesh Development Studies* 3 (October 1975).

362. Shah, S. L., and Singh, L. R. "The Impact of New Agricultural Technology on Rural Employment in North-West Uttar Pradesh." *Indian Journal of Agricultural Economics* 25 (July–September 1970): 29–33.

363. Staub, William J. *Agricultural Development and Farm Employment in India.* Foreign Agricultural Economics Report no. 84. Washington, D. C.: Economic Research Service, US Department of Agriculture, January 1973.

364. Wills, Ian R. "Green Revolution and Agricultural Employment and Incomes in Western UP." *Economic and Political Weekly* 6 (27 March 1971): A2–A10.

365. ______. "Projections of Effects of Modern Inputs on Agricultural Income and Employment in a Community Development Block, Uttar Pradesh, India." *American Journal of Agricultural Economics* 54 (August 1972): 452–460.

366. Yudelman, Montague; Butler, Gavan; and Banerji, Ranadev. *Technological Change in Agriculture and Employment in Developing Coun-*

tries. Employment Series no. 4. Paris: Organization for Economic Cooperation and Development, 1971.

Rural Industrialization

An increasingly important aspect of rural employment is the creation of rural industries to serve farm communities. Here, the experience of China has been of particular interest. Sigurdson is the best source to consult on rural industrialization in China, particularly entries 376 and 377. Perkins et al. and Riskin also discuss Chinese rural industries. Readers interested in India should consult Behari. The article by Suárez Melo examines a successful experiment under which a rural community enterprise took over a sugar mill. (Rural community enterprises are discussed in the section entitled "Agrarian Change and Land Reform: Latin America," pages 166–171.)

367. Anderson, Dennis, and Leiserson, Mark. *Rural Enterprise and Nonfarm Employment.* World Bank Paper. Washington, D. C.: World Bank, January 1978.

368. Behari, Bepin. *Rural Industrialization in India.* New Delhi: Vikas, 1976.

369. Cartillier, Michel. "Role of Small-Scale Industries in Economic Development: Irrigation Pumpsets Industry in Coimbatore." *Economic and Political Weekly* 10 (1 November 1975): 1732–1741.

370. Chuta, Enyinna, and Liedholm, Carl. *The Role of Small Scale Industry in Employment Generation and Rural Development: Initial Research Results from Sierra Leone.* African Rural Employment Paper no. 11. East Lansing: Department of Agricultural Economics, Michigan State University, 1975.

371. Gandhi, M. K. *The Economics of Village Industrialization.* Ahmedabad: Navajivan, n.d.

372. Jain, O. P. *Rural Industrialization: India's Experience and Programs for Developing Countries.* New Delhi: Commercial Publications Bureau, 1975.

373. Kaneda, Hiromitsu, and Child, Frank. *Small-Scale Agriculturally Related Industry in the Punjab.* Working Paper Series, no. 11. Davis: Department of Economics, University of California, 1971.

374. Perkins, Dwight, et al. *Rural Small-Scale Industry in the People's Republic of China.* Berkeley: University of California Press, 1977.

375. Riskin, Carl. "Intermediate Technology in China's Rural Industries." *World Development* 6 (November–December 1978): 1297–1311.

376. Sigurdson, Jon. *The Role of Small Scale and Rural Industry and its Interaction with Agriculture and Large Scale Industry in China.* Stockholm: Economic Research Institute, Stockholm School of Economics, 1974.

377. ______. *Rural Industrialization in China.* Cambridge, Mass.: Council on East Asian Studies, distributed by Harvard University Press, 1977.

378. ______. "Rural Industrialization in China: A Case Study." *Expert Group Meeting on Rural Industrialization.* Bucharest, September 1973.

379. Simmons, Emmy B. "The Small-Scale Rural Food-Processing Industry in Northern Nigeria." *Food Research Institute Studies* 14:2 (1975).

380. Suárez Melo, Mario. "La Empresa Comunitaria en Colombia: El Caso de la Bertha." *Desarrollo Rural en las Américas* 2:3 (1970): 215–218.

381. United Nations, Industrial Development Organization. "Industrialization and Rural Development," pp. 269–285. In *World Industry Since 1960.* Special Issue of the Industrial Development Survey for the Third General Conference of UNIDO. New York: United Nations, 1979.

382. Vyas, V. S., and Mathai, George. "Farm and Non-Farm Employment in Rural Areas: A Perspective for Planning." *Economic and Political Weekly* 13:6–7 (Annual Number 1978): 333–347.

Role of Public Works Programs

Public works programs are sometimes seen as an important element of rural development policies, helping to solve both the problem of insufficient rural infrastructure and the problem of rural unemployment/underemployment (see, for example, Lewis). However, there is increasing evidence that rural public works programs are not really a long-term solution to the employment problem. For one thing, it is rarely the poorest who profit from these programs, either in terms of employment or in terms of non-wage benefits (for example, greater access to irrigation water). The rural employment problem is structural in nature and only if structural obstacles are removed can long-term solutions be implemented.

One analyst has concluded that in South Asia, "The existing distribution of scarce resources, especially land, is the single most important determinant of the flows of non-wage benefits from works programs" (entry 934, pp. 169–170). A similar assessment is offered by Sau who finds that the main stumbling block to rural development in India is the power of the kulaks who use their land less intensively than small farmers. Sau argues that the state should establish norms for yield per acre and employment per acre. When farmers do not attain these levels, they should be deprived of their land. However, Sau says, because planners do not want to undertake such structural reforms, they frequently "seize" upon rural works programs as the "remedy" for rural employment problems. In addition to entry 934 and the article by Sau, the study by Burki and the articles by Rodgers address the question of the usefulness of public works programs.

Kikuchi, Dozina, and Hayami study the mobilization of labor and other resources at the community level for an irrigation project in the Philippines. Guha surveys the Indian strategy for stimulating capital formation by mobilizing the rural unemployed. Guha reports that this idea never got beyond the stage of a "modest relief programme," due in part to the lack of resources made available to Indian rural works programs.

383. Burki, S. J. *Public Works Programs in Developing Countries: A Comparative Analysis.* Working Paper no. 224. Washington, D. C.: World Bank, February 1976.

384. Dantwala, M. L. "Some Neglected Issues in Employment Planning." *Economic and Political Weekly* 13:6–7 (Annual Number 1978): 291–294.

385. Guha, Sunil. *Rural Manpower and Capital Formation in India.* Bombay: Academic, 1969.

386. Gupta, Ranjit. "Rural Works Programme: Where It Has Gone Astray." *Economic and Political Weekly* 6 (15 May 1971): 995–1004.

387. Kikuchi, Masao; Dozina, Geronimo, Jr.; and Hayami, Yujiro. "Economics of Community Work Programs: A Communal Irrigation Project in the Philippines." *Economic Development and Cultural Change* 26 (January 1978): 211–225.

388. Lewis, John P. "The Public Works Approach to Low-End Poverty Problems: The New Potentialities of an Old Answer." *Journal of Development Planning* no. 5 (1973): 85–113.

389. Rodgers, G. B. "Effects of Public Works on Rural Poverty: Some Case Studies from the Kosi Area of Bihar." *Economic and Political Weekly* 8:4–6 (Annual Number 1973): 255–268.

390. Rodgers, Gerry. "Poverty and Public Works in India." *Institute of Development Studies Bulletin* 5:4 (May 1974): 37–42.

391. Sau, Ranjit. "Growth, Employment and Removal of Poverty." *Economic and Political Weekly* 13:31–33 (Special Number 1978): 1279–1284.

392. Thomas, John W.; Burki, S. J.; Davies, D. G.; and Hook, R. M. *Employment and Development: A Comparative Analysis of the Role of Public*

Works Programs. Cambridge, Mass.: Harvard Institute for International Development, 1975.

393. Thomas, John W. "Employment Creating Public Works Programs: Observations on Political and Social Dimensions." In *Employment in Developing Nations.* Ed. Edgar O. Edwards. New York: Columbia University Press, 1974.

394. Thormann, Peter H. "Labour Intensive Irrigation Works and Some Constructions." *International Labour Review* 106 (August 1972): 151–164.

Impact of Agrarian Reform

With the exception of the article by Joshi, all of the entries in this section belong to a series of articles published in the *International Labour Review.* The first article by Sternberg (entry 400) summarizes the main findings of the other articles in this series and places the problem of agrarian reform and rural employment in a broader context. In general, the *ILR* series demonstrates that agrarian reforms can lead to increased employment opportunities and incomes in the agricultural sector. In fact, "agrarian reform may well be a prerequisite to the achievement of employment objectives (entry 401, p. 1).

Three major sets of constraints on increased employment in agriculture were identified in most of the *ILR* series articles: high concentration of land ownership, undue land fragmentation, and land tenure institutions themselves (notably the lack of security of tenure). Each of these could be altered by agrarian reform measures. However, Sternberg cautions against seeing agrarian reform as a panacea for all employment-related problems. "Many agrarian reforms have bought valuable time, have bought relief from pressure of mass rural exodus and mass unemployment and underemployment. But such problems may reappear if the rest of the economy is not reformed at the same time" (entry 400, p. 476).

395. Ahmad, Zubeida M., and Sternberg, Marvin J. "Agrarian Reform and Employment With Special Reference to Asia." *International Labour Review* 99 (February 1969): 159–183.

396. Clayton, Eric S. "Agrarian Reform, Agricultural Planning and Employment in Kenya." *International Labour Review* 102 (November 1970): 431–453.

397. Dorner, Peter P., and Felstehausen, Herman. "Agrarian Reform and Employment: The Colombian Case." *International Labour Review* 102 (September 1970): 221–240.

398. Joshi, P. C. "Agrarian Structure and Employment: Some Aspects of Historical Experience." *Economic and Political Weekly* 13:6–7 (Annual Number 1978): 315–331.

399. Koo, Anthony Y. C. "Agrarian Reform, Production and Employment in Taiwan." *International Labour Review* 104 (July–August 1971): 1–22.

400. Sternberg, Marvin J. "Agrarian Reform and Employment: Potential and Problems." *International Labour Review* 103 (May 1971): 453–476.

401. ______. "Agrarian Reform and Employment, With Special Reference to Latin America." *International Labour Review* 95 (January–February 1967): 1–26.

402. Warriner, Doreen. "Employment and Income Aspects of Recent Agrarian Reforms in the Middle East." *International Labour Review* 101 (June 1970): 605–625. (Discusses Egypt, Iraq, Iran)

Part II: Rural Development

General

The entries in this section reflect the fact that for most of the last three decades change in the rural sector has been associated with agricultural development, that is, raising agricultural output. A number of entries deal with the broader topics of rural development and alleviating rural poverty. Of these, the following are suggested as introduction to the topic: the book by Coombs and Ahmed, the volume edited by Bengtsson, the special issue of *Revue Tiers-Monde* edited by Goussault, and the articles by Stavenhagen and by King.

Most of the remainder of the entries in this section deal very broadly with agricultural development as well as with topics not covered elsewhere in Part II such as rural cooperatives, education, rural extension and training, rural transportation systems, and agricultural research.

Books and Monographs

The FAO publication *The State of Food and Agriculture* (entry 431) is an annual review of the world food and agricultural situation. Each volume features a detailed examination of a particular subject. *World Agriculture: The Last Quarter Century* (entry 434), also a FAO publication, reviews post-World War II agriculture up to the end of the 1960s. Technical progress and agricultural development policies are also discussed.

In recent years, there has been considerable interest in issues pertaining to "participation" in rural development. However, as is often the case, while there is a consensus on the desirability of promoting participation, there is much less agreement on what participation may be, how it should occur, or whom it should benefit. The monograph by Uphoff, Cohen, and Goldsmith is a state-of-the-art review of participation as it pertains to rural development and is recommended as an introduction to the topic. A bibliographic supplement to this monograph can be found in entry 3157.

The monograph by Whyte considers deficiencies in the contributions of behavioral scientists to the formulation of agricultural and rural development strategies. Whyte also proposes an "organizational framework designed to advance both theory and practice" of agricultural development. The study by Rice documents the failure of the USAID-sanctioned extension model widely used in Latin America in the 1950s and 1960s. Rice concludes that extension results in increased agricultural productivity only when "it offers a profitable new technology in an economic regime that reduces risks, guarantees prices and/or offers credit." The shortcomings of extension services are also discussed, *inter alia,* by Coombs and Ahmed.

Dahlberg uses contextual analysis to examine the "real-world contexts" of agricultural development theories. He is particularly interested in encouraging social scientists to take a longer-term view of agricultural development—especially in terms of its ecological, social, and technological components—than is inherent in the policy-oriented time-frame which is normally adopted. Other recommended items are Dumont, Kayser, Griffin, Hopkins, Talbot and Puchala, and the volume edited by Bengtsson. The latter contains a useful short bibliography.

403. The Agribusiness Council. *Agricultural Initiative in the Third World—A Report on the Conference: Science and Agribusiness in the Seventies.* Lexington, Mass.: Heath/Lexington, 1975.

404. Agricultural Cooperative Development International. *Building Farmer-Owned Enterprises. Annual Report 1972.* Contract AID/csd–2219. Washington, D. C.: 1972.

405. ———. *The Role of Agricultural Cooperatives in Development Strategies.* Washington, D. C.: 1974.

406. Ahmed, R. *Agriculture in Integrated Rural Development. A Critique.* Washington, D. C.: International Food Policy Research Institute, 1977.

407. Aldrich, Daniel G., Jr., ed. *Research for the World Food Crisis.* AAAS Publication no. 92. Washington, D. C.: American Association for the Advancement of Science, 1970.

408. Axinn, George H., and Thorat, Sudhakar. *Modernizing World Agriculture: A Comparative Study of Agricultural Extension Education Systems.* New York: Praeger, 1972.

409. Bengtsson, Bo, ed. *Rural Development Research—The Role of Power Relations.* Sarec Report R4:1979. Stockholm: Swedish Agency for Research Cooperation with Developing Countries, 1979.

410. Birowo, A. T. *Research on Rural Development to Improve the Rural Poor in the Third World.* Jakarta: Agro-Economic Survey, 1978.

411. Bunting, A. H., ed. *Change in Agriculture.* London: Duckworth, 1970.

412. Cernea, Michael M., and Tepping, Benjamin J. *A System of Monitoring and Evaluating Agricultural Extension Projects.* Working Paper no. 272. Washington, D. C.: World Bank, December 1977.

413. Cohen, John M., and Uphoff, Norman T. *Rural Development Participation: Concepts and Measures for Project Design, Implementation and Evaluation.* Ithaca, N. Y.: Rural Development Committee, Center for International Studies, Cornell University, January 1977.

414. Coombs, Philip H., with Manzoor Ahmed. *Attacking Rural Poverty: How Nonformal Education Can Help.* Baltimore, Md.: Johns Hopkins University Press, 1974.

415. Courtenay, Philip P. *Plantation Agriculture.* New York: Praeger, 1965.

416. Csáki, Norbert. *Land Supply and International Specialization in Agriculture.* Budapest, Akadémiai Kiadó, 1974.

417. Cummings, Ralph W. *Food Crops in the Low-Income Countries: The State of Present and Expected Agricultural Research and Technology.* New York: Rockefeller Foundation, 1976.

418. Dahlberg, Kenneth A. *Beyond the Green Revolution: The Ecology and Politics of Global Agricultural Development.* New York: Plenum, 1979.

419. Dalrymple, Dana G. *Survey of Multiple Cropping in Less Developed Nations.* Foreign Agricultural Economics Report no. 91. Washington, D. C.: Economic Research Service, US Department of Agriculture, October 1971.

420. ______. *Technological Change in Agriculture: Effects and Implications for the Developing Nations.* Washington, D. C.: Foreign Agriculture Service, US Department of Agriculture, April 1969.

421. ______. *The Diversification of Agricultural Production in Less Developed Countries.* Washington, D. C.: International Agricultural Development Service, US Department of Agriculture, August 1968.

422. Dorner, Peter P., ed. *Cooperative and Commune: Group Farming in the Economic Development of Agriculture.* Madison: University of Wisconsin Press, 1977.

423. Dorner, Peter P., and Kanel, Don. *Group Farming Issues and Prospects: A Summary of International Experience.* Seminar Report. New York: The Agricultural Development Council, November 1975.

424. Duckham, Alec N., and Masefield, Geoffrey Bussell. Assisted by R. W. Wiley and Kathleen Down. *Farming Systems of the World.* London: Chatto & Windus, 1970.

425. Dumett, Raymond E., and Brainard, Lawrence J. *Problems of Rural Development: Case Studies and Multi-Disciplinary Perspectives.* Leiden: Brill, 1975.

426. Dumont, René. *Utopia or Else.* Trans. Vivienne Menkes. New York: Universe, 1975.

427. ______. *Types of Rural Economy. Studies in World Agriculture.* London: Methuen, 1957. (Chapters 1–5 and Conclusion are relevant.)

428. Dumont, René, with Marcel Mazoyer. *Socialisms and Development.* Trans. Rupert Cunningham. New York and Washington, D. C.: Praeger, 1973.

429. Evenson, Robert E., and Kislev, Yoav. *Agricultural Research and Productivity.* New Haven and London: Yale University Press, 1975.

430. Food and Agriculture Organization. *Agricultural Policies at Different Levels of Development.* Rome: 1975.

431. ______. *The State of Food and Agriculture.* Rome: annually from 1947.

432. ______. *Studies in Agricultural Economics and Statistics.* Rome: 1978.

433. ______. *World Agricultural Structure: Study No. 1. General Introduction: Number and Size of Holdings.* FAO/61/J/13839–p. Rome: 1961.

434. ______. *World Agriculture: The Last Quarter Century.* World Food Problems Series, no. 13. Rome: 1970.

435. Gable, Richard W., and Springer, J. Fred. *Administering Agricultural Development in Asia: A Comparative Analysis of Four National Programs.* Boulder, Colo.: Westview, 1977.

436. Hayami, Yujiro, and Ruttan, Vernon. *Agricultural Development: An International Perspective.* Baltimore, Md.: Johns Hopkins University Press, 1971.

437. Hodder, B. W. *Economic Development in the Tropics.* 2nd ed. London: Methuen, 1973. (Chapters 1–9 are particularly relevant.)

438. Hopkins, Raymond F.; Talbot, Ross; and Puchala, Don. *Food, Politics, and Agricultural Development: Case Studies in Public Policy in Rural Modernization.* Boulder, Colo.: Westview, 1979.

439. Indian Society of Agricultural Economics. *Seminar on Rural Development for Weaker Sections.* Bombay: Indian Society of Agricultural Economics, in collaboration with Centre for Management in Agriculture, Indian Institute of Management (Ahmedabad), 1974.

440. Islam, Nurul. *Agricultural Policies in Developing Countries.* New York: Wiley, 1974.

441. Jodha, N. S. *Resource Base as a Determinant of Cropping Patterns.* PN–AAF–062. Washington, D. C.: US Agency for International Development, 1977.

442. Jurion, F., and Henry, J. *Can Primitive Farming be Modernized?* Trans. Agra Europe. Brussels [?]: Hors Series, 1969.

443. Kayser, Bernard. *L'Agriculture et la Société Rurale des Régions Tropicales.* Paris: Société d'Edition d'Enseignement Supérieur, 1969.

444. Leakey, C. L. A., and Wills, J. B., eds. *Food Crops of the Lowland Tropics.* Oxford: Oxford University Press, 1977.

445. Mann, Amy G., and Miracle, Jan, eds. *Rural Development: The Interplay of Analysis and Action.* Bloomington: Indiana University, International Development Research Center, 1975.

446. Mazumdar, Dipak. *An International Comparison of Low Income in the Agricultural Sector in Selected Less Developed Countries.* Working Paper no. 118. Washington, D. C.: World Bank, October 1971.

447. *Mechanisation and the World's Rice Crop.* Oxford: Massey-Ferguson (Export), distributed by Basil Blackwell, 1967.

448. Meier, Gerald M. *Leading Issues in Economic Development.* 3rd ed. New York: Oxford University Press, 1976. (The section entitled "Agricultural Strategy," pp. 561–628, is particularly relevant.)

449. Meta Systems, Inc. *Systems Analysis of Rural Transportation.* Working Paper no. 77. Washington, D. C.: World Bank, May 1970.

450. Millikan, Max F., and Hapgood, David. *No Easy Harvest: The Dilemma of Agriculture in Developing Countries.* Boston: Little, Brown, 1967.

451. Mosher, Arthur T. *Creating a Progressive Rural Structure.* New York: Agricultural Development Council, 1969.

452. ———. *Getting Agriculture Moving: Essentials for Development and Modernization.* New York: Praeger, 1966.

453. Myrdal, Gunnar. *The Challenge of World Poverty.* New York: Pantheon, 1970. (Chapters 4, 12–15 are especially relevant.)

454. Myren, D. T., ed. *Communications in Agricultural Development.* Mexico City: First Inter-American Research Symposium, October 1964.

455. National Research Council, Commission on International Relations. *World Food and Nutrition Study. The Potential Contributions of Research. Vol. III.* Washington, D. C.: National Academy of Sciences, 1977.

456. Norman, David W. *Inter-Disciplinary Research on Rural Development. The Experience of the Rural Economy Research Unit in Northern Nigeria.* OLC Paper no. 6. Washington, D. C.: Overseas Liaison Committee, American Council on Education, April 1974.

457. Owens, Edgar, and Shaw. Robert d'A. *Development Reconsidered.* Lexington, Mass.: Lexington, 1972. (Chapter 5 is relevant.)

458. Parsons, Kenneth H. *The Political Economy of Agricultural Development.* LTC no. 16. Madison: Land Tenure Center, University of Wisconsin, April 1978.

459. Pawley, W. H. *Possibilities of Increasing World Food Production.* FFHC Basic Study no. 10. Rome: FAO, 1963.

460. Rice, E. B. *Extension in the Andes: An Evaluation of Official US Assistance to Agricultural Extension Services in Central and South America.* Washington, D. C.: Agency for International Development, 1971.

461. Robinson, Edward A. G., and Kidron, Michael, eds. *Economic Development in South Asia.* London: Macmillan; New York: St. Martin's, 1970. (The chapter by Raj entitled "Some Questions Concerning Growth, Transformation and Planning of Agriculture in the Developing Countries" is particularly relevant.)

462. Rockefeller Foundation. *Program in the Agricultural Sciences.* New York: 1959–1966, annually.

463. ______. *Strategy for the Conquest of Hunger. Proceedings of a Symposium.* New York: 1–2 April 1968.

464. ______. *Toward the Conquest of Hunger.* Progress Report, Program in the Agricultural Sciences. New York: 1965–1966.

465. Schultz, Theodore W., ed. *Distortions of Agricultural Incentives.* Bloomington: Indiana University Press, 1978.

466. Schuster, Helmut. *Agricultural Reader.* EDI Sem. 7. Washington, D. C.: World Bank, 1973.

467. *Science, Technology and Development. United States Papers Prepared for the United Nations Conference on the Application of Science and Technology For the Benefit of Less Developed Areas. Vol. III: Agriculture.* Washington, D. C.: US Printing Office, c.1962.

468. Scrimshaw, Nevin S., and Béhar, Moisés. *Nutrition and Agricultural Development. Significance and Potential for the Tropics.* New York and London: Plenum, 1974.

469. Thiesenhusen, William C. *Hill Land Farming: An International Dimension.* LTC no. 109. Madison: Land Tenure Center, University of Wisconsin, December 1976.

470. *Toward the Integration of World Agriculture.* Tripartite Report. Washington, D. C.: The Brookings Institution, 1973.

471. United Nations, Economic Commission for Africa. *A Survey of Economic Conditions in Africa, 1967.* New York: 1969. (See especially, Part One, III. Agriculture, pp. 30–61; and Part Two, II. The Export of Primary Products, pp. 149–166.)

472. United Nations, Research Institute for Social Development. *Rural Cooperatives as Agents of Change: A Research Report and a Debate.* Geneva: 1975.

473. United States, Department of Agriculture, Economic Research Service. *Changes in Agriculture in 26 Developing Nations, 1948 to 1963.* Foreign Agricultural Economic Report no. 27. Washington, D. C.: November 1965.

474. ______. *Economic Progress of Agriculture in Developing Nations, 1950–68.* Foreign Agricultural Economic Report no. 59. Washington, D. C.: May 1970. (Includes detailed studies of Taiwan, Mexico, Colombia, Brazil, India, and Nigeria.)

475. Uphoff, Norman T.; Cohen, John M.; and Goldsmith, Arthur A. *Feasibility and Application of Rural Development Participation: A State of the Art Paper.* Monograph Series, no. 3. Ithaca, N. Y.: Rural Development Committee, Center for International Studies, Cornell University, January 1979.

476. Virone, L. E.; Pellizzi, C.; Upton, M.; and Marcano, L. *The Transformation of Rural Communities. Some Implications of Promoting Change from Subsistence to Marketing Agriculture in Contrasted Geographical Regions.* The World Land Use Survey, Occasional Papers no. 7. Bude, UK: Geographical Publications, 1966.

477. Whyte, William F. *Organizing for Agricultural Development.* New Brunswick, N. J.: Transaction, 1975.

478. Wortman, Sterling, and Cummings, Ralph W., Jr. *To Feed This World.* Baltimore, Md.: Johns Hopkins University Press, 1975.

Articles

The articles by Kötter and Rondinelli are suggested as introductions to Integrated Rural Development. Other recommended articles include Bairoch, Dandekar, Stavenhagen, and the issue of *Revue Tiers-Monde* edited by Goussault.

479. Bairoch, Paul. "Evolution et Rôle de l'Agriculture dans le Tiers-Monde." *Civilisations* 20:1 (1970): 25–36.

480. Broadbent, Kieran P. "An 'Invisible' Good." *Ceres* no. 63 (May–June 1978): 19–23.

481. Brookfield, H. C. "New Directions in the Study of Agricultural Systems in Tropical Areas," pp. 413–439. In *Evolution and Environment.* Ed. Ellen T. Drake. New Haven: Yale University Press, 1968.

482. Butani, D. H., ed. "Agricultural Productivity" (Special Issue). *Productivity* (New Delhi) 6:2–3 (1965): 174–482.

483. Chambers, Robert. "Rural Development in Africa and South Asia." *Institute of Development Studies Bulletin* 5:4 (May 1974): 54–58.

484. Chang Jen-hu. "The Agricultural Potential of the Humid Tropics." *The Geographical Review* 63 (July 1968): 333–361.

485. ______. "Tropical Agriculture: Crop Diversity and Crop Yields." *Economic Geography* 53 (July 1977): 241–254.

486. Chedd, Graham. "Famine or Sanity?" *New Scientist* 44 (23 October 1969): 178–182.

487. Dandekar, V. M. "Agricultural Growth with Social Justice in Overpopulated Countries." *Economic and Political Weekly* 5:29–31 (Special Number 1970): 1231–1238.

488. Enke, Stephen. "Agricultural Innovations and Community Development." In *Problems of the Developing Countries: Readings and Case Studies.* Ed. Lewis P. Fickett, Jr. New York: Crowell, 1966.

489. Evenson, Robert E., and Kislev, Yoav. "Investment in Agricultural Research and Extension: A Survey of International Data." *Economic Development and Cultural Change* 23 (April 1975): 507–521.

490. Goussault, Y., ed. "Le Développement Rural" (Special Issue). *Revue Tiers-Monde* 14 (April–June 1973): 227–436.

491. Grist, D. H. "Cultivation of Rice." *World Crops* 21 (March–April 1969): 17–21.

492. Hervé, Alain. "Multilateral Investment in Agriculture." *Ceres* no. 5 (September–October 1968): 29–31.

493. Hibler, Michelle. "Less Waste, More Food." *IDRC Reports* 7 (June 1978): 19–21.

494. Highsmith, Richard M., Jr. "How Types of Farming Divide World Agriculture into Regions." *Foreign Agriculture,* 14 March 1966, pp. 3–5.

495. Joy, Leonard. "Strategy for Agricultural Development," pp. 174–202. In *Development in a Divided World.* Ed. Dudley Seers and Leonard Joy. Harmondsworth, UK: Penguin Books, 1971.

496. King, David J. "Rural Development: A Proposed New Perspective." *LTC Newsletter* no. 44 (April–June 1974): 1–7.

497. Kötter, H. R. "Some Observations on the Basic Principles and General Strategy Underlying Integrated Rural Development." *Monthly Bulletin of Agricultural Economics and Statistics* 23:4 (1974).

498. Meister, Albert. "Characteristics of Community Development and Rural Animation in Africa." *International Review of Community Development* nos. 27–28 (Summer 1972): 75–132.

499. Mellor, John W. "The Process of Agricultural Development in Low-Income Countries." *Journal of Farm Economics* 44 (August 1962): 700–716.

500. Ooi, Jin Bee. "Rural Development in Tropical Areas with Special Reference to Malaya." *Journal of Tropical Geography* 12 (March 1959): 1–222.

501. "Report of the Group Farming Conference" (Special Issue). *Land Tenure Center Newsletter* no. 49 (July–September 1975). (Includes a bibliography of English-language sources on group farming.)

502. "The Role of Agriculture in the World Economy." *Journal of Farm Economics* 43 (May 1961): 320–346.

503. Rondinelli, Dennis A. "Administration of Integrated Rural Development Policy: The Politics of Agrarian Reform in Developing Countries." *World Politics* 31 (April 1979): 389–416.

504. Ruttan, Vernon W. "Integrated Rural Development Programs: A Skeptical Perspective." *International Development Review* 17:4 (1975): 9–16.

505. Shastry, B. D. "Quickening the Pace of Agricultural Development." *Economic and Political Weekly* 6 (26 June 1971): A95–A98.

506. Stavenhagen, Rodolfo. "Basic Needs, Peasants and the Strategy for Rural Development," pp. 40–65. In *Another Development. Approaches and Strategies.* Ed. Marc Nerfin. Uppsala: Dag Hammarskjöld Foundation, 1977.

507. Tagumpay-Castillo, Gelia. "Propensity to Invest in Agriculture. Observations from a Developing Country—the Philippines." *International Journal of Agrarian Affairs* 5 (July 1968): 282–310.

508. Thurston, H. David. "Tropical Agriculture. A Key to the World Food Crisis." *BioScience* 19:1 (1969): 29–34.

509. Uphoff, Norman T., and Esman, Milton J. "Local Organization for Rural Development in Asia." *Development Digest* 13 (July 1975): 31–46. (An extended version of this has been published as *Local Organization for Rural Development: An Analysis of Asian Experience.* Monograph RLG no. 19. Ithaca, N. Y.: Rural Development Committee, Center for International Studies, Cornell University, November 1974.)

510. Waddell, Eric. "The Return to Traditional Agriculture: The Only Means of Solving the World Food Problem." *The Ecologist* 7 (May 1977): 144–147.

511. Wickizer, V. D. "The Plantation System in the Development of Tropical Economies." *Journal of Farm Economics* 40 (February 1958): 63–77.

512. Zuvekas, Clarence, Jr. "Determining Agricultural Sector Growth Rates in Less Developed Countries: The Case of Ecuador." *Inter-American Economic Affairs* 27 (Autumn 1973): 67–83.

Contribution to National Development

The emphasis in conventional development strategies on achieving rapid rates of industrial expansion has led to the relative neglect of agriculture in most developing countries. However, even in the 1960s it was evident that a stagnant agricultural sector could jeopardize overall economic growth. The FAO identified four major areas in which agriculture had to make a strong contribution if industrial development were to take place: supplier of food and raw materials, earner of foreign exchange, supplier of finance and labor, and market for industrial goods (entry 522, pp. 2–10). The necessity of agricultural and industrial development proceeding simultaneously is the topic of a number of items below (such as el-Beblaoui, FAO, Khan, Waterson, Mkandawire, and Johnson and Mellor). Additional sources can be found in entry 77. At the same time, through the entire post-World War II period, some analysts have argued that agricultural development must be given priority over industrial expansion (see, for example, Badouin, Lindholm, Sayigh, and Traoré).

Books and Monographs

An introduction to the argument that the development of agriculture and industry must proceed simultaneously is found in the FAO study, *Agriculture and Industrialization.* The FAO suggests that "agro-oriented industrialization" should be given far more attention:

> This would concentrate particularly on the consumer goods and inputs needed by the agricultural population, who would thus be assisted and stimulated to produce the increasing quantities of food and other agricultural products demanded by the industrial population, and would in turn, as a result of having higher incomes, become better customers for the products of industry. (entry 522, p. 10)

To some extent, this sort of development strategy sounds similar to the one which has dominated Chinese thinking for much of the past two decades, notwithstanding the "four modernizations," in which the priorities have been agriculture, light industry, and heavy industry. However, when one examines the roles assigned to the agricultural sector by the FAO, one discovers that self-reliant development is the last thing that is being promoted:

> The capital goods required for industrialization are still largely produced in the developed countries, and the developing countries must therefore spend foreign exchange in order to purchase them. The same

applies to many of the intermediate goods needed in industry and also to many of the consumer goods for which the demand increases as the industrial labor force expands. (entry 522, p. 5)

It was recognized before the 1970s that a stagnant agricultural sector means a stagnant economy. Nevertheless, although large numbers of people in rural areas were living in absolute poverty, it was only after the urban-industrial centers failed to absorb a sufficiently large portion of the third world work force and the per capita food production failed to increase significantly or actually declined that lending agencies such as the World Bank and USAID were forced to emphasize programs for the rural sector. Whether increased lending to the agricultural sector will actually improve the situation of the poorest and help promote self-reliant growth, as these lending agencies claim it will, remains to be seen. Critics of these groups and of the entire Western aid system claim that the aid agencies' rural-oriented strategy will only benefit the world's wealthy—urban and rural, in rich and poor nations—and will not benefit the rural poor at all. (See for example entries 1607, 1887, and 1890.)

513. Badouin, Robert. *Agriculture et Accession au Développement.* Paris: Editions A. Pedone, 1967.

514. Bawa, Ujagar S. *Agricultural Production and Industrial Capital Formation, India, 1951–52 to 1964–65.* Cornell International Agricultural Development Bulletin 17. Ithaca, N. Y.: Cornell University, March 1971.

515. el-Beblaoui, Hazem. *L'Interdépendance Agriculture-Industrie et le Développement Economique (L'Exemple de la R. A. U.).* Paris: Editions Oujas, 1967.

516. Bhatia, Balmokand M. *Poverty, Agriculture and Economic Growth.* New Delhi: Vikas, 1977.

517. Brenner, Y. S. *Agriculture and the Economic Development of Low Income Countries.* The Hague and Paris: Mouton, 1971.

518. Dasgupta, Ajit Kumar. *Agriculture and Economic Development in India.* New Delhi: Associated, 1973.

519. Eicher, Carl, and Witt, Lawrence. *Agriculture in Economic Development.* New York: McGraw-Hill, 1964.

520. Fletcher, Lehman B.; Graber, E.; Thorbecke, E.; and Merrill, W. C. *Guatemala's Economic Development: The Role of Agriculture.* Ames: Iowa State University Press, 1971.

521. Flores, Xavier-André. *Agricultural Organizations and Economic and Social Development in Rural Areas.* Studies and Reports, New Series, no. 77. Geneva: ILO, 1971.

522. Food and Agriculture Organization. *Agriculture and Industrialization.* FFHC Basic Study no. 17. Rome: 1967.

523. Heuberger, Aloys. *Economic Growth and the Role of Agriculture in Developing Countries: With Special Reference to India.* Bern and Frankfurt-am-Main: Herbert Lang & Peter Lang, 1974.

524. Japan Economic Research Center. *Agriculture and Economic Development: Structural Readjustment in Asian Perspective.* JERC Center Paper, no. 17. Tokyo: 1972.

525. Khan, Mahmood Hasan. *The Role of Agriculture in Economic Development.* Wageningen: Centre for Agricultural Publications and Documentation, 1966.

526. Lipton, Michael. *Transfer of Resources from Agriculture to Non-Agricultural Activities: The Case of India.* IDS Communication 109. Brighton, UK: Institute of Development Studies, University of Sussex, c. 1973.

527. Merrill, William C.; Fletcher, L. B.; Hoffman, R. A.; and Applegate, M. J. *Panama's Economic Development: The Role of Agriculture.* Ames: Iowa State University Press, 1975.

528. Oluwasanmi, H. A. *Agriculture and Nigerian Economic Development.* Ibadan: Oxford University Press, 1966.

529. Reynolds, Lloyd G., ed. *Agriculture in Development Theory.* New Haven: Yale University Press, 1975.

530. Rosier, Bernard. *Structures Agricoles et Développement Economique.* Paris: Mouton, 1968.

531. Rudra, Ashok. *Relative Rates of Growth—Agriculture and Industry.* Series in Economics no. 14. Bombay: University of Bombay, 1967.

532. Schultz, Theodore W. *Economic Growth and Agriculture.* New York: McGraw-Hill, 1968.

533. Sinha, Sachchidanand. *The Bitter Harvest: Agriculture and the Economic Crisis.* New Delhi: Manas, 1975.

534. Southworth, Herman M., and Johnston, Bruce F. *Agricultural Development and Economic Growth.* Ithaca, N. Y.: Cornell University Press, 1967.

535. Sundrum, R. M., and Hlaing, U Aye. *The Role of Agriculture in Economic Development. The Burmese Experience.* Economics Papers, no. 6. Rangoon: Department of Economics, Statistics and Commerce, University of Rangoon, 1961.

536. Thorbecke, Erik, ed. *The Role of Agriculture in Economic Development.* New York: National Bureau of Economic Research, distributed by Columbia University Press, 1969.

537. Thornton, D. S. *Agriculture in Economic Development.* Reprint no. 124. Madison: Land Tenure Center, University of Wisconsin, c. 1973.

538. Waterston, Albert. *Preparing a Program for Agriculture.* EDI Sem. 5. Washington, D. C.: World Bank, 1973.

539. Wells, Jerome C. *Agricultural Policy and Economic Growth in Nigeria.* Ibadan: Oxford University Press, 1974.

Articles

Klatzmann argues that without agricultural development there can be no overall economic development and he discusses a number of political, economic, and social reasons why agricultural development has been slow in many countries. Cownie claims that the belief that the agricultural and the industrial sectors are in competition with each other for scarce resources has caused planners to allocate resources in a way which gives preference to capital-intensive development. This tendency is aggravated, according to Cownie, by the dependence on aggregate statistics (especially GNP) to measure economic progress. Cownie argues in favor of the use of scarce capital and foreign exchange to bring labor and land into the development process. He also supports the creation of alternative means of measuring economic and social progress (such as distribution-of-income or employment-creation indicators). Cartillier discusses the role played by small industries in Indian agricultural development, taking as his example the diffusion of irrigation pumps (largely manufactured by small firms) as one result of the introduction of Green Revolution technology.

Amin argues that the Green Revolution cannot be used as a substitute for "total, self-centered development, agricultural and industrial." Also recommended are Mkandawire and entry 2516. The latter discusses the relationship between industrial and agricultural development in Taiwan.

540. Amin, Samir. "The Limits of the 'Green Revolution.' " *Ceres* no. 16 (July–August 1970): 49–52.

541. Azam, K. M. A. "Role of Agriculture and Industrialisation in Economic Growth," pp. 35–65. In his *Planning and Economic Growth.* Lahore: Maktaba-tul-Arafat, 1968.

542. Barter, P. G. H. "The Role of Agriculture in Economic Development," pp. 45–54. In *Agricultural Planning Course, 1963.* Food and Agriculture Organization. Agricultural Planning Studies no. 4. Rome: 1964.

543. Cartillier, Michel. "La Révolution Verte en Inde et le Rôle des Petites Industries: Le Cas des Pompes d'Irrigation." *Revue Tiers-Monde* 18 (April–June 1977): 397–412.

544. Cownie, John. "Agriculture, Domestic Manufacturing, and Structural Transformation: Assessing Economic Development." *African Studies Review* 17 (April 1974): 123–132.

545. Gutman, G. O. "A Note on Economic Development with Subsistence Agriculture." *Oxford Economic Papers* (New Series) 9 (October 1957): 323–329.

546. Hsieh, S. C., and Lee, T. H. "Agricultural Development and its Contribution to Economic Growth in Taiwan." *Economic Digest Series.* no. 17. Taipei: Joint Commission on Rural Reconstruction, 1966.

547. Johnson, D. Gale. "The Role of Agriculture in Economic Development," pp. 3–26. In *Natural Resources and International Development.* Ed. Marion Clawson. Baltimore, Md.: Johns Hopkins University Press, 1964.

548. Johnston, Bruce F. "Agricultural Strategy and Industrial Growth," pp. 181–192. In *Economic Growth in Developing Countries—Material and Human Resources.* Ed. Yohanan Ramati. Praeger Special Studies in International Economics and Development. New York: Praeger, 1975.

549. Johnston, Bruce F., and Mellor, John W. "The Role of Agriculture in Economic Development." *American Economic Review* 51 (September 1961): 566–593.

550. Klatzmann, Joseph. "Les Blocages du Développement dans le Secteur Agricole." *Revue Tiers-Monde* 8 (January–March 1967): 45–56.

551. Lindholm, Richard W. "The Farm: The Misused Income Expansion Base of Emerging Nations." *Journal of Farm Economics* 43 (May 1961): 236–246.

552. Mkandawire, P. Thandika. "Employment Strategies in the Third World: A Critique." *Journal of Contemporary Asia* 7:1 (1977): 27–43.

553. Onwubuemeli, Emeka. "Agriculture, the Theory of Economic Development and the Zande Scheme." *Journal of Modern African Studies* 12:4 (1974): 569–587.

554. Reddaway, William. "The Roles of Industry and Agriculture in the Development of Developing Countries," pp. 193–201. In *Economic Growth in Developing Countries—Material and Human Resources.* Ed. Yohanan Ramati. Praeger Special Studies in International Economics and Development. New York: Praeger, 1975.

555. Sau, Ranjit. "Some Aspects of Inter-Sectoral Resource Flow." *Economic and Political Weekly* 9:32–34 (Special Number 1974): 1277–1284.

556. Sayigh, Y. A. "The Place of Agriculture in Economic Development." *Agricultural Situation in India* 14 (Annual Number 1959).

557. Traoré, Aly. "Rapports Agriculture-Industrie et 'Socialisme Ujamaa' en Tanzanie." *Revue Tiers-Monde* 16 (October–December 1975): 805–820.

558. Wils, Frits C. M. "Agriculture and Industrial Development in Peru: Some Observations on Their Relationship." *Development and Change* 5:2 (1973–74): 76–100.

Economic Aspects

This section contains items covering a wide variety of topics related to the economic aspects of agricultural development.

Books and Monographs

In *The Conditions of Agricultural Growth,* Boserup sets forward the argument that too small a population can be a handicap when a country seeks to promote agricultural development. She argues the case that innovations have often resulted from the pressure of rising populations on traditional cultivation methods. This is a position that a number of developing nations, particularly in Africa, have found attractive. In *Transforming Traditional Agriculture,* Schultz argues that the agricultural sector is the closest approximation of a neoclassical competitive equilibrium in existence. Therefore, he believes that institutional change and the reallocation of resources will not increase production; rather, the problem is one of a lack of inputs.

Hill calls for the creation of "indigenous economics" based on the actual functioning of developing country economies. Such a formulation would enable Western-biased concepts to be avoided when dealing with the third world. This book is recommended as is the one by Gudeman.

559. Behrman, Jere R. *Development, The International Economic Order and Commodity Agreements.* Reading, Mass.: Addison-Wesley, 1978.

560. Boserup, Ester. *The Conditions of Agricultural Growth: The Economics of Agrarian Change Under Population Pressure.* Chicago, Ill.: Aldine, 1965.

561. Dovring, Folke. *Land Reform and Productivity: The Mexican Case, Analysis of Census Data.* LTC no. 63. Madison: Land Tenure Center, University of Wisconsin, January 1969.

562. Eddie, Scott M. *The Simple Economics of Land Reform: The Expropriation-Compensation Process and Income Distribution.* LTC no. 75. Madison: Land Tenure Center, University of Wisconsin, February 1971.

563. Gittinger, J. Price. *The Economic Analysis of Agricultural Projects.* Baltimore, Md.: Johns Hopkins University Press, 1972.

564. Gudeman, Stephen. *The Demise of a Rural Economy: From Subsistence to Capitalism in a Latin American Village.* London: Routledge & Kegan Paul, 1978. (Discusses Panama)

565. Hallett, Graham. *The Economics of Agricultural Policy.* Oxford: Blackwell, 1968.

566. Haswell, Margaret. *Tropical Farming Economics.* London: Longman, 1973.

567. Hill, Polly. *Studies in Rural Capitalism in West Africa.* Cambridge: Cambridge University Press, 1970.

568. Jain, Sharad Chandra. *Price Behaviour and Resource Allocation in Indian Agriculture.* Bombay and New York: Allied, 1968.

569. Johnston, Bruce F., and Kilby, Peter. *Agricultural and Structural Transformation: Economic Strategies in Late-Developing Countries.* New York: Oxford University Press, 1975.

570. Mellor, John W. *The Economics of Agricultural Development.* Cornell Paperbacks. Ithaca, N. Y.: Cornell University Press, 1970.

571. Myrdal, Gunnar. *Asian Drama: An Inquiry into the Poverty of Nations.* New York: Pantheon, 1968.

572. Schultz, Theodore W. *Economic Crises in World Agriculture.* Ann Arbor: University of Michigan Press, 1966.

573. ______. *The Economic Organization of Agriculture.* New York: McGraw-Hill, 1953.

574. ______. *Transforming Traditional Agriculture.* reprint ed. New Haven: Arno, 1976.

575. Shulka, Tara, ed. *Economics of Underdeveloped Agriculture.* Bombay: Vora, 1969.

576. Tyagi, D. S. *Farmers' Response to Agricultural Prices in India (A Study in Decision Making).* Delhi: Heritage, 1974.

577. United States, General Accounting Office. *Providing Economic Incentives to Farmers Increases Food Production in Developing Countries.* ID–76–34. Washington, D. C.: 13 May 1976.

578. van de Wetering, H. *The Demand Induced Impact of Land Redistribution.* LTC no. 91. Madison: Land Tenure Center, University of Wisconsin, July 1973.

579. Whitaker, Morris; Glenn, G.; Lebaron, A.; and Wennergren, B. *Effect of Increased Water Supply on Net Returns to Dairy Farms in Sonsonate, El Salvador.* Logan: Department of Economics, Utah State University, February 1973.

580. Yudelman, Montague. *Africans on the Land: Economic Problems of African Agricultural Development in Southern, Central and East Africa. With Special Reference to Southern Rhodesia.* Cambridge, Mass.: Harvard University Press, 1964.

Articles

In "Peasant Economic Behavior," Wong argues that if peasants operate efficiently under traditional agricultural systems, then institutional changes such as land reform will not have the effect of increasing output. Rather, technological improvements will increase productivity. According to Wong, the Chinese experience substantiates this thesis: only after 1962 when the Chinese government shifted its attention from the redistribution of land to technical improvements in the methods of production did productivity rise.

The articles by Feder, Schultz (entries 593 and 592), and Adams (in that order) form an interesting debate initiated by Feder in his review of Schultz's *Transforming Traditional Agriculture* (entry 574). Feder takes issue with Schultz's contention that the increased provision of inputs and not institutional change or the reallocation of productive resources (i.e. land and capital) is the key to increased agricultural productivity. In the third article in this series, Schultz is mainly concerned with demonstrating that traditional farmers respond to economic stimuli, something which mainstream economic thought had long held them incapable of doing.

The articles by Chandra and Sau should be read together.

581. Adams, Dale W. "Resource Allocation in Traditional Agriculture: Comment." *Journal of Farm Economics* 49 (November 1967): 930–933.

582. Ahsanullah, M. "Economics and Management of Tubewell Irrigation in One Area of Bangladesh." *LTC Newsletter* no. 40 (April–June 1973): 30–35.

583. Barker, Randolph. "The Economics of Rice Production." *Teaching Forum* no. 5. New York: The Agricultural Development Council, June 1971.

584. Beckford, George L. "The Economics of Agricultural Resource Use and Development in Plantation Economies." *Social and Economic Studies* 18 (December 1969): 321–347.

585. Chandra, Nirmal K. "Farm Efficiency Under Semi-Feudalism: A Critique of Marginalist Theories and Some Marxist Formulations." *Economic and Political Weekly* 9:32–34 (Special Number 1974): 1309–1332.

586. Feder, Ernest. "The Latifundia Puzzle of Professor Schultz: Comment." *Journal of Farm Economics* 49 (May 1967): 507–510.

587. Lipton, Michael. "Population, Land and Decreasing Returns to Agricultural Labour." *Oxford University Insitute of Economics and Statistics* 26 (May 1964): 123–157.

588. ______. "The Theory of the Optimising Peasant." *Journal of Development Studies* no. 4 (April 1968): 327–351.

589. Raynaut, Claude. "Transformation du Système de Production et Inégalité Economique: Le Cas d'un Village Haoussa (Niger)." *Canadian Journal of African Studies* 10:2 (1976): 279–306.

590. Robinson, Warren C. "Some Negative Thoughts About Labor-Intensive Development." *The Malayan Economic Review* 20 (April 1975): 12–26.

591. Sau, Ranjit. "Farm Efficiency under Semi-Feudalism. A Critique of Marginalist Theories and Some Marxist Formulations: A Comment." *Economic and Political Weekly* 10 (29 March 1975): A18–A21.

592. Schultz, Theodore W. "Resource Allocation in Traditional Agriculture: Comment." *Journal of Farm Economics* 49 (November 1967): 933–935.

593. ______. "The Latifundia Puzzle of Professor Schultz: Reply." *Journal of Farm Economics* 49 (May 1967): 511–514.

594. Singh, Bhagat. "Economics of Tractor Cultivation—A Case Study." *Indian Journal of Agricultural Economics* 23 (January–March 1968): 83–88.

595. Taylor, Donald C. "Formulating Financial Policies in Large-Scale Canal Irrigation Projects." *Land Tenure Center Newsletter* no. 54 (October–December 1976): 13–20.

596. Thornton, D. S., and Wynn, R. F. "An Economic Assessment of the Sudan's Khasm el Girba Scheme." *East African Journal of Rural Development* 1:2 (1968): 1–21.

597. Wong, John. "Peasant Economic Behavior: The Case of Traditional Agricultural Cooperation in China." *The Developing Economies* 9 (September 1971): 332 ff.

598. Young, Maurice de. "Some Notes on the Economics of the Beef Industry in the West African Sub-Region." *Agricultural Economics Bulletin for Africa* no. 10 (July 1968): 49–60.

Sociological Aspects

Books and Monographs

The study by Long surveys and critiques the relevant sociological and anthropological literature. The volume edited by Newby covers rural sociology in both Western and third world societies. Chapters dealing with the third world discuss such topics as rural poverty, the Green Revolution, and power in rural communities. These two books are recommended along with the studies by de Castro, Okwuosa, Pearse, Stavenhagen, and the volume edited by Huq.

599. Apter, David E. *The Politics of Modernization.* Chicago: The University of Chicago Press, 1967.

600. Chambers, Robert, ed. *The Volta Resettlement Experience.* London: Pall Mall, 1970.

601. Constandse, A. K., and Hofstee, E. W. *Rural Sociology in Action.* 3rd ed. FAO Agricultural Development Paper no. 79. FAO Economic and Social Development Series no. 10. Rome: Food and Agriculture Organization, 1978.

602. de Castro, Josué. *Death in the Northeast.* New York: Random House, 1966.

603. Desai, A. R., ed. *Rural Sociology in India.* 4th ed. Bombay: Popular Prakashan, 1969.

604. Hinderink, Jan, and Kiray, Mübeccel B. *Social Stratification as an Obstacle to Development. A Study of Four Turkish Villages.* New York: Praeger, 1970.

605. Hoyois, Giovanni. *Sociologie Rurale.* Paris: Encyclopédie Universitaire, Editions Universitaires, 1968.

606. Huq, Ameerul, ed. *Exploitation and the Rural Poor: A Working Paper on the Rural Power Structure in Bangladesh.* Comilla: Bangladesh Academy for Rural Development, 1976.

607. Kivlin, Joseph E., et al. *Innovation in Rural India.* Bowling Green, Ohio: Bowling Green University Press, 1971.

608. Lambert, Claire, ed. *Village Studies.* Brighton, UK: Institute of Development Studies, University of Sussex, 1976.

609. Long, Norman. *An Introduction to the Sociology of Rural Development.* Boulder, Colo.: Westview, 1977.

610. MacDonald, Alphonse L. *Agricultural Technology in Developing Countries: Social Factors Related to the Use of Modern Techniques in Two Rural Areas in Peru.* Rotterdam: University Press, 1976.

611. Meister, Albert. *Participation, Animation et Développement: A Partir d'une Etude Rurale en Argentine.* Paris: Editions Anthropos, 1969.

612. Migdal, Joel S. *Peasants, Politics, and Revolution.* Princeton, N. J.: Princeton University Press, 1974.

613. Moerman, Michael. *Agricultural Change and Peasant Choice in a Thai Village.* Berkeley, Calif.: University of California Press, 1968.

614. Newby, Howard, ed. *International Perspectives in Rural Sociology.* Chichester, UK: John Wiley, 1978.

615. Okwuosa, Adoaha Chibuzo. *Consequences of the Cash-Crop Economy for the Family Structure of Selected Societies of West Africa (Nigeria and Ghana).* Freiburg: Albert-Ludwigs-Universität, 1975.

616. Pearse, Andrew. *The Latin American Peasant.* London: Cass, 1976.

617. Petras, James, and Zemelman Merino, Hugo. *Peasants in Revolt. A Chilean Case Study, 1965–1971.* Trans. Thomas Flory. Austin and London: University of Texas Press, 1972.

618. Post, Ken. *On "Peasantisation" and Rural Class Differentiation in Western Africa.* ISS Occasional Papers, no. 2. The Hague: Institute for Social Studies, 1970.

619. Rajagopalan, C., and Singh, Jaspal. *Adoption of Agricultural Innovations.* Delhi: National, 1971.

620. Scott, James C. *The Moral Economy of the Peasant.* New Haven: Yale University Press, 1976.

621. Scott, James C., and Kerkvliet, Benedict J. *How Traditional Rural Patrons Lose Legitimacy: A Theory with Special Reference to Southeast Asia.* Louvain: Université Catholique de Louvain, 1973.

622. Shanin, Teodor, ed. *Peasants and Peasant Societies.* Baltimore, Md.: Penguin, 1971.

623. Solari, Aldo. *Sociología Rural Latino-Americana.* 2nd ed. Buenos Aires: Paidós, 1968.

624. Stavenhagen, Rodolfo. *Social Classes in Agrarian Societies.* Garden City, N. Y.: Anchor/Doubleday, 1975.

625. Tullis, F. LaMond. *Lord and Peasant in Peru: A Paradigm of Political and Social Change.* Cambridge, Mass.: Harvard University Press, 1970.

626. Urquidi, Arturo. *Las Comunidades Indígenas en Boliva.* Cochabamba: Los Amigos del Libro, 1970.

627. Wilkie, Raymond. *San Miguel: A Mexican Collective Ejido.* Stanford, Calif.: Stanford University Press, 1971.

628. Young, Frank W. *The Rural Development Inventory.* 2 vols. Honolulu: East-West Technology and Development Institute, 1975.

629. Zagorin, Ruth K. *The Sociology of Food.* IDRC–99e. Ottawa: International Development Research Centre, December 1977.

Articles

The article by D'Souza should be read in conjunction with the book by Desai (entry 603).

630. Alavi, Hamza. "Peasant Classes and Primordial Loyalties." *The Journal of Peasant Studies* 1:1 (1973): 23–62.

631. Alexander, K. C. "Some Characteristics of the Agrarian Social Structure of Tamil Nadu." *Economic and Political Weekly* 10 (19 April 1975): 664–672.

632. Blanckenburg, Peter von. "Who Leads Agricultural Modernisation? A Study of Some Progressive Farmers in Mysore and Punjab." *Economic and Political Weekly* 7 (30 September 1972): A94–A112.

633. Bose, Santi Priya. "Characteristics of Farmers Who Adopt Agricultural Practices in Indian Villages." *Rural Sociology* 26 (June 1961): 138–145.

634. Bowden, Edgar, and Moris, Jon. "Social Characteristics of Progressive Baganda Farmers." *East African Journal of Rural Development* 2:1 (1969): 56–62.

635. Colin, Roland. "L'Animation et le Développement en Afrique Noire Francophone." *Archives Internationale de Sociologie de la Coopération* no. 20 (July–December 1966): 133–199.

636. D'Souza, Victor S. "Rural Sociology." *Economic and Political Weekly* 6 (20 February 1971): 493–494.

637. Erasmus, Charles J. "Upper Limits of Peasantry and Agrarian Reform: Bolivia, Venezuela, and Mexico Compared." *Ethnology* 6 (October 1967): 349–380.

638. Huizer, G. "The Utilization of Conflict in Community Development and Peasant Organization: A Case from Chile." *International Review of Community Development* nos. 27–28 (Summer 1972): 133–148.

639. Kellerhals, Jean. "Fonctions de la Participation Organisée: Quelques Tendances de la Sociologie Américaine." *International Review of Community Development* nos. 17–18 (1967): 257–270.

640. Khan, A. M. "Impact of Changes in Agriculture on Political Life in Asia." *Sociologia Ruralis* 4:3–4 (1964): 343–359.

641. Kiray, Mübeccel, and Hinderink, Jan. "Interdependence Between Agroeconomic Development and Social Change: A Comparative Study Conducted in the Cukurova Region of Southern Turkey." *The Journal of Development Studies* 4 (July 1968): 497–529.

642. Lawson, R. "Innovation and Growth in Traditional Agriculture of the Lower Volta, Ghana." *The Journal of Development Studies* 4 (October 1967): 138–149.

643. Merriam, Alan P. "Social and Cultural Change in a Rural Zairian Village." *African Studies Review* 17 (September 1974): 345–359.

644. Scott, James C. "The Erosion of Patron-Client Bonds and Social Change in Rural Southeast Asia." *Journal of Asian Studies* 32 (November 1972): 5–37.

645. ______. "Exploitation in Rural Class Relations: A Victim's Perspective." *Comparative Politics* 7:4 (1975): 489–532.

646. Stinchcombe, Arthur L. "Agricultural Enterprise and Rural Class Relations." *American Journal of Sociology* 67 (September 1961): 165–176.

647. Wickham, Gekee Y. "The Sociology of Irrigation: Insights from a Philippine Study." *Philippine Sociological Review,* January–April 1972. (A shortened version of this is found in *Teaching Forum.* no. 32. New York: The Agricultural Development Council, June 1973.)

Green Revolution

Most country studies dealing with the Green Revolution are found below, in the sections on Latin America, Asia, and Africa, rather than in "Part V: Country-Specific Studies," pages 241–326.

General

Along with land reform, the Green Revolution is one of the most widely debated aspects of rural development. The studies in this first section dealing with the Green Revolution touch on many points raised in the course of this debate. Entry 699 is a useful introductory essay, discussing a variety of topics such as the implications of Green Revolution strategy for technical and economic aid, the role to be played by institutional reform, and the contribution of the Green Revolution to national growth.

The story of the beginning of the Green Revolution is told in the book by Stakman, Bradfield, and Mangelsdorf. A good deal of what has been written on the Green Revolution is optimistic, particularly the writings of the late 1960s and early 1970s. However, as the passage of time has allowed the evaluation of different experiences in applying Green Revolution technology, discussion has focused in large part on the ways in which this technology interacts with the social, economic, political, and environmental settings into which it is introduced.

Books and Monographs

Recommended studies include Griffin, Palmer, UNRISD, Pearse, and Havens and Flinn. *Beyond the Green Revolution* (entry 418) and Part 4 ("Modernizing Hunger") of *Food First* (entry 1890) are also relevant here.

648. Borlaug, Norman. *The Accelerated Crop Improvement and Production Programs and the Agricultural Revolution: Suggestions for Future Development.* Mexico: CIMMYT, 1968.

649. Bosso, N'Guetta. *CIMMYT and the International Maize Research/Production Programs.* Cornell International Agricultural Mimeograph 47. Ithaca, N. Y.: Cornell University, February 1975.

650. Brown, Lester R. *Seeds of Change.* New York: Praeger, 1970.

651. ———. *The Social Impact of the Green Revolution.* New York: Carnegie Endowment for International Peace, 1971.

652. Centro Internacional de Mejoramiento de Maiz y Trigo (CIMMYT). *Annual Report.* Mexico: 1966/67–1972.

653. ———. *CIMMYT Report on Maize Improvement.* Mexico: 1973–. (Supersedes entry 652)

654. ———. *CIMMYT Report on Wheat Improvement.* Mexico: 1973–. (Supersedes entry 652)

655. Dalrymple, Dana G. *Development Spread of High Yielding Varieties of Wheat and Rice in the Less Developed Nations.* Foreign Economic Development Report 95. Washington, D. C.: United States Department of Agriculture, July 1974.

656. ———. *Imports and Plantings of High-Yielding Varieties of Wheat and Rice in the Less-Developed Nations.* Washington, D. C.: Foreign Agricultural Service, US Department of Agriculture, November 1969.

657. ———. *Measuring the Green Revolution: The Impact of Research on Wheat and Rice Production.* Foreign Agricultural Economic Report no. 106. Washington, D. C.: Economic Research Service, US Department of Agriculture, July 1975.

658. Gonzáles Iñigo, J. F. *CIMMYT and the Green Revolution.* Mexico: CIMMYT, 1970.

659. Griffin, Keith. *The Green Revolution: An Economic Analysis.* Report no. 72.6. Geneva: UNRISD, 1972.

660. ———. *The Political Economy of Agrarian Change: An Essay on the Green Revolution.* Cambridge, Mass.: Harvard University Press, 1974.

661. Havens, A. Eugene, and Flinn, William L. *Green Revolution Technology and Community Development. The Limits of Action Programs.* LTC no. 93. Madison: Land Tenure Center, University of Wisconsin, 1973. (A shortened version is available in *Economic Development and Cultural Change* 23 (April 1975): 469–481.)

662. Indian Agricultural Research Institute. *Five Years of Research on Dwarf Wheats.* New Delhi: 1968.

663. International Rice Research Institute (IRRI). *IRRI Annual Reports.* Los Baños, Philippines: 1961/62–.

664. Lele, Uma. *The Green Revolution: Income Distribution and Nutrition.* Department of Agricultural Economics Occasional Paper no. 48. Ithaca, N. Y.: Cornell University, 1971.

665. Palmer, Ingrid. *Science and Agricultural Production.* Geneva: UNRISD, 1972.

666. Pearse, Andrew. *The Social and Economic Implications of the Large-Scale Introduction of New Varieties of Food Grains: Summary of Conclusions.* Geneva: UNRISD, 1975.

667. ———. *The Socio-Economic Implications of Large Scale Introduction of New Varieties of Foodgrains.* Geneva: UNRISD, 1977.

668. Pohekar, G. S., ed. *Studies in Green Revolution.* Bombay: United Asia, 1970.

669. Poleman, Thomas T., and Freebairn, Donald. *Food, Population, and Employment: The Impact of the Green Revolution.* New York: Praeger, 1973. (See especially Chapters 1–4, 6, 11, and 12.)

670. Randhawa, M. S. *Green Revolution.* New York: Wiley, 1974.

671. Ruttan, Vernon W.; Houck, J. P.; and Evenson, R. E. *Technical Change and Agricultural Trade: Three Examples (Sugar Cane, Bananas, and Rice).* Agricultural Economics Staff Paper P68–4. St. Paul: University of Minnesota, December 1968.

672. Stakman, E. C.; Bradfield, Richard; and Mangelsdorf, Paul C. *Campaigns Against Hunger.* Cambridge, Mass.: Belknap Press of the Harvard University Press, 1967.

673. United Nations Research Institute for Social Development (UNRISD). *A Selection of Readings.* Report no. 71.6. Geneva: 1971.

674. United States, House of Representatives, Committee on Foreign Affairs, Subcommittee on National Security Policy and Scientific Developments. Proceedings: *Symposium on Science and Foreign Policy: The Green Revolution.* 91st Cong., 1st Sess. Washington, D. C.: US Printing Office, 5 December 1969.

Articles

Readers will want to look at the article by Borlaug and Aresvik in order to have some understanding of the way in which a major figure in the creation of Green Revolution technology views the spread of the improved seeds. Recommended articles are those by Greenland, Ladejinsky, Coward and Schutjer, Staub and Blase, and Lipton.

675. Allen, Robert. "New Strategy for the Green Revolution." *New Scientist* 63 (8 August 1974): 320–321.

676. Anderson, Alan, Jr. "The Green Revolution Lives." *New York Times Magazine,* 27 April 1975, pp. 15, 80–83, 90, 94.

677. Barker, Randolph. "Green Revolution." *Current Affairs Bulletin* 45 (January 1970): 66–79.

678. Borlaug, Norman. "Wheat Breeding and Its Impact on World Food Supply." Paper presented to the Third International Wheat Genetics Symposium, 1968.

679. Borlaug, Norman, and Aresvik, Oddvar H. "The Green Revolution: An Approach to Agricultural Development and Some of Its Economic Implications." *Journal of Agrarian Affairs* 5:6 (1972): 385–403.

680. Cleaver, Harry M., Jr. "The Contradictions of the Green Revolution." *Monthly Review* 24 (June 1972): 80–111.

681. Coward, E. Walter, Jr., and Schutjer, Wayne A. "The Green Revolution: Initiating and Sustaining Change." *Civilisations* 20:4 (1970): 473–483.

682. Flores, Edmundo. "Why There is a Crisis." *Ceres* no. 38 (March–April 1974): 8–11.

683. Greenland, D. J. "Bringing the Green Revolution to the Shifting Cultivator." *Science* 190 (28 November 1975): 841–844.

684. Harpstead, D. D. "High-Lysine Corn." *Scientific American* 225 (August 1971): 34–47.

685. Harris, M. "How Green the Revolution." *Natural History,* June–July 1972, pp. 28–30.

686. Hopper, W. David, and Freeman, Wayne H. "From Unsteady Infancy to Vigorous Adolescence: Rice Development." *Economic and Political Weekly* 4 (29 March 1969): A17–A21.

687. Ladejinsky, Wolf. "Agricultural Production and Constraints." *World Development* 4 (January 1976): 1–10.

688. Lipton, Michael. "Inter-Farm, Inter-Regional and Farm–Non-Farm Income Distribution: The Impact of the New Cereal Varieties." *World Development* 6 (March 1978): 319–337.

689. Oswald, Ursula. "Agribusiness, Green Revolution, and Cooperatives," pp. 276–282. In *Peace, Development, and New Interna-*

tional Economic Order. Proceedings of the 7th IPRA General Conference. Eds. Luis Herrera and Raimo Väyrynen. Tampere, Finland: International Peace Research Association, 1979.

690. Paddock, William. "How Green is the Green Revolution?" *BioScience* 20 (15 August 1970): 897–902.

691. Paddock, William and Elizabeth. "The Browning of the Green Revolution." *The Progressive* 37 (June 1973): 29–32.

692. Reinton, Per Olav. "The Green Revolution Experience." *Instant Research on Peace and Violence* 3:2 (1973): 58–73.

693. Reitz, Louis. "New Wheats and Social Progress." *Science* 169 (9 September 1970): 952–955.

694. Rice, Edward B. "Spring Review of the New Cereal Varieties." US Agency for International Development Evaluation Paper 2. Washington, D. C.: US Agency for International Development, January 1970.

695. Saito, Kazuo. "On the Green Revolution." *The Developing Economies* 9 (March 1971): 16–30.

696. Schuler, Alexanderina. "Of Seed and Man—II: International Institute of Tropical Agriculture Wages Battle to Improve Food Crops in Poor Lands." *War on Hunger* 10 (June 1976): 1–4, 11–13.

697. Skorov, Georgy. "The Green Revolution and Social Progress." *World Development* 1 (November 1973): 13–21.

698. Staub, William J., and Blase, Melvin G. "Genetic Development and Agricultural Development." *Science* 173 (9 July 1971): 119–123.

699. "The Green Revolution: Second Generation Problems." *American Journal of Agricultural Economics* 52 (December 1970): 698–722.

700. Wharton, Clifton R., Jr. "The Green Revolution: Cornucopia or Pandora's Box?" *Foreign Affairs* 47:3 (1969): 464–476.

701. Wortman, Sterling. "Extending the Green Revolution." *World Development* 1 (December 1973): 45–51.

702. Zeven, A. C. "Breeding Green Revolutions." *World Crops and Livestock* 29 (May–June 1977): 123–124.

Asia

Books and Monographs

Recommended studies include Dasgupta, Hameed, et al., Palmer, Shigemochi, and Wood and Huq.

703. Atkinson, L. Jay, and Kunkel, David E. *High-Yielding Varieties of Rice in the Philippines. Progress of the Seed-Fertilizer Revolution.* Foreign

Agricultural Economic Report no. 113. Washington, D. C.: Economic Research Service, US Department of Agriculture, February 1976.

704. Dasgupta, Biplab. *Agrarian Change and the New Technology in India.* Report no. 77.2. Geneva: UNRISD, 1977.

705. Farmer, Bertram H., ed. *Green Revolution? Technology and Change in Rice-Growing Areas of Tamil Nadu and Sri Lanka.* Boulder, Colo.: Westview, 1977.

706. Frankel, Francine R. *India's Green Revolution: Economic Gains and Political Losses.* Princeton, N. J.: Princeton University Press, 1971.

707. Hameed, N. D. Abdul, et al. *Rice Revolution in Sri Lanka.* Report no. 76.7. Geneva: UNRISD, 1977.

708. Hutchinson, Joseph, ed. *Evolutionary Studies in World Crops: Diversity and Change in the Indian Subcontinent.* Cambridge, UK: Cambridge University Press, 1974.

709. International Rice Research Institute. *Changes in Rice Farming in Selected Areas of Asia.* Los Baños, Philippines: 1975.

710. Khan, Mahmood Hasan. *The Economics of the Green Revolution in Pakistan.* New York: Praeger, 1975.

711. Mandal, G. C., and Ghosh, M. G. *Economics of the Green Revolution: A Study in East India.* London: Asia, 1976.

712. Mudahar, Mohinder S. *Dynamic Analysis of Direct and Indirect Implications of Technological Change in Agriculture—The Case of Punjab, India.* Occasional Paper 79. Ithaca, N. Y.: Technological Change in Agriculture Project, Department of Agricultural Economics, Cornell University, December 1974.

713. Nulty, Leslie. *The Green Revolution in West Pakistan: Implications of Technological Change.* Praeger Special Studies in International Economics and Development. New York: Praeger, 1972.

714. Palmer, Ingrid. *The New Rice in Asia: Conclusions from Four Countries.* Geneva: UNRISD, 1976. (Deals with Indonesia, Philippines, Malaysia, and Thailand.)

715. ______. *The New Rice in Indonesia.* Report no. 77.1. Geneva: UNRISD, 1977.

716. ______. *The New Rice in the Philippines.* Report no. 75.2. Geneva: UNRISD, 1975.

717. Parker, John B., Jr. *New Technology in India's Agriculture and Outlook for Grain Production.* ERS-Foreign 341. Washington, D. C.: Economic Research Service, US Department of Agriculture, June 1972.

718. Sen, Bandhudas. *The Green Revolution in India: A Perspective.* New York: Wiley, 1974.

719. Shigemochi, Hirashima. *The Structure of Disparity in Developing Agriculture: A Case Study of the Pakistan Punjab.* Tokyo: Institute of Developing Economies, 1978.

720. Singh, Jasbir. *The Green Revolution in India: How Green It Is!* Kurukshetra, Haryana, India: Vishal, 1974.

721. Stevens, Robert D., et al. *Rural Development in Bangladesh and Pakistan.* Honolulu: The University Press of Hawaii, 1976.

722. Streeter, Carroll P. *A Partnership to Improve Food Production in India.* New York: Rockefeller Foundation, December 1969.

723. von Vorys, Karl, and Frankel, Francine. *The Political Challenge of the Green Revolution: Shifting Patterns of Participation in India and Pakistan.* Policy Memorandum no. 38. Princeton, N. J.: Center for International Studies, Princeton University, 1972.

724. Willett, Joseph. *The Impact of New Grain Varieties in Asia.* Washington, D. C.: Economic Research Service, US Department of Agriculture, 1969.

725. Wood, G. D., and Huq, M. Ameerul. *The Socio-Economic Implications of Introducing HYV in Bangladesh.* Comilla: Bangladesh Academy for Rural Development, November 1975.

Articles

The *Economic and Political Weekly* has, over the course of the last decade, run a number of articles dealing with the socio-economic impact of the Green Revolution in India. The two articles by Ladejinsky and the ones by Bardhan and by Junankar discuss the growing rural disparities arising out of the implementation of the Green Revolution. The articles by Chowdhury, Lahiri, Gough, Herdt and Baker, Nayyar, and Saini all deal with the specific problem of income disparities. Herdt and Baker find that in most of India the increased demand for labor generated by the introduction of Green Revolution technology has not increased wages for agricultural laborers. Gough finds that in Punjab and Haryana wages did increase significantly. However, he stresses that the wage rate alone is not sufficient to determine income; one must know both the wage rate *and* the number of days worked. Agricultural laborers who work fewer days following the introduction of Green Revolution technology may not see their income increased by rising wage rates. The article by Wetsch discusses how the introduction of high-yielding varieties of grain could work to the disadvantage of Thai farmers in terms of income distribution.

Other recommended articles include Mencher, Singh and Day, Ojha, Franke, Dasgupta, and Ahmad. The articles by Tharpar and Roy should be read together.

726. Admed, Saleem, and Khalid, S. Abu. "Why Did Mexican Dwarf Wheat Decline in Pakistan?" *World Crops* 23 (July–August 1971): 211–215.

727. Ahmad, Zubeida Manzoor. "The Social and Economic Implications of the Green Revolution in Asia." *International Labour Review* 105 (January 1972): 9–34.

728. Bardhan, Kalpana, and Bardhan, Pranab. "The Green Revolution and Socio-Economic Tensions: The Case of India." *International Social Science Journal* 25:3 (1973): 285–292.

729. Bardhan, Pranab. "'Green Revolution' and Agricultural Labourers." *Economic and Political Weekly* 5:29–31 (Special Number 1970): 1239–1246. (A revised version is available in *Teaching Forum.* no. 8. New York: The Agricultural Development Council, July 1971.)

730. Brown, Lester. "The Agricultural Revolution in Asia." *Foreign Affairs* 46:4 (1968): 688–698.

731. Chowdhury, B. K. "Disparity in Income in Context of HYV." *Economic and Political Weekly* 5 (26 September 1976): A90–A96.

732. Dasgupta, Biplab. "India's Green Revolution." *Economic and Political Weekly* 12:6–8 (Annual Number 1977): 241–259.

733. Franda, Marcus F. "Policy Responses to India's Green Revolution." *LTC Newsletter* no. 39 (January–March 1973): 9–11.

734. Franke, Richard W. "Miracle Seeds and Shattered Dreams in Java." *Challenge* 17 (July–August 1974): 42–47.

735. Gough, James W. "Agricultural Wages in Punjab and Haryana: A Note." *Economic and Political Weekly* 6 (27 March 1971): A19–A20.

736. "Green Revolution: Halting in Mid-Track?" *Economic and Political Weekly* 8 (1 September 1973): 1591–1593.

737. Herdt, Robert W., and Baker, Edward A. "Agricultural Wages, Production and the High-Yielding Varieties." *Economic and Political Weekly* 7 (25 March 1972): A23–A30.

738. Hoskins, Martin. "The Green Revolution and Cropping Intensity." *Institute of Development Studies Bulletin* 5:4 (May 1974): 43–50.

739. Jacoby, Erich. "Effects of the Green Revolution in South and South East Asia." *Modern Asian Studies* 6:1 (1972): 63–69.

740. Jayaprakash, R. K. "The Technological Breakthrough in Agriculture and Its Possible Socio-Economic Impact in India." *World Crops* 25 (March–April 1973): 78–84.

741. Johl, S. S. "Gains of the Green Revolution: How They Have Been Shared in the Punjab." *The Journal of Development Studies* 11 (April 1975): 178–189.

742. Junankar, P. N. "Green Revolution and Inequality." *Economic and Political Weekly* 10 (29 March 1975): A15–A18.

743. Ladejinsky, Wolf. "How Green is the Indian Green Revolution?" *Economic and Political Weekly* 8 (December 1973): A133–A144.

744. ______. "Ironies of India's Green Revolution." *Foreign Affairs* 48:4 (1970): 758–768.

745. ______. "The Green Revolution in Bihar—The Kosi Area: A Field Trip." *Economic and Political Weekly* 4 (27 September 1969): A147–A162.

746. ______. "The Green Revolution in Punjab: A Field Trip." *Economic and Political Weekly* 4 (28 June 1969): A73–A82.

747. Lahiri, R. K. "Impact of HYVP on Rural Labour Market." *Economic and Political Weekly* 5 (26 September 1970): A111–A114.

748. Lockwood, Brian, and Moulik, T. K. "Seeds of Development in a Delhi Village." *Economic and Political Weekly* 6 (27 March 1971): A11–A18.

749. Mann, K. S.; Moore, C. V.; and Johl, S. S. "Estimates of Potential Effects of New Technology on Agriculture in Punjab, India." *American Journal of Agricultural Economics* 50 (May 1968): 278–290.

750. Mencher, Joan P. "Conflicts and Contradictions in the 'Green Revolution': The Case of Tamil Nadu." *Economic and Political Weekly* 9:6–8 (Annual Number 1974): 309–323.

751. ______. "Why Grow More Food? An Analysis of Some Contradictions in the 'Green Revolution' in Kerala." *Economic and Political Weekly* 13 (23–30 December 1978): A98–A104.

752. Michie, Barry H. "Variations in Economic Behaviour and the Green Revolution: An Anthropological Perspective." *Economic and Political Weekly* 8 (30 June 1973): A67–A75.

753. Munthe-Kaas, Harald. "The Landed and the Hungry." *Far Eastern Economic Review* (12 March 1970): 27–30.

754. Nayyar, Rohini. "Wages of Agricultural Labourers in Uttar Pradesh: A Note." *Economic and Political Weekly* 11 (6 November 1976): 1771–1772.

755. Ojha, Gyaneshwar. "Small Farmers and HYV Programme." *Economic and Political Weekly* 5 (4 April 1970): 603–605.

756. Parthasarathy, G. "Economics of IR8 Paddy: Factors Influencing its Adoption in a Tank Irrigated District." *Economic and Political Weekly* 4 (20 September 1969): 1519–1523.

757. Parthasarathy, G., and Prasad, D. S. "Season-Wise Progress of High-Yielding Varieties in Andhra Pradesh: Role of Economic Variables." *Economic and Political Weekly* 6 (25 September 1971): A117–A122.

758. Patel, Surendra J. "What is Holding up Agricultural Growth?" *The Economic Weekly* 16:5–7 (Annual Number February 1964): 327 ff.

759. Roy, Probhat. "The Green Revolution in India: Land Reforms First." *Ceres* no. 29 (September–October 1972): 40–43.

760. Roy, Shyamal. "Profitability of HYV Paddy Cultivation." *Economic and Political Weekly* 6 (26 June 1971): A75–A78.

761. Ruttan, Vernon W. "Planning Technological Advance in Agriculture: The Case of Rice Production in Taiwan, Thailand and the Philippines," pp. 52–77. In *Inducing Technological Change for Economic Growth and Development.* Eds. Robert A. Solo and Everett M. Rogers. East Lansing: Michigan State University Press, 1972.

762. Ryan, James G., and Subrahmanyam, K. V. "Package of Practices Approach in Adoption of High-Yielding Varieties: An Appraisal." *Economic and Political Weekly* 10 (27 December 1975): A101–A110.

763. Sagar, Vidya. "Contribution of Individual Technological Factors in Agricultural Growth. A Case Study of Rajasthan." *Economic and Political Weekly* 13 (24 June 1978): A63–A69.

764. Saini, G. R. "Green Revolution and Disparities in Farm Incomes: A Comment." *Economic and Political Weekly* 11 (13 November 1976): 1804–1806.

765. Singh, Inderjit, and Day, Richard H. "Factor Utilization and Substitution in Economic Development: A Green Revolution Case Study." *The Journal of Development Studies* 11 (April 1975): 155–177.

766. Stein, Leslie. "The Green Revolution and Asian Development Strategy." *Studies in Comparative International Development* 12 (Summer 1977): 58–69.

767. Tharpar, Ashok. "The Green Revolution in India: Infrastructure, Not Land Reform." *Ceres* 5 (September–October 1972): 36–40.

768. Wetsch, Delane E. "Technological Change and Income Effects in Thailand." *LTC Newsletter* no. 37 (July–October 1972): 7–10.

Latin America

The studies by CIMMYT, Alcantara, and Thiesenhusen are recommended as is Alcantara's longer study on Mexico found in entry 2937.

769. Alcantara, Cynthia Hewitt de. "The Green Revolution as History: The Mexican Experience." *Development and Change* 5:2 (1973–74): 25–44.

770. Centro Internacional de Mejoramiento de Maiz y Trigo (CIMMYT). *The Puebla Project: Seven Years of Experience 1967–73, Analysis of a Program to Assist Small Subsistence Farmers to Increase Crop Production in a Rainfed Area of Mexico.* El Batan, Mexico: 1974.

771. Rockefeller Foundation. *A Review of the Mexican Agricultural Program.* New York: 1950–1958, annually.

772. Thiesenhusen, William C. *Technological Change and Income Distribution in Latin American Agriculture.* LTC no. 78. Madison: Land Tenure Center, University of Wisconsin, August 1971. (A shortened version can be found in *LTC Newsletter* no. 33 (February–July 1971): 13–17.)

773. Tuckman, B. H. "The Green Revolution and the Distribution of Agricultural Income in Mexico." *World Development* 4 (January 1976): 17–24.

Africa

Both entries are recommended.

774. Cohen, John M. "Effects of Green Revolution Strategies on Tenants and Small-Scale Landowners in the Chilalo Region of Ethiopia." *Developing Areas* 9 (April 1975): 335–358.

775. Dumont, René. *Notes sur les Implications Sociales de la "Révolution Verte" en Quelques Pays d'Afrique.* Report no. 71.5. Geneva: UNRISD, 1971.

Women in Development

The role of women in the development process has been largely ignored—both in academic works and in actual development programs—until quite recently. Some 90 percent of the items in the following sections were published during or after 1975, International Women's Year. The majority of the studies deal with the role and situation of women in rural development although a few, for example, Boserup in entry 776 and Youssef in entry 802, discuss the role played by women in the non-agricultural sector.

Probably more than in any other section of this bibliography, the studies listed here tend to reach similar conclusions. The "modernization" process has not benefited women because women are frequently excluded from training or agricultural extension programs or because what they are taught does not enhance their agricultural skills. As a result, "modernization" programs have widened the knowledge and skills gaps between men and women and upgraded the status of men to the detriment of women. Very little research is directed at women, particularly women in the agricultural sector, and very little money has been spent on them. Theorists, especially of rural development, have not put forward many explicit ideas of the role women might play in the development process.

Books and Monographs

Boserup (entry 776) analyzes women's participation in the labor force—rural, urban, and traditional sectors—in Africa, Asia, and Latin America. Pala (entry 794) provides a useful introduction to the topic of the role of women in rural development in Africa. Curtain discusses the progress made in improving the status of women in China but points out that discrimination still exists there. Dixon (entry 782) suggests that producer cooperatives owned and operated by women should be established to strengthen the position of rural women in South Asia. In entry 783, Dixon demonstrates that as women's rights increase, their fertility decreases. The report by O'Kelly is particularly useful for people who are actively involved in development work. The UNICEF report analyzes the obstacles to the participation of Latin American women in the development process. The volume edited by Mazumdar contains a series of case studies which examine projects aimed at improving the situation of rural women in the Cameroons, India, Indonesia, Panama, Jamaica, and Ghana.

There are a number of entries in the section entitled "International Agency Approaches," pages 142–145, which are of relevance here.

776. Boserup, Ester. *Women's Role in Economic Development.* New York: St. Martin's, 1970. (The argument in this book is summarized in *Development Digest* 9 (April 1971): 97–122.)

777. ______. *Women and Their Role in Peasant Societies.* London: Centre of International and Area Studies, University of London, 1974.

778. Boulding, Elise. *Women, Bread and Babies: Directing Aid for Fifth World Farmers.* International Women's Year Studies on Women, Paper no. 4. Boulder: Program of Research on General Social and Economic Dynamics, Institute of Behavioral Sciences, University of Colorado, 1975.

779. Bukh, Jette. *The Village Woman in Ghana.* Uppsala: Institute of African Studies, 1979.

780. Curtain, Katie. *Women in China.* New York: Pathfinder, 1975.

781. Development Alternatives, Inc. *Seven Country Survey of the Role of Women in Rural Development.* Prepared for USAID. Washington, D. C.: 1974.

782. Dixon, Ruth B. *Rural Women at Work, Strategies for Development in South Asia.* Baltimore, Md.: Johns Hopkins University Press, for Resources for the Future, 1978.

783. ______. *Women's Rights and Fertility.* Reports on Population/Family Planning, no. 17. New York: Population Council, 1975.

784. Etienne, M., and Leacock, E. *Women and Colonization.* New York: Praeger, 1980.

785. Food and Agriculture Organization. *The Missing Half: Women 1975.* Rome: 1975.

786. ______. *Report on the Seminar on the Role of Women in Integrated Rural Development with Emphasis on Population Problems.* F1141. Rome: 1975.

787. ______. *Status of Rural Women, Especially Agricultural Workers, Programme of Concerted International Action to Promote the Advancement of Women and their Integration in Development.* E/CN.6/583/Add. 2. Rome: December 1973.

788. Giele, Janet Z., and Smock, Audrey C., eds. *Women: Roles and Status in Eight Countries.* New York: Wiley-Interscience, 1977.

789. Hafkin, N., and Bay, E., eds. *Women in Africa.* Stanford, Calif.: Stanford University Press, 1976. (The chapters by Hay, Mullings, and Brain are relevant.)

790. Henriquez de Paredes, Querubina; Izaguirre P., Maritza; and Vargas Delauny, Inés. *Participación de la Mujer en el Desarrollo de América Latina y del Caribe.* Santiago: UN Children's Fund, 1975.

791. Mazumdar, Vira, ed. *Role of Rural Women in Development.* Delhi: Indian Council of Social Science Research, 1978.

792. Mickelwait, Donald R. M.; Riegelman, Mary Ann; and Sweet, Charles F. *Women in Rural Development: A Survey of the Roles of Women in Ghana, Lesotho, Kenya, Nigeria, Bolivia, Paraguay and Peru.* Boulder, Colo.: Westview, 1976.

793. O'Kelly, Elizabeth. *Rural Women: Their Integration in Development Programmes and How Simple Intermediate Technologies Can Help Them.* London: 1978. (Available from the author, 3 Cumberland Gardens, Lloyd Square, London WC1X 9AF.)

794. Pala, Achola O. *African Women in Rural Development: Research Trends and Priorities.* OLC Paper no. 12. Washington, D. C.: Overseas Liaison Committee, American Council on Education, December 1976.

795. ______. *The Role of Women in Rural Development: Research Priorities.* Institute for Development Studies Discussion Paper no. 203. Nairobi: University of Nairobi, 1975.

796. Simmons, Emmy B. *Economic Research on Women in Rural Development in Northern Nigeria.* OLC Paper no. 10. Washington, D. C.: Overseas Liaison Committee, American Council on Education, September 1976.

797. Spencer, Dunstan S. C. *African Women in Agricultural Development. A Case Study in Sierra Leone.* OLC Paper no. 9. Washington, D. C.:

Overseas Liaison Committee, American Council on Education, June 1976. (Also available as Working Paper no. 11. East Lansing: African Rural Economy Program, Michigan State University, April 1976.)

798. United Nations, Children's Fund, Regional Office for Latin America. *Servicios de Apoyo: Mecanismos para la Incorporación de la Mujer al Desarrollo.* Santiago: 1975.

799. United Nations, Educational, Scientific and Cultural Organization. *Study on the Equality of Access of Girls and Women to Education in the Context of Rural Development.* Paris: 1972.

800. United Nations, Protein-Calorie Advisory Group. *Women in Food Production, Food Handling and Nutrition, With Special Emphasis on Africa.* New York: June 1977.

801. Verny, Régine. *Fonction Sociale et Familiale de la Femme Ivoirienne.* Abidjan: Institut d'Ethno-Sociologie, Université d'Abidjan, May 1975.

802. Youssef, Nadia H. *Women and Work in Developing Societies.* Population Monograph Series, no. 15. Berkeley, Calif.: Institute of International Studies, University of California, 1974.

Articles

Davin and Eberstadt corroborate Curtain's (entry 780) findings on China. Davin points out that women are expected to work outside the home but that for the most part men do not in turn assume a proportionate share of the housework. Mbilinya argues that while Tanzanian authorities are conscious of the contradictions that have developed in the Tanzanian economy due to the dependence on foreign capital, they have largely ignored the contradictions arising between men and women due to the shift from a subsistence-based economy to a cash crop, money-oriented one. The UN Commission for Africa has produced a number of interesting studies on the status of women in African societies. Entry 835 discusses how women's second-class status has contributed to Africa's high birth rates and the high rates of mortality for infants, children, and women. In entry 838, the ECA summarizes the work done by African women in food production and family care and compares that to the minimal role women are assigned by development plans. Entry 843 demonstrates that despite their traditional importance in the agricultural sector, Indian women are largely ignored by extension programs. The importance of training women in modern farm techniques is stressed and suggestions are offered for possible training programs that would meet this objective.

Articles that are particularly recommended are the one by Moore, the ECA article in the *African Studies Review* (entry 836), the selections edited by Wipper and by Young, and the two articles by Gulati. Also relevant are entry 1950, entry 310, Chapter 5 of entry 475, and the article by Thorberg in entry 2322. The latter surveys post-Liberation policies for the employment of women in China, particularly in the rural sector.

803. African Training and Research Centre for Women (ECA). "The Role of Women in African Development." *Economic Bulletin for Africa* 11:1 (1975): 57–78.

804. Ashraf, Malik. "Notes on the Role of Rural Pakistani Women in Farming in the Northwest Frontier Province." *Land Tenure Center Newsletter* no. 55 (January–March 1977): 10–13.

805. Boulding, Elise. "Village Woman and World Food: Some Policy Perspectives," pp. 294–310. In *Peace, Development and New International Economic Order. Proceedings of the 7th IPRA General Conference.* Eds. Luis Herrera and Raimo Väyrynen. Tampere, Finland: International Peace Research Association, 1979.

806. Brain, J. L. "The Position of Women on Rural Development Schemes in Tanzania." *Ufahamu* 6:1 (1975): 40–59.

807. Braun, Armelle. "Escape from the Passive Past." *Ceres* no. 64 (July–September 1978): 40–44.

808. Chutikul, Saisuree. "Women in Rural Northeast Society in Thailand." Khon Kaen, Thailand: Khon Kaen University, n.d., mimeo.

809. Cordonnier, Rita. "De la Condition Socio-Economique des Femmes Africaines." *Cultures et Développement* 9:3 (1977): 387–411.

810. Davin, Delia. "Women in the Countryside of China," pp. 243–273. In *Women in Chinese Society.* Ed. Margery Wolf and Roxane Witke. Stanford, Calif.: Stanford University Press, 1975.

811. Deere, C. D. "Rural Women's Subsistence Production in the Capitalist Periphery." *Review of Radical Political Economics* 8:1 (1976): 9–17.

812. Eberstadt, Nick. "Women and Education in China: How Much Progress?" *New York Review of Books* (19 April 1979): 41–45.

813. Elmendorf, Mary. "The Dilemma of Peasant Women: A View from a Village in Yucatan," pp. 88–94. In *Women and World Development.* Ed. Irene Tinker and Michèle Bo Bramsen. Washington, D. C.: Overseas Development Council, 1976.

814. "La Femme et l'Economie/Women and the Economy," pp. 259–309. In *La Civilisation de la Femme dans la Tradition Africaine.* Meeting Organized by the Society of African Culture, Abidjan, 3–8 July 1972. Paris: Présence Africaine, 1975.

815. Gulati, Leela. "Profile of a Female Agricultural Labourer." *Economic and Political Weekly* 13 (25 March 1978): A27–A35.

816. ______. "Unemployment Among Female Agricultural Labourers." *Economic and Political Weekly* 11 (27 March 1976): A31–A39.

817. Henry, Natalie D. "A Forgotten Resource in Development—Women." Prepared for the 13th World Conference of the Society for International Development, San José, Costa Rica, 22–25 February 1973, mimeo.

818. Jedlicka, Allen. "Diffusion of Technical Innovation: A Case for the Non-Sexist Approach Among Rural Villages." Presented to Seminar on Women in Development. Sponsored by the American Association for the Advancement of Science; UN Development Programme; UN Institute for Training and Research. Mexico City: 1975, mimeo.

819. Kokuhirwa, Hilda. "Towards the Social and Economic Promotion of Rural Women in Tanzania." Dar-es-Salaam: Institute for Adult Education, 1975, mimeo.

820. Lindenbaum, Shirley. "The Social and Economic Status of Women in Bangladesh." New York: Department of Anthropology, York College, City University of New York, 1974, mimeo.

821. Mbilinya, Marjorie J. "The 'New Woman' and Traditional Norms in Tanzania." *Journal of Modern African Studies* 10:1 (1972):57–72.

822. Mead, Margaret. "A Comment on the Role of Women in Agriculture," pp. 9–11. In *Women and World Development.* Eds. Irene Tinker and Michèle Bo Bramsen. Washington, D. C.: Overseas Development Council, 1976.

823. Mitchnik, David. "The Role of Women in Rural Development in Zambia." London: Oxfam, 1972, mimeo.

824. Moore, M. P. *Some Economic Aspects of Women's Work and Status in the Rural Areas of Africa and Asia.* IDS Discussion Paper no. 43. Brighton, UK: Institute of Development Studies, University of Sussex, 1974.

825. Olmstead, Judith. "Farmer's Wife, Weaver's Wife: Women and Work in Two Southern Ethiopian Communities." *African Studies Review* 18 (December 1975): 85–98.

826. Omvedt, Gail. "Women and Rural Revolt in India." *The Journal of Peasant Studies* 5 (April 1978): 370–403.

827. Oppong, Christine; Okali, Christine; and Houghton, Beverly. "Women Power: Retrograde Steps in Ghana." *African Studies Review* 18 (December 1975): 71–84.

828. Rogers, Barbara,. "Women and Land Rights." *ISIS International Bulletin* no. 11 (Spring 1979).

829. "Rural Women and Development," pp. 61–117. In *Role of Women in Socio-Economic Development in Bangladesh.* Proceedings of a Seminar held in Dacca, May 9–10, 1976. Dacca: Bangladesh Economic Association, 1977.

830. Simmons, Emily Bartz. "Cultural Assumptions and Women's Roles in Development." Monrovia: Liberian Institute of Public Administration, n.d., mimeo.

831. Stoler, Ann. "Land, Labor and Female Autonomy in a Javanese Village." New York: Department of Anthropology, Columbia University, 1975, mimeo.

832. Swanson, Rebecca L. "Role of Women in the Yemen Arab Republic." Washington, D. C.: US Agency for International Development, 1975, mimeo.

833. Swedish International Development Authority. "Rural Women in Kenya and Tanzania." *Development Digest* 13 (July 1975): 53–60.

834. Tinker, Irene. "The Adverse Impact of Development on Women," pp. 22–34. In *Women and World Development.* Eds. Irene Tinker and Michèle Bo Bramsen. Washington, D. C.: Overseas Development Council, 1976.

835. United Nations, Economic Commission for Africa. "The Data Base for Discussion on the Interrelations between the Integration of Women in Development, Their Situation, and Population Factors in Africa." Paper presented to the Regional Seminar on the Integration of Women in Development with Special Reference to Population Factors, Addis Ababa, 1974.

836. United Nations, Economic Commission for Africa, African Training and Research Center for Women, Human Resources and Development Division. "Women and National Development in African Countries: Some Profound Contradictions." *African Studies Review* 18 (December 1975): 47–70.

837. ______. "Women: The Neglected Human Resource for African Development." *Canadian Journal of African Studies* 6:2 (1972): 359–370.

838. ______. "The Integration of Women in African Development." Prepared for the 14th World Conference of the Society for International Development, Abidjan, Ivory Coast, 1974, mimeo.

839. United Nations, Economic and Social Council, and United Nations, Children's Fund. "Summary of the Report on Women and Girls in National Development." E/ICEF/616/Add. 3/Annex. 11 February 1972. (Deals with Egypt, Sudan, and Lebanon.)

840. Von-Harder, Gudrun M. "Women's Role in Rice Processing." In *Women for Women: Bangladesh 1975*. Dacca: Bangladesh University Press, 1975.

841. Wipper, Audrey, ed. "Rural Women: Development or Underdevelopment?" *Rural Africana* no. 29 (Winter 1975–1976). (Includes a selected bibliography)

842. "Women: A Long-Silent Majority" (Issue Title). *Ceres* no. 44 (March–April 1975).

843. "Women in Agriculture" (Issue Title). *Indian Farming* 25:8 (1975). (Copies are available from the Indian Council of Agricultural Research, New Delhi.)

844. Young, Kate, ed. "Women in Development" (Issue Title). *IDS Bulletin* 10 (March 1979).

845. Youssef, Nadia H. "Women and Agricultural Production in Muslim Societies." *Studies in Comparative International Development* 12 (Spring 1977): 41–58.

Pastoralism

For a long time, it was widely believed that pastoralists wandered more or less aimlessly in search of food and water for their animals and that they were constantly at the mercy of natural phenomena, notably drought. A substantial body of evidence now proves that these notions have no basis in reality. Far from wandering aimlessly, pastoralists have devised systems of pasture division designed to regulate conflicts between different groups and to minimize the danger of over-grazing. Pastoral societies and economies have been shaped by the necessity of existing within an essentially hostile environment. The level of technology at the disposal of a pastoral society is low, but that does not mean that pastoralists are at the mercy of natural forces. They have an extensive knowledge of the soil, plant life, and water resources of the areas in which they live. They have developed means of mitigating the harmful effects of climatic changes such as migrations of varying lengths and changes in herd composition.

As developing countries have been progressively integrated into the commercialized economic system, the situation of pastoralists has worsened. Whether attempts have been directed at integrating the pastoralists themselves into the national economy (by encouraging them to sell more and more of their animals) or at expanding agricultural production, the results have been much the same: increasing impoverishment of herders and growing vulnerability to natural phenomena.

The droughts in West and East Africa in the late 1960s and early 1970s caused the plight of pastoral societies to become familiar to large numbers of people around the world. However, anthropologists have long been interested in the dynamics of pastoral societies. More recently, they have begun to study the functioning of pastoral economic systems. It is primarily these two strands of the anthropological literature that form the sections below.

Books and Monographs

The book by Dahl and Hjort focuses on the economic aspects of herding which, in the past, have taken second place in academic discussions to the "social value" of herds. Dahl and Hjort argue that such an approach has tended to ignore, or at least downplay, the herders' need to maintain a certain number of animals to satisfy household consumption requirements. If pastoralism is to survive as a viable system, its economic basis clearly will have to be understood by the people who are responsible for drawing up and implementing development plans. This book, which contains a useful short bibliography, is highly recommended. Also of relevance here is entry 1644, a monograph by Dahl and Hjort, which discusses "the effects of drought on herd structures and the possible economic implications of these for the pastoral household." It too contains a useful bibliography. Another good bibliography is found in Irons and Dyson-Hudson. Other recommended studies are Nicolaisen, Johnson, and Baker.

846. Abercrombie, Frank D. *Range Development and Management in Africa.* Washington, D. C.: US Agency for International Development, August 1974.

847. Baker, Randall. *Perceptions of Pastoralism.* Development Studies Discussion Paper. Norwich, UK: University of East Anglia, 1974.

848. Dahl, Gudrun, and Hjort, Anders. *Having Herds: Pastoral Herd Growth and Household Economy.* Stockholm Studies in Social Anthropology 2. Stockholm: Department of Anthropology, University of Stockholm, 1976.

849. Demirüren, A. S. *The Improvement of Nomadic & Transhumance Animal Production Systems.* Rome: FAO, 1974.

850. Doornbos, Martin R., and Lofchie, Michael F. *Ranching and Scheming: A Case Study of the Ankole Ranching Scheme.* ISS Occasional Paper, no. 3. The Hague: Institute of Social Studies, c. 1971.

851. Food and Agriculture Organization. *Near East Regional Study—Animal Husbandry, Production and Health, Fodder Production and Range Management in the Near East and FAO's Policies and Plans for Promoting the Animal Industry.* Rome and Cairo: 1972.

852. France, Secrétariat d'Etat aux Affaires Etrangères, Direction de l'Aide au Développement, Service des Etudes Techniques, Département de l'Elevage. *La Reconstitution du Cheptel et le Développement de la Production Animale en Zone Sahélienne et Sudano-Sahélienne. Esquisse d'une Stratégie Nationale et Régionale.* Paris: August 1973.

853. Frantz, Charles. *Pastoral Societies, Stratification and National Integration.* Research Report no. 30. Uppsala: Scandinavian Institute of African Studies, 1975.

854. Hess, Oleen. *The Establishment of Cattle Ranching Associations in Tanzania.* Occasional Paper no. 7. Ithaca, N. Y.: Rural Development Committee, Center for International Studies, Cornell University, 1976.

855. Irons, William, and Dyson-Hudson, Neville, eds. *Perspectives on Nomadism.* Leiden: Brill, 1972.

856. Johnson, Douglas. *The Nature of Nomadism.* Research Paper no. 118. Chicago, Ill.: Department of Geography, University of Chicago, 1969.

857. Konczacki, Z. A. *The Economics of Pastoralism.* London: Cass, 1978.

858. Leeds, Anthony, and Vayda, Andrew P., eds. *Man, Culture and Animals.* Publication no. 78. Washington, D. C.: American Association for the Advancement of Science, 1965. (The chapters by Sweet, Deshler, Downs and Ekvall, Murra, and Strickon are of interest.)

859. Lewis, Ioan M. *A Pastoral Democracy: A Study of Pastoralism and Politics among the Northern Somali of the Horn of Africa.* London: Oxford University Press, for the International African Institute, 1961.

860. Monod, T., ed. *Pastoralism in Tropical Africa.* London: International African Institute, 1975.

861. Nicolaisen, J. *Ecology and Culture of the Pastoral Tuareg.* Copenhagen: National Museum of Copenhagen, 1963.

862. Raay, Hans G. T. van. *Fulani Pastoralists and Cattle.* ISS Occasional Paper. The Hague: Institute of Social Studies, May 1974.

863. Sjöberg, K-E, and Persson, S. *Cattle Production in Africa.* Stockholm: College of Agriculture, 1974.

864. Société d'Etudes pour le Développement Economique et Social. *L'Elevage en Cote d'Ivoire: Diagnostic et Perspectives.* Paris: October 1973.

865. ______. *Projet de Modernisation de L'Elevage en Zone Pastorale, Niger.* Paris: July 1973.

866. Stenning, Derrick J. *Savannah Nomads.* London: Oxford University Press, 1959.

867. United Nations, Educational, Scientific and Cultural Organization. *Nomades et Nomadisme au Sahara.* Arid Zone Research, no. 19. Paris: 1963.

868. Whyte, Robert Orr. *Land, Livestock and Human Nutrition in India.* New York: Praeger, 1968.

Articles

Widstrand argues that the survival of nomads depends on the precise manipulation of ecological conditions, rational decision-making, and risk management. Pastoralists are capable of all these, but Widstrand demonstrates that factors outside their control (such as water development, veterinary and health services, international boundaries restricting herd movement) have contributed in large part to overstocking and thus to the economic and ecological marginalization of herders. The article by Rada and Neville Dyson-Hudson offers a good short summary of the human ecology of Karamojong herding practices. Glantz discusses many of the problems confronting herders in the West African Sahel. Also recommended are entry 1620, the chapter by Hoyle in entry 990, and all the articles by Swift. The chapter by Swift in entry 1650 is also relevant.

869. Chatty, Dawn. "Structuring Forces of Pastoral Nomadism in S. W. Asia (With Emphasis on Camel Pastoral Nomadism)." *Development and Change* 4:3 (1972–73): 51–72.

870. Dyson-Hudson, Rada. "Men, Women and Work in a Semi-Arid Area." *Natural History* (December 1960): 42–57.

871. Dyson-Hudson, Rada and Neville. "Subsistence Herding in Uganda." *Scientific American* 220 (February 1969): 76–89.

872. Glantz, Michael H. "Value of a Reliable Long Range Weather Forecast for the West African Sahel." *Bulletin of the American Meteorological Society* 58:2 (1977): 150–158.

873. Marx, Emanuel. "The Tribe as a Unit of Subsistence: Nomadic Pastoralism in the Middle East." *American Anthropologist* 79 (June 1977): 343–363.

874. Rigby, P. "Pastoralism & Prejudice. Ideology and Rural Development in East Africa." *Nkanga* no. 4 (1971).

875. Sall, Alioune. "Quel Aménagement Pastoral Pour le Sahel?" *Revue Tiers-Monde* 19 (January–March 1978): 161–169.

876. Stryker, J. Dirck. "The Malian Cattle Industry: Opportunity and Dilemma." *Journal of Modern African Studies* 12:3 (1974): 441–457.

877. Swift, Jeremy. "In Defence of Nomads." *Mazingira* no. 2. (1977): 26–30.

878. ______. "Nomadisme et Utilisation des Terres." *Etudes Maliennes* 2 (1972): 49–53.

879. ______. "Sahelian Pastoralists—Underdevelopment, Desertification and Famine." *Annual Review of Anthropology* 6 (1977): 457–478.

880. Toupet, Charles. "Pastoralisme et Milieu Naturel." *Notes et Documents Voltaiques* 6 (1973): 8–9.

881. Widstrand, Carl Gösta. "The Rationale of Nomad Economy." *Ambio* 4:4 (1975): 146–153.

882. Wilson, R. T. "Temporal Changes in Livestock Numbers and Patterns of Transhumance in Southern Darfur, Sudan." *Journal of Developing Areas* 11 (July 1977): 493–508.

Reaching the Small Farmer

The need to reach "the poorest of the poor" in developing countries—that is, the subsistence farmer—has been increasingly emphasized by international aid agencies such as USAID and the World Bank. Critics of these agencies have, however, argued that aid agency rhetoric has not yet been translated into effective action. For one thing, these agencies have shown themselves unwilling to promote the structural changes necessary for the majority of the people in the third world to benefit from development programs. Without changes in the power structure of many third world countries, aid designed to reach the very poor risks ending up in the pockets of the better-off, as it has all too frequently in the past. For example, in Guatemala, the World Bank has defined a smallholding as a parcel of land which covers less than 112 acres. This certainly is small compared to many US farms. However, fully 97 percent of all holdings in Guatemala are smaller than 112 acres (entry 3173, p. 45). There simply can be no guarantee that the truly smallholder who has only an acre or two of land will be more likely to benefit from World Bank programs than the "smallholder" who farms 100 acres; in fact, there is every likelihood that the truly smallholder will be bypassed (see, for example, Davis).

Aid agencies also have financed or otherwise promoted the third world activities of agribusiness, which, in most cases, becomes involved in developing countries to obtain food and other cash crops for export or to provision the elites in third world countries. Helping the poor to feed themselves has not been high on the list of priorities of any agribusiness firm (see entry 1607, pp. 30, 44–46; entry 1605, Part II; and entry 1887, pp. 214–234).

The World Bank and USAID have sometimes attempted to turn subsistence farmers into cash-crop producers. However, the results have not always been beneficial to smallholders. The report by Development Alternatives, Inc. discusses how increased coffee production by Haitian smallholders under a USAID-financed project has increased the participants' economic vulnerability.

But perhaps the most serious flaw in the new interest in the smallholder is that it is unlikely to help those who really *are* "the poorest of the poor," the landless and near-landless agricultural laborers. According to World Bank figures, the landless and near-landless now comprise 40 to 60 percent of the population in many third world countries. It should come as no surprise that aid agencies like the World Bank prefer to channel their aid to "those with investment opportunities sufficient to produce a significant marketable surplus" as "the best way to reduce the level of default" on loans (entry 1607, p. 25). If this sort of preference militates against lending to farmers with only a few acres of land, or less, it is not hard to imagine what happens to the landless and near-landless who have *no* "investment opportunities" at all. The issue of landlessness and near-landlessness is discussed in entries 1391, 1399, 1404, and 1407.

General

Books and Monographs

The monograph by Streeter is probably the best source to consult for an understanding of the "liberal" position on this issue. A thoughtful introduction to the function of peasant societies is provided by Greenwood. He suggests that peasants are considerably more rational in their judgments and more willing to adapt themselves to change than the development experts' traditional view of them suggests. Other recommended studies are Halperin and Dow, Lundahl, Vallianatos, and Wolf. Items discussing the availability of agricultural credit to smallholders can be found on pages 190–193.

883. Badouin, Robert. *Les Agricultures de Subsistence et le Développement Economique.* Paris: Editions A. Pedrone, 1975.

884. Biggs, Huntley H., and Tinnermeier, R. L., eds. *Small Farm Agricultural Development Problems.* Fort Collins, Colo.: Colorado State University, 1974.

885. Clark, Colin, and Haswell, Margaret. *The Economics of Subsistence Agriculture.* New York: St. Martin's, 1964.

886. Development Alternatives, Inc. *Strategies for Small Farmer Development: An Empirical Study of Rural Development Projects.* 2 vols. Boulder, Colo.: Westview, 1976.

887. Greenwood, Davydd J. *The Political Economy of Peasant Family Farming: Some Anthropological Perspectives on Rationality and Adaptation.* Occasional Paper no. 2. Ithaca, N. Y.: Rural Development Committee, Cornell University, 1973. (A shortened, revised version appeared as "Political Economy and Adaptive Processes: A Framework for the Study of Peasant States." *Peasant Studies Newsletter* 3 (July 1973): 1–10.)

888. Halperin, Rhoda, and Dow, James, eds. *Peasant Livelihood. Studies in Economic Anthropology and Cultural Ecology.* New York: St. Martin's, 1977.

889. Hunter, Guy. *Modernizing Peasant Societies: A Comparative Study in Asia and Africa.* New York: Oxford University Press, 1971.

890. International Labour Office. *Conditions of Life and Work of Share-Croppers, Tenant Farmers, and Similar Categories of Semi-Independent and Independent Workers in Agriculture.* Report 3, International Labour Organization Asian Regional Conference, New Delhi, November 1957. Geneva: 1957.

891. Lundahl, Mats. *Peasants and Poverty: A Study of Haiti.* New York: St. Martin's, 1979.

892. Nash, Manning. *Primitive and Peasant Economic Systems.* San Francisco: Chandler, 1966.

893. Potter, Jack M.; Diaz, May N.; and Foster, George M., eds. *Peasant Society: A Reader.* The Little Brown Series in Anthropology. Boston: Little, Brown, 1967.

894. Stevens, Robert D., ed. *Tradition and Dynamics in Small-Farm Agriculture: Economic Studies in Asia, Africa and Latin America.* Ames: Iowa State University Press, 1977.

895. Streeter, Carroll P. *Reaching the Developing World's Small Farmer.* New York: Rockefeller Foundation, c. 1972.

896. Vallianatos, E. G. *Fear in the Countryside: The Control of Agricultural Resources in the Poor Countries by Nonpeasant Elites.* Cambridge, Mass.: Ballinger, 1976.

897. Wharton, Clifton R., ed. *Subsistence Agriculture and Economic Development.* Chicago, Ill.: Aldine,1969.

898. Wolf, Eric R. *Peasants.* Foundations of Modern Anthropology Series. Englewood Cliffs, N. J.: Prentice-Hall, 1966.

Articles

Scott argues that peasant societies are organized to minimize risk, not to maximize production. The economic structure of peasant societies provides their members with security without compromising social stability. The importance of the risk-minimizing function is stressed by Schluter and Mellor. They find that while access to credit is important, uncertainty is the most important variable influencing the adoption of high-yielding varieties by small farmers.

The articles by Hossain and by Chadha discuss the issue of farm size and productivity in Bangladesh and India respectively. Both agree that smaller farms tend to be more productive than larger ones. Hossain takes the position that this occurs because smaller farms have more labor per unit of land than larger ones and can thus take better care of their crops. Chadha discusses the factors driving smaller farmers to more intensive cultivation. He believes that if these intensive-cultivation practices were combined with the proper inputs provided by a network of cooperatives, small farms could compete with larger ones in all areas except that of size-biased machines. Other recommended articles are Beckford and Feder, as well as entry 506.

899. Abercrombie, K. C. "Who are They, Where are They?" *Ceres* no. 45 (May–June 1975): 49–51.

900. Beckford, George L. "Agricultural Development in 'Traditional' and 'Peasant' Economies: A Review Article." *Social and Economic Studies* 15 (March 1966): 151–161.

901. Belloncle, Guy. "Listening to the Peasant." *Ceres* no. 33 (May–June 1973): 24–27.

902. Bharadwaj, Krishna. "Notes on Farm Size and Productivity." *Economic and Political Weekly* 9 (30 March 1974): A11–A24.

903. Castro, Leandro. "Las Cooperativas del Campo y el Mercado de los Productos Agrarios." *Revista de Estudios Agro-Socioles* 12:44 (1963): 99–118.

904. Chadha, G. K. "Farm Size and Productivity Revisited. Some Notes from Recent Experience of Punjab." *Economic and Political Weekly* 13 (30 September 1978): A87–A96.

905. Chattapadhya, Manabendu, and Rudra, Ashok. "Size-Productivity Revisited." *Economic and Political Weekly* 11 (25 September 1976): A104–A116.

906. Feder, Ernest. "Six Plausible Theses about the Peasants' Perspectives in the Developing World." *Development and Change* 5:2 (1973–74): 1–24.

907. Grant, James P. "Development: The End of Trickle Down?" *Foreign Policy* no. 12 (Fall 1973): 43–65.

908. Hendry, Peter. "A Touch of Social Engineering." *Ceres* no. 64 (July–August 1978): 36–39.

909. Hossain, Mahabub. "Farm Size, Tenancy and Land Productivity: An Analysis of Farm Level Data in Bangladesh Agriculture." *The Bangladesh Development Studies* 5 (July 1977): 285–348.

910. Mouzelis, N. P. "Modernisation, Development and the Peasant" (Review Article). *Development and Change* 4:3 (1972–73): 73–88.

911. Pearse, Andrew. "Subsistence Farming is Far From Dead." *Ceres* no. 10 (July–August 1969): 38–43.

912. Sachs, Ignacy. "Nobody Asks Him." *Ceres* no. 10 (July–August 1969): 54–56.

913. Schluter, Michael, and Mellor, John W. "New Seed Varieties and the Small Farm." *Economic and Political Weekly* 7 (25 March 1972): A31–A38.

914. Scott, James C. "The Subsistence Ethic: A Peasant View of Security." *The New Ecologist* no. 3 (May–June 1978): 75–76.

915. Vail, D. J. "Induced Farm Innovation and Derived Scientific Research Strategy: The Choice of Techniques in Developing Smallholder Agriculture in Land Abundant Areas." *Journal of Rural Development* 6:1–2 (1973): 1–17.

916. Watters, R. F. "The Nature of Shifting Cultivation: A Review of Recent Research." *Pacific Viewpoint* 1 (1960): 59–99.

917. Watts, R. "Attitudes to Small Farmers are Changing, World-Wide." *World Crops and Livestock* 29 (July–August 1977): 153, 156–157.

918. Wood, Geof. "A Peasantry and the State." *Development and Change* 5:2 (1973–1974): 45–75.

Asia and Oceania

Entry 926, the article by Jose, and the monograph by Singh all discuss different aspects of the problem of agricultural laborers in Asia. The latter is typical of World Bank reports in that it discusses ways of increasing small-farmer productivity and of expanding opportunities for rural employment of the landless *in the absence of major land redistribution.* Another article discussing the risk-minimizing strategy of small farmers is by Schluter and Mount. Rochin reports on the responsiveness of subsistence farmers to innovations. The monograph by Whyte is a useful introduction to the topic of developing rural Asia.

The article by Krishna reviews the operations of the Small Farmer Development Agency (SFDA) in India during its first eight years. Krishna concludes that the economic status of farmers can be improved through the SFDA's provision of productive assets and adequate supporting services. The main problems confronting the SFDA are said to be the low number of smallholders reached (one-eighth of the estimated 49 million smallholders in India), administrative apathy, and the failure to organize necessary support mechanisms.

919. Barran, Jacques. *Subsistence Agriculture in Melanesia.* Bulletin 219. Honolulu: Bernice P. Bishop Museum, 1958.

920. Delvert, Jean. *Le Paysan Cambodgien.* Paris: Mouton, 1961.

921. Gaikwad, V. R. *Small Farmers. State Policy and Programme Implementation.* Hyderabad: National Institute of Community Development, 1971.

922. Geertz, Clifford. *The Impact of Capital-Intensive Agriculture on Peasant Societies. A Case Study.* Cambridge, Mass.: Center for International Studies, Massachusetts Institute of Technology, 1956.

923. "Getting Poorer." *Economic and Political Weekly* 13 (14 October 1978): 1726–1727.

924. Gilpatrick, Chadbourne. "Problems and Prospects of Small Farmers in Uttar Pradesh." *LTC Newsletter* no. 37 (July–October 1972): 1–6.

925. Hunter, Guy, and Bottrall, Anthony, eds. *Serving the Small Farmer: Policy Choices in Indian Agricultural Development.* London: Croom-Helm, 1974.

926. Jose, A. V. "Real Wages, Employment, and Income of Agricultural Labourers." *Economic and Political Weekly* 13 (25 March 1978): A16–A20.

927. Krishna, Raj. "Small Farmer Development." *Economic and Political Weekly* 14 (26 May 1979): 913–918.

928. Lok, Siepko H. "Smallholders' Rubber Production." *Monthly Bulletin of Agricultural Economics and Statistics* 26 (March 1977).

929. Mahapatra, Sitakant. "Modernisation of Tribal Agriculture. Technological and Cultural Constraints." *Economic and Political Weekly* 13 (1 April 1978): 581–585.

930. Reddy, V. N., and Murthy, C. S. "Backward Castes and Tenancy: A Village Study." *Economic and Political Weekly* 13 (1 July 1978): 1061–1076.

931. Rochin, Refugio I. "Responsiveness of Subsistence Farmers to New Ideas: Dwarf Wheats on Unirrigated Small Holdings in Pakistan." *Teaching Forum.* no. 17. New York: The Agricultural Development Council, May 1972.

932. Schluter, Michael G. G., and Mount, Timothy D. "Some Management Objectives of the Peasant Farmer: An Analysis of Risk Aversion in the Choice of Cropping Pattern, Surat District, India." *The Journal of Development Studies* 12 (April 1976): 246–261.

933. Shah, C. H. "Small Farmers: Policy and Problems." *Economic and Political Weekly* 13 (21 October 1978): 1771–1775.

934. Singh, Inderjit. *Small Farmers and the Landless in South Asia.* Working Paper 320. Washington, D. C.: World Bank, 1979.

935. Vyas, V. S. "Structural Change in Agriculture and the Small Farm Sector." *Economic and Political Weekly* 11 (10 January 1976): 24–32.

936. Vyas, V. S.; Tyagi, D. S.; and Misra, V. N. "New Agricultural Strategy and Small Farmers. A Case Study in Gujarat." *Economic and Political Weekly* 4 (29 March 1969): A49–A53.

937. Whyte, Robert Orr. *The Asian Village as a Basis for Rural Modernization.* Occasional Paper no. 44. Singapore: Institute of Southeast Asian Studies, 1976.

Latin America

The articles by Myren and by Winkelmann discuss the Puebla project. Finkler shows how the Mexican *ejido* system, initially designed to be egalitarian, has "unwittingly contributed to economic differentiation" and has helped to defeat the objectives of Mexico's agrarian reform. The article by Nicholls should be read with the book by Forman. The articles by Davis, Whyte, and Development Alternatives, Inc. are recommended.

938. Belshaw, Michael. *A Village Economy: Land and People of Huecorio.* New York and London: Columbia University Press, 1967. (Deals with Mexico)

939. Bernstein, Richard H., and Herdt, Robert W. "Towards an Understanding of *Milpa* Agriculture: The Belize Case." *The Journal of Developing Areas* 11 (April 1977): 373–392.

940. Brierly, John S. *Small Farming in Grenada, West Indies.* Winnipeg: Geographical Studies, University of Manitoba, 1974.

941. Davis, L. Harlan. "Foreign Aid to the Small Farmer: The El Salvador Experience." *Inter-American Economic Affairs* 29 (Summer 1975): 81–91.

942. Development Alternatives, Inc. "Evaluation of Haiti Small Farm Project." Washington, D. C.: 1977.

943. Eckstein, Shlomo, and Carroll, Thomas F. "Peasant Cooperation in Land Reform Programs: Some Latin American Experiences." In *Popular Participation in National Development.* Ed. June Nash, Jorge Dandler, and Nicholas S. Hopkins. The Hague: Mouton, 1976.

944. Erven, Bernard L., and Rask, Norman. *Credit Infusion as a Small Farmer Development Strategy—The Ibiruba Pilot Project in Southern Brazil.* Occasional Paper no. 48. Columbus: Ohio State University, December 1971.

945. Finkler, Kaja. "From Sharecroppers to Entrepreneurs: Peasant Household Strategies under the Ejido System of Mexico." *Economic Development and Cultural Change* 27 (October 1978): 103–120.

946. Forman, Shepard. *The Brazilian Peasantry.* New York and London: Columbia University Press, 1975.

947. Garcia-Huidobro, Francisca Rosene. "Attitudes Toward Collectivization Held by Chilean Campesinos." *Land Tenure Center Newsletter* no. 51 (January–March 1976): 16–24.

948. Handelman, Howard. *Struggle in the Andes: Peasant Mobilization in Peru.* Austin: University of Texas Press, 1974.

949. Haney, Emil. *Progressive Deterioration of Minifundia Agriculture in Colombia: Structural Reform Not in Sight.* Latin American Research Briefs no. 14. Madison: Land Tenure Center, University of Wisconsin, April 1971.

950. Johnson, Allen W. *Sharecroppers of the Sertão; Economics and Dependence on a Brazilian Plantation.* Stanford, Calif.: Stanford University Press, 1971.

951. Keatinge, Elsie B. "Latin American Peasant Corporate Communities: Potentials for Mobilization and Political Integration." *Journal of Anthropological Research* 29 (Spring 1973).

952. Landsberger, Henry A., ed. *Latin American Peasant Movements.* Ithaca, N. Y. and London: Cornell University Press, 1969.

953. MacDonald, A. L. *Agricultural Technology in Developing Countries: Social Factors Related to the Use of Modern Techniques in Two Rural Areas in Peru.* Rotterdam: University Press, 1976.

954. Moran, Michael. "La Commercialización Agropecuaria y su Significación para el Desarrollo Socioéconomico del Campesino." *Desarrollo Rural en las Américas* 7:2 (1975): 137–146.

955. Myren, Delbert T. *Strategies for Increasing Agricultural Production on Small Holdings.* International Conference. Puebla, Mexico: CIMMYT [?], August 1970.

956. Nash, June. "Social Resources of a Latin Peasantry: The Case of a Maya Indian Community." *Social and Economic Studies* 15 (December 1966): 353–367.

957. Nicholls, William H. "Review Article: Professor Forman on the Brazilian Peasantry." *Economic Development and Cultural Change* 26 (January 1978): 359–383.

958. Powell, John Duncan. *The Role of the Federacion Campesina in the Venezuelan Agrarian Reform Process.* LTC Research Paper no. 26. Madison: Land Tenure Center, University of Wisconsin, December 1967.

959. Rask, Norman. *Technological Change and the Traditional Small Farmer of Rio Grande do Sul—Brazil.* Occasional Paper no. 85. Columbus: Ohio State University, June 1972.

960. Santos de Morais, Clodomir. "The Role of the Campesino Sector in the Honduran Agrarian Reform." *Land Tenure Center Newsletter* no. 47 (January–March 1975): 16–22.

961. Whittenbarger, Robert L., and Havens, A. Eugene. *A Longitudinal Analysis of Three Small-Farm Communities in Colombia: A Compendium of Descriptive Statistics.* LTC no. 87. Madison: Land Tenure Center, University of Wisconsin, June 1973.

962. Whyte, William F. "Rural Peru—Peasants as Activists." In *Contemporary Culture and Societies of Latin America.* 2nd ed. Eds. Dwight E. Heath and Richard N. Adams. New York: Random House, 1974.

963. Winkelmann, Don. "Factors Inhibiting Farmer Participation in the Plan Puebla." *LTC Newsletter* no. 39 (January–March 1973): 1–5.

Africa

The articles by Moody and Norman discuss risk-minimizing strategies of the peasantry in Africa. Norman finds that planting a mixed crop in an area where precipitation tends to be low is a rational strategy from the point of view of maximizing profit and minimizing risk. It is even more rational than growing a single crop with modern agricultural technology. Thus, reluctance on the part of farmers to adopt a monoculture strategy is sensible. Moody looks at Kenyan smallholders and concludes that their economy is a composite of giving production priority to subsistence crops and a "cautious approach" to earning money through crop diversification. However, Moody stresses that cash crop production is but one of several options available to Kenyan peasants interested in obtaining money. Furthermore, Kenyan peasants do not see their land merely as a vital element in the process of income maximization. Land offers security in terms of food, capital savings, income, and as an important inheritance for future generations.

A review of the literature concerning peasant resistance to change is found in the chapter by Hutton and Cohen in entry 43.

The article by Leitner discusses agricultural laborers in Kenya. The book edited by Smith and Welch is also recommended.

964. Benneh, G. "The Ecology of Peasant Farming Systems in Ghana." *Environment in Africa* 1:1 (1974): 35–50.

965. Cleave, John H. *African Farmers: Labor Use in the Development of Smallholder Agriculture.* New York: Praeger, 1974.

966. Goussault, Yves. "Participation Paysanne au Développement et aux Structures Nouvelles." *Présence Africaine* 43 (1962): 183–189.

967. Guillermou, Yves. "La Réforme Agraire Algérienne. Portée et Limites: Les Exploitations Familiales. Eléments d'Analyse Régionale." *Revue Tiers-Monde* 18 (July–September 1977): 603–616.

968. Johnston, Bruce. "Agricultural Production Potentials and Small Farmer Strategies in Sub-Saharan Africa," pp. 65–127. In *Two Studies of Development in Sub-Saharan Africa.* Shankar N. Acharya and Bruce Johnston. Working Paper 300. Washington, D. C.: World Bank, October 1978.

969. Lamb, Geoff. "The Neocolonial Integration of Kenya Peasants." *Development and Change* 8:1 (1977): 45–59.

970. Leander, Lars. *A Case Study of Peasant Farming in the Digelu and Yeloma Areas. Chilalo Awraja, Ethiopia.* Addis Ababa: Planning and Evaluation Section, Chilalo Agricultural Development Unit, 1969.

971. Leitner, Kerstin. "The Situation of Agricultural Workers in Kenya." *Review of African Political Economy* no. 6 (May–August 1976): 34–50.

972. Mann, R. D. *Rural African Development Project: Identifying the Problems of Small Farmers. A Farm-Level Survey Technique to Identify Labour, Machinery and Other Input Requirements, With an Example of Its Use in Zambia.* Revised by John Boyd. rev. ed. London: Intermediate Technology, 1976.

973. Moody, Tony. "Peasant Agriculture, Commercial Production, and Employment in Kenya." *Africa Development* 1 (September 1976): 62–72.

974. Norman, David W. "Rationalising Mixed Cropping Under Indigenous Conditions: The Example of Northern Nigeria." *Journal of Development Studies* 11 (October 1974): 3–21.

975. Smith, Alan K., and Welch, Claude E., Jr., eds. *Peasants in Africa.* Waltham, Mass.: Crossroads Press, 1978. (Also available in *African Studies Review* 20 (December 1977): 1–130.)

976. Spencer, Dunstan, S. C., and Byerlee, Derek. *Small Farms in West Africa: A Descriptive Analysis of Employment, Incomes, and Productivity in Sierra Leone.* Working Paper no. 19. East Lansing: African Rural Economy Program, Michigan State University, February 1977.

977. ———. *Technical Change, Labor Use and Small Farmer Development: Evidence from Sierra Leone.* Working Paper no. 15. East Lansing: African Rural Economy Program, Michigan State University, August 1976.

978. Waters, Alan R. "Understanding African Agriculture and Its Potential for Change." *Journal of Modern African Studies* 12:1 (1975): 45–56.

979. Whetham, Edith H., and Currie, Jean I., eds. *Readings in the Applied Economics of Africa. Volume I.* Cambridge, UK: Cambridge University Press, 1967. (The chapters by Abercrombie, Clayton, and Davis Fogg are relevant.)

Resource and Ecological Considerations

General

Books and Monographs

Although only the chapter by Farvar deals directly with agricultural development, the entire volume edited by Matthews is recommended, particularly the contributions by Sachs and Farvar. Other recommended studies are Crosson and Frederick, O'Keefe and Wisner, and the volume edited by Vayda.

980. Bergeret, A., et al. *Nourrir en Harmonie avec l'Environnement—Trois Etudes de Cas.* Paris: Mouton, 1978.

981. Clawson, Marion, ed. *Natural Resources and International Development.* Baltimore, Md.: Johns Hopkins University Press, 1964. (See especially the chapters by Gaitskell and Grunwald.)

982. Conway, Gordon, and Romm, Jeff. *Ecology and Resources Development in Southeast Asia.* New York: Office for Southeast Asia, Ford Foundation, August 1973.

983. Crosson, Pierre R., and Frederick, Kenneth D. *The World Food Situation: Resource and Environmental Issues in the Developing Countries and the United States.* Baltimore, Md.: Johns Hopkins University Press, 1977.

984. Curry-Lindahl, Kai. *Conservation for Survival: An Ecological Strategy.* New York: Morrow, 1972.

985. *Development and Environment. Report and Working Papers of a Panel of Experts Convened by the Secretary-General of the United Nations Conference on the Human Environment (Founex, Switzerland, June 4–12, 1971).* Paris and The Hague: Mouton, 1972.

986. International Rice Research Institute. *Proceedings of the Symposium on Climate & Rice.* Los Baños, Philippines: 1976.

987. Loftas, Tony. *Food and the Environment.* Rome: FAO, 1976.

988. Matthews, William H., ed. *Outer Limits and Human Needs. Resource and Environmental Issues of Development Strategies.* Uppsala: Dag Hammarskjöld Foundation, distributed by Almqvist & Wiksell (Stockholm), 1976.

989. National Academy of Sciences-National Research Council, Committee on Resources and Man. *Resources and Man.* San Francisco: Freeman, 1969. (See especially Introduction, Chapters 2 and 4.)

990. O'Keefe, Phil, and Wisner, Ben. *Land Use and Development: African Environment.* African Environment Special Report 5. London: International African Institute, 1977.

991. Phillips, John F. V. *Agriculture and Ecology in Africa: A Study of Actual and Potential Development South of the Sahara.* New York: Praeger, 1966.

992. Richards, Paul, ed. With the assistance of Nicola Harris. *African Environment: Problems and Perspectives.* African Environment Special Report 1. London: International African Institute, 1975.

993. Sasson, Albert. *Dêveloppement et Environnement.* Paris and The Hague: Mouton, 1974.

994. *Science, Technology, and Development: United States Papers Prepared for the United Nations Conference on the Application of Science and Technology for the Benefit of the Less Developed Areas. Volume I: Natural Resources—Energy, Water, and River Basin Development.* Washington, D. C.: US Printing Office, 1962.

995. Stamp, L. Dudley. *Land for Tomorrow: The Underdeveloped World.* Bloomington and New York: Indiana University Press and the American Geographical Society, 1952. (Chapters 1–4 are relevant.)

996. Thomas, Michel Frederic, and Whittington, G. W., eds. *Environment and Land Use in Africa.* London: Methuen, 1969.

997. United States Department of Agriculture-United States Agency for International Development Watershed Management Team. *Resource Management for the Rainfed Region of West Pakistan. Final Draft Report. Volume One: Summary of Findings and Recommendations* and *Volume Two: General Background and Analyses of Specific Problem Areas.* Washington, D. C.: May 1968–February 1969.

998. Vayda, Andrew P., ed. *Environment and Cultural Behavior, Ecological Studies in Cultural Anthropology.* Garden City, N. Y.: The Natural History Press, 1969.

Articles

Brush (entries 1001 and 1002) points out that peasant farming systems are of necessity adapted to local ecological conditions; if they were not, they would not be viable. Therefore, one must be extremely careful when seeking to alter such systems, particularly in areas where ecological conditions are difficult for one reason or another. If farmers in the Peruvian highlands were to adopt high-yielding varieties of potatoes or grains as has been suggested, they would run the risk of losing their entire crop to pests or bad weather. Brush argues that in a difficult environment such as the Peruvian highlands, it is safest to plant many varieties of potatoes or grain, as has traditionally been the practice, and thus be assured of at least something to harvest.

The articles by Sigurdson, Kapp, and Orleans and Suttmeier all discuss aspects of Chinese environmental policies. Other recommended articles are Carruthers, Dasgupta, and Wittwer.

999. Beets, W. C. "The Agricultural Environment of Eastern and Southern Africa and Its Uses." *Agriculture and Environment* 4 (April 1978): 5–25.

1000. Bolin, Bert, and Arrhenius, Erik, eds. "Nitrogen—An Essential Life Factor and a Growing Environmental Hazard. Report from Nobel Symposium No. 38." *Ambio* 6:2–3 (1977): 96–105.

1001. Brush, Stephen B. "Farming the Edge of the Andes." *Natural History* (May 1977): 32–40.

1002. ______. "A Study of Subsistence Activities in Uchumarca, Peru." *LTC Newsletter* no. 40 (April–June 1973): 10–18.

1003. Carruthers, Ian. "Raking-Up Muck and Magic for Agricultural Progress." *Economic and Political Weekly* 13 (20 May 1978): 834.

1004. Chenery, Hollis B. "Land: The Effect of Resources on Economic Growth," pp. 19–49. In *Economic Development with Special Reference to East Asia.* Ed. Kenneth Berrill. New York: St. Martin's, 1964.

1005. Commoner, Barry. "Improving Resources' Productivity: A Way to Support the Growing World Population." *Ambio* 3:3–4 (1974): 136–138.

1006. Dasgupta, Biplab. "The Environment Debate: Some Issues and Trends." *Economic and Political Weekly* 13:6–7 (Annual Number 1978): 385–400.

1007. DeSoet, F. "Agriculture and the Environment." *Agriculture and Environment* 1 (June 1974): 1–15.

1008. Erlich, Paul R. "Ecology and the War on Hunger." *War on Hunger* 4 (December 1970): 1–3.

1009. Felger, Richard S., and Nabhan, Gary Paul. "Deceptive Barrenness." *Ceres* no. 50 (March–April 1976): 34–39.

1010. Johnson, Brian. "Who Cares?" *Mazingira* no. 9 (1979): 66–71.

1011. Kapp, K. William. "'Recycling' in Contemporary China." *World Development* 3 (July–August 1975): 565–573.

1012. Leeuw, P. N. de. "Fodder Resources and Livestock Development in North-East Nigeria." *Savannah* 5 (June 1976): 61–73.

1013. Manning, H. L. "The Statistical Assessment of Rainfall Probability and Its Application in Uganda Agriculture." *Proceedings of the Royal Society* Series B, 144 (1956): 460–480.

1014. Nabhan, Gary Paul. "Who is Saving the Seeds to Save Us?" *Mazingira* no. 9 (1979): 55–59.

1015. Netting, Robert M. "Heritage of Survival." *Natural History* (March 1965): 14–21.

1016. Orleans, Leo A., and Suttmeier, R. P. "The Mao Ethic and Environmental Quality." *Science* 170 (11 December 1970): 1173–1176.

1017. Radwanski, Stanislaw A. "East African Catenas in Relation to Land Use and Farm Planning." *World Crops* 23 (September–October 1971): 265–273.

1018. Ranganathan, Shankar. "A Plan for Rural India." *The New Ecologist* no. 1 (January–February 1978): 10–12.

1019. Sigurdson, Jon. "Resources and Environment in China." *Ambio* 4:3 (1975): 112–119.

1020. Trenbath, R. B. "Diversify or be Damned?" *The Ecologist* 5 (March–April 1975): 76–83.

1021. Vohra, B. B. "A Charter for the Land." *Economic and Political Weekly* 8 (31 March 1973): A2–A16.

1022. Voorhoeve, Joris J. C. "Treasure in the Dustbin." *Ceres* no. 50 (March–April 1976): 48–50.

1023. Wittwer, S. H. "Maximum Production Capacity of Food Crops." *BioScience* 24 (April 1974): 216–224.

Tropical Agriculture

One of the major problems arising out of attempts to "develop" third world agricultural systems has been that the methods suggested by development officials originated in and are best suited to the temperate climates of the industrialized countries. It is now recognized that research must focus on the development of improved farming methods and crops that are suited to tropical environments.

Ruthenberg is suggested as an introduction to the sorts of production systems found in tropical areas.

1024. Bene, J. G.; Beall, H. W.; and Coté, A. *Trees, Food and People: Land Management in the Tropics.* IDRC–084e. Ottawa: International Development Research Centre, August 1977.

1025. Blaut, James. "The Ecology of Tropical Farming Systems." *Revista Geografica* no. 54 (1961): 47–67.

1026. Brokensha, David, ed. *Ecology and Economic Development in Tropical Africa.* Research Series no. 9. Berkeley: Institute of International Studies, University of California, 1965.

1027. Devred, R. "Agricultural Research Programmes—Ecological Bases—Basic Principles and General Measures for Strengthening

Co-Operation." In *Agricultural Research Priorities for Economic Development in Tropical Africa. Volume II.* Abidjan, Ivory Coast: National Research Council, National Academy of Sciences, 5–12 April 1968.

1028. Dhua, S. P. "Need for Organo-Mineral Fertilizer in Tropical Agriculture." *The Ecologist* 5 (June 1975): 153–157.

1029. Donahue, Roy L. *Soils of Equitorial Africa and their Relevance to Rational Agricultural Development.* Research Report no. 7. East Lansing: Institute of International Agriculture, Michigan State University, February 1970.

1030. Gourou, P. *The Tropical World.* Trans. S. H. Beaver and E. D. Laborde. 4th ed. London: Longmans, Green, 1966.

1031. Lee, Douglas H. K. *Climate and Economic Development in the Tropics.* New York: Harper, 1957.

1032. Litzenberger, Samuel C., ed. *Guide for Field Crops in the Tropics and the Subtropics.* Washington, D. C.: Office of Agriculture, Technical Assistance Bureau, US Agency for International Development, 1974.

1033. Manshard, Walter. *Tropical Agriculture: A Geographical Introduction and Appraisal.* London: Longmans, 1974.

1034. Owen, Denis F. *Man in Tropical Africa: The Environmental Predicament.* New York: Oxford University Press, 1973. (The English title of this book is *Man's Environmental Predicament: An Introduction to Human Ecology in Tropical Africa.*)

1035. Phillips, John F. V. *The Development of Agriculture and Forestry in the Tropics: Patterns, Problems and Promises.* 2nd ed. London: Faber, 1966.

1036. Ruthenberg, Hans. *Farming Systems in the Tropics.* 2nd ed. New York: Clarendon, 1976.

1037. Webster, Cyril C., and Wilson, Peter N. *Agriculture in the Tropics.* London: Longmans, 1966.

1038. Whyte, Robert Orr. *Tropical Grazing Lands: Communities and Constituent Species.* The Hague: Junk, 1974.

1039. Williams, C. N., and Joseph, K. T. *Climate, Soil, and Crop Production in the Humid Tropics.* Oxford: Oxford University Press, 1970.

WATER

The special issue of *Ambio* entitled "Water" (entry 1053) is recommended.

1040. Brancker, A. V. "Solar Energy—I: The Water Problem and Its Relation to Solar Energy." *World Crops* 8 (September 1956): 339–344.

1041. Crosson, Pierre R.; Cummings, Ronald G.; and Frederick, Kenneth D., eds. *Selected Water Management Issues in Latin American Agriculture.* Baltimore, Md.: Johns Hopkins University Press, 1978.

1042. Dijon, Robert. "The Search for Ground-Water in the Crystalline Regions of Africa." *Natural Resources Forum* 1:1 (1971): 32–38.

1043. Falkenmark, Malin, and Lindh, Gunnar. "How Can We Cope with the Water Resources Situation by the Year 2015?" *Ambio* 3:3–4 (1974): 114–122.

1044. ______. *Water for a Starving World.* Trans. Roger B. Tanner. Boulder, Colo.: Westview, 1977.

1045. Food and Agriculture Organization. *The Environmental Aspects of Water Resources Development and Management with Suggestions for Action.* Presented to the UN Conference on the Human Environment, Stockholm, 1972. Rome: 17 August 1971.

1046. ______. *Water in Agriculture.* E/CONF.70/11. Rome: 20 January 1977.

1047. Furon, Raymond. *The Problem of Water: A World Study.* Trans. Paul Barnes. New York: American Elsevier, 1967.

1048. Saunders, Robert J., and Warford, Jeremy J. *Village Water Supply: Economics and Policy in the Developing World.* Baltimore, Md.: Johns Hopkins University Press, 1976.

1049. United Nations, Department of Economic and Social Affairs. *National Systems of Water Administration.* ST/ESA/17. New York: 1974. (Discusses India, Mexico, and Algeria)

1050. United Nations, Economic Commission for Asia and the Far East and United Nations, Educational, Scientific, and Cultural Organization. *The Development of Groundwater Resources with Special Reference to Deltaic Areas.* Water Resources Series, no. 24. New York: 1963.

1051. ______. *Methods and Techniques of Ground-Water Investigation and Development.* Water Resources Series, no. 33. ST/ECAFE/SER.F/33. New York: 1968.

1052. United States, Agency for International Development. *Water Quality Standards and International Development.* TA/OST/72–4. Washington, D. C.: Office of Science and Technology, October 1971.

1053. "Water" (Special Issue). *Ambio* 6:1 (1977).

1054. Williams, Rosemary. "The Analysis of Rainfall Reliability for Probability Estimates of Crop Water Deficits." *Institute of Development Studies Bulletin* 5:4 (May 1974): 51–53.

Soils

The FAO frequently puts out monographs dealing with agricultural soils. The eight FAO entries listed here (including those by Penn and Wright and Bennema) are recommended.

1055. Food and Agriculture Organization. *Guide to Sixty Soil and Water Conservation Practices.* Soils Bulletin no. 4. Rome: 1966.

1056. ______. *Improving Soil Fertility in Africa.* Soils Bulletin no. 14. Rome: 1971.

1057. ______. *Sandy Soils.* Soils Bulletin no. 25. Rome: 1973.

1058. ______. *Shifting Cultivation and Soil Conservation in Africa.* Soils Bulletin no. 24. Rome: 1974.

1059. ______. *Soil Erosion by Water: Some Measures for Control on Cultivated Lands.* FAO Agricultural Development Paper no. 81. FAO Land and Water Development Series no. 7. 4th printing. Rome: 1978.

1060. ______. *Soil Erosion by Wind and Measures for Its Control on Agricultural Land.* FAO Agricultural Development Paper no. 71. FAO Land and Water Development Series no. 6. 4th printing. Rome: 1978.

1061. Kellogg, Charles E. *Agricultural Development: Food, Soil, and People.* Madison, Wis.: Soil Science Society of America, 1975.

1062. Khan, Abdul Rashid, and Choudhuri, M. A. Hameed. *Farming Erodable Lands in West Pakistan.* Lahore: West Pakistan Agriculture Department, 1967.

1063. Kovda, Victor. "The Management of Soil Fertility." *Nature and Resources* 8:2 (April–June 1972): 2–4.

1064. Maher, Colin. "Soil Conservation. 1: The Fight Against Erosion." *World Crops* 24 (March–April 1972): 94–97.

1065. ______. "Soil Conservation. 2: Land-Capability Classification." *World Crops* 24 (May–June 1972): 160–162.

1066. ______. "Soil Conservation. 3: Physical Measures of Conservation." *World Crops* 24 (November–December 1972): 324–327.

1067. National Academy of Sciences. *Soils of the Humid Tropics.* Washington, D. C.: Agricultural Board, Committee on Tropical Soils, National Research Council, 1972.

1068. Penn, Raymond J. *Environmental Aspects of Natural Resource Management: Agriculture and Soils.* AgS: ASB/14. Rome: Food and Agriculture Organization, 1972.

1069. Sanchez, Pedro A. *Properties and Management of Soils in the Tropics.* New York: Wiley, 1976.

1070. Wright, A. C. S., and Bennema, J. *The Soil Resources of Latin America.* FAO/UNESCO Project on World Soil Resources Report no. 18. Rome: Food and Agriculture Organization, 1965.

Energy

All the entries in this section are recommended. The study by Odum is a useful introduction, particularly Chapter 4 which discusses energy use and food production. The reports by UNIDO, the Tanzanian National Scientific Research Council, the US National Academy of Sciences, and the US Research Council discuss the use of solar energy for development. The nature and uses of biogas technology are reviewed in the three studies authored by Barnett, Pyle, and Subramanion, Rao, and Prasad, Prasad, and Reddy. Makhijani and Poole focus on the economics of decentralized energy production in third world rural areas. More general discussion of the use of renewable energy resources for development is found in Hayes and in the volume edited by Brown.

1071. Barnett, Andrew; Pyle, Leo; and Subramanion, S. K. *Biogas Technology in the Third World: A Multidisciplinary Review.* IDRC–103e. Ottawa: International Development Research Centre, c.1978.

1072. Brown, Norman L., ed. *Renewable Energy Resources and Rural Applications in the Developing World.* Boulder, Colo.: Westview, 1978.

1073. Hayes, Denis. *Energy for Development: Third World Options.* Worldwatch Paper 15. Washington, D. C.: Worldwatch Institute, 1977.

1074. Makhijani, Arjun, with Alan Poole. *Energy and Agriculture in the Third World.* Cambridge, Mass.: Ballinger, 1975.

1075. National Academy of Sciences. *Solar Energy in Developing Countries: Prospectives and Prospects.* Report of an Ad Hoc Advisory Panel of the Board on Science and Technology for International Development. Washington, D. C.: 1972.

1076. National Research Council, Commission on International Relations. *Energy for Rural Development: Renewable Resources and Alternative Technologies for Developing Countries.* Washington, D. C.: National Academy of Sciences, 1976.

1077. Odum, Howard T. *Environment, Power and Society.* New York: Wiley-Interscience, 1971.

1078. Prasad, C. R.; Prasad, K. Krishna; and Reddy, A. K. N. "Bio-Gas Plants: Prospects, Problems, and Tasks." *Economic and Political Weekly* 9:32–34 (Special Number 1974): 1347–1364.

1079. Rao, T. Shivaji. "The Handling of Nitrogenous Wastes in Rural India." *Ambio* 6:2–3 (1977): 134–136.

1080. Tanzania National Scientific Research Council. *Workshop on Solar Energy for the Villages of Tanzania, Dar es Salaam: August 11–19, 1977.* Dar-es-Salaam: 1978.

1081. United Nations, Industrial Development Organization. *Technology for Solar Energy Utilization.* Development and Transfer of Technology Series no. 5. Vienna: c.1979.

Arid Lands

Glantz and Katz discuss the problem of determining what is "normal" rainfall in arid regions. Also recommended are the volumes edited by Stamp and by Rapp, Le Houérou and Lundholm.

1082. Arnon, I. *Crop Production in Dry Regions. Volume I: Background and Principles.* London: Leonard Hill (Intertext), 1972.

1083. Boudet, Gabriel. *The Sahel: Ecological Approaches to Land Use.* MAB Technical Notes. Paris: UNESCO, 1975.

1084. Glantz, Michael H., and Katz, Richard W. "When is a Drought a Drought?" *Nature,* 19 May 1977, pp.192–193.

1085. Hills, Edwin S., ed. *Arid Lands: A Geographical Appraisal.* London: Methuen, and Paris: UNESCO, 1966.

1086. Larmuth, John. "Desert and Man: A Future." *Third World Quarterly* 1 (July 1979): 104–111.

1087. Mundlak, Yair, and Singer, S. Fred. eds. *Arid Zone Development. Potentialities and Problems.* Cambridge, Mass.: Ballinger, 1977.

1088. Rapp, Anders; Le Houérou, H. H.; and Lundholm, B., eds. *Can Desert Encroachment Be Stopped? A Study with Emphasis on Africa.* Ecological Bulletins, no. 24. Stockholm: NFR, 1976.

1089. Stamp, Lawrence Dudley, ed. *A History of Land Use in Arid Regions.* Arid Zone Research no. 17. Paris: UNESCO, 1961.

1090. United Nations, Educational, Scientific, and Cultural Organization. *Salinity Problems in Arid Zones.* Arid Zone Research, no. 14. Paris: 1961.

1091. United States, Agency for International Development, Technical Assistance Bureau, Office of Agriculture. *Improving Farm Production in Tropical and Sub-Tropical Regions of Limited Rainfall.* Technical Series Bulletin, no. 4. Washington, D. C.: November 1971.

1092. World Meteorological Organization. *Agroclimatology in the Semi-Arid Areas South of the Sahara.* WMO–no. 340. Geneva: 1973.

Forests

All entries in this section are recommended.

1093. Allen, Robert. "The Year of the Rain Forest." *New Scientist* 66 (24 April 1975): 178–180.

1094. Beresford-Peirse, H. *Forests, Food and People.* FFHC Basic Studies no. 20. Rome: FAO, 1968.

1095. Hamilton, Lawrence S. *Tropical Rainforest Use and Preservation.* New York: Sierra Club Office of International Environmental Affairs, March 1976.

1096. Poulsen, Gunnar. *Man and Tree in Tropical Africa: Three Essays on the Role of Trees in the African Environment.* IDRC–101e. Ottawa: International Development Research Centre, August 1978.

1097. Rappaport, Roy A. "Forests and Man." *The Ecologist* 6 (August–September 1976): 241–246.

1098. United States, Department of State and United States, Agency For International Development. *Proceedings of the U. S. Strategy Conference on Tropical Deforestation.* Washington, D. C.: 12–14 June 1978.

Planning

Books and Monographs

As an introduction to the conventional approach to agricultural planning, the study by Mosher is suggested. A radical critique of planning methods based on the economic microanalysis of projects is made by Amin, Franco, and Sow. A summary of topics which should be taken into consideration when planning for agricultural development is found in entry 538. Other recommended studies are Chambers and entry 413.

1099. Amin, Samir; Franco, Mark; and Sow, Samba. *La Planification du Sous-Développement. Critique de l'Analyse de Projets.* Paris: Editions Anthropos-IDEP, 1975.

1100. Bansil, Puran Chand. *Agricultural Planning for 700 Million. A Perspective Study.* Bombay: Lalvani, 1971.

1101. Barbour, Kenneth Michael, ed. *Planning for Nigeria: A Geographical Approach.* Ibadan: Ibadan University Press, 1972.

1102. Bottomley, Anthony. *Planning for Innovation in African Agriculture.* E/CN.14/CAP/19. Addis Ababa: UN Economic and Social Council, 29 August 1967. (A short version of this is available in *Agricultural Economics Bulletin for Africa* no. 9 (October 1967): 64–78.)

1103. Chambers, Robert. *Managing Rural Development: Ideas and Experience from East Africa.* Uppsala: The Scandinavian Institute of African Studies, 1974.

1104. Cochrane, Willard W. *Agricultural Development Planning: Economic Concepts, Administrative Procedures, and Political Process.* Praeger Special Studies in International Economics and Development. New York: Praeger, 1974.

1105. Collinson, M. *Farm Management in Peasant Agriculture: A Handbook for Rural Development Planning in Africa.* New York: Praeger, 1972.

1106. Food and Agriculture Organization. *Report of the FAO/ECAFE Expert Groups on Selected Aspects of Agricultural Planning in Asia and the Far East.* C/CN.11/L.91. Rome: 1960.

1107. Gittinger, J. Price. *Planning for Agricultural Development: The Iranian Experience.* Planning Experience Series no. 2. Washington, D. C.: Center for Development Planning, National Planning Association, August 1965.

1108. Helleiner, Gerald K. *Agricultural Planning in East Africa.* Nairobi: East African, 1968.

1109. Honey, John C. *Planning and the Private Sector. The Experience in Developing Countries: A Comparative Analysis.* New York: Dunellen, 1970.

1110. *Joint Seminar on Problems and Approaches in Planning Agricultural Development (16 October–17 November 1967, Addis Ababa).* Addis Ababa: German Foundation for Developing Countries/Economic Commission for Africa/Food and Agriculture Organization, 1968.

1111. Mehretu, Assefa. *Area/Regional Planning for Rural Development Strategies with Special Reference to the Eastern ORD of Upper Volta.* PN–AAF–27. Washington, D. C.: US Agency for International Development, 1977.

1112. Mosher, Arthur T. *To Create a Modern Agriculture: Organization and Planning.* New York: The Agricultural Development Council, 1971.

1113. Norton, Roger D., and Bassoco, Luz María. *A Quantitative Agricultural Planning Methodology.* Working Paper 180. Washington, D. C.: World Bank, May 1974. (Deals with Mexico)

1114. Sarkar, Prafulla C. *The Planning of Agriculture in India.* Rotterdam: Rotterdam University Press, 1966.

1115. Upton, M. *Farm Management in Africa: The Principles of Production and Planning.* London: Oxford University Press, 1973.

1116. Weitz, Raanan, gen. ed. *Rural Planning in Developing Countries.* Cleveland, Ohio: The Press of Western Reserve University, 1966.

Articles

Myers argues that too much attention has been given to manpower planning for the urban sector. The case of Zambia is used to demonstrate how devoting more attention to rural manpower can contribute to the development process. Abel and Easter present a framework for agricultural policy and program planning based on the concept of agroclimatic regions and on the identification of key regional and natural constraints on agricultural development. Battacharjee believes that Indian planners have been too concerned with the economic aspects of planning and growth to the detriment of social and political considerations. Rudra charges that planning in India "primarily consists in setting targets representing aspirations . . ." and has a predictive capacity which is less than that of weather forecasting. Another critique of planning in India can be found in entry 89. A useful critical summary of post-World War II development planning is made by Villamil.

1117. Abel, Martin E., and Easter, K. William. "Agricultural Planning and Programme Evaluation: Focus on Regional Restraints." *Economic and Political Weekly* 6 (Special Number 1971): 1577–1596.

1118. Belshaw, D. G. R. "Dynamics and Operational Aspects of the Equity Objective in Rural Development Planning." In *Agricultural Employment and Labour Migration in East Africa.* Ed. V. F. Amann. Makerere, Uganda: Makerere University, 1974.

1119. Bhattacharjee, Jayabrata. "Socio-Political Parameters of Economic Planning." *Economic and Political Weekly* 5 (8 August 1970): 1337, 1339, 1341.

1120. Dandekar, V. M. "Effectiveness in Agricultural Planning." *Teaching Forum.* no. 19. New York: The Agricultural Development Council, July 1972.

1121. Food and Agriculture Organization-United Nations Economic Commission for Africa. "Agricultural Development Planning in West Africa." In *Intra-Sub-Regional Co-Operation and Trade in West Africa in the Field of Agriculture. Phase 1.* Rome: Food and Agriculture Organization, 1971.

1122. Ijere, M. O. "The Planning Experience in Nigerian Agriculture. *Journal of Administration Overseas* 16 (January 1977): 17–23.

1123. Lewis, John P. "Development Planning: Some Lessons from Experience," pp. 36–43. In *Economic Growth in Developing Countries—Material and Human Resources.* Ed. Yohanan Ramati. Praeger Special Studies in International Economics and Development. New York: Praeger, 1975.

1124. Myers, Robert J. "Rural Manpower Planning in Zambia." *International Labour Review* 102 (July 1970): 15–28.

1125. Ramati, Yohanan, ed. "Part IV: Planning and Implementation," pp. 341–486. In *Economic Growth in Developing Countries—Material and Human Resources.* Praeger Special Studies in International Economics and Development. New York: Praeger, 1975.

1126. Rudra, Ashok. "Planning and the New Agricultural Strategy." *Economic and Political Weekly* 6 (6 February 1971): 429–430.

1127. Villamil, José J. "Planning for Self-Reliant Growth," pp. 307–322. In *Transnational Capitalism and National Development: New Perspectives on Dependence.* Ed. José J. Villamil. Hassocks, UK: Harvester Press, 1979.

Irrigation

Books and Monographs

The book edited by Hagan, Haise, and Edminster covers all aspects of irrigation. Many of the contributions are quite technical, but the book is useful to anyone who is very interested in irrigation. The monograph by Booher provides a comprehensive survey of all existing surface irrigation systems. The report by the National Research Council discusses a variety of irrigation technologies useful for arid regions. Worthington looks at some of the environmental aspects of arid land irrigation. Brannon, Alton, and Davis consider the reasons why farmers in Northeast Thailand have not adopted dry-season irrigation and set forward ideas for encouraging them to do so.

Pillsbury examines a number of sprinkler irrigation systems operating under various conditions and then outlines the factors that affect their performance. Sprinkler irrigation is popular in Israel and in parts of the United States, notably California. This method conserves water, reduces run-off (making marginal land cultivatable), suppresses weed growth but is, at present, rather expensive and unsuitable for grains. It is not clear what the future of sprinkler irrigation will be in developing countries.

The report from the Trilateral Commission by Colombo, Johnson, and Shishido argues that efforts to increase food output in Asia should focus on expanding and improving irrigation facilities. The authors propose a plan for doubling rice production in South and Southeast Asia within ten years by improving existing irrigation systems, largely through ditch construction and maintenance. They point out that a major benefit of this strategy is that large amounts of capital are not necessary for its implementation. The political content of this report is, however, limited. While it is recognized that one way of approaching the hunger problem is by "achieving a more equal distribution of food and income," it is concluded that "Strategies to increase food production and reduce waste can be most readily implemented and are the ones stressed in this report" (entry 1137, p. 9).

How those who are now too poor to buy sufficient food will be able to improve their diets simply because rice production is increased is left unclear. Land reform is seen as necessary because "the participation of community members in communal irrigation projects is greater and more uniform in a village where farmers are more homogeneous in terms of tenure and farm size" (entry 1137, p. 29). However, there is no recognition of the fact that most governments in South and Southeast Asia have avoided implementing effective land reform programs for domestic political reasons.

1128. Addison, Herbert. *Land, Water and Food.* 2nd rev. ed. London: Chapman & Hall, 1961. (See especially Chapters 1, 2, 5–11, 14, and 15.)

1129. Asian Development Bank. *Regional Workshop on Irrigation Water Management.* Manila: 1973.

1130. Bergman, Hellmuth, and Boussard, Jean-Marc. *Guide to the Economic Evaluation of Irrigation Projects.* rev. ed. Paris: Organization for Economic Cooperation and Development, 1976.

1131. Biggs, Stephen D.; Edwards, Chris; and Griffith, Jon. *Irrigation in Bangladesh.* IDS Discussion Paper D–126. Brighton, UK: Institute of Development Studies, University of Sussex, 1978.

1132. Booher, L. J. *Surface Irrigation.* FAO Agricultural Development Paper no. 95. FAO Land and Water Development Series no. 3. 2nd printing. Rome: FAO, 1976.

1133. Brannon, R. J.; Alton, C. T.; and Davis, J. T. *Irrigated Dry Season Crop Production in Northeast Thailand.* Department of Agricultural Economics Staff Paper no. 63. PN–AAF–270. Washington, D. C.: US Agency for International Development, 1978.

1134. Cantor, Leonard M. *A World Geography of Irrigation.* New York: Praeger, 1970.

1135. Chaudhari, Ali Muhammad. *Man, Water & Economy. A Socio-Economic Analysis of Fourteen Rural Communities in Mona Project.* Lyallpur: West Pakistan Agricultural University; and Lahore: Water and Power Development Authority, 1970.

1136. Clark, Colin. *The Economics of Irrigation.* 2nd ed. New York: Pergamon, 1970.

1137. Colombo, Umberto; Johnson, D. Gale; and Shishido, Toshio. *Reducing Malnutrition in Developing Countries: Increasing Rice Production in South and Southeast Asia.* The Triangle Papers: 16. New York, Tokyo, and Paris: The Trilateral Commission, 1978.

1138. Duane, Paul. *A Policy Framework for Irrigation Water Charges.* Working Paper 218. Washington, D. C.: World Bank, July 1975.

1139. Food and Agriculture Organization. *Successful Irrigation Planning, Development, and Management.* Rome: 1970.

1140. Hagan, Robert M.; Haise, Howard P.; and Edminster, Talcott W., eds. *Irrigation of Agricultural Lands.* Madison, Wis.: American Society of Agronomy, 1967.

1141. The Indian Society of Agricultural Economics, in collaboration with The Institute for Social and Economic Change. *Role of Irrigation in the Development of India's Agriculture.* Seminar Series—XIII. Bombay: Shri T. R. Sundaram, 1976.

1142. *Irrigated Agriculture in Northern Thailand.* National Seminar Report no. 5. New York and Chian Mai, Thailand: The Agricultural Development Council, 1974.

1143. Lazaro, Rogelio C., et al. *Irrigation Systems in Southeast Asia.* Teaching and Research Forum Seminar Report no. 6. New York: The Agricultural Development Council, 1977.

1144. Lieftnick, Pieter; Sadove, A. Robert; and Creyke, Thomas C. *Water and Power Resources of West Pakistan. A Study in Sector Planning, Volume I: The Main Report.* Baltimore, Md.: Johns Hopkins University Press, 1968.

1145. Metzer, James D. *A Study of Water Utilization for Increasing Agricultural Production in Nepal.* USAID Duplicated Report. Washington, D. C.: US Agency for International Development, 1966.

1146. National Research Council, Ad Hoc Panel on Promising Technologies for Arid-Land Water Development. *More Water for Arid Lands.* Washington, D. C.: National Academy of Sciences, 1974.

1147. Norton, Roger D.; Bassoco, Luz María; and Silos, José S. *Appraisal of Irrigation Projects and Related Policies and Investments.* Working Paper 184. Washington, D. C.: World Bank, August 1974. (Deals with Mexico)

1148. Otten, Adrianus J. H., and Reutlinger, Shlomo. *Performance Evaluation of Eight Ongoing Irrigation Projects.* Working Paper 40. Washington, D. C.: World Bank, March 1969. (Focuses on India, Mexico, Pakistan, Taiwan, and Turkey)

1149. Pillsbury, A. F. *Sprinkler Irrigation.* FAO Agricultural Development Paper no. 33. 3rd printing. Rome: FAO, 1975.

1150. Rydzewsky, Janusz R. *Irrigation Development in Africa South of the Sahara: Potentials and Possibilities 1965–1985.* Rome: Food and Agriculture Organization, 1968.

1151. Sally, Hari Lai. *Irrigation Planning for Intensive Cultivation.* New York: Asia, 1968.

1152. Stutler, R. Kern; Kidman, D. C.; Tosso, J.; and Fritsch, N. *Irrigated Corn Production in Chile: Increasing Yields Through Intensive Irrigation Management.* Logan: Utah State University, December 1974.

1153. United Nations, Economic Commission for Asia and the Far East; and United Nations, Office of Technical Cooperation. *Planning Water Resources Development.* Water Resources Series no. 37. ST/ECAFE/SER.F/37. Sales no. E.69.II.F.13. New York: 1969.

1154. University of Reading. *The Economics of Irrigation Development.* Development Study no. 6. Reading, UK: Department of Agricultural Economics, University of Reading, May 1969.

1155. Upton, M. *Irrigation in Botswana.* Development Study no. 5. Reading, UK: Department of Agricultural Economics, University of Reading, May 1969.

1156. van der Tak, Herman G., and Schmedtje, Jochen K. *Economic Aspects of Water Utilization in Irrigation Projects.* EC–132. Washington, D. C.: World Bank, January 1965.

1157. Worthington, E. Barton. *Arid Lands Irrigation in Developing Countries: Environmental Problems and Effects.* New York: Pergamon, 1977.

Articles

Lanois and Sow both discuss the relationship between irrigation and the spread of bilharzia. Tewari finds that the use of wind power for irrigation is economical for small farmers for whom electric- or diesel-powered pumps are too expensive or whose villages do not have electricity. However, Tewari cautions that wind-powered irrigation is still relatively expensive and suggests that it should be government-subsidized.

V. M. Rao argues that, while irrigation is generally considered a technical problem, the crucial constraints facing Indian irrigation are institutional and socio-economic. Wade identifies such obstacles and discusses ways of overcoming them in the four articles he has written for *Economic and Political Weekly* (entries 1177–1180). In entry 1178, Wade discusses the technical, economic, and organizational attributes of canal irrigation schemes that prevent them from being used to capacity and cause them to contribute less than anticipated to agricultural development. In entry 1180, he discusses the problems arising from the adoption of water-intensive crops in the upper reaches of irrigation projects. He outlines an administrative strategy employed in Andhra Pradesh to prevent farmers from adopting such crops in the first years of an irrigation project so that they would not make excessive demands on the water once the irrigation project was extended farther downstream.

S. K. Rao finds that the most important proximate cause of disparities in the rate of growth of crop output in India between 1952/53 and 1964/65 was the difference in the rate of growth of irrigation systems. Public investment was largely responsible for the expansion of irrigation in India. Because public irrigation investment tended to be concentrated in the wealthier agricultural regions and tended to benefit the wealthier farmers in those regions, the expansion of irrigation in India has had the effect of widening the gap between regions and between rich and poor farmers.

The article by Nelson and Tileston surveys the technical, managerial, social, financial, and environmental problems that can cause irrigation projects to fail.

1158. Bhatia, Ramesh, and Mehta, Meera. "Tubewell Irrigation: Analysis of Some Technical Alternatives." *Economic and Political Weekly* 10 (27 December 1975): A111–A119.

1159. Bottomley, Anthony. "Is Irrigation Worthwhile?" *Agricultural Economics Bulletin for Africa* no. 16 (December 1974): 10–20.

1160. Dastane, N. G. "New Concepts in Irrigation. Necessary Changes for New Strategy." *Economic and Political Weekly* 4 (29 March 1969): A27–A30.

1161. Dhawan, B. D. "Utilisation of Ground Water Resources: Public versus Private Tubewells." *Economic and Political Weekly* 9 (28 September 1974): A75–A81.

1162. ______. "Economics of Groundwater Utilisation: Traditional versus Modern Agriculture." *Economic and Political Weekly* 10 (28 June 1975): A31–A42.

1163. Gustafson, W. Eric, and Reidinger, Richard B. "Delivery of Canal Water in North India and West Pakistan." *Economic and Political Weekly* 6 (25 December 1971): A157–A162.

1164. Kaneda, Hiromitsu, and Ghaffar, Mohammed. "Output Effects of Tubewells on the Agriculture of the Punjab: Some Empirical Results." *The Pakistan Development Review* 10 (Spring 1970): 68–87.

1165. Kanwar, J. S. "From Protective to Productive Irrigation." *Economic and Political Weekly* 4 (29 March 1969): A21–A26.

1166. Lanois, Joseph N. "Relations Between Agricultural Engineering and Bilharziasis." *Bulletin of the World Health Organization* 18 (1958): 1011–1035.

1167. Loftas, Tony. "The Rajasthan Canal Project." *World Crops* 23 (January–February 1971): 20–23.

1168. Mellor, John W., and Moorti, T. V. "Dilemma of State Tubewells." *Economic and Political Weekly* 6 (27 March 1971): A37–A44.

1169. Mohammad, Ghulam. "Private Tubewell Development and Cropping Patterns in West Pakistan." *The Pakistan Development Review* 5 (Spring 1965): 1–53.

1170. Nelson, Gary, and Tileston, Fred M. "Why Irrigation Projects May Become 'Enduring Monuments to Failure.'" *International Development Review* 19:3 (1977): Focus 22–24.

1171. Rao, S. K. "Inter-Regional Variations in Agricultural Growth, 1952–53 to 1964–65: A Tentative Analysis in Relation to Irrigation." *Economic and Political Weekly* 6 (3 July 1971): 1333–1346.

1172. Rao, V. M. "Linking Irrigation with Development. Some Policy Issues." *Economic and Political Weekly* 13 (17 June 1978): 993–997.

1173. Rydzewski, Janusz R. "Towards Increased Efficiency of Irrigation Projects: The Civil Engineer's Point of View." *World Crops* 23 (January–February 1971): 17–18.

1174. Shahi, H. N. "Surface Methods of Irrigation." *World Crops* 23 (January–February 1971): 12–15.

1175. Sow, A. "Bilharzia and Irrigation in Mauritania." *African Environment* 3:2 (1978): 83–93.

1176. Tewari, Sharat K. "Economics of Wind Energy Use for Irrigation in India." *Science* 202 (3 November 1978): 481–486.

1177. Wade, Robert. "Administration and the Distribution of Irrigation Benefits." *Economic and Political Weekly* 10 (1 November 1975): 1743–1747.

1178. ———. "Performance of Irrigation Projects." *Economic and Political Weekly* 11 (17 January 1976): 63–66.

1179. ———. "Water Accounting in Irrigation Projects: A Technique from Maharastra." *Economic and Political Weekly* 11 (28 August 1976): 1436–1439.

1180. ———. "Water Supply as an Instrument of Agricultural Policy: A Case Study." *Economic and Political Weekly* 13 (25 March 1978): A9–A13.

1181. Williams, Donald A. "Water Management in the Seventies." *Economic and Political Weekly* 5 (27 June 1970): A53–A60.

Agricultural Chemicals

General

This section focuses on the use of fertilizers. Of the two entries in which the role of pesticides is considered (entries 1192 and 1193), the book by Headley and Lewis draws on the US experience, but the discussion is relevant to all countries. Several entries discuss non-chemical methods of fertilization, such as biological nitrogen fixation (Ayanaba and Dort, and Stewart) and the use of organic fertilizers (Bredero, McGarry, and entries 1188 and 1202). Annual statistics on fertilizer use, production, and trade can be found in entries 1185 and 1186. The articles by Parikh and Vaidyanathan should be read together. In addition, the sections on fertilizers and pesticides in *How the Other Half Dies* (entry 1887, pp. 301–317, Penguin edition) and *Food First* (entry 1890, chapter 9) are worth looking at.

1182. Ayanaba, A., and Dort, P. J., eds. *Biological Nitrogen Fixation in Farming Systems of the Tropics.* Chichester, N. Y.: Wiley, 1977.

1183. Bredero, T. J. "The Role of Farmyard Manure and Green Manures in Soil Fertility Restoration in the Humid Tropics." *Abstracts on Tropical Agriculture* (October 1977): 9–17.

1184. Desai, Gunvant M. *Growth of Fertilizer Use in Indian Agriculture.* Cornell International Agricultural Development Bulletin 18. Ithaca, N. Y.: Cornell University, 1971.

1185. Food and Agriculture Organization. *Annual Fertilizer Review.* Rome: 1970–. (Supersedes entry 1186 below)

1186. ______. *Fertilizers: An Annual Review of World Production, Consumption and Trade.* Rome: 1951–1969.

1187. ______. *Fertilizer Legislation.* Soils Bulletin no. 20. Rome: 1973.

1188. ______. *Organic Materials as Fertilizers.* Soils Bulletin no. 27. Rome: December 1974.

1189. ______. *Planning and Organization of Fertilizer Use in Africa.* Soils Bulletin no. 16. Rome: 1972.

1190. Goldsworthy, P. R. *Response of Cereals to Fertilizers in Northern Nigeria: 1. Sorghum.* Zaria: Institute for Agricultural Research, Ahmadu Bello University, 1967.

1191. Gray, Robert C., and Waitzman, Donald. *Tunisia: Nitrogen Fertilizer Needs, Alternatives to Meet Needs.* Muscle Shoals, Ala.: National Fertilizer Development Center, Tennessee Valley Authority, 1968.

1192. Gunther, Francis A., and Jeppson, L. R. *Modern Insecticides and World Food Production.* London: Chapman & Hall, 1960.

1193. Headley, J. C., and Lewis, J. N. *The Pesticide Problem: An Economic Approach to Public Policy.* Baltimore, Md.: Johns Hopkins University Press, distributor, 1967.

1194. Heathcote, R. G., and Stockinger, K. R. *Soil Fertility Under Continuous Cultivation in Northern Nigeria: 2. Responses to Fertilizers in the Absence of Organic Manures.* Samaru Research Bulletin 135. Zaria: Institute for Agricultural Research, Ahmadu Bello University, 1971.

1195. Hicks, G. C.; Young, R. D.; Strumpe, J. J.; Norton, M. M.; and Richards, M. J. *Technical and Economic Evaluation of Fertilizer Intermediates for Use by Developing Countries.* Muscle Shoals, Ala.: National Fertilizer Development Center, Tennessee Valley Authority, 1970.

1196. Hughes, Helen, and Pearson, Scott. *Principle Issues Facing the World Fertilizer Economy.* New York: The Agricultural Development Council, 1975.

1197. Ingestad, Torsten. "Nitrogen and Plant Growth: Maximum Efficiency of Nitrogen Fertilizers." *Ambio* 6: 2–3 (1977): 146–151.

1198. McGarry, Michael G. "The Taboo Resource: The Use of Human Excreta in Chinese Agriculture." *The Ecologist* 6 (May 1976): 150–156.

1199. Olkowski, Dennis. "Strategies to Feed a Hungry World." *East-West Center Magazine* (Spring 1977): 9–11.

1200. Parikh, Kirit S. "HYV Fertilisers: Synergy or Substitution: Implications for Policy and Prospects for Agricultural Development." *Economic and Political Weekly* 13 (25 March 1978): A2–A8.

1201. Parker, Frank W. *Fertilizers and Economic Development.* Rome: Food and Agriculture Organization, 1962.

1202. "Production of Bio-Fertilizer and Bio-Gas from Agricultural Waste Materials (in India)." *Research and Industry* 11:1 (1966): 24–25.

1203. Robinson, K. L., and Falusi, A. O. *The Present and Potential Role of Fertilizer in Meeting Nigeria's Food Requirement.* Cornell International Agriculture Mimeograph 46. Ithaca, N. Y.: Cornell University, November 1974.

1204. Sheldrick, W., and Stier, H. *World Potash Survey.* Working Paper 293. Washington, D. C.: World Bank, c. 1978.

1205. Slack, Archie Vivian. *Defense Against Famine: The Role of the Fertilizer Industry.* New York: Doubleday, 1970.

1206. Soermarwoto, Otto. "Nitrogen in Tropical Agriculture." *Ambio* 6:2–3 (1977): 162–165.

1207. Stewart, William D. P. "Present-Day Nitrogen-Fixing Plants." *Ambio* 6:2–3 (1977): 166–173.

1208. Tennessee Valley Authority. *Projected Fertilizer Needs for Korea, 1967–1971.* Wilson Dam: TVA Fertilizer Consultant Team, 30 June 1965.

1209. "The Role of Fertiliser in Solving the World Food Problem." *OECD Observer* no. 28. (June 1967): 13–15.

1210. Vaidyanathan, A. "HYV and Fertilisers: Synergy or Substitution? A Comment." *Economic and Political Weekly* 13 (24 June 1978): 1031–1035.

1211. Zimdahl, R. L., ed. *Weed Science in the Development Countries of the World.* Contract AID/csd-3296. Berkeley: University of California, 1973.

Production in Developing Countries

The report by Gas Developments Corporation discusses factors to be considered in the development of pesticide production; all other entries concern the development of fertilizer production in specific third world countries and regions or in developing areas in general. The article by Coulson looks at the failure of an attempt in Tanzania to set up a fertilizer factory in conjunction with a German firm.

1212. Coulson, Andrew C. "Tanzania's Fertilizer Factory." *Journal of Modern African Studies* 15:1 (1977): 119–125.

1213. Fertilizer Study Group. *Report on the Development of the Turkish Fertilizer Industry.* Ankara: State Planning Organization, August 1966.

1214. Gas Developments Corporation. *Bolivian Pesticide Production: A Feasibility Study of Technical, Economic, Marketing and Institutional Aspects for the Government of Bolivia. Volume III.* La Paz and Chicago, Ill.: November 1969.

1215. Liu Jung-chao. *China's Fertilizer Economy.* Chicago, Ill.: Aldine, 1970.

1216. Organization of American States, General Secretariat, Department of Economic Affairs, Sectoral Studies Unit. *The Fertilizer Situation in Costa Rica.* Washington, D. C.: 1970.

1217. United Nations, Economic Commission for Asia and the Far East. *Proceedings of the Seminar on Sources of Mineral Raw Materials for the Fertilizer Industry in Asia and the Far East.* Mineral Resources Development Series no. 32. E/CN.11/837. New York: 1968.

1218. United Nations, Industrial Development Organization. *Chemical Fertilizer Projects: Their Creation, Evaluation and Establishment.* Fertilizer Industry Series, Monograph no. 1. New York: 1968.

1219. ______. *Factors Inhibiting the Indigenous Growth of the Fertilizer Industry in Developing Countries.* Report of the Ad Hoc Group of Experts from Fertilizer Deficit Countries. New York: 1969.

1220. ______. *Fertilizer Industry.* UNIDO Monographs on Industrial Development no. 6. New York: 1969.

1221. ______. *Guide to Building an Ammonia Fertilizer Complex.* Fertilizer Industry Series, Monograph no. 2. New York: 1969.

1222. Zalla, Tom; Diamond, Ray B.; and Mudahar, Mohinder S. *Economic and Technical Aspects of Fertilizer Production and Use in West Africa.* Working Paper no. 22. East Lansing: African Rural Economy Program, Michigan State University, September 1977.

The Safety Debate

The entries in this section debate the hazards involved in the intensive use of agricultural chemicals. Most deal with pest control although there are problems associated with the intensive use of fertilizers as well (see entries 1228 and 1000). Nonetheless, the USAID bulletin (entry 1240) argues that urban/industrial pollution has caused far greater environmental hazards than the use of nitrogen fertilizers.

The article by Borlaug, "Father of the Green Revolution," was written nearly ten years after the publication of *The Silent Spring*, yet it is reminiscent of the attacks on Rachel Carson by members of the chemicals industry and other special interest groups. Borlaug charges that environmentalists who oppose the use of pesticides are out of touch with reality because those chemicals are of vital importance to the success of the Green Revolution. This view has been echoed, at least in part, by many government officials in developing countries. They fear that industrialized countries, which have banned the domestic use of certain chemicals, such as DDT, may refuse to import commodities treated with these chemicals from developing countries.

While it is true that some industrialized countries, notably the United States, have regulations banning food containing residues of specific chemicals, it is unclear to what extent these regulations actually impinge on the exports of developing countries. Even at the end of the 1970s, it was suspected that a large portion of the food imported into the United States contained what are considered to be unsafe levels of pesticide residues.

Despite all this, evidence is mounting that the intensive application of agricultural chemicals throughout the world is giving rise to serious problems. One of the most important is that pests are becoming more and more resistent to pesticides. The 1979 Annual Report of the United Nations Environment Programme (entry 1238) points out that the FAO has identified 364 species of insects and mites which have become resistant to the pesticides used against them. While in some cases it is possible to switch to another kind of pesticide, some 223 agricultural pests have become resistant to nine of the major *groups* of pesticides. Included in this number are many of the major pests of major crops: the boll weevil, the rice stem borer, the Colorado potato beetle and the cotton leafworm. Resistance to fungicides and rodenticides is also growing. Entries 1229 and 1230 provide detailed discussions of the resistance problem.

Other hazardous side-effects of the intensive use of agricultural chemicals include pollution of lakes and streams and the growing exposure of people and animals to substances that are known or suspected to be dangerous to their health. Interest is increasingly turning to non-chemical means of controlling pests (see Collins, Dinther, Lever, Robinson, the UNEP report, and entry 1231). However, these alternatives are not without their shortcomings (see Tucker and Tolba). "Integrated pest control," the mixture of environmental, biological, chemical, and behavioral pest control methods, is considered the best long-term solution. David and Marcia Pimentel argue that chemical pesticides should only be used as "an emergency weapon."

The articles by Tucker and by the Pimentels, the 1979 UNEP report and the book by David Pimentel are especially recommended.

1223. Borlaug, Norman E. "Ecology Fever." *Ceres* no. 25 (January–February 1972): 21–25.

1224. Collins, Peter. "Pest Control—The Natural Way." *Development Forum* 7 (April 1979): 3.

1225. Dinther, John B. M. "Insect Control and New Approaches." *World Crops* 24 (July–August 1972): 180–183.

1226. Dorst, Jean. "The Age of Agricultural Chemical Warfare is Over." *Ceres* no. 25 (January–February 1972): 31–34.

1227. Edwards, Clive A. "Soil Pollutants and Soil Animals." *Scientific American* 220 (April 1969).

1228. Food and Agriculture Organization. *Effects of Intensive Fertilizer Use on the Human Environment.* Soils Bulletin no. 16. Rome: 1972.

1229. ______. *FAO Global Survey of Pesticide Resistance.* AGP: 1976/17/10. Rome: 1977.

1230. ______. *Report of the First Session of the FAO Panel of Experts on Pest Resistence to Pesticides and Crop Loss Assessment.* FAO Plant Production and Protection Papers no. 6. Rome: 1977.

1231. Food and Agriculture Organization–United Nations Environment Programme. *The Development and Application of Integrated Pest Control.* ACP:1974/M/8. Rome: 1975.

1232. Gunn, D., and Stevens, J., eds. *Pesticides and Human Welfare.* Oxford: Oxford University Press, 1976.

1233. Irvine, David E. G., and Knights, Brian, eds. *Pollution and the Use of Chemicals in Agriculture.* London: Butterworths, 1974.

1234. Lever, R. J. A. W. "Former and Current Control Methods for Insect Pests of Some Tropical Crops." *World Crops* 24 (July–August 1972): 184–187.

1235. Pimentel, David, ed. *World Food, Pest Losses and the Environment.* Boulder, Colo.: Westview, 1978.

1236. Pimentel, David and Marcia. "The Risks of Pesticides." *Natural History* (March 1979): 24,28,30,32.

1237. Robinson, R. A. "Crop Resistance May be Our Best Crop Protection." *World Crops and Livestock* 29 (May–June 1977): 104–106.

1238. Tolba, Mostafa Kamal. *The State of the World Environment.* Nairobi: UN Environment Programme, 1979, 5–7.

1239. Tucker, William. "Of Mites and Men." *Harper's* (August 1978): 43–58.

1240. United States, Agency for International Development, Technical Assistance Bureau, Office of Agriculture. *Agricultural Production in Relation to the Environment.* Technical Series Bulletin no. 7. Washington, D. C.: August 1972.

1241. United States, Department of Health, Education, and Welfare. *Report of the Secretary's Commission on Pesticides and Their Relationship to Environmental Health. Parts I and II.* Washington, D. C.: December 1969.

1242. Watson, D. L., and Brown, A. W. *Pesticide Management and Insect Resistence.* London: Academic Press, 1977.

1243. World Health Organization. *Resistence of Vectors and Reservoirs of Disease to Pesticides.* Technical Report Series no. 585. Geneva: 1976.

International Agency Approaches

Agency Positions

The 1973 speech by McNamara to the Board of Governors of the World Bank (entry 1253) is now considered a landmark in Bank history, since it stated the Bank's revised policy toward the rural sector. Entry 2190, which outlines World Bank policy toward the forestry sector in third world countries, is also relevant here.

1244. "Agricultural Development at the World Bank. A Conversation with Dr. Montague Yudelman." *Trialogue* no. 17 (Spring 1978): 8–10.

1245. Food and Agriculture Organization. *An Approach to Food/Population Planning.* F1471. Rome: 1977.

1246. _____. *Indicative World Plan for Agricultural Development to 1975 and 1985: South America.* Rome: 1968–1969.

1247. _____. *Indicative World Plan for Agricultural Development, 1965–85: Near East.* Rome: 1966.

1248. _____. *Indicative World Plan for Agricultural Development to 1975 and 1985: Africa, South of the Sahara.* Rome: 1968–1969.

1249. _____. *Provisional Indicative World Plan for Agricultural Development.* 2 vols. Rome: 1970.

1250. _____. *Provisional Indicative World Plan for Agricultural Development: Summary and Main Conclusions.* Rome: 1970.

1251. _____. *The Role of Women in Rural Development.* E/CONF.66/BP/11. Rome: 24 March 1975.

1252. Goering, Theodore, coord. *Agricultural Land Settlement.* Issues Paper. Washington, D. C.: World Bank, January 1978.

1253. McNamara, Robert S. "Address to the Board of Governors, Nairobi." Washington, D. C.: World Bank, 1973.

1254. Organization for Economic Cooperation and Development. *Food Aid—Its Role in Economic Development.* Paris: 1963.

1255. _____. *The Food Problem of the Developing Countries.* Paris: 1968.

1256. _____. "Problems of the Least-Developed Countries. III. Sectoral Problems. a) Agriculture," pp. 107–112. In *Development Cooperation, 1972 Review.* Paris: OECD, December 1972.

1257. _____. *Rural Development in a Basic Needs Perspective—The Role of Aid in Increasing the Production of the Small Farmer.* Paris: Development Assistance Committee, OECD, April 1978.

1258. United Nations, Economic Commission for Africa. *The Role of Women in African Development.* E/CONF.66/BP/8. Addis Ababa: 10 April 1975.

1259. United Nations, Economic Commission for Africa, Human Resources Development Division, Women's Programme Unit. "Women and National Development in African Countries: Some Profound Contradictions." Position Paper prepared for the Ford Foundation Task Force on Women. Addis Ababa: February 1973, mimeo.

1260. _____. "Women of Africa: Today and Tomorrow." Addis Ababa: 1975, mimeo.

1261. United States, Department of Agriculture, Economic Research Service. *Multilateral Assistance for Agricultural Development.* ERS-521. Washington, D. C.: October 1973.

1262. World Bank. *Agricultural Credit.* World Bank Paper. Washington, D. C.: May 1975.

1263. ———. *Agriculture: Sector Working Paper.* Washington, D. C.: June 1972.

1264. ———. *The Assault on World Poverty: Problems of Rural Development, Education and Health.* Baltimore, Md.: Johns Hopkins University Press, 1975.

1265. ———. *Environment and Development.* Washington, D. C.: May 1975.

1266. ———. *Integrating Women into Development.* Washington, D. C.: August 1975.

1267. ———. *Land Reform.* World Bank Paper. Washington, D. C.: May 1975.

1268. ———. *Rural Development: Sector Policy Paper.* Washington, D. C.: February 1975.

1269. ———. *Rural Electrification.* World Bank Paper. Washington, D. C.: October 1975.

1270. ———. *Water for Economic Development: Two Papers Presented by the World Bank to the International Conference on Water for Peace, May 23–31, 1967.* Washington, D. C.: 1967.

Critical Appraisals

All of the entries in this section are recommended. With the exception of entries 1274 and 1281, these articles deal solely with the World Bank, a reflection of that organization's growing importance and influence as a lending agency. Critiques of the FAO and USAID (as well as the World Bank) are found in *How the Other Half Dies* (entry 1887, especially pages 158–267, Penguin edition) and *The Aid Debate* (entry 1607). Entry 30 critically examines World Bank policies in Latin America while entry 44 focuses on International Monetary Fund programs and policies.

Reid, Nsekela, and "World Bank, IMF and the Poor" offer specific suggestions for revising international agency positions. The other articles listed here are less optimistic about the ability of international agencies to contribute in any meaningful way to the development process. Of this latter group, the articles by Stryker and Payer are especially recommended.

1271. Feder, Ernest. "Capitalism's Last-Ditch Effort to Save Underdeveloped Agricultures: International Agribusiness, the World Bank and the Rural Poor." *Journal of Contemporary Asia* 7:1 (1977): 56–78.

1272. ______. "McNamara's Little Green Revolution: World Bank Scheme for Self-Liquidation of Third World Peasantry." *Economic and Political Weekly* 11 (3 April 1976): 532–541.

1273. Lappé, Frances M., and Collins, Joseph. "Does the World Bank Bind the Poor to Poverty?" *Economic and Political Weekly* 14 (12 May 1979): 853–856. Also available in *Reprint Packet 1.* San Francisco, Calif.: Institute for Food and Development Policy (March 1979): 11–13.

1274. Lappé, Frances Moore; Collins, Joseph; and Kinley, David. *Aid as Obstacle.* San Francisco, Calif.: Institute for Food and Development Policy, May 1980.

1275. Nsekela, Amon J. "The World Bank and the New International Economic Order." *Development Dialogue* 1 (1977): 75–84.

1276. Oppenheim, V. H. "Whose World Bank?" *Foreign Policy* no. 19 (Summer 1975): 98–108.

1277. Payer, Cheryl. "The World Bank and the Small Farmers." *Journal of Peace Research* 16:4 (1979): 293–312.

1278. Reid, Escott. "The World Bank Group: An Unequal Partnership." *Cooperation Canada* (November–December 1973): 14–21.

1279. Stryker, Richard E. "The World Bank and Agricultural Development: Food Production and Rural Poverty." *World Development* 7 (March 1979): 325–336.

1280. van de Laar, Aart J. M. "The World Bank and the World's Poor." *World Development* 4 (October 1976): 837–851.

1281. "World Bank, IMF and the Poor." *Economic and Political Weekly* 13 (7 October 1978): 1693–1695.

Historical Studies

General

Grigg identifies major historical periods and processes that have affected the evolution of modern agriculture and offers a description of agriculture at each stage of its development. The study by Lewis is a good introductory survey of the history of a number of tropical countries in Latin America, Asia, and Africa. The volume edited by Struever discusses why agriculture may have developed, how early agriculture affected different parts of the world, and the role played by agriculture in social development. Tuma concludes that most agrarian reforms have ended in failure. Also recommended is Bairoch, who looks only at the twentieth century.

1282. Bairoch, Paul. *The Economic Development of the Third World Since 1900.* Trans. C. Poslan. Berkeley: University of California Press, 1975. (See especially Chapters 2 and 6.)

1283. Darlington, C. D. "The Origins of Agriculture." *Natural History* (May 1970): 47–57.

1284. Fussell, George E. *Farming Technique from Prehistoric to Modern Times.* London: Pergamon, 1965.

1285. Grigg, David Brian. *The Agricultural Systems of the World.* London: Cambridge University Press, 1974.

1286. Lewis, W. Arthur, ed. *Tropical Development 1880–1913.* Evanston, Ill.: Northwestern University Press, 1970.

1287. Spitz, Pierre. "L'Arme de l'Aide Alimentaire: Les Années d'Apprentissage, 1914–1947." *Critiques de l'Economie Politique* no. 15 (January–March 1974): 105–135.

1288. Struever, Stuart, ed. *Prehistoric Agriculture.* American Museum Sourcebooks in Anthropology. Garden City, N. Y.: Natural History Press, 1971.

1289. Tuma, Elias H. *Twenty-Six Centuries of Agrarian Reform.* Berkeley: University of California Press, 1965.

1290. Wallerstein, Immanuel M. *The Modern World System: Capitalist Agriculture and the Origins of the European World-Economy in the Sixteenth Century.* New York: Academic Press, 1974.

Latin America

Taylor looks at an area in which the indigenous population was not totally subjugated by the Spanish conquerors and where the Indians were able to hold on to a relatively large portion of their lands. He discusses the reasons why this group managed to retain a measure of autonomy. The study of Chile by MacBride is considered a classic. Other recommended studies are Stein and Stein, De Shazo, and the volume edited by Duncan, Rutledge, and Harding.

1291. Adamson, Alan. *Sugar Without Slaves: The Political Economy of British Guiana, 1838–1904.* New Haven: Yale University Press, 1972.

1292. Browning, David. *El Salvador: Landscape and Society.* Oxford: Clarendon, 1971.

1293. Carmagani, Marcello. *Les Méchanismes de la Vie Economique dans une Société Coloniale: le Chili, 1680–1830.* Paris: SEVPEN, 1973. (Part III, Chapters 2–4 are especially relevant.)

1294. Dean, Warren. *Rio Claro: A Brazilian Plantation System.* Stanford, Calif.: Stanford University Press, 1976.

1295. De Shazo, Peter. *The Colonato System of the Bolivian Altiplano from Colonial Times to 1952.* LTC no. 83. Madison: Land Tenure Center, University of Wisconsin, c. 1972.

1296. Duncan, Kenneth, and Rutledge, Ian, eds. With Colin Harding. *Land and Labour in Latin America: Essays on the Development of Agrarian Capitalism in the Nineteenth and Twentieth Centuries.* Cambridge, UK: Cambridge University Press, 1977.

1297. Dunn, Richard S. *Sugar and Slaves.* Chapel Hill: University of North Carolina Press, 1972.

1298. Frank, André Gunder. *Capitalism and Underdevelopment in Latin America: Historical Studies of Chile and Brazil.* New York: Monthly Review, 1967.

1299. Guerra y Sánchez, Ramiro. *Sugar and Society in the Caribbean: An Economic History of Cuban Agriculture.* Caribbean Series no. 7. New Haven: Yale University Press, 1964.

1300. Harrison, Peter D., and Turner, B. L., II. *Pre-Hispanic Maya Agriculture.* Albuquerque: University of New Mexico Press, 1978.

1301. Keith, Robert G. *Conquest and Agrarian Change: The Emergence of the Hacienda System on the Peruvian Coast.* Cambridge, Mass.: Harvard University Press, 1976.

1302. MacBride, George. *Chile: Land and Society.* New York: American Geographical Society Research Series, 1936.

1303. Moreno Fraginals, Manuel. *The Sugarmill: The Socioeconomic Complex of Sugar in Cuba, 1760–1860.* Trans. Cedric Belfrage. New York and London: Monthly Review, 1976.

1304. Panday, R. M. N. *Agriculture in Surinam, 1650–1950: An Inquiry into the Causes of Its Decline.* Amsterdam: H. J. Paris, 1959.

1305. San Estaban, Ricardo. *El Agro Argentino: Progreso Histórico.* Buenos Aires: Editorial Cartago, 1975.

1306. Sheridan, Richard. *The Development of Plantations to 1750. An Era of West Indian Prosperity 1750–1775.* Kingston, Jamaica: Caribbean Universities Press, 1970.

1307. ______. "The Plantation Revolution and the Industrial Revolution." *Caribbean Studies* 9 (October 1969): 7–71.

1308. ______. *Sugar and Slavery: An Economic History of the British West India, 1623–1775.* Baltimore, Md.: Johns Hopkins University Press, 1973.

1309. Stein, Stanley J., and Stein, Barbara H. *The Colonial Heritage of Latin America: Essays on Economic Dependence in Perspective.* New York: Oxford University Press, 1970.

1310. Taylor, William B. *Landlord and Peasant in Colonial Oaxaca.* Stanford, Calif.: Stanford University Press, 1972.

Africa and the Middle East

Baldwin analyzes the failure of a colonial-period project designed to promote the production of oilseeds. Harroy examines the relationship between colonial domination and soil degradation. The monograph by Gellar documents some of the negative economic and political consequences of French colonial rule for Senegal. These three studies are recommended.

1311. Baldwin, Kenneth D. S. *The Niger Agricultural Project.* Cambridge, Mass.: Harvard University Press, 1957.

1312. Flannery, Kent V. "The Ecology of Early Food Production in Mesopotamia." *Science* 147 (12 March 1965): 1247–1255.

1313. Gellar, Sheldon. *Structural Changes and Colonial Dependency: Senegal, 1885–1945.* Beverly Hills, Calif. and London: Sage, 1976.

1314. Harroy, Jean-Paul. *Afrique: Terre Qui Meurt. La Dégradation des Sols Africains Sous l'Influence de la Colonisation.* 2nd ed. Brussels: Hayez, 1949.

1315. Hellen, John A. *Rural Economic Development in Zambia, 1890–1965.* Afrika-Studien no. 32. Munich: Weltforum Verlag, 1968.

1316. Kjekshus, Helge. *Agricultural Initiatives in Pre-colonial Tanzania.* NUPI Notat no. 133. Oslo: Norsk Utenrikspolitisk Institutt, December 1976.

1317. ______. *Ecology Control and Economic Development in East African History: The Case of Tanganyika, 1850–1950.* London: Heinemann; and Berkeley: University of California Press, 1977.

1318. Pankhurst, Richard. "The Great Ethiopian Famine of 1888–1892: A New Assessment (Part Two)." *Journal of the History of Medicine and Allied Sciences* 21 (July 1966): 271–294.

1319. Richards, Alan. "Technical and Social Change in Egyptian Agriculture: 1890–1914." *Economic Development and Cultural Change* 26 (July 1978): 725–745.

1320. Youé, Christopher P. "Peasants, Planters, and Cotton Capitalists: The 'Dual' Economy in Colonial Uganda." *Canadian Journal of African Studies* 12:2 (1978): 163–184.

Asia

Readers interested in the history of Chinese agriculture will want to consult Perkins. Ho discusses the development of Taiwanese agriculture during the Japanese occupation. Whitcombe's study shows how

Western attitudes concerning the role of public works, economic efficiency, and land tenure in rural areas served to undermine the natural and social environments of colonial India. For example, irrigation canals were built with the stated dual purpose of protecting the local population from famine and of increasing export crop production. However, the diet of the ordinary Indian declined in nutritional value following the construction of these canals because the autumn crops of millet and pulses were abandoned in the process of expanding export crop production. The impact of the irrigation canals on the natural environment was no better as marginal lands succumbed to salinity or to overcultivation. As Whitcombe demonstrates, similar problems arose from the construction of roads and railways and from the institution of legal and administrative "reforms."

1321. Adams, Robert M. "Agriculture and Urban Life in Early Southwest Iran." *Science* 136 (13 April 1962): 109–122.

1322. Fei Hsiao-tung, and Chang Chih-I. *Earthbound China: A Study of Rural Economy in Yunnan.* Chicago, Ill.: University of Chicago Press, 1945.

1323. Ghose, Kamal Kumar. *Agricultural Labourers in India. A Study of Their Growth and Economic Condition.* Calcutta: Indian Publications, 1969.

1324. Ho, Samuel Pao-san. "Agricultural Transformation Under Colonialism: The Case of Taiwan." *The Journal of Economic History* 28 (September 1968): 313–340.

1325. Indian Council of Agricultural Research. *Agriculture in Ancient India.* New Delhi: 1964.

1326. Lee, Mabel Ping-hua. *The Economic History of China, With Special Reference to Agriculture.* New York: Columbia University, 1921.

1327. Myers, Ramon, and Ching, Adrienne. "Agricultural Development in Taiwan Under Japanese Colonial Rule." *Journal of Asian Studies* 23 (August 1964): 555–570.

1328. Ngo Vinh Long. *Before the Revolution: The Vietnamese Peasant Under the French.* Cambridge, Mass.: The MIT Press, 1973.

1329. Panikkar, K. N. "Agrarian Legislation and Social Classes. A Case Study of Malabar." *Economic and Political Weekly* 13 (27 May 1978): 880–888.

1330. Perkins, Dwight H. *Agricultural Development in China: 1368–1968.* Chicago, Ill.: Aldine, 1969.

1331. Singh, K. S. "Colonial Transformation of Tribal Society in Middle India." *Economic and Political Weekly* 13 (29 July 1978): 1221–1232.

1332. Stokes, Eric. *The Peasant and the Raj—Studies in Agrarian Society and Peasant Rebellion in Colonial India.* Cambridge, UK: Cambridge University Press, 1978.

1333. Whitcombe, Elizabeth. *Agrarian Conditions in Northern India: The United Provinces Under British Rule 1860–1900.* Berkeley: University of California Press, 1972.

Mechanization

Because the dominant development strategy of the 1950s and 1960s envisaged the third world following the same path to "modernization" as had been taken by the industrialized countries, it was assumed that a "progressive" agricultural sector would absorb a declining portion of the third world labor force and that agricultural machinery of the kind used in industrialized countries would become commonplace in fields throughout Asia, Africa, and Latin America. However, as population growth has outstripped the absorptive capacity of the industrial sector in developing countries, rural employment has become an issue of considerable importance.

Over the last decade, numerous questions have been posed about the labor-augmenting versus labor-saving characteristics of agricultural machinery, the suitability of agricultural machinery designed in industrialized countries to tropical conditions, and the impact of mechanization on social relations in the countryside. There is now a growing acceptance of the notion that third world countries should practice "selective" mechanization in labor-abundant regions. Some agricultural machinery is inherently labor-saving (for example, the combine harvester); indeed, Western agricultural machinery has been *designed* to cope with the problem of labor shortages, not labor abundance. All too often, larger landowners in the third world turn to mechanization as a means of reducing their dependence on hired labor. This has frequently occurred where agricultural wages have risen for one reason or another. Western-produced agricultural machinery is also of little if any use to small landholders and tenant farmers, since it is most economically employed on large holdings.

Books and Monographs

The FAO studies authored by Hopfen and by Hopfen and Biesalski describe the most important hand tools and animal-drawn equipment available to third world farmers. The study by Stavis examines Chinese mechanization strategies and is recommended.

1334. Abdel-Raouf, Mohamed Mahmoud. *Agricultural Mechanization in The Arab Republic of Egypt.* Memo no. 410. Cairo: The Institute of National Planning, November 1974.

1335. Central Treaty Organization. *CENTO Traveling Seminar on Farm Tools and Implements. Iran, Pakistan, Turkey.* Ankara: Office of United States Economic Coordinator for CENTO Affairs, September 1968.

1336. Donaldson, Graham F., and McInerney, John P. *The Consequences of Farm Tractors in Pakistan.* Working Paper 210. Washington, D. C.: World Bank, February 1975.

1337. Food and Agriculture Organization. *Report on the Meeting of the FAO/OECD Expert Panel on the Effects of Farm Mechanization on Production and Employment.* Rome: 1975.

1338. Gemmill, Gordon, and Eicher, Carl. *The Economics of Farm Mechanization and Processing in Developing Countries.* RTN no. 4. New York: The Agricultural Development Council, December 1973.

1339. ______. *A Framework for Research on the Economics of Farm Mechanization in Developing Countries.* African Rural Employment Paper no. 6. East Lansing: Department of Agricultural Economics, Michigan State University, April 1973.

1340. Hopfen, H. J. *Farm Implements for Arid and Tropical Regions.* FAO Agricultural Development Paper no. 91. 2nd rev. ed. Rome: Food and Agriculture Organization, 1976.

1341. Hopfen, H. J., and Biesalski, E. *Small Farm Implements.* FAO Agricultural Development Paper no. 32. FAO Agricultural Series no. 5. Rome: Food and Agriculture Organization, 1978.

1342. Johl, S. S. *Mechanization, Labor-Use, and Productivity in Indian Agriculture.* Economics and Sociology Occasional Paper no. 23. Columbus: Department of Agricultural Economics and Rural Sociology, Ohio State University, 1970.

1343. Kline, C. K.; Green, D. A. G.; Donahue, R. L.; and Stout, B. A. *Agricultural Mechanization in Equatorial Africa.* Research Report no. 6. East Lansing: Institute of International Agriculture, Michigan State University, 1969.

1344. Lönnemark, H. *Multifarm Use of Agricultural Machinery.* FAO Agricultural Development Paper no. 85. FAO Agricultural Series no. 6. Rome: Food and Agriculture Organization, 1978.

1345. Southworth, Herman, ed. *Farm Mechanization in East Asia.* New York: The Agricultural Development Council, 1972.

1346. Stavis, Benedict. *The Politics of Agricultural Mechanization in China.* Ithaca, N. Y.: Cornell University Press, 1978.

1347. United Nations, Industrial Development Organization. *The Role of UNIDO in Promoting the Agricultural Machinery and Implements Industry.* Vienna: 1972.

Articles

Articles dealing with the topic of selective mechanization include Abercrombie, Anker, Hanumantha Rao, Inukai, Lockwood, and Njoku. Njoku discusses a case in which selective mechanization helped to increase employment and productivity in an African country. Lockwood provides a useful summary of the situation in India up to the early 1970s.

Some of the effects of mechanization on social relations are discussed in Raj and in Barker et al. The latter find that, in the Philippines, mechanization had not caused a drop in rural employment up to the early 1970s because reductions in labor needed for land preparation were offset by increased labor requirements for weeding and harvesting. However, they estimate that the higher minimum rural wage adopted at the beginning of the 1970s is likely to increase the rate of mechanization and reduce overall rural employment. Barker et al. argue that mechanization can either hurt or help smallholders; in the case of the Philippines, while government policy has been to aid smallholders, the credit to purchase tractors has gone primarily to the larger landholders. It is the tenant farmers who, Barker et al. find, will be most threatened by expanded mechanization. In general, they conclude the widespread adoption of mechanization can rapidly destroy small-scale, labor-intensive farming.

Raj cites "considerable evidence" from several areas in India and Sri Lanka that demonstrates an important reason behind mechanization has been the desire on the part of large landowners to reduce their dependence on casual labor. Because smallholders do not have the same access as larger ones to scarce resources such as capital and thus cannot adopt even high-productivity machinery, Raj argues that landownership must be equalized to prevent growing disparities in the countryside.

The adaptation of agricultural machinery to tropical conditions is discussed by Deutsch and by Khan. In a similar vein, Chopra notes that small tractors are more suited to Indian conditions where farms tend to be small. However, farmers must buy large tractors because that is all that is available. In this context, readers will want to look at entry 1784 which discusses problems encountered in the production of an indigenously designed tractor in India.

Additional items discussing the relationship between mechanization and employment can be found in the section entitled "Rural Employment: Impact of the Green Revolution and Mechanization" on pages 57–61.

1348. Abercrombie, K. C. "Agricultural Mechanization and Employment in Latin America." *International Labour Review* 106 (July 1972): 11–45.

1349. Anker, Desmond L. W. "Some Effects of Farm Mechanisation." *International Labour Review* 71 (March 1955): 236–254.

1350. Barker, Randolph; Meyers, W. H.; Chrisotomo, C. M.; and Duff, B. "Employment and Technological Change in Philippine Agriculture." *International Labour Review* 106 (August–September 1972): 111–139.

1351. Barwell, Ian J. "Mechanisation: Chinese Two-Wheeled Tractor." *World Crops and Livestock* 29 (July–August 1977): 176–178.

1352. Boshoff, W. H. "Development of Uganda Small Tractor." *World Crops* 24 (September–October 1972): 238–240.

1353. Chopra, Kusum. "Tractorisation and Changes in Factor Inputs: A Case Study of Punjab." *Economic and Political Weekly* 9 (28 December 1974): A119–A127.

1354. Clayton, Eric S. "Mechanisation and Employment in East African Agriculture." *International Labour Review* 105 (April 1972): 309–334.

1355. de Coene, R. "La Place du Machinisme Agricole dans les Modèles Successifs d'Exploitation Marquant l'Intensification des Cultures au Pays Sous-Développés." *Options Méditerranéennes* no. 4 (New Series) (December 1970): 34–40.

1356. Dawlaty, Khairullah. "The Effects of Tractors on Farm Output, Income and Employment During the Initial Stages of Farm Mechanization in Afghanistan." In *Employment and Unemployment Problems of the Near East and South Asia. Volume II.* Eds. Ronald G. Ridker and Harold Leibell. Delhi: Vikas, 1971.

1357. Deutsch, Allan E. "Tractor Dilemma for the Developing Countries." *World Crops* 24 (September–October 1972): 234–236.

1358. Dias, G. R. W. "Rice Mechanisation in Ceylon." *World Crops* 8 (October 1956): 405–407.

1359. Gordon, James. "Mechanisation and the Small Farmer: The Need for a Broader Approach to the Problem in West Africa." *World Crops* 23 (September–October 1971): 250–251.

1360. Gotsch, Carl H. "Tractor Mechanisation and Rural Development in Pakistan." *International Labour Review* 107 (February 1973): 133–166.

1361. Hanumantha Rao, C. H. "Farm Mechanization in a Labour Abundant Economy." *Economic and Political Weekly* 7:5–7 (Annual Number 1972): 393–400.

1362. Inukai, I. "Farm Mechanisation Output and Labour Input: A Case Study of Thailand." *International Labour Review* 101 (May 1970): 453–473.

1363. Jodha, N. S. "A Case of the Process of Tractorisation." *Economic and Political Weekly* 9 (28 December 1974): A111–A118.

1364. Kaneda, Hiromitsu. "Economic Implications of the 'Green Revolution' and the Strategy of Agricultural Development in West Pakistan." *The Pakistan Development Review* 9 (Summer 1969): 111–143.

1365. Khan, Amir U. "Agricultural Mechanisation: The Tropical Farmer's Dilemma." *World Crops* 24 (July–August 1972): 208–213.

1366. Lidman, Russell M. "The Tractor Factor: Agricultural Mechanization in Peru." *Public and International Affairs* no. 1 (1968): 5–30.

1367. Lockwood, Brian. "Patterns of Investment in Farm Machinery and Equipment." *Economic and Political Weekly* 7 (30 September 1972): A113–A124.

1368. Lombard, P. "Méchanisation Partielle de la Culture Contonière au Maroc." *Options Méditerranéennes* no. 4 (New Series) (December 1970): 106–110.

1369. McFarguhar, A. M. M., and Hall, M. "Mechanization and Agricultural Development: No Miracle in Africa." *Options Méditerranéennes* no. 4 (New Series) (December 1970): 26–32.

1370. Nervik, Ottar, and Haghjoo, E. "Mechanization in Underdeveloped Countries." *Journal of Farm Economics* 43 (August 1961): 663–666.

1371. Njoku, Athanasius. "The Impact of Technological Change in a Rural Economy." *Civilisations* 25:1–2 (1975): 52–59.

1372. Orev, Y. "Animal Draught in W. Africa." *World Crops* 24 (September–October 1972): 236–237.

1373. Pothecary, B. P. "Out-of-Season Work for Agricultural Machinery." *World Crops* 23 (July–August 1971): 215, 217.

1374. Raj, K. N. "Mechanisation of Agriculture in India and Sri Lanka (Ceylon)." *International Labour Review* 106 (October 1972): 315–334.

1375. Rana, A. S. "Introduction and Scope for Power Tillers in Nigeria." *World Crops* 23 (September–October 1971): 256–259.

1376. Robinson, R. D. "Tractors in the Village—A Study of Turkey." *Journal of Farm Economics* 34 (November 1952): 451–462.

1377. Schertz, Lyle P. "The Role of Farm Mechanization in the Developing Countries." *Foreign Agriculture* 6 (25 November 1968): 2–4.

1378. Singh, Gajendra, and Chancellor, William. "Energy Inputs and Agricultural Production under Various Regimes of Mechanization." *Transactions* 18:2 (1975): 252–259.

1379. Venkatappiah, B. "Issues in Farm Mechanization." *Teaching Forum* no. 11. New York: The Agricultural Development Council, January 1972.

Part III: Constraints on Rural Development

Land Tenure and the Need for Agrarian Reform

The following sections contain many studies concerned with land tenure and agrarian reform in specific countries. Thus, they supplement, to some extent, "Part V: Country-Specific Studies." In addition, land tenure and agrarian reform are discussed in the context of technological innovation in agriculture in many of the studies in the section in Part II entitled "Green Revolution," pages 88–98.

Agrarian Structures and Land Tenure Patterns

Inequitable land tenure patterns pose one of the most serious obstacles to rural development. The classic image of inequitable land tenure patterns is that of the *latifundia* versus the *minifundia* in Latin America, but the differences in the size of landholdings need not be so large for inequalities to exist.

Inequitable land tenure is one manifestation of the maldistribution of power within society as a whole. Despite attempts at land reform in many countries, land is being concentrated in the hands of fewer and fewer people throughout the world. This trend is evidenced by the growing number of landless and near-landless. While estimates of the degree of landlessness vary widely, and the data on which these estimates are based generally are sketchy, there can be no doubt that landlessness is a problem whose dimensions are constantly expanding. Landlessness has been recognized as a problem of major proportions by many international aid agencies. Yet it is not clear how these agencies can deal with this problem, since they have so far been unwilling to promote the sort of social and political reforms necessary to reduce the power of third world elites and to give "the poorest of the poor" a chance to become major actors in the process of rural development.

Inappropriate land tenure patterns are also of concern here. In the literature surveyed, the emphasis is on Africa, where communal land tenure systems are increasingly being replaced by freehold systems. Fragmented landholdings also come under the heading of "inappropriate" land tenure patterns.

Books and Monographs

Land tenure as an obstacle to rural development and as a cause of landlessness is discussed in entry 2262, the second Asian agricultural survey of the Asian Development Bank. Although this report fails to come to terms with the necessity of socio-political change and limits itself largely to technical recommendations, its survey sections very clearly link skewed patterns of land ownership with growing Asian rural poverty. Readers interested in Latin America should begin by consulting Barraclough, Feder, and Barraclough and Collarte. The study by Dayal and Elliott is a good general survey.

Looking at land tenure in Africa, Parsons argues that traditional land tenure systems and traditional agricultural methods have no future in that continent. Sounding a more cautious note, Barrows explains that it is the traditional land tenure systems' apparent inability to adjust quickly to the changing requirements of economic development that causes critics to suggest that traditional communal forms of tenure be replaced by individual ownership. Barrows suggests that there are ways of altering traditional tenure systems to eliminate the constraints they place on development without actually changing to a different system. He stresses that, if governments are to change land tenure systems, it is crucial to understand the functions performed by the old system and the mechanisms by which these are performed. It is then necessary to provide for the performance of these functions if the new system eliminates the mechanisms through which they have been performed in the past. Finally, Barrow argues that governments would be well-advised to weigh the costs and benefits of alternative methods of instituting change.

Four studies on landlessness and near-landlessness are recommended: Esman, Rosenberg and Rosenberg, Lassen, and the one by the International Labour Office.

The book by Griffin is also recommended.

1380. Asfaw, Lulseged. *The Role of State Domain Lands in Ethiopia's Agricultural Development.* LTC no. 106. Madison: Land Tenure Center, University of Wisconsin, April 1975.

1381. Barraclough, Solon. *Notes on Land Tenure.* Santiago de Chile: Instituto de Capacitación e Investigación en Reforma Agraria, c. 1970.

1382. Barraclough, Solon, ed., with the collaboration of Juan Carlos Collarte. *Agrarian Structure in Latin America.* Lexington, Mass.: Lexington, 1973.

1383. Barrows, Richard L. *Individualized Land Tenure and African Agricultural Development: Alternatives for Policy.* LTC no. 85. Madison:

Land Tenure Center, University of Wisconsin, April 1973. (A shortened version appears in *LTC Newsletter* no. 39 (January–March 1973).)

1384. Biebuyck, Daniel, ed. *African Agrarian Systems.* London: Oxford University Press, 1963.

1385. Centre National de la Recherche Scientifique. *Les Problèmes Agraires des Amériques Latines.* Paris: Editions du Centre National de la Recherche Scientifique, 1967.

1386. Centro Interamericano de Desarrollo Agrícola. *Chile: Tenencia de la Tierra y Desarrollo Socio-económico del Sector Agrícola.* Santiago: 1966.

1387. Crocombe, R. G. *Land Tenure in the Cook Islands.* Melbourne: Oxford University Press, 1964.

1388. Crocombe, Ron, ed. *Land Tenure in the Pacific.* Melbourne: Oxford University Press, 1971.

1389. Dayal, Ram, and Elliott, Charles. *Land Tenure, Land Concentration, and Agricultural Output.* Geneva: UN Research Institute for Social Development, 1966.

1390. Emmanuel, Hailu W. *Land Tenure, Land Use and Development in the Awash Valley—Ethiopia.* LTC no. 105. Madison: Land Tenure Center, University of Wisconsin, 1975.

1391. Esman, Milton. *Landless and Near-Landless in Developing Countries.* LNL no. 1. Ithaca, N. Y.: Rural Development Committee, Center for International Studies, Cornell University, September 1978.

1392. Feder, Ernest, ed. *Rape of the Peasantry: Latin America's Landholding System.* New York: Doubleday, 1972.

1393. Food and Agriculture Organization. *World Agricultural Structure. Study No. 2: Land Tenure.* FAO/61/G/11268. Rome: 1961.

1394. Griffin, Keith B. *Land Concentration and Rural Poverty.* London: Macmillan, 1976.

1395. Harms, Robert. *Land Tenure and Agricultural Development in Zaire, 1895–1961.* LTC no. 99. Madison: Land Tenure Center, University of Wisconsin, June 1974.

1396. Inter-American Committee for Agricultural Development. *Land Tenure Conditions and Socio-Economic Development of the Agricultural Sector. Argentina.* Washington, D. C.: Pan American Union, 1965.

1397. ______. *Land Tenure Conditions and Socio-Economic Development of the Agricultural Sector: Brazil.* Washington, D. C.: Pan American Union, 1966.

1398. ______. *Land Tenure Conditions and Socioeconomic Development of the Agricultural Sector in Seven Latin American Countries: Regional Report. Preliminary Version. Part I.* Washington, D. C.: Pan American Union, 1966.

1399. International Labour Office. *Poverty and Landlessness in Rural Asia.* Geneva: 1977. (This includes case studies of Bangladesh, Malaysia, Indonesia, Pakistan, Philippines, Sri Lanka, and four Indian States—Punjab, Uttar Pradesh, Bihar, and Tamil Nadu.) (A summary of the main empirical findings of this study is available as Griffin, Keith, and Khan, Azizur Rahman. "Poverty in the Third World: Ugly Facts and Fancy Models." *World Development* 6 (March 1978): 295–304.)

1400. James, Roden William. *Land Tenure and Policy in Tanzania.* Nairobi: East African Literature Bureau, 1971.

1401. Jannuzi, F. Tomasson. *Agrarian Crisis in India: The Case of Bihar.* Austin: University of Texas Press, 1974.

1402. Kawharu, I. H. *Maori Land Tenure. Studies of a Changing Institution.* Oxford: Clarendon, 1977.

1403. Korea Land Economics Research Center. *A Study of Land Tenure System in Korea.* Seoul: 1966.

1404. Lassen, Cheryl. *Landlessness and Near-Landlessness in Latin America.* Ithaca, N. Y.: Rural Development Committee, Center for International Studies, Cornell University, c. 1979.

1405. Lundsgaarde, Henry P., ed. *Land Tenure in Oceania.* ASAO Monograph no. 2. Honolulu: The University Press of Hawaii, 1974.

1406. Parsons, Kenneth H. *Customary Land Tenure and the Development of African Agriculture.* LTC. no. 77. Madison: Land Tenure Center, University of Wisconsin, 1971.

1407. Rosenberg, David A., and Rosenberg, Jean G. *Landless Peasants and Rural Poverty in Selected Asian Countries.* LNL no. 2. Ithaca, N. Y.: Rural Development Committee, Center for International Studies, Cornell University, 1978. (Focuses on Bangladesh, India, Indonesia, the Philippines, and Sri Lanka.)

1408. Starns, William W., Jr. *Land Tenure Among the Rural Hausa.* LTC no. 104. Madison: Land Tenure Center, University of Wisconsin, December 1974.

1409. Sund, Michael. *Land Tenure and Economic Performance of Agricultural Establishments in Northeast Brazil.* Research Paper no. 17. Madison: Land Tenure Center, University of Wisconsin, April 1965.

1410. Tesfai, Alemseged. *Communal Land Ownership in Northern Ethiopia and Its Implications for Government Development Policies.* LTC no. 88. Madison: Land Tenure Center, University of Wisconsin, June 1973.

1411. Verdier, Jean-Maurice; Desanti, Pierre; and Karila, Juhana. *Structures Foncières et Développement Rural au Maghreb*. Paris: Presses Universitaires de France, 1969. (Focuses on Algeria, Tunisia, and Morocco.)

Articles

King discusses why it is wrong to ignore the importance of land tenure conditions as a constraint on agricultural development. He critically examines the view adopted by many agricultural development officials and experts that, if sufficient inputs, adequate price incentives, and technology are made available to third world farmers, the land tenure situation will "evolve" so that these incentives can be used effectively.

Dorner finds that a large farm using hired labor or share-croppers is the *least* productive of many possible forms of land tenure. He argues that simply because the trend in the US and Western Europe is toward larger and larger farms, a similar trend should not be promoted in most developing countries where the industrial sector is less able to absorb surplus labor than it is in the industrialized countries.

Two opposing views on the benefits of changing to a freehold land tenure system are offered by Ike and Brock. Investigating the situation in Western Nigeria, Ike tentatively concludes that a communal land tenure system is inferior to a freehold system. Discussing Uganda, Brock sees a freehold system as but one alternative to traditional systems. She argues that simply granting freehold title does not by itself ensure that agricultural development will follow. Nor does she see any necessary connection between the consolidation of fragmented land and freehold tenure systems. Land fragmentation can occur under different forms of tenure system. In addition, Brock finds that the customary land tenure system is more resilient and flexible than many experts believe it to be.

Readers interested in Latin America will want to consult Barraclough.

1412. Appu, P. S. "Agrarian Structure and Rural Development." *Economic and Political Weekly* 9 (28 September 1974): A70–A75.

1413. Barraclough, Solon. "The Agrarian Problem," pp. 487–500. In *Latin America and the Caribbean: A Handbook*. Ed. Claudio Veliz. New York: Praeger, 1968.

1414. Benneh, G. "Communal Land Tenure and the Problem of Transforming Traditional Agriculture in Ghana." *Journal of Administration Overseas* 15 (January 1976): 26–33.

1415. Blume, Helmut. "Types of Agricultural Regions and Land Tenure in the West Indies." *Revista Geográfica* no. 67 (1967): 1–20.

1416. Brock, Beverley. "Customary Land Tenure, 'Individualization' and Agricultural Development in Uganda." *East African Journal of Rural Development* 2:2 (1969): 1–27.

1417. Clark, Ronald James. "Land-Holding Structure and Land Conflicts in Bolivia's Lowland Cattle Region." *Inter-American Economic Affairs* 28 (Autumn 1974): 15–38.

1418. Dorner, Peter P. "Manpower Policies and Programs for Agriculture in Developing Countries," pp. 182–188. In *Manpower: Employment Strategies for Economic Development.* Washington, D. C.: International Manpower Institute, US Department of Labor, 1969.

1419. Famoriyo, Segun. "Land Tenure and Food Production in Nigeria." *LTC Newsletter* no. 41 (July–September 1973): 10–15.

1420. ______. "Some Issues in the Social Development of Nigerian Agriculture." *Journal of Administration Overseas* 14 (October 1975): 251–258.

1421. Finkel, Herman J. "Patterns of Land Tenure in the Leeward and Windward Islands and Their Relevance to Problems of Agricultural Development." *Economic Geography* 40 (April 1964): 163–174.

1422. Goddard, A. D. "Land Tenure, Land Holding and Agricultural Development in the Central Sokoto Close-Settled Zone, Nigeria." *Savanna* 1 (June 1972): 29–41.

1423. Hammons, V. Alvin, ed. "Land Use in Rural Africa." *Rural Africana* no. 23 (Winter 1974). (Deals with Nigeria, Kenya, Sierra Leone, and Angola.)

1424. Harkin, Duncan A. "The Nature of the Problem and Land Tenure in the Philippines." *Land Tenure Center Newsletter* no. 50 (October–December 1975): 1–5.

1425. Ijere, M. O. "A Positive Approach to the African Land Tenure Questions." *Agricultural Economics Bulletin for Africa* no. 16 (December 1974): 21–30.

1426. Ike, Don Nnaemeka. "A Comparison of Communal, Freehold and Leasehold Land Tenure: A Preliminary Study in Ibadan and Ife, Western Nigeria." *American Journal of Economics and Sociology* 36 (April 1977): 187–195.

1427. King, David J. "Problems of Recent Agricultural Development Policy in Nigeria." *LTC Newsletter* no. 37 (July–October 1972): 28–32.

1428. Minhas, B. S. "Rural Poverty, Land Distribution and Development." *Indian Economic Review* 5 (New Series) (April 1970): 97–128.

1429. Patnaik, Utsa. "Economics of Farm Size and Farm Scale: Some Assumptions Re-Examined." *Economic and Political Weekly* 7:31–33 (Special Number 1972): 1613–1624.

1430. Penn, Raymond J. "Malaysia: Land Tenure and Land Development." *LTC Newsletter* no. 33 (February–July 1971): 6–12.

1431. Segal, Aaron. "The Politics of Land in East Africa." *Economic Development and Community Change* 16 (July 1968): 275–296.

1432. Sternberg, Marvin J. "The Economic Impact of the *Latifundista.*" *Land Reform, Land Settlement and Cooperatives* no. 2 (1970): 21–34.

1433. Tiffany, Sharon W. "Principles of Land Tenure Relations in Oceania: An Overview." *Land Tenure Center Newsletter* no. 54 (October–December 1976): 21–27.

1434. Ward, Alan. "The Land Question in Independent Papua New Guinea." *Journal of Administration Overseas* 16 (January 1977): 4–16.

Agrarian Change and Land Reform

If inequitable land tenure patterns pose one of the most serious blocks to rural development, it does not follow that land reform is high on the list of priorities of most third world governments. It is true that most developing countries can point to some measure of land reform legislated or implemented in the last two decades or so. But very often these reforms have only been partially implemented or have not been intended to produce significant changes in rural landholding patterns.

At the same time, land reform by itself (that is, simply the redistribution of land) cannot solve the problem of the rural sector. If rural development is to occur, land reform must be coupled with agrarian reform—the creation of a physical and institutional framework designed to promote the participation and well-being of smallholders (see Cummings et al.).

It is possible that the World Conference on Agrarian Reform and Rural Development (held in Rome in July 1979) may help to generate renewed interest in land reform and agrarian reform. That does not seem likely, however. No government willingly destroys its own power base and too many governments in the third world rely on the rural elite to maintain themselves in power for land reform or agrarian reform to be politically advantageous.

GENERAL

For the general reader, the studies by Eckholm and by the Jacobys are good introductions to the subject of the relationship between land reform and agricultural productivity and progress. A summary of agrarian reform from the mid-1960s to the end of the 1970s is found in the reference document prepared for the World Conference on Agrarian Reform and Rural Development (entry 1441). Land reform as a necessary but not sufficient condition for rural development is discussed in Sidhu, Warriner, Lehmann, and Cummings et al. The book by Warriner (entry 1463) is best when the Middle East is discussed.

Prosterman argues that, since most foreign aid is irrelevant to the needs of developing countries, the US should finance land reform by using its aid to guarantee that landlords will be reimbursed for expropriated property. (The *actual* use of aid to promote land reform is outlined in entries 1466 and 1601.)

In addition, readers will want to consult the section entitled "Rural Employment: Impact of Agrarian Reform," pages 64–65, for an interesting series of articles discussing the importance of agrarian reform to the resolution of the rural employment problem.

1435. Brown, Marion, ed. "International Seminar: Agrarian Reform, Institutional Innovation, and Rural Development. Major Issues in Perspective. Proceedings: Part I." *Land Tenure Center Newsletter* no. 56 (April–June 1977): 1–32; "Part II." no. 57 (July–September 1977): 1–56.

1436. Chaney, Elsa. *Agrarian Reform and Politics.* LTC no. 74. Madison: Land Tenure Center, University of Wisconsin, November 1970.

1437. Cummings, Ralph W., Jr. and Staff Members of the Land Tenure Center. *Land Tenure and Agricultural Development.* LTC no. 117. Madison: Land Tenure Center, University of Wisconsin, July 1978.

1438. Dorner, Peter P. "Changing the Concept of Economic Development." *LTC Newsletter* no. 33 (February–July 1971): 2–6.

1439. ______. *Land Reform and Economic Development.* Baltimore, Md.: Penguin, 1972.

1440. Eckholm, Erik P. *The Dispossessed of the Earth: Land Reform and Sustainable Development.* Worldwatch Paper 30. Washington, D. C.: Worldwatch Institute, 1979.

1441. Food and Agriculture Organization, World Conference on Agrarian Reform and Rural Development. *Review and Analysis of Agrarian Reform and Rural Development in the Developing Countries since the Mid 1960's.* Reference Document. Rome: January 1979.

1442. Food and Agriculture Organization-International Labour Organization. *Progress in Land Reform.* 6 vols. New York: UN, 1954, 1956, 1962, 1966, 1970, and 1976.

1443. Grac, Pierre. "La Réforme Agraire et les Idéologues." *Critique de l'Economie Politique* no. 15 (January–March 1974): 5–18.

1444. Jacoby, Erich H. *Agrarian Reconstruction.* FFHC Basic Studies no. 18. Rome: Food and Agriculture Organization, 1968.

1445. ______. *Inter-Relationship between Agrarian Reform and Agricultural Development.* FAO Agricultural Studies no. 26. Rome: Food and Agriculture Organization, 1953.

1446. Jacoby, Erich H., with Charlotte F. Jacoby. *Man and Land: The Essential Revolution.* New York: Knopf, 1971.

1447. Jones, E. L., and Woolf, S. J., eds. *Agrarian Change and Economic Development.* London: Methuen, 1969.

1448. Lalive d'Epinay, Christian, and Zylberberg, Jacques. "Une Variable Oubliée de la Problématique Agraire: Le Prolétariat Urbain (Le Cas du Chili)." *Civilisations* 23–24: 1–2 (1973–1974): 51–63.

1449. "Land Reform" (Special Issue). *Ceres* no. 12 (November–December 1969).

1450. "Land Reform: Its Reasons and Meaning" (Editorial). *Civilisations* 20:3 (1970): 301–333.

1451. Lehmann, David. "The Death of Land Reform: Polemic." *World Development* 6 (March 1978): 339–345.

1452. Lehmann, David, ed. *Agrarian Reform and Agrarian Reformism: Studies of Peru, Chile, China and India.* London: Faber & Faber, 1974.

1453. ______. *Peasants, Landlords and Governments: Agrarian Reform in the Third World.* New York: Holmes & Meier, 1974.

1454. "National Resources and Land Reforms" (Editorial). *Civilisations* 20:4 (1970): 452–470.

1455. Prosterman, R. L. "Land Reform as Foreign Aid." *Foreign Policy* no. 6 (Spring 1972): 128–141.

1456. Sachs, Ignacy, ed. *Agriculture, Land Reforms and Economic Development. Studies on Developing Countries, Volume 2.* Warsaw: PWN-Polish Scientific, 1964.

1457. Santa Cruz, Hernán. "The Three Tiers of 'Basic Needs' for Rural Development." *Finance & Development* 16 (June 1979): 29–31.

1458. Sazama, G. W., and Davis, L. Harlan. "Land Taxation and Land Reform." *Economic Development and Cultural Change* 21 (July 1973, Part I): 642–654.

1459. Sidhu, B. S. *Land Reform, Welfare and Economic Growth.* Bombay: Vora, 1976.

1460. Tai Hung-chao. *Land Reform and Politics: A Comparative Analysis.* Berkeley, Los Angeles, and London: University of California Press, 1974.

1461. United States Department of Agriculture, Economic Research Service, Farm Economics Division. *Agrarian Reform & Economic Growth in Developing Countries.* Papers from a Seminar on Research Perspective and Problems. Washington, D. C.: March 1962.

1462. Walinsky, Louis J., ed. *The Selected Papers of Wolf Ladejinsky: Agrarian Reform as Unfinished Business.* New York: Oxford University Press, 1977.

1463. Warriner, Doreen. *Land Reform in Principle and Practice.* Oxford: Clarendon, 1969.

1464. ______. "Results of Land Reform in Asian and Latin American Countries." *Food Research Institute Studies in Agricultural Economics, Trade and Development* 12:2 (1973): 115–131.

1465. Wilkie, James W. *Measuring Land Reform.* Los Angeles: UCLA Latin American Center, 1974.

LATIN AMERICA

Alexander's survey of land reform in Latin America is a useful introduction to the topic. Adams examines the relationship between land reform and the policies of aid agencies. He finds that one reason so little land reform had been carried out in Latin America by the end of the 1960s was that aid agencies had failed to promote such reforms actively. This situation stood in direct contradiction to the official position of the US-sponsored Alliance for Progress, that land reform was to be encouraged as a means of reducing rural poverty. Adams looks at three reasons aid agencies have given for not supporting land reform: land reform reduces productivity, urbanization is a better means of reducing poverty, land colonization is a better means of reducing poverty, and then discusses the flaws in these arguments.

The relationship between land reform and increased agricultural output has been a topic of some debate. Mueller stresses the importance of land reform in improving agricultural output, especially over the long-term. Burke finds that land reform by itself is not sufficient to produce large increases in agricultural output. Eckstein, Donald, Horton, and Carroll conclude, *inter alia,* that in Bolivia, Chile, Mexico, Peru, and Venezuela the overall impact of reform on agricultural production has been positive. Adams argues that there is little empirical evidence to support claims that land reform reduces productivity. The key would seem to be to provide the necessary services to enable smallholders to exploit their new holdings successfully.

The articles by Aranjo, Pinto, Suárez Melo, Flores Quiróz, Noguera, and Orchard and Ortiz form an interesting discussion of the rural community enterprise, a Latin American experiment developed in the 1970s to overcome the shortcomings of previous attempts at land reform. A community enterprise is a self-managed unit of production whose members make equal contributions of capital and labor and share the profits. Such an entity is said to be central to a development strategy in which the *campesino* takes an active, not a passive, role and where peasant participation in the benefits of development is a guiding principle. The articles by Aranjo and Pinto are suggested as introductions to this topic.

Other recommended studies include all Barraclough entries, Barraclough and Affonso, Barraclough and Fernández, Senior, and the volume edited by Stavenhagen.

1466. Adams, Dale W. *The Economics of Land Reform in Latin America and the Role of Aid Agencies.* AID Discussion Paper no. 21. Washington, D. C.: US Agency for International Development, 1969.

1467. Alexander, Robert J. *Agrarian Reform in Latin America.* New York and London: Macmillan and Collier Macmillan, 1974.

1468. Aranjo, José E. "La Reforma Agraria y la Empresa Comunitaria." *Desarrollo Rural en las Américas* 2:3 (1970): 193–206.

1469. Barraclough, Solon. "Agricultural Policies and Strategies of Land Reform," pp. 95–171. In *Masses in Latin America.* Ed. Irving L. Horowitz. New York: Oxford University Press, 1970.

1470. ———. "Estrategia de Desarrollo Rural y Reforma Agraria." *Desarrollo Rural en las Américas* 4:1 (1972): 61–79.

1471. ———. "Latin American Agrarian Reform in Action," pp. 202–215. In *Economic Growth in Developing Countries—Material and Human Resources.* Ed. Yohanan Ramati. Praeger Special Studies in International Economy and Development. New York: Praeger, 1975.

1472. Barraclough, Solon, and Affonso, Almino. *Critical Appraisal of the Chilean Agricultural Reform.* Santiago: ICIRA, 1972. (This is a translation of "Diagnóstico de la Reforma Agraria Chilena." *Cuadernos de la Realidad Nacional* no. 16 (April 1973).)

1473. Barraclough, Solon, and Fernández, José Antonio, coords. *Diagnóstico de la Reforma Agraria Chilena.* Mexico: Siglo Veintiuno Editores, SA, 1975.

1474. Barriga, Claudio. "Chile: Peasants, Politics and Land Reform." *LTC Newsletter* no. 36 (April–June 1972): 11–14.

1475. Benavides M., Guillermo A. *Reforma Social Agraria.* Bogotá: Editorial Temis, 1970.

1476. Blankstein, Charles S., and Zuvekas, Clarence, Jr. *Agrarian Reform in Ecuador.* LTC no. 100. Madison: Land Tenure Center, University of Wisconsin, September 1974.

1477. Burke, Melvin. "Land Reform and Its Effect upon Production and Productivity in the Lake Titicaca Region." *Economic Development and Cultural Change* 18 (April 1970): 410–450.

1478. Clark, Ronald J. *Land Reform and Peasant Market Participation on the Northern Highlands of Bolivia.* LTC Reprint no. 42. Madison: Land Tenure Center, University of Wisconsin, n.d.

1479. Cline, William R. *Economic Consequences of a Land Reform in Brazil.* Amsterdam: North-Holland, 1970.

1480. Cuba, Delegation to World Land Reform Conference, Rome, 1966. *Cuba: Report on Land Reform.* RU:WLR-C/66/19. Rome: Food and Agriculture Organization, 1966.

1481. Dorner, Peter P., ed. *Land Reform in Latin America: Issues and Cases.* Land Economic Monographs, no. 3. Madison: Land Tenure Center, University of Wisconsin, 1971.

1482. Dovring, F. *Land Reform and Productivity: The Mexican Case.* LTC no. 63. Madison: Land Tenure Center, University of Wisconsin, 1969.

1483. Eckstein, Shlomo; Donald, G.; Horton, D.; and Carroll, T. *Land Reform in Latin America: Bolivia, Chile, Mexico, Peru, and Venezuela.* Working Paper 275. Washington, D. C.: World Bank, April 1978.

1484. Egginton, Everett, and Ruhl, J. Mark. "The Influence of Agrarian Reform Participation on Peasant Attitudes: The Case of Colombia." *Inter-American Economic Affairs* 28 (Winter 1974): 27–43.

1485. Flores, Edmundo. "Financing Land Reform: A Mexican Casebook," pp. 331–344. In *Masses in Latin America.* Ed. Irving L. Horowitz. New York: Oxford University Press, 1970.

1486. Flores Quiróz, Luis. "La Empresa Comunitaria y la Participación Campesina." *Desarrollo Rural en las Américas* 6:3 (1974): 77–95.

1487. Foland, Frances M. "Agrarian Reform in Latin America." *Foreign Affairs* 48:1 (1969): 97–112.

1488. García, José María. *Reforma Agraria y Liberación Nacional.* Buenos Aires: Editorial Porvenir, 1964.

1489. Goussault, Yves. "La Réforme Agraire Chilienne: Hésitations ou Impasse?" *Revue Tiers-Monde* 13 (July–September 1972): 541–558.

1490. Graeff, Peter. *The Effects of Continued Landlord Presence in the Bolivian Countryside During the Post-Reform Era: Lessons to be Learned.* LTC no. 103. Madison: Land Tenure Center, University of Wisconsin, October 1974.

1491. Greenshields, Bruce L. *Agricultural Reforms and Productivity and Trade in Chile Since 1965.* ERS-Foreign 345. Washington, D. C.: Economic Research Service, US Department of Agriculture, October 1972.

1492. Guido Pastorino, Juan. *Reforma Agraria y Reforma Política: La Salida de la Crisis Argentina.* Buenos Aires: Ediciones Líberia, 1971.

1493. Haisman, I. "The Village Corporation: Mexican Experience with a New Land Tenure System." *Land Reform, Land Settlements and Cooperatives.* no. 2. Rome: FAO, 1972.

1494. Hautfenne, Stéphane. "Les Structures et la Réforme Agraire Chiliennes (1er Partie)." *Civilisations* 20:3 (1970): 364–376; "(2e Partie)." 20:4 (1970): 516–536.

1495. Heath, Dwight B.; Erasmus, Charles J.; and Buechler, Hans C. *Land Reform and Social Revolution in Bolivia.* New York and London: Praeger, 1969.

1496. Herzog, Jesús Silva. *El Agrarismo Mexicano y la Reforma Agraria.* 2nd ed. Mexico City: Fondo de Cultura Económica, 1964.

1497. Heyduk, Daniel. "Bolivia's Land Reform Hacendados." *Inter-American Economic Affairs* 27 (Summer 1973): 87–96.

1498. Horton, Douglas. *Haciendas and Cooperatives: A Preliminary Study of Latifundist Agriculture and Agrarian Reform in Northern Peru.* Research Paper no. 53. Madison: Land Tenure Center, University of Wisconsin, September 1973.

1499. Huizer, Gerrit. "Peasant Organization in Agrarian Reform in Mexico," pp. 445–502. In *Masses in Latin America.* Ed. Irving L. Horowitz. New York: Oxford University Press, 1970.

1500. Kaufman, Robert R. *The Chilean Political Right and Agrarian Reform: Resistance and Moderation.* Political Study no. 2. Washington, D. C.: Institute for the Comparative Study of Political Systems, 1967.

1501. Lehmann, David. *Political Incorporation vs. Political Stability: The Case of the Chilean Agrarian Reform, 1965–1970.* IDS Communication. Brighton, UK: Institute of Development Studies, University of Sussex, 1971.

1502. McCoy, Terry L. *The Politics of Structural Change in Latin America: The Case of Agrarian Reform in Chile.* Research Paper no. 37. Madison: Land Tenure Center, University of Wisconsin, August 1969.

1503. Mathiason, John R. *Caicara de Maturin: Case Study of an Agrarian Reform Settlement in Venezuela.* Research Papers on Land Tenure and Agrarian Reform, no. 1. Washington, D. C.: Inter-American Committee for Agricultural Development, issued by Pan American Union, 1967.

1504. Mueller, Marnie W. "Changing Patterns of Agricultural Output and Productivity in the Private and Land Reform Sectors in Mexico, 1940–60." *Economic Development and Cultural Change* 18 (January 1970): 252–266.

1505. Nisbet, Charles T., ed. *Latin America: Problems in Economic Development.* New York: Free Press, 1969. (Chapters by Barraclough and Domike, and Flores are relevant.)

1506. Noquera, Anibal. "La Empresa Comunitaria Como Estrategia del Desarrollo Rural." *Desarrollo Rural en las Américas* 2:3 (1970): 207–214.

1507. Orchard, Jorge, and Ortiz, Jaime. "Presión Campesina, Reforma Agraria y Empresas Comunitarias." *Desarrollo Rural en las Américas* 5:2 (1973): 97–120.

1508. Parsons, Kenneth H. "Agrarian Reform in Southern Honduras." *Land Tenure Center Newsletter* no. 50 (October–December 1975): 6–14.

1509. ______. *Key Policy Issues for the Reconstruction and Development of Honduran Agriculture Through Agrarian Reform.* LTC no. 114. Madison: Land Tenure Center, University of Wisconsin, January 1978.

1510. Pinto, Bosco. "Analisis Científico de las Empresa Comunitarias Campesinos." *Desarrollo Rural en las Américas* 4:3 (1972): 236–248.

1511. Ringlien, Wayne R. "Some Economic and Institutional Results of the Agrarian Reform in Peru." *LTC Newsletter* no. 41 (July–September 1973): 5–14.

1512. Rivarola, Domingo. "Freins et Obstacles à la Réforme Agraire au Paraguay." *Civilisations* 25:3–4 (1975): 286–292.

1513. Sandoval, Rigoberto. *The Role of Peasants' and Rural Workers' Associations in Agrarian Reform: Latin America.* Rome: Food and Agriculture Organization, 1973.

1514. Seligson, Mitchell A. *Agrarian Reform in Costa Rica, 1942–1976: The Evolution of a Program.* LTC no. 115. Madison: Land Tenure Center, University of Wisconsin, January 1978.

1515. Senior, Clarence. "Reforma Agraria y Democracia en la Comarca Lagunera." *Problemas Agrícolas e Industriales de México* 8:2 (1956).

1516. Sentilhes, Henri. "Réforme Agraire au Pérou." *Revue Tiers-Monde* 11 (October–December 1970): 759–766.

1517. Simpson, Eyler N. *The Ejido: Mexico's Way Out.* Chapel Hill: The University of North Carolina Press, 1937.

1518. Stanfield, David. "The Chilean Agrarian Reform, 1975." *Land Tenure Center Newsletter* no. 52 (April–June 1976): 1–13.

1519. Stavenhagen, Rudolfo, ed. *Agrarian Problems & Peasant Movements in Latin America.* Garden City, N. Y.: Anchor, Doubleday, 1970.

1520. Steenland, Kyle. *Agrarian Reform Under Allende: Peasant Revolt in the South.* Albuquerque: University of New Mexico Press, 1977.

1521. Strasma, John. "The Economic Background to Allende's Reform." *LTC Newsletter* no. 43 (January–March 1974): 1–10.

1522. Suárez Melo, Mario. "Empresas Comunitarias en América Latina." *Desarrollo Rural en las Américas* 4:2 (1972): 139–159.

1523. Swift, Jeannine. *Agrarian Reform in Chile: An Economic Study.* Lexington, Mass.: Lexington, Heath, 1971.

1524. Thiesenhusen, William Charles. *Chile's Experiments in Agrarian Reform.* Land Economics Monographs, no. 1. Madison: University of Wisconsin Press, 1966.

1525. van de Wetering, H. "The Current State of Land Reform in Peru." *LTC Newsletter* no. 40 (April–June 1973): 5–9.

1526. van der Pluijm, Theodore. "An Analysis of the Venezuelan Land Reform." *Land Reform* no. 2 (1972).

1527. Vellard, Jehan. "Problèmes Agraires de la Bolivie Andine." *Civilisations* 20:2 (1970): 227–236.

AFRICA AND THE MIDDLE EAST

The monograph by King is recommended as a general introduction to the topic of land reform in Africa. Radwan demonstrates that Egyptian land reform has not changed the pattern of land distribution significantly. In 1972, landless laborers accounted for 50 percent of the rural population in Egypt. While there has been some improvement in income distribution among land*owners* due to the land reform, if one takes the landless into account, some 44 percent of Egypt's rural households had incomes below the poverty line in the early 1970s. A similar argument is made by Boeck.

Omosule discusses a group in Kenya that did not want to participate in a land consolidation program. Other problems arising out of the Kenyan land consolidation are considered in Barber. Van Malder concludes that the agrarian reform in Algeria has in fact favored the industrial sector at the expense of agriculture. Also recommended are Springborg, Ståhl, and Cohen, Goldsmith, and Mellor.

1528. Abdel Fadil, Mahmoud. *Development, Income Distribution and Social Change in Rural Egypt (1952–1970): A Study in the Political Economy* *of Agrarian Transition.* Department of Applied Economics Occasional Paper no. 45. New York: Cambridge University Press, 1975.

1529. Barber, William J. "Land Reform and Economic Change Among African Farmers in Kenya." *Economic Development and Cultural Change* 19 (October 1970): 6–24.

1530. Boeckx, Cécile. "Réforme Agraire et Structures Sociales en Egypte Nassérienne." *Civilisations* 21:4 (1971): 373–390.

1531. Brietzke, Paul. "Land Reform in Revolutionary Ethiopia." *Journal of Modern African Studies* 14:4 (1976): 637–660.

1532. Brokensha, David, and Glazier, Jack. "How Land Reform is Affecting the Mbeere of Central Kenya." *LTC Newsletter* no. 44 (April–June 1974): 8–14.

1533. Bruce, John W. "Ethiopia: Nationalization of Rural Lands Proclamation." *Land Tenure Center Newsletter* no. 47 (January–March 1975): 1–15.

1534. Charbonnier, François. *Les Réformes Agraires en Afrique du Nord: La Tunisie.* Paris: Fondation Nationales des Sciences Politiques, 1964.

1535. Cohen, John M.; Goldsmith, Arthur A.; and Mellor, John W. "Rural Development Issues Following Ethiopian Land Reform." *Africa Today* 23 (April–June 1976): 7–28.

1536. Djeghloul, Adelkader. "Révolution Agraire et Problèmes de la Transition en Algérie." *Cultures et Développement* 9:4 (1977): 577–599.

1537. Harbeson, John W. "Land Reforms and Politics in Kenya, 1954–70." *Journal of Modern African Studies* 9:2 (1971): 231–251.

1538. Khader, Bichara. "Propriété Agricole et Réforme Agraire en Syrie." *Civilisations* 25:1–2 (1975): 62–82.

1539. King, David J. *Land Reform and Participation of the Rural Poor in the Development Process of African Countries.* LTC no. 101. Madison: Land Tenure Center, University of Wisconsin, September 1974.

1540. Nashrty, Ahmed H. *Agrarian Reform in the U. A. R.* rev. ed. Cairo: Agrarian Reform Organization, c.1966.

1541. Omosule, Monone. "Kikuyu Reaction to Land Consolidation 1955–9." *Transafrican Journal of History* 4: 1–2 (1974): 115–134.

1542. Pedraza, G. J. W. "Land Consolidation in the Kikuyu Area of Kenya," pp. 58–66. In *Readings in Applied Economics, Volume I.* Ed. Edith H. Whetham and Jean I. Currie. Cambridge, UK: Cambridge University Press, 1967. (Reprinted from *Journal of African Administration* 8:2 (1956): 82–87.)

1543. Radwan, Samir. *Agrarian Reform and Rural Poverty, Egypt, 1952–1975.* Geneva: International Labour Office, 1977.

1544. Rogers, M. "The Kenya Land Reform Programme: A Model for Modern Africa?" *Verfassung und Recht in Ubersee* 6:1 (1973): 49–63.

1545. Saab, Gabriel S. *The Egyptian Agrarian Reform: 1952–1962.* London and New York: Oxford University Press, 1967.

1546. Smith, Tony. "The Political and Economic Ambitions of Algerian Land Reform, 1962–1974." *The Middle East Journal* 29 (Summer 1975): 259–278.

1547. Springborg, Robert. "New Patterns of Agrarian Reform in the Middle East and North Africa." *The Middle East Journal* 31 (Spring 1977): 127–142.

1548. Ståhl, Michael. *New Seeds in Old Soil: A Study of the Land Reform Process in Western Wollega, Ethiopia 1975–76.* Research Report no. 40. Uppsala: The Scandinavian Institute of African Studies, 1977.

1549. Tuma, Elias H. "Agrarian Reform and Urbanization in the Middle East." *The Middle East Journal* 24 (Spring 1970): 163–177.

1550. Van Dooren, P. J. *The Cooperative Approach in Implementing Land Reform Programs: The Tunisian and Egyptian Experience.* LTC no. 113. Madison: Land Tenure Center, University of Wisconsin, October 1977.

1551. van Malder, René. "La Révolution Agraire en Algérie: Tournant Politique ou Infléchissement Technique." *Civilisations* 25:3–4 (1975): 251–270.

1552. Verhelst, Thierry G. *Réflexions en Marge des Projets de Réforme Agraire en Ethiopie.* Brussels: Académie Royale des Sciences d'Outre-Mer, 1974.

ASIA

Sanderatre concludes that land reforms instituted in the early 1970s in Pakistan (entry 1579) and Sri Lanka (entry 1578) will not lead to significant changes in the rural sector of either country. Taiwan is considered a major Asian "success story" in terms of the development of its agricultural sector. Koo underlines the importance of the relationship between stable land tenure arrangements and progress in the agricultural sector. The editorial in *Civilisations* (entry 1555) suggests that Taiwan's land reform program has been so successful because of the very large subsidies provided by the US to the Taiwanese government after 1949. Griffin (entry 2516) takes the opposite view, arguing that in some cases US aid may even have retarded economic growth, in both the industrial and the agricultural sectors.

Readers interested in issues relating to land reform and agrarian reform in India should survey the *Economic and Political Weekly* on a regular basis. The article by Rao discusses the redistribution of land to the landless and to tenant-tillers. Rao looks at the ways in which land reform has been dealt with to date in India and how it should be dealt with in the future. The articles by Ladejinsky, Mencher, and Hanumantha Rao all have to do with the question of land ceilings (limiting the amount of land which can legally be owned by one person). Hanumantha Rao states that the point of land ceilings is that they prevent the growth of capitalist farming. Since the smaller holdings tend to have more labor available per unit of land farmed than larger ones (see also entry 909) and thus tend to be more productive per unit of land farmed, Hanumantha Rao argues that the enforcement of land ceilings and the provision of capital resources to small holders would lead to an important increase in Indian agricultural output.

Mencher holds the opposite view of the effect of land ceilings. She argues that they tend to *encourage* the growth of capitalist farming by leading farmers to view agriculture as a business even though *zamindar*-type farming is curbed by land ceilings. Land ceilings, as they have been legislated and implemented, have not changed the power relations in rural India nor have they significantly altered the way in which land is distributed. Ladejinsky takes the position that land ceilings are an essential feature of successful land reforms but that one should not concentrate on enforcing land ceilings at this time because larger farmers are seen by the Indian government as crucial actors in the adoption of Green Revolution technology. Furthermore, Ladejinsky argues that emphasis on land ceilings can detract attention from other very important components of rural progress such as land consolidation, the implementation of fair land-rents, security of tenure, and rights for tenants and sharecroppers.

1553. Ajami, Ismail. "Land Reform and Modernisation of the Farming Structure in Iran." *Oxford Agrarian Studies* 2:2 (New Series) (1973): 120–131.

1554. Aktan, Reşat. "Problems of Land Reform in Turkey." *The Middle East Journal* 20 (Summer 1966): 317–334.

1555. "A Successful Land Reform: The Case of Taiwan (Formosa)." *Civilisations* 21:1 (1971): 3–14.

1556. Chao, Kang. *Economic Effects of Land Reforms in Taiwan, Japan, and Mainland China.* LTC no. 80. Madison: Land Tenure Center, University of Wisconsin, 1972.

1557. Dorner, Peter P. "The Experiences of Other Countries in Land Reform: Lessons for the Philippines?" *Land Tenure Center Newsletter* no. 48 (April–June 1975): 12–17.

1558. Hanumantha Rao, C. H. "Ceiling on Agricultural Landholding: Its Economic Rationale." *Economic and Political Weekly* 7 (24 June 1972): A59–A62.

1559. Harkin, Duncan. *Land Reform, Land-Use Changes, and Capital Gains: The Philippine Case.* LTC no. 108. Madison: Land Tenure Center, University of Wisconsin, April 1976.

1560. Hautfenne, Stéphane. "Les Etapes de la Collectivisation des Campagnes en République Populaire de Chine." *Civilisations* 22:1 (1972): 35–45.

1561. Herring, Ronald, and Chaudery, M. Ghaffar. "The 1972 Land Reforms in Pakistan and Their Economic Implications." *Pakistan Development Review* 13:3 (1974): 245–279. (Also available as Reprint no. 126. Madison: Land Tenure Center, University of Wisconsin, 1974.)

1562. Hunt, Chester L. "The Philippine Compact Farm: Right Answer or Wrong Question?" *Journal of Rural Cooperation* 5:2 (1977): 121–140.

1563. Joshi, P. C. "Land Reforms Implementation and Role of Administrator." *Economic and Political Weekly* 13 (30 September 1978): A78–A83.

1564. Keddie, Nikki R. "The Iranian Village Before and After Land Reform." *Journal of Contemporary History* 3:3 (July 1968): 69–91.

1565. Khan, Akhter Hameed. *Land Reforms in Pakistan, 1947–72.* Karachi: National Institute of Social and Economic Research, 1972.

1566. Klatt, Werner. "Agrarian Issues in Asia: II. Reform and Insurgency." *International Affairs* 48 (July 1972): 395–413.

1567. Koo, Anthony Y. C. *The Role of Land Reform in Economic Development. A Case Study of Taiwan.* New York and London: Praeger, 1968.

1568. Krishna, R. "Agrarian Reform in India: The Debate on Ceilings." *Economic Development and Cultural Change* 7 (1959): 302–317.

1569. Ladejinsky, Wolf. "Land Ceilings and Land Reform." *Economic and Political Weekly* 7:5–7 (Annual Number 1972): 401–408.

1570. ———. "New Ceiling Round and Implementation Prospects." *Economic and Political Weekly* 7 (30 September 1972): A125–A132.

1571. Lakshman, T. K.; Ramadas, K. L.; and Kauthi, Mahendra S. "Land Ceilings in Karnataka: A Case Study." *Economic and Political Weekly* 8 (29 September 1973): A111–A115.

1572. Lambton, Ann K. S. *The Persian Land Reform, 1962–1966.* Oxford: Clarendon, 1969.

1573. Lippit, Victor D. *Land Reform and Economic Development in China: A Study of Institutional Change and Development Finance.* White Plains, N. Y.: International Arts and Sciences, 1974.

1574. Mencher, Joan P. "Land Ceilings in Tamil Nadu: Facts and Fiction." *Economic and Political Weekly* 10:5–7 (Annual Number 1975): 241–254.

1575. Omvedt, Gail. "Agrarian Crisis in India" (Review Article). *Bulletin of Concerned Asian Scholars* 6 (November–December 1974): 17–23.

1576. Porter, D. Gareth. *The Myth of the Bloodbath: North Vietnam's Land Reform Reconsidered.* IREA Project Interim Report no. 2. Ithaca, N. Y.: Cornell University, September 1972.

1577. Rao, V. M. "Two Perspectives on Redistribution of Land." *Economic and Political Weekly* 9 (30 March 1974): A2–A10.

1578. Sanderatre, Nimal. "New Land Reform in Sri Lanka (Ceylon)." *LTC Newsletter* no. 37 (July–October 1972): 18–22.

1579. ______. "Pakistan's Land Reform of 1972." *LTC Newsletter* no. 42 (October–December 1973): 17–20.

1580. ______. "Tenancy in Ceylon's Paddy Lands: The 1958 Reform." *South Asian Review* 5 (January 1972): 117–136.

1581. Sinha, Arun. "Legal Loopholes: To Landlord's Rescue." *Economic and Political Weekly* 13 (21 October 1978): 1758–1760.

1582. Tjondronegoro, Sediono M. P. *Land Reform or Land Settlement: Shifts in Indonesia's Land Policy.* LTC no. 81. Madison: Land Tenure Center, University of Wisconsin, December 1972.

1583. Tran Buu-khanh. "Certains Aspects Sociaux de la Réforme Agraire en Asie du Sud-Est." *Civilisations* 20:4 (1970): 485–493.

1584. Tran Ngoc Bich. "Stratégie de Développement et Evolution du Cadre Socio-Economique au Nord-Vietnam." *Civilisations* 22:1 (1972): 49–75.

1585. Utrecht, Ernst. "Land Reform and 'Bimas' in Indonesia." *Journal of Contemporary Asia* 3:2 (1973): 149–164.

1586. Wong, John. *Land Reform in the People's Republic of China: Institutional Transformation in Agriculture.* New York: Praeger, 1973.

RESETTLEMENT SCHEMES

Land settlement, or colonization, is considered an important alternative—in land-abundant areas—to redistribution of land. However, on a worldwide basis, past attempts at using land settlement as an alternative to land reform have generally ended in failure. One problem has been, as Higgs points out, that most settlement schemes only reproduce the old land tenure system in a different place. He also finds that settlers have unrealistic assumptions of what settlement life will offer them and so it is relatively easy for them to speak of "failure."

Higgs enumerates a series of problems that must be resolved or avoided if settlement schemes are to succeed as a land reform measure. The article by Riding is a journalistic piece. However, it clearly illustrates the reproduction of old land tenure systems discussed by Higgs.

All but two of the articles in this section deal with African settlement schemes. This is at least in part a reflection of the fact that land colonization really is a viable alternative only in Africa and parts of Latin America. The articles by Domike and by Leo are also recommended. In addition, entry 1582 is relevant here.

1587. Adegeye, A. J. "Re-examination of Issues Involved in the Farm Settlement Scheme of the Western State of Nigeria." *Oxford Agrarian Studies* 3:2 (New Series) (1974): 79–88.

1588. Apthorpe, Raymond, ed. "Land Settlement and Rural Development in Eastern Africa." *Nkanga* no. 3 (n.d.).

1589. Chambers, Robert. *Settlement Schemes in Tropical Africa: A Study of Organizations and Development.* New York: Praeger, 1969.

1590. Domike, Arthur A. "Colonization as an Alternative to Land Reform." *AID Spring Review of Land Reform. Volume XI: Analytic Papers.* 2nd ed. Washington, D. C.: US Agency for International Development, June 1970.

1591. Elder, Joseph W. "Planned Resettlement in Nepal's Terai." *Land Tenure Center Newsletter* no. 50 (October–December 1975): 24–32.

1592. Haugwitz, Hans-Wilhelm von. *Some Experiences with Smallholder Settlement in Kenya 1963/64 to 1966/67.* Afrika-Studien no. 72. Munich: Weltforum Verlag, 1972.

1593. Higgs, John. "Land Settlement in Africa and the Near East: Some Recent Experiences." *Land Reform* no. 2. (1978): 1–24.

1594. Leo, Christopher. "The Failure of the 'Progressive Farmer' in Kenya's Million-Acre Settlement Scheme." *Journal of Modern African Studies* 16:4 (1978): 619–638.

1595. Riding, Alan. "Guatemala Opening New Lands But the Best Goes to Rich." *New York Times* (5 April 1979): A2.

1596. Roider, Werner. *Farm Settlements for Socio-Economic Development: The Western Nigeria Case.* Afrika-Studien no. 66. Munich: Weltforum Verlag, 1971.

1597. Whetham, Edith H. *Cooperation, Land Reform and Land Settlement: Report on a Survey in Kenya, Uganda, Sudan, Ghana, Nigeria and Iran.* London: Plunkett Foundation for Co-Operative Studies, 1968.

1598. ______. "Land Reform and Resettlement in Kenya." *East African Journal of Rural Development* 1:1 (1968): 18–29.

Aid and Neocolonialism

As a group, the studies listed below present the argument that economic development "aid" and the expansion of multinational corporations into third world regions are major contributing factors to the failure of third world countries to initiate self-sustaining, self-reliant economic growth, agricultural and industrial. Aid is used by developed countries primarily to further their political, economic, and military goals while multinational corporations are, by definition, interested in profit. The needs of the agricultural sector as a whole have frequently been ignored and now, even with the renewed emphasis on agricultural development and reaching "the poorest of the poor," the welfare of the smallholder and the landless or near-landless are rarely advanced by the intervention of aid agencies or multinational corporations.

Books and Monographs

Recommended studies include Franke and Chasin, Khan, Feder, Davis, George, Ledogar, the monograph by the Institute for Food and Development Policy Staff (entry 1607), and the volume edited by Byres. Also of relevance are pages 7–13 of entry 281.

1599. Billaz, René. *La Recherche Agronomique en Afrique de l'Ouest Francophone Fait-Elle Fausse Route?* Paris: Institut de Recherche et d'Application des Méthodes de Développement, 1973.

1600. Byres, T. J., ed. *Foreign Resources and Economic Development: A Symposium on the Report of the Pearson Commission.* London: Cass, 1972.

1601. Davis, L. Harlan. *United States Assistance to Agriculture in Latin America Through the Agency for International Development.* LTC no. 71. Madison: Land Tenure Center, University of Wisconsin, June 1970.

1602. DeMarco, Susan, and Sechler, Susan. *The Fields Have Turned Brown: Four Essays on World Hunger.* Washington, D. C.: Agribusiness Accountability Project, c. 1975.

1603. Feder, Ernest. *Strawberry Imperialism: An Enquiry into the Mechanisms of Dependency in Mexican Agriculture.* The Hague: Institute of Social Studies, 1977.

1604. Franke, Richard W., and Chasin, Barbara H. *Seeds of Famine: Ecological Destruction and the Development Dilemma in the West African Sahel.* Montclair, N. J.: Allanheld, Osmum, 1980.

1605. George, Susan. *Feeding the Few: Corporate Control of Food.* Washington, D. C.: Institute for Policy Studies, 1979. (Part I is also available, in a somewhat revised form, as "Le Tiers-Monde Face à Ses Riches Clients." *Le Monde Diplomatique* (March 1979): 19–20.)

1606. Goldberg, Ray A., project director. *Agribusiness Management for Developing Countries with Special Reference to the Central American Fruit, Vegetable and Floriculture Export Industries.* Cambridge, Mass.: Agribusiness Program, School of Business Administration, c. 1974.

1607. Institute for Food and Development Policy Staff. *The Aid Debate: Assessing the Impact of U. S. Foreign Assistance and the World Bank.* Working Paper no. 1. San Francisco: Institute for Food and Development Policy, January 1979.

1608. Khan, Akhter Hameed. *Ten Decades of Rural Development: Lessons from India.* MSU Rural Development Paper no. 1. East Lansing: Department of Agricultural Economics, Michigan State University, 1978.

1609. Ledogar, Robert J. *Hungry for Profits: U. S. Food & Drug Multinationals in Latin America.* New York: IDOC/North America, 1975.

1610. Lipton, Michael, ed. *Rural Poverty and Agribusiness: Conference Proceedings.* Discussion Paper 104. Brighton, UK: Institute of Development Studies, University of Sussex, 1977.

1611. Mende, Tibor. *From Aid to Re-Colonization, Lessons of a Failure.* New York: Pantheon, 1973.

1612. Weissman, Steve, et al. *The Trojan Horse.* San Francisco: Ramparts, 1974.

Articles

Recommended articles include Ball, Feder, Flood, Meillassoux, Streeten, Rudra, and Sterling. Chapter 7 of *How the Other Half Dies* (entry 1887) deals with agribusiness.

1613. Adams, Dale W. "What Can Underdeveloped Countries Expect From Foreign Aid to Agriculture: Case Study. Brazil—1950–1970." *Inter-American Economic Affairs* 25 (Summer 1971): 47–63.

1614. Ball, Nicole. "Drought and Dependence in the Sahel." *International Journal of Health Services* 8:2 (1978): 271–298.

1615. ______. "The Myth of the Natural Disaster." *The Ecologist* 5 (December 1975): 368–371.

1616. Burback, Roger, and Flynn, Patricia. "Agribusiness Targets Latin America." *NACLA Report on the Americas* 12 (January–February 1978): 2–36.

1617. Colin, Roland. "Politique de Participation et Développement Technologique." *Développement et Civilisations* nos. 49–50 (1972): 11–18.

1618. Feder, Ernest. "Agribusiness in Underdeveloped Agricultures." *Economic and Political Weekly* 11 (17 July 1976): 1065–1080.

1619. ______. "How Agribusiness Operates in Underdeveloped Agricultures." *Development and Change* 7 (October 1976): 413–443.

1620. Flood, Glynn. "Nomadism and its Future: The 'Afar.'" *RAIN: Royal Anthropological Institute News* no. 6 (January–February 1975): 5–9.

1621. Franco, Marco. "La Rentabilité, Critère du Développement Rural en Afrique?" *Revue Tiers-Monde* 19 (January–March 1978): 139–148.

1622. Goldsmith, Edward. "The Fallacy of Triage." *The Ecologist* 6 (May 1976): 124–127.

1623. Gordon, Victor. "Aid—The Arch Enemy." *The Ecologist* 6 (May 1976): 123–124.

1624. Grossman, Rachael, and Siegel, Lenny. "Weyerhaeuser in Indonesia." *Pacific Research* 9 (November–December 1977): 1–12.

1625. Meillassoux, Claude. "Is the Sahel Famine Good Business?" *Review of African Political Economy* no. 1 (August–November 1974): 27–33.

1626. Mukhopadhyay, Asim. "Bangladesh: The Economic Millstone of Foreign Aid." *Economic and Political Weekly* 13 (28 October 1978): 1797–1799.

1627. North American Congress on Latin America (NACLA). "Del Monte: Bitter Fruits." *NACLA's Latin America and Empire Report* 10 (September 1976).

1628. ______. "Harvest of Anger: Agro-Imperialism in Mexico's Northwest." *NACLA's Latin America and Empire Report* 10 (July–August 1976): 2–30.

1629. Petras, James F., and La Porte, Robert, Jr. "Part Four: The United States and Socio-Political Change in Latin America." *Cultivating Revolution: The United States and Agrarian Reform in Latin America.* New York: Random House, 1971.

1630. Roux, Bernard. "Expansion du Capitalisme et Développement du Sous-Développement: L'Intégration de l'Amérique Centrale au Marché Mondiale de la Viande Bovine." *Revue Tiers-Monde* 16 (April–June 1975): 355–380.

1631. Rudra, Ashok. "New Urgency About Aid." *Economic and Political Weekly* 5 (8 August 1970): 1341, 1343–1345.

1632. Shankman, Paul. "A Forestry Scheme in Samoa." *Natural History* (October 1975): 60–69.

1633. Sinha, Radha. "Agribusiness: A Nuisance in Every Respect?" *Mazingira* nos. 3–4 (1977): 16–23.

1634. Sterling, Claire. "Nepal." *Atlantic* (October 1976): 14–25.

1635. Streeten, Paul. "A Primer for Aid Recipients." *Economic and Political Weekly* 14 (23 June 1979): 1042–1044.

1636. Swift, Jeremy. "Desertification and Man in the Sahel." *Africa Development* 1 (September 1976): 1–8.

1637. Tobis, David. "United Fruit is Not Chiquita." *NACLA's Newsletter* 5 (October 1971): 7–15.

1638. Wade, Nicholas. "Sahelian Drought: No Victory for Western Aid." *Science* 185 (19 July 1974): 234–237.

1639. Wallerstein, Immanuel. "Rural Economy in Modern World-Society." *Studies in Comparative Interntional Development* 12 (Spring 1977): 29–40.

1640. Wilson, Ernest J., III. "The Energy Crisis and African Underdevelopment." *Africa Today* 22 (October–December 1975): 11–37.

Ecology and Resources

Both capitalist and socialist-communist economic systems have tended to assume that mankind can prove its ascendency over nature through the mastery of technological processes. Both seek to shape the natural world to meet the perceived material needs of human societies. The works in this section demonstrate that the natural environment is not infinitely malleable and that a failure to recognize and act in accordance with ecological constraints will inevitably lead to disaster. The items included here are, however, generally less political than the ones in the preceeding section. Works discussing the links between environmental degradation and the progressive integration of the third world into the dominant economic system are found in the preceeding section (for example, entries 1604, 1614, 1615, 1620, 1625, and 1634).

Books and Monographs

The books by Borgstrom and Eckholm (entry 1645) and the monographs put out by the Worldwatch Institute (entries 1643, 1646, and 1647) are useful introductions for the general reader. The book by Jacks and Whyte is also for the general reader and demonstrates that human mismanagement of the ecology is not a recent phenomenon. Readers should not be deterred by the authors' racial biases as there is a good deal of interesting information contained in this volume. In fact, in a number of cases (when discussing Kenya for example), Jacks and Whyte demonstrate that many ecological problems had their roots in, or were exacerbated by, colonial patterns of land use. The ecological consequences of colonial land use is also the theme of entry 1313.

The book edited by Glantz is, despite its title, largely concerned with environmental degradation in Africa. The volume by Myers deals largely with the degradation of tropical forest zones. The *World Conservation Strategy* (entry 1654) outlines steps that should be taken to combat such ecological problems as deforestation, overfishing, soil erosion, desertification.

Other recommended studies are Farvar and Milton, Pimentel, and Rapp. *Beyond the Green Revolution* (entry 418) is also of relevance to this topic.

1641. Allaby, Michael. *Who Will Eat? The World Food Problem — Can We Solve It?* London: Stacey, 1972.

1642. Borgstrom, Georg. *Too Many: A Study of Earth's Biological Limitations.* New York: Macmillan, 1969.

1643. Brown, Lester. *The World Loss of Cropland.* Worldwatch Paper 24. Washington, D. C.: Worldwatch Institute, 1978.

1644. Dahl, Gudrun, and Hjort, Anders. *Pastoral Change and the Role of Drought.* Sarec Report R2:1979. Stockholm: Swedish Agency for Research Cooperation with Developing Countries, 1979. (Contains a useful short bibliography.)

1645. Eckholm, Erik P. *Losing Ground: Environmental Stress and World Food Prospects.* New York: Norton, 1976.

1646. ______. *The Other Energy Crisis: Firewood.* Worldwatch Paper 1. Washington, D. C.: Worldwatch Institute, 1975. (Excerpted in *The Ecologist* 6 (March–April 1976): 80–86.)

1647. Eckholm, Erik P., and Brown, Lester R. *Spreading Deserts—The Hand of Man.* Worldwatch Paper 13. Washington, D. C.: Worldwatch Institute, August 1977.

1648. Farvar, Taghi, and Milton, John, eds. *The Careless Technology: Ecology and International Development. The Record.* Garden City, N. Y.: Natural History, 1972. (Excerpts appeared under the title "The Unforeseen International Ecological Boomerang" (Special Supplement). *Natural History* (February 1969): 42–72.)

1649. Furon, Raymond. *L'Erosion du Sol.* Paris: Payot, 1947.

1650. Glantz, Michael H., ed. *Desertification: Environmental Degradation in and Around Arid Lands.* Boulder, Colo.: Westview, 1977.

1651. Guerrin, André. *Humanité et Subsistances.* Neuchâtel: Editions du Griffon, 1957. (Pages 132–238 are relevant.)

1652. Henriksen, G. *Economic Growth and Ecological Balance: Problems of Development in Turkana.* Bergen: University of Bergen, 1974.

1653. Horowitz, Michael M., ed. *Colloquium on the Effects of Drought on the Productive Strategies of Sudano-Sahelian Herdsmen and Farmers.* Binghamton, N. Y.: Institute for Development Anthropology, September 1976.

1654. International Union for Conservation of Nature and Natural Resources, World Wildlife Fund, and United Nations Environment Programme. *World Conservation Strategy.* Gland, Switzerland: IUCN, 1980.

1655. Jacks, G. V., and Whyte, R. O. *Vanishing Lands: A World Survey of Soil Erosion.* New York: Doubleday, Doran, 1939.

1656. Kamarck, Andrew M. *The Tropics and Economic Development: A Provocative Inquiry into the Poverty of Nations.* Baltimore, Md.: Johns Hopkins University Press, 1976.

1657. Myers, Norman. *The Sinking Ark.* New York: Pergamon, 1979.

1658. National Academy of Sciences. *Nitrates: An Environmental Assessment (Scientific and Technical Assessments of Environmental Pollutants).* Washington, D. C.: Panel on Nitrates, Environmental Studies Board, NAS, 1978.

1659. Newman, James L., ed. *Drought, Famine, and Population Movements in Africa.* Eastern Africa Series 17. Syracuse, N. Y.: Maxwell School of Citizenship and Public Affairs, Syracuse University, 1975.

1660. Osborn, Fairfield. *Our Plundered Planet.* Boston: Little, Brown, 1948.

1661. Oyer, Edwin B. *Constraints on Increasing Agricultural Production in the Tropics: Research and Implementation Needs.* Grant Report to the Science and Technology Policy Office of the National Science Foundation. Ithaca, N. Y.: New York State College of Agriculture and Life Sciences, Cornell University, 1976.

1662. Phillips, John. *Agriculture and Ecology in Africa.* New York: Praeger, 1960.

1663. Pimentel, David. *Energy Needs, Uses, and Resources in the Food Systems of Developing Countries.* Report 78–2. Ithaca, N. Y.: Department of Entomology & Section of Ecology and Systematics, Cornell University, June 1978.

1664. ______. *Energy Use in World Food Production.* Environmental Biology Report 74–1. Ithaca, N. Y.: Cornell University, 1974.

1665. Program for International Development and Social Change. *International Cooperation to Combat Desertification: Demographic, Social and Behavioral Review.* 3rd draft. Worcester, Mass.: Clark University, 1976.

1666. Rapp, Anders. *A Review of Desertization in Africa: Water, Vegetation, and Man.* Stockholm: Secretariat for International Ecology, Sweden, 1974.

1667. Secretariat of the United Nations Conference on Desertification. *Desertification: Its Causes and Consequences.* Oxford and New York: Pergamon, 1977.

1668. Stewart, P. J. *Algerian Peasantry at the Crossroads: Fight Erosion or Migrate.* IDS Discussion Paper 69. Brighton, UK: Institute of Development Studies, University of Sussex, 1975.

1669. Thompson, Louis M. *Weather Variability and the Need for a Food Reserve.* CAED Report 26. Ames: Iowa State University, 1966.

1670. United States Agency for International Development. *Desert Encroachment on Arable Lands: Significance, Causes and Control.* TA/OST 72–10. Washington, D. C.: Office of Science and Technology, August 1972.

1671. ———. *Environmental Problems in Selected Developing Countries (Preliminary Survey).* TA/OST 71–2. Washington, D. C.: Office of Science and Technology, July 1971.

Articles

The articles by Leach and by Pimentel et al discuss the problems that are likely to arise out of developing countries' widespread adoption of the sort of energy-intensive food production methods on which agriculture in the industrialized countries is dependent. Stressing the importance of using locally available energy sources, Leach considers the role to be played by solar energy and biogas generation. Pimentel et al. point out that in 1973, energy equivalent to 80 gallons of gasoline was necessary to produce one acre of corn in the US. They conclude that the adoption of high-energy, Green Revolution technology could decrease, rather than increase, world food stability. The article by David and Marcia Pimentel deals solely with the US but is relevant nonetheless.

Other recommended articles include Ormerod, Eckholm (entry 1687), Enloe & Phoenix, Harris, Jahoda and O'Hearn, Janzen, Lowdermilk, Rapp, and Biswas and Biswas.

1672. Ashish, Sri Madhava. "Agricultural Economy of Humaon Hills: Threat of Ecological Disaster." *Economic and Political Weekly* 14 (23 June 1979): 1058–1064.

1673. Baier, Stephen, and King, David J. "Drought and the Development of Sahelian Economies: A Case Study of Hausa-Tuareg Interdependence." *LTC Newsletter* no. 45 (July–September 1974): 11–21.

1674. Ball, Nicole. "Deserts Bloom . . . and Wither." *The Ecologist Quarterly* no. 1 (Spring 1978): 20–31.

1675. Biswas, Margaret R., and Biswas, Asit K. "Environment Impacts of Increasing the World's Food Production." *Agriculture and Environment* 2 (December 1975): 291–309.

1676. Brown, Lester R. "Human Food Production as a Process in the Biosphere." *Scientific American* 223 (September 1970): 160–170.

1677. Campbell, Ian. "Human Mismanagement as a Major Factor in the Sahelian Drought Tragedy." *The Ecologist* 4 (June 1974): 164–169.

1678. Campbell, Robert. "A Timely Reprieve or a Death Sentence for the Amazon" *Smithsonian* (October 1977): 100–110.

1679. Candell, Arthur. "Haiti is an Object Lesson in Ecological Disaster." *World Environment Report,* September 1975.

1680. "Case Studies in Ecological Results of Development Activities." *Development Digest* 9 (January 1971): 25–33.

1681. Conway, Gordon. "Current Environmental Priorities for the Third World." *Institute of Development Studies Bulletin* 4 (December 1971): 4–11.

1682. Dagg, Matthew, and Gwynne, Michael. "Water Supplies in Less Developed Countries: Some Fallacies." *Institute of Development Studies Bulletin* 2 (October 1969): 35–37.

1683. Dahlberg, Kenneth A. "Ecological Effects of Current Development Processes in Less Developed Countries," pp. 71–91. In *Human Ecology and World Development.* Eds. Anthony Vann and Paul Rogers. New York and London: Plenum, 1974.

1684. De Bivort, L. H. "World Agricultural Development Strategy and the Environment." *Agriculture and Environment* 2 (June 1975): 1–14.

1685. Dennison, E. B. "Problems of Reclaiming Certain Infertile Areas in the Sudan Zone of Northern Nigeria (Kano Province)." *World Crops* 8 (April 1956): 131–133, 136.

1686. "Drought in Africa" (Issue Title). *Savanna* 2 (December 1973): 97–164.

1687. Eckholm, Erik P. "Desertification: A World Problem." *Ambio* 4:4 (1975): 137–145.

1688. ______. "The Politics of Soil Conservation." *The Ecologist* 6 (February 1976): 54–59.

1689. El-Baz, Farouk. "Expanding Desert Creates Grim Beauty But Also Threatens Crucial Crop Land." *Smithsonian* (June 1977): 35–40.

1690. Elderidge, Edward F. "Irrigation as a Source of Water Pollution." *Journal of the Water Pollution Control Federation* 35 (May 1963): 614–625.

1691. Enloe, Cynthia, and Phoenix, Michael. "Reforestation in the Philippines: Case Study no. 1," pp. 1–27. In *Workshops in Techniques of Environmental Investigation: Training Course for Preparing Initial Environmental Examinations.* Worcester, Mass.: Program for International Development, Clark University, February 1978.

1692. Floyd, Barry. "Soil Erosion and Deterioration in Eastern Nigeria." *The Nigerian Geographical Journal* 8 (June 1965): 33–44.

1693. Glantz, Michael H. "The Sahelian Drought: No Victory for Anyone." *Africa Today* 22 (April–June 1975): 57–61.

1694. Grant, James P. "Energy Shock and the Development Process," pp. 31–50. In *The U.S. and the Developing World. Agenda for Action, 1974.* Ed. James W. Howe. New York: Praeger, 1974.

1695. Grigg, David B. "Ecological Problems in Agricultural Development," pp. 155–281. In his *The Harsh Lands: A Study in Agricultural Development.* New York: St. Martin's, 1970.

1696. Harris, M. "The Human Strategy: The Withering Green Revolution." *Natural History* (March 1973): 20–22.

1697. Hewitt, Kenneth. "Earthquake Hazards in the Mountains." *Natural History* (May 1976): 30–37.

1698. "How Much Good Land is Left?" *Ceres* no. 64 (July–August 1978): 13–16.

1699. Jahoda, John C., and O'Hearn, Donna L. "The Reluctant Amazon Basin." *Environment* 17 (October 1975): 16–20, 25–30.

1700. Janzen, Daniel H. "The Uncertain Future of the Tropics." *Natural History* (November 1972): 80–89.

1701. Jodha, N. S. "A Strategy for Dry Land Agriculture." *Economic and Political Weekly* 7 (25 March 1972): A7–A12.

1702. ———. "Drought and Scarcity in the Rajasthan Desert." *Economic and Political Weekly* 4 (19 April 1969): 699–703.

1703. ———. "Effectiveness of Farmers' Adjustments to Risk." *Economic and Political Weekly* 13 (24 June 1978): A38–A48.

1704. Keylitz, N. "World Resources and the World Middle Class." *Scientific American* 235 (July 1976): 28–35.

1705. Kneese, Allen V. "Development and Environment." *RFF Reprint Series.* no. 161. Washington, D. C.: Resources for the Future, 1979.

1706. Lardner, G. E. A. "Africa is Still in Time." *Ceres* no. 20 (March–April 1971): 27–30.

1707. Leach, Gerald. "Energy and Food Production." *Food Policy* (November 1975): 62–73.

1708. Lees, Susan H. "Oxaca's Spiralling Race for Water." *The Ecologist* 6 (January 1976): 20–23.

1709. Long, Frank. "A Major Obstacle." *Mazingira* no. 5 (1978): 82–86.

1710. Lowdermilk, Walter C. "History of Civilization Without Soil and Water Management Planning." In *The Proceedings of the International Seminar on Soil and Water Utilization.* Brookings: South Dakota State University, 1962.

1711. Omerod, W. E. "Drought in the Sahel: The Debit Side of Development?" *Tropical Doctor* (October 1976): 163–167.

1712. ______. "Ecological Effect of Control of African Trypanosomiasis." *Science* 191 (27 February 1976): 815–821.

1713. ______. "The Relationship Between Economic Development and Ecological Degradation: How Degradation has Occurred in West Africa and How Its Progress Might be Halted." *Journal of Arid Environments* 1 (1978): 357–379.

1714. Openshaw, Keith. "Wood Fuels the Developing World." *New Scientist* 61 (31 January 1974): 271–272.

1715. Pimentel, David, et al. "Food Production and the Energy Crisis." *Science* 182 (2 November 1973): 443–449.

1716. Pimentel, David and Marcia. "Counting the Kilocalories." *Ceres* no. 59 (September–October 1977): 17–21.

1717. Rapp, Anders. "Soil Erosion and Sedimentation in Tanzania and Lesotho." *Ambio* 4:4 (1975): 154–163.

1718. Ray, S. K. "Weather and Reserve Stocks of Foodgrains." *Economic and Political Weekly* 6 (25 September 1971): A131–A142.

1719. Ross, John E., and Bryson, Reid A. "The Potential For a World Food Crisis." *LTC Newsletter* no. 40 (April–June 1973): 1–4.

1720. Sanchez, P. A., and Buol, S. W. "Soils of the Tropics and the World Food Crisis." In *Food: Politics, Economics, Nutrition and Research.* Washington, D. C.: American Association for the Advancement of Science, 1975.

1721. Seaman, J.; Holt, J.; and Murlis, J. "An Enquiry into the Drought Situation in Upper Volta." *The Lancet* (6 October 1973): 774–778.

1722. "Time to Call a Halt" (Issue Title). *Ceres* no. 56 (March–April 1977).

1723. Tinker, Jon. "Sudan Challenges the Sand-Dragon." *New Scientist* 73 (24 February 1977): 448–450.

1724. Walls, James. "Man's Desert: The Mismanaged Earth." *Mazingira* no. 2 (1977): 18–25.

1725. Watt, Kenneth E. F. "Man's Efficient Rush Toward Deadly Dullness." *Natural History* (February 1972): 74–77, 80, 82.

1726. White, Gilbert F. "Flood Damage Prevention Policies." *Natural Resources Forum* 1:1 (1971): 39–45.

Agricultural Credit

Access to credit is crucial if farmers are to make improvements in their production methods that will lead to higher output. In particular, the adoption of Green Revolution technology—with its seed, water, and fertilizer requirements—has been to some degree dependent on a farmer's access to credit. In general, the larger farmers have benefited most from rural credit schemes. They are the best "credit risks," less likely in the eyes of the provider of credit to default than small farmers with relatively few assets. The small farmers have tended to be dependent on local moneylenders, whose interest rates are higher than those of formal credit schemes. The new interest in reducing rural poverty has led to a corresponding interest in channeling credit to smallholders. How successful such smallholder-oriented schemes will prove to be in the long term remains to be seen, for their success would clearly alter rural power relations in many parts of the third world.

General

As an introduction to the topic of agricultural credit, the monograph by Blair is suggested. Bhat finds that where credit has failed to promote agricultural development, it has often been diverted to purposes other than those for which it was originally granted. Sheira discusses aspects of agricultural credit programs that are designed to change land-tenure conditions so that they will act as a stimulus to agricultural development. The articles by Dantwala and Datta on rural banks in India should be read together.

1727. Adams, Dale W. "Agricultural Credit in Latin America: A Critical Review of External Funding Policy." *American Journal of Agricultural Economics* 53 (May 1971).

1728. "Agricultural Credit" (Section Title). *Development Digest* 9 (April 1971): 49–86.

1729. *Agricultural Credit for Development.* World Conference on Credit for Farmers in Developing Countries, Rome, 14–21 October 1975. Milan: Cassa di Risparmio delle Provincie Lombarde, 1975.

1730. Amore, Giordano dell'. *Agricultural Credit in African Countries.* Milan: Cassa di Risparmio delle Provincie Lombarde, 1973.

1731. Belloncle, Guy. "Problèmes du Crédit Coopératif à l'Agriculture Africaine Traditionelle." *Archives Internationales de Sociologie de la Coopération* no. 19 (January–June 1966): 19–43.

1732. ———. *Problèmes Généraux du Crédit Agricole dans les Pays d'Afrique d'Expression Française au Sud du Sahara.* Rome: Food and Agriculture Organization, 1968.

1733. Bhat, M. L. "Diversion of Long-Term Agricultural Finance: A Study of Past Trends and Future Strategy." *Economic and Political Weekly* 6 (9 October 1971): 2151–2158.

1734. Blair, Harry W. *The Political Economy of Distributing Agricultural Credit and Benefits.* Occasional Paper no. 3. Ithaca, N. Y.: Rural Development Committee, Center for International Studies, Cornell University, c. 1975.

1735. Dantwala, M. L. "Regional Rural Banks. A Clarification." *Economic and Political Weekly* 13 (21 October 1978): 1776–1777.

1736. Datey, C. D. *The Financial Cost of Agricultural Credit: A Case Study of Indian Experience.* Working Paper 296. Washington, D. C.: World Bank, c. 1978.

1737. Datta, Bhabatosh. "Regional Rural Banks." *Economic and Political Weekly* 13 (9 September 1978): 1553–1556.

1738. Desai, B. M. "Costs of Operations in Agricultural Financing by Formal Agencies." *Economic and Political Weekly* 13 (24 June 1978): A70–A74.

1739. Desai, B. M., and Desai, D. K. "Is Inadequacy of Institutional Credit a Problem in Changing Agriculture?" *Economic and Political Weekly* 5 (26 September 1970): A101–A110.

1740. Food and Agriculture Organization. *Credit for Agriculture in the Developing World.* Rome: 1976.

1741. ———. *New Approach to Agricultural Credit.* 3rd ed. FAO Agricultural Development Paper no. 77. Rome: 1971. (Based on experiences of Brazil, Mexico, and India.)

1742. Harrison, Alan. *Agricultural Credit in Botswana.* Development Studies no. 4. Reading, UK: Department of Agricultural Economics, University of Reading, December 1967.

1743. Harvey, Charles. "Rural Credit in Zambia." *Development and Change* 6 (April 1975): 89–105.

1744. Lelart, Michel. "L'Evolution des Coopératives Agricoles de Crédit en Thailande." *Communauté: Archives Internationales de la Sociologie de la Coopération et du Développement* no. 40 (July–December 1976): 97–124.

1745. Narasimhan, M. "National Agricultural Credit Policy." *Economic and Political Weekly* 6 (9 January 1971): 97–102.

1746. National Council of Applied Economic Research. *Credit Requirements for Agriculture.* New Delhi: 1974.

1747. Ohio State University-Columbus, Capital Formation and Technological Change Project. *Agricultural Credit and Rural Savings.* Washington, D. C.: US Agency for International Development, 1972.

1748. Onchan, Tongroj. *Agricultural Credit Problems in Thailand.* National Seminar Report no. 1. New York: The Agricultural Development Council, 1971.

1749. Paul, Arthur. "Credit's Role in Improving Agriculture." *Asia Foundation Program Bulletin* no. 36 (September 1965).

1750. Reserve Bank of India. *Regional Rural Bank: Report of the Review Committee.* Bombay: 1978.

1751. Schmandt, L. *Le Crédit Agricole dans les Pays en Voie de Développement.* Paris: Caisse Centrale de Coopération Economique, 1964.

1752. Sheira, A. Z. "Credit Aspects of Land Reform in Africa." *Agricultural Economics Bulletin for Africa* no. 7 (September 1965): 36–53.

1753 Sheth, N. R., and Shah, B. G. "Personnel Management for Rural Banks." *Economic and Political Weekly* 10 (17 May 1975): 802–806.

1754. Zalla, Tom. *A Proposed Structure for the Medium-Term Credit Program in the Eastern ORD of Upper Volta.* Working Paper no. 10. East Lansing: African Rural Economy Program, Michigan State University, February 1976.

Credit and the Smallholder

Ames's study of large farmers in India (entry 1758) leads him to conclude that the larger landholders have controlled credit cooperatives from their inception and have been the primary beneficiaries of the credit and inputs (largely fertilizer) provided by these organizations. Partly in recognition of this problem, the Small Farmers' Development Agency (SFDA) was set up in Mysore to channel credit to the small farmer. The SFDA had not been taken over by the larger farmers at the time of Ames's study in 1975, but he suggested that, if government supervision of the SFDA were to be relaxed, such a take over might well occur. The first eight years of SFDA activity (1971–1979) are reviewed in entry 927. A certain degree of success is noted and problems confronting the SFDA are analyzed.

Gonzales-Vega looks at the performance of small, decentralized bank offices that provide credit to small farmers in rural Costa Rica. He concludes that they have been relatively successful, particularly when compared to other small farmer credit programs in other developing countries. Nonetheless, Gonzales-Vega concludes that more farmers might have been reached had some changes in policies and methods of functioning been implemented.

Rao and Acharlu state that in India the tendency has been to concentrate on providing short- to medium-term credit. The provision of long-term credit, particularly to small farmers, has been somewhat neglected. Vasthoff discusses the need to accompany the provision of credit to small farmers with advice and supervision. For example, he found that loans for ploughing or planting in East Africa have generally not been successful because farmers are unfamiliar with the new methods of cultivation which the loans have enabled them to employ.

1755. Adams, Dale W.; Davis, L. Harlan; and Bettis, Lee. "Is Inexpensive Credit a Bargain for Small Farmers? The Recent Brazilian Experience." *Inter-American Economic Affairs* 26 (Summer 1972): 47–58. (Also available as Occasional Paper no. 58. Columbus: Ohio State University, January 1972.)

1756. Adams, Dale W., and Tommy, Joseph L. *Changes in Small Farmer Credit Use in Southern Brazil, 1965–1969*. Occasional Paper no. 61. Columbus: Ohio State University, February 1972.

1757. Ames, Glenn W. "Small Farmer Associations and Development Programs: Case of the Dominican Republic." *Land Tenure Center Newsletter* no. 52 (April–June 1976): 14–21.

1758. ———. "Who Benefits from Credit Programs and Who Repays? Large Farmers in Village-Level Cooperatives in Mysore State, India." *Land Tenure Center Newsletter* no. 47 (January–March 1975): 23–32.

1759. Bardhan, Pranab, and Rudra, Ashok. "Interlinkage of Land, Labour and Credit Relations: An Analysis of Village Survey Data in East India." *Economic and Political Weekly* 13:6–7 (Annual Number 1978): 367–384.

1760. Beyene, Michael. *An Analysis of CADU Credit Progamme 1971/72–1972/73*. CADU Publication no. 92. Asella, Ethiopia: Chilalo Agricultural Development Unit, January 1973.

1761. Brown, Albert L. "The Agricultural Credit Project of the Agricultural Sector Program of Costa Rica." *A. I. D. Spring Review of Small Farm Credit* 2:SR 102 (February 1973): 1–50.

1762. "Credit for Small Farmers." *Economic and Political Weekly* 4 (9 August 1969): 1293–1294.

1763. Donald, Gordon. *Credit for Small Farmers in Developing Countries.* Boulder, Colo.: Westview, 1976.

1764. Felstehausen, Herman. "The Puebla Project: An Additional Perspective." *LTC Newsletter* no. 39 (January–March 1973): 6–8.

1765. Gillette, Cynthia, and Uphoff, Norman. *Small Farmer Credit—Cultural and Social Factors Affecting Small Farmer Participation in Formal Credit Programs.* Occasional Paper no. 3. Ithaca, N. Y.: Rural Development Committee, Center for International Studies, Cornell University, c. 1975.

1766. Gonzales-Vega, Claudio. "Small Farmer Credit in Costa Rica: The Junta Rurales." *A. I. D. Spring Review of Small Farm Credit* 2:SR 102 (February 1973).

1767. Ijere, M. O. "Credit Infusion as Small Farmer Development Strategy: The NTC-Nsukka Project." *The Developing Economies* 14 (March 1976): 72–84.

1768. "Indebtedness Among the Poor." *Economic and Political Weekly* 11 (17 July 1976): 1057–1058.

1769. Jodha, N. S. "Land-Based Credit Policies and Investment Prospects for Small Farmers." *Economic and Political Weekly* 6 (25 September 1971): A143–A148.

1770. Kifle, Henock. *An Analysis of the CADU Credit Programme 1968/69–1970/71 and Its Impact on Income Distribution.* CADU Publication no. 66. Addis Ababa: Chilalo Agricultural Development Unit, August 1971.

1771. Krul, Nicholas G. "But They Still Prefer the Money-Lender." *Ceres* no. 10 (July–August 1969): 44–47.

1772. Rao, R. M. Mohana, and Archarlu, P. Jagannadha. "Small Farmer and Long-Term Finance." *Economic and Political Weekly* 7 (24 June 1972): A83–A86.

1773. Soles, Roger E. *Agricultural Credit in Latin America: Persistent Problems and Potential Promises.* LTC no. 96. Madison: Land Tenure Center, University of Wisconsin, December 1973.

1774. Stickley, T., and Hayek, M. *Small Farmer Credit in Jordan.* Beirut: Agricultural Economics, Extension and Rural Sociology Department, Faculty of Agriculture, American University of Beirut, 1972.

1775. Thirsk, Wayne Robert. *Rural Credit and Income Distribution in Colombia.* Paper no. 51. Houston, Texas: Program of Development Studies, William Marsh Rice University, 1974.

1776. Vasthoff, Josef. *Small Farm Credit and Development. Some Experiences in East Africa with Special Reference to Kenya.* Afrika-Studien no. 33. Munich: Weltforum Verlag, 1968.

1777. Wells, R. J. G. "An Input Credit Programme for Small Farmers in West Malaysia." *Journal of Administration Overseas* 17 (January 1978): 4–16.

Bureaucratic and Political Constraints

It would be wrong to see external influences as the sole, or even the major, constraint on agricultural development. Government officials and other third world elites have their own interests which may or may not coincide with those of foreign governments and corporations. The entries in this section look at the domestic component of underdevelopment in the rural sector.

The book by Lipton identifies the neglect of the rural sector, in favor of the urban-industrial sector, as the primary cause of third world poverty. However, Hanumantha Rao (entry 1793) points out that by opposing the interests of "the rural sector" to those of "the urban-industrial sector," Lipton has created a false dichotomy. The interests of the rural elite are not synonymous with those of the mass of the rural population, as Lipton has assumed them to be. Hanumantha Rao argues that basing a rural development strategy on that assumption, as Lipton has done, can only lead to the strengthening of disparities between rich and poor in rural areas.

The power of the large farmers in India to influence and formulate policies on land reform, taxation, credit, and prices that are to their own advantage is the subject of Hanumantha Rao's article (entry 1792). These large farmers, unlike the zamindars, are rooted in the villages and have considerable influence over the peasantry. They constitute a social base and a "vote bank" for various political parties. They exert considerable political power at the state level in India.

Botera Gonzalez discusses how agrarian reform in Colombia has come to benefit the large landowners. Blair discusses particular bureaucratic factors which have biased the operation of the Comilla project in Bangladesh in favor of the larger farmers. These factors have operated independently of class relations and Blair argues that they would bias any rural development program in favor of rural elites, whatever the social context.

Valier discusses the political and bureaucratic decisions that have created problems in Cuba's agricultural and industrial sectors. Krotz describes how the Mexican government has used rural cooperatives to prevent the political mobilization of the peasantry rather than to promote development, thus stifling the grass-roots initiative so necessary for the success of cooperatives. A good introduction to the political and bureaucratic constraints confronting agricultural development in Africa is found in McLoughlin.

Bhatt tells the story of how a tractor developed indigenously for small and medium farmers in north India had great difficulty in finding funding despite the official policy of encouraging the indigenous development of technology. This article is particularly recommended.

The articles by Barnett and by Muller outline some of the bureaucratic problems facing irrigation schemes in Sudan. Peasants have evolved more efficient and effective methods of irrigating, but bureaucrats refuse to accept, or even officially acknowledge, these innovations. This problem is also discussed in entry 2684.

Entries 2728 and 2729 discuss bureaucratic constraints on agricultural development in Tanzania. Chapter 3 of entry 475 considers the relationship between local elites, decentralization of authority, and greater popular participation. Part 2 of entry 1494 is also relevant.

1778. Ahmad, Saghir. *Class and Power in a Punjabi Village.* New York: Monthly Review, 1977.

1779. Ary, Gláucio. "The Web of Exploitation: State and Peasants in Latin America." *Studies in Comparative International Development* 12 (Fall 1977): 3–24.

1780. Barnett, Tony. "Why are Bureaucrats Slow Adapters? The Case of Water Management in the Gezira Scheme." *Sociologia Ruralis* 19:1 (1979): 60–70.

1781. Barraclough, Solon. "Rol de las Organizaciones Agrarias en Programas de Desarrollo Rural." *Desarrollo Rural en las Américas* 2:2 (1970): 161–180.

1782. Bates, Robert H. "The Politics of Rural Development: A Case Study from Central Africa." Pasadena: California Institute of Technology, c. 1975, mimeo. (Deals with Zambia)

1783. Beckford, George L. "Comparative Rural Systems, Development and Underdevelopment." *World Development* 2 (June 1974): 35–43.

1784. Bhatt, V. V. "Decision Making in the Public Sector: Case Study of Swaraj Tractor." *Economic and Political Weekly* 13 (27 May 1978): M30–M45.

1785. Blair, Harry W. "Rural Development, Class Structure and Bureaucracy in Bangladesh." *World Development* 6 (January 1978): 65–82.

1786. Botero Gonzalez, César. "La Réforme Agraire en Colombie." *Civilisations* 20:3 (1970): 336–344.

1787. Breman, Jan. *Patronage and Exploitation: Agrarian Relations in South Gujarat, India.* Berkeley: University of California Press, 1974.

1788. Burki, Shahid Javed. "Interest Group Involvement in West Pakistan's Rural Works Program." *Public Policy* 19 (Winter 1971): 167–206.

1789. Elliott, Charles, assisted by Françoise de Marsier. *Patterns of Poverty in the Third World: A Study of Social and Economic Stratification.* New York: Praeger, 1975. (Chapters 1–5, 13 are relevant.)

1790. Glantz, Michael H. "Man, State and the Environment: An Inquiry into Whether Solutions to Environmental Problems are Known but not Applied." Boulder, Colo.: Environmental and Societal Impact Group, National Center for Atmospheric Research, 1979, mimeo.

1791. Griffin, Keith. "Agrarian Policy: The Political and Economic Context." *World Development* 1 (November 1973): 1–11.

1792. Hanumantha Rao, C. H. "Socio-Political Factors and Agricultural Policies." *Economic and Political Weekly* 9:32–34 (Special Number 1974): 1285–1292.

1793. ______. "Urban vs Rural or Rich vs Poor?" *Economic and Political Weekly* 13 (7 October 1978): 1699–1702.

1794. Krotz, Esteban. "Las Cooperativas en el Campo Mexicano: Perspectivas." *Controversia* 1:3 (1977): 72–80.

1795. "Land Reform: Concealing the Surplus." *Economic and Political Weekly* 13 (1 July 1978): 1051–1052.

1796. Lipton, Michael. *Why Poor People Stay Poor: Urban Bias in World Development.* Cambridge, Mass.: Harvard University Press, 1977.

1797. McLoughlin, Peter F. M. "The Farmer, the Politician and the Bureaucrat: Local Government and Agricultural Development in Independent Africa." *African Studies Review* 15 (December 1972): 413–436.

1798. Mencher, Joan P. "Agrarian Relations in Two Rice Regions of Kerala." *Economic and Political Weekly* 13:6–7 (Annual Number 1978): 349–366.

1799. Muller, Mike. "Experts Cling to Water Myths." *New Scientist* 70 (24 June 1976): 692–693.

1800. Nalapat, M. D. "Irrigation Muddle." *Economic and Political Weekly* 13 (20 May 1978): 836–837.

1801. Oyugi, W. Ouma. *Bureaucracy and Rural Development in Africa.* IDS Discussion Paper D–133. Brighton, UK: Institute of Development Studies, University of Sussex, 1978.

1802. Rikken, G. *The Unequally Distributed Benefits of Rural Development Programs.* Manila: Asian Social Institute, 1976.

1803. Samoff, Joel and Rachel. "The Local Politics of Underdevelopment." *The African Review* 6:1 (1976): 69–97.

1804. Silva, José Gomes da. "Obstacles à une Réforme Agraire: Le Cas du Brésil." *Civilisations* 23–24:3–4 (1973–1974): 248–261.

1805. Valier, Jacques. "Cuba 1968–1971: Le Développement des Déformations Bureaucratiques et des Difficultés Economiques." *Critique de l'Economie Politique* no. 6 (January–March 1972): 112–141.

1806. Weinbaum, Marvin G. "Agricultural Development and Bureaucratic Politics in Pakistan." *Journal of South Asian and Middle Eastern Studies* 2 (Winter 1978): 42–62.

Part IV: Food

General

The general tenor of the works in this section is that the world food problem can be overcome, but only if certain measures are adopted: reduction of populations, more equitable distribution of land, more widespread use of "modern" agricultural techniques, more foreign aid, etc. However, as a whole, these studies do not take adequate account of the significant structural changes—economic, social, and political—that must take place in both industrialized and developing countries if those measures, or any others designed to reduce hunger, are to be successfully implemented.

Books and Monographs

The following studies are suggested as introductions to the subjects they cover: Allaby, the FAO's Fourth World Food Survey, the National Academy of Sciences' study of postharvest food losses, and the special issue of *Science* entitled "Food" (entry 1827). Two studies dealing specifically with the role of animals in the world food situation are Phillips and the conference report from the Rockefeller Foundation.

1807. Abeleson, Philip H. *Food: Politics, Economics, Nutrition and Research.* Washington, D. C.: American Association for the Advancement of Science, 1975.

1808. Allaby, Michael. *World Food Resources. Actual and Potential.* London: Applied Science, 1977.

1809. Amin, G. *Food Supply and Economic Development: With Special Reference to Egypt.* London: Cass, 1966.

1810. Aziz, Sartaj. *Hunger, Politics and Markets: The Real Issues in the World Food Crisis.* New York: New York University Press, 1975.

1811. Bergesen, Helge Ole. *Towards a Global Food Regime?* NUPI Rapport no. 3. Oslo: Norsk Utenrikspolitisk Institutt, November 1976. (See especially the section on the International Fund for Agricultural Development, pp. 63–78.)

1812. ———. *When Interdependence Doesn't Work: A Study in World Food Politics.* NUPI Rapport no. 34. Oslo: Norsk Utenrikspolitisk Institutt, August 1977.

1813. Blakeslee, Leroy L.; Heady, Earl O.; and Framingham, Charles F. *World Food Production, Demand and Trade.* Ames: Iowa State University Press, 1973.

1814. Borgstrom, Georg. *Focal Points: A Global Food Strategy.* New York: Macmillan, 1973.

1815. ———. *The Food and People Dilemma.* North Scituate, Mass.: Duxbury, 1973.

1816. Bourne, M. C. *Promising Avenues for Increased Efforts in Reducing Post Harvest Food Losses in Developing Countries.* PN–AAF–298. Washington, D. C.: US Agency for International Development, 1976.

1817. Brown, Lester R. *Man, Land and Food: Looking Ahead at World Food Needs.* Foreign Agricultural Economic Report no. 11. Washington, D. C.: US Department of Agriculture, 1963. (Chapters 8–10 are particularly relevant.)

1818. ———. *The Politics and Responsibility of the North American Breadbasket.* Worldwatch Paper no. 2. Washington, D. C.: Worldwatch Institute, 1975.

1819. Brown, Lester R., and Finsterbusch, Gail W. *Man and His Environment: Food.* New York: Harper and Row, 1972.

1820. Brown, Lester R., with Erik P. Eckholm. *By Bread Alone.* New York and Washington, D. C.: Praeger, 1974.

1821. Buringh, P.; Heemst, H. D. J. van; and Staring, G. J. *Computation of the Absolute Maximum Food Production of the World.* Wageningen, Holland: Department of Tropical Soil Sciences, Agricultural University, 1975.

1822. Burki, Shahid Javed, and Goering, T. J. *A Perspective on the Foodgrain Situation in the Poorest Countries.* Working Paper 251. Washington, D. C.: World Bank, 1977.

1823. Chou, Marylin. *World Food Prospects and Agricultural Potential.* Praeger Special Studies in International Economics and Development. New York: Praeger, 1977.

1824. Clark, Colin. *Starvation or Plenty?* New York: Taplinger, 1970.

1825. Drogat, Noel, S. J. *The Challenge of Hunger.* Trans. J. R. Kirwan. Westminster, Md.: Newman, 1962.

1826. Evans, Luther H., et al. *The Decade of Development: Problems and Issues.* Dobbs Ferry, N. Y.: Oceana, 1966. (Chapters 13 and 31 are relevant.)

1827. "Food" (Issue Title). *Science* 188 (9 May 1975): 501–653.

1828. Food and Agriculture Organization. *Food and Nutrition Strategies in National Development. Ninth Report of the Joint FAO/WHO*

Expert Committee on Nutrition. Rome, 11–20 December 1974. 2nd ed. FAO Nutrition Meetings Report Series no. 56. FAO Food and Nutrition Series no. 5. Rome: 1977.

1829. ______. *The Fourth World Food Survey.* F1359. Rome: 1977.

1830. ______. *The Stabilization of International Trade in Grains: An Assessment of Problems and Possible Solutions.* FAO Commodity Policy Studies no. 20. Rome: 1970.

1831. ______. *The World Rice Economy.* 2 vols. Commodity Bulletin Series no. 36. Rome: 1962–1963.

1832. FAO Staff Members. "Rice: An Economic and Agronomic Summary." *World Crops* 8 (August 1956): 299–302.

1833. *Food: One Tool in International Development.* Ames: Iowa State University Press, 1962.

1834. Garst, Jonathan. *No Need for Hunger.* New York: Random House, 1963.

1835. Hardin, Clifford M., ed. *Overcoming World Hunger.* Englewood Cliffs, N. J.: Prentice-Hall, 1969.

1836. Hopper, W. David. *The Politics of Food.* IDRC–100e. Ottawa: International Development Research Centre, December 1977.

1837. International Food Policy Research Institute. *Food Needs of Developing Countries: Projections of Production and Consumption to 1990.* Research Report 3. Washington, D. C.: December 1977.

1838. Iowa State University Center for Agricultural and Economic Development. *Alternatives for Balancing World Food Production and Needs.* Ames: Iowa State University Press, 1967.

1839. Johnson, D. G. *World Food Problems and Prospects.* Washington, D. C.: American Enterprise Institute for Public Policy Research, 1975.

1840. Mitrany, David. *Food and Freedom.* London: Batchworth, 1954.

1841. National Academy of Sciences. *Postharvest Food Losses in Developing Countries.* Washington, D. C.: 1978.

1842. ______. *Prospects of the World Food Supply. Proceedings of a Symposium.* Washington, D. C.: 1966.

1843. ______. *World Food and Nutrition Study: The Potential Contributions of Research.* Washington, D. C.: National Research Council, 1977.

1844. Organization for Economic Cooperation and Development. *The Food Problems of Developing Countries.* Paris: 1968.

1845. Osvald, Hugo. *The Earth Can Feed Us.* Trans. B. Nesfield-Cookson, London: Allen & Unwin, 1966.

1846. Oury, Bernard. *Estimation of Long-Run Changes in Domestic Demand for Food in Less Developed Countries.* Working Paper 83. Washington, D. C.: World Bank, January 1969.

1847. Phillips, Ralph W. *Animal Agriculture and the World's Food Supply.* International Agriculture Series 6. St. Paul: Institute of Agriculture, University of Minnesota, c. 1967.

1848. Rockefeller Foundation. *The Role of Animals in the World Food Situation.* Conference Held at the Rockefeller Foundation. New York: 1975.

1849. United States, Department of Agriculture, Economic Research Service. *World Demand Prospects for Grain in 1980. With Emphasis on Trade by the Less Developed Countries.* Foreign Agricultural Economics Report no. 75. Washington, D. C.: December 1971.

1850. United States, Department of Agriculture, Economics, Statistics and Cooperatives Service. *Alternative Futures for World Food in 1985. Volume 1: World GOL Model Analytical Report.* Foreign Agricultural Economics Report no. 146. Washington, D. C.: April 1978.

1851. Vries, Egbert de. *World Food Crisis and Agricultural Trade Problems.* Beverly Hills, Calif.: Sage, 1974.

1852. Wellhausen, Edwin J. *Plant Sciences and the World Food Supply.* International Agriculture Series 4. St. Paul: Institute of Agriculture, University of Minnesota, c. 1966.

1853. West, Quentin M. *World Food Needs.* Washington, D. C.: Foreign Regional Analysis Division, US Department of Agriculture, 16 February 1966.

1854. Willett, Joseph W., comp. *The World Food Situation: Problems and Prospects to 1985.* 2 vols. Dobbs Ferry, N. Y.: Oceana, 1976.

1855. Wortman, Sterling. *The World Food Situation: A New Initiative.* New York: The Rockefeller Foundation, May 1976.

Articles

The article by Almeida et al. surveys the views that have been set forward on the world food question and is a good introductory essay. "A Stocktaking on Food" (entry 1856) discusses the lack of progress in increasing third world food production since the World Food Conference in 1974. In this summary, technical and resource obstacles are seen as secondary to political ones.

1856. "A Stocktaking on Food." *Development Forum* 7 (June–July 1979): 13.

1857. Almeida, S., et al. "Assessment of the World Food Situation—Present and Future." *International Journal of Health Services* 5:1 (1975):95–120.

1858. Bergeret, Anne, and Théry, Daniel. "Weeds into Crops." *Ceres* no. 50 (March–April 1976): 29–32.

1859. Brown, Lester R. "World Food: Growing Dependence on North America." *Cooperation Canada* (November–December 1975): 3–9.

1860. Ezekiel, Mordecai. "Food Needs and World Agricultural Production," pp. 1–6. In *Proceedings: Symposium on Food, People & Trade.* Seattle, Wash.: 17–18 January 1963.

1861. "Food and Agriculture" (Issue Title). *Scientific American* 235 (September 1976).

1862. "Food for Asia—1969" (Special Section). *Far Eastern Economic Review* (9 October 1969): 101–120.

1863. "Food from One Earth" (Special Issue). *Ekistics* (January 1975).

1864. "Freedom from Hunger" (Special Double Issue). *The UNESCO Courier* (July–August 1962).

1865. "The Global Political Economy of Food" (Special Issue). *International Organization* 32 (Summer 1978): 581–871.

1866. Grant, James P. "The Trilateral Stake: More Food in the Developing Countries or More Inflation in the Industrial Democracies." *Trialogue* no. 17 (Spring 1978): 3–6, 13.

1867. Hopper, W. David. "To Conquer Hunger: Opportunity and Political Will." *Cooperation Canada* (July–August 1975): 22–26.

1868. Mellor, John W. "Food Price Policy and Income Distribution of Low-Income Countries." *Economic Development and Cultural Change* 27 (October 1978): 1–26.

1869. Ogbu, John U. "Seasonal Hunger in Tropical Africa as a Cultural Phenomenon." *Africa* 43 (October 1973): 317–332.

1870. Pirie, N. W. "Waste Not, Want Not." *New Scientist* 75 (28 July 1977): 233–235.

1871. "Preventing Food Losses" (Issue Title). *Ceres* no. 60 (November–December 1977).

1872. Schertz, Lyle P. "World Food: Prices and the Poor." *Foreign Affairs* 52 (April 1974): 511–537.

1873. Stanley, Bob. "Triticale: Closing the Gap Between Scientist and Farmer." *IDRC Reports* 5:4 (1976): 12–14.

1874. Sutton, Vic. "Thought for Food." *New Internationalist* no. 14 (April 1974): 22–24.

1875. "Total World Agricultural Production at a Standstill." *World Crops* 23 (January-February 1971): 8–11. (This is a brief summary of the FAO publication, *The State of Food and Agriculture, 1970*.)

1876. Underwood, E. J. "Man, Land and Food." *Australian Journal of Science* 29 (May 1967): 395–401.

1877. Walton, P. D. "World Cereal Crops." *World Crops* 21 (July-August 1969): 188–190.

1878. Weber, E. J. "New Beginnings for an Ancient Crop." *IDRC Reports* 7:3 (1978): 3–5.

1879. "What Will Their Children Eat?" (Issue Title). *Agenda* 1 (September 1978): 1–21.

1880. Wholey, Douglas W. "Versatile Cassava is at Home in Asia." *IDRC Reports* 5:3 (1976): 3–4.

Economic and Political Roots of Hunger

The books and articles in this section introduce a political and economic element into the discussion of the causes and likely cures of world hunger. The causes of hunger most frequently identified by the authors in this section are the same as those described as blocking self-reliant, self-sustaining economic growth (see Part III, "Aid and Neocolonialism," pages 178–181). Indeed, hunger is the inevitable result of development strategies that have ignored the needs of the poor while catering to the interests of the wealthy in urban and rural areas. Many of the items in this section demonstrate that famines are in no way "natural" disasters and that they do not have as their primary cause some natural phenomenon such as a drought or a flood, although a drought or a flood may well act as a triggering mechanism. Rather, the roots of global hunger are to be found in socioeconomic and political inequality.

Books and Monographs

To anyone familiar with the history of Britain's economic domination of Ireland, it will come as no surprise that the factors cited by Woodham-Smith as causing famine—monoculture, absentee landlords demanding high rents, lack of investment in agriculture, subdivision of land, and so on—are the same as those identified by the authors of more recent studies as causing hunger in the dependent regions of today's world.

The USAID report is of interest because it documents the problem of the diversion of famine assistance. Much of the relief food sent to Ghana by USAID eventually ended up in the hands of government officials and merchants, not in the stomachs of those who were actually starving. This phenomenon is not by any means unique to Ghana, as the Comité Information Sahel volume shows, nor to Africa, as the studies by Hartmann and Boyce and entries 1965 and 1944 demonstrate.

Particularly recommended are Woodham-Smith, Sinha, Robbins and Ansari, Hartmann and Boyce, Comité Information Sahel, Copans, Lappé and Collins, and George.

1881. Bhatia, Balmokand M. *Famines in India. A Study in Some Aspects of the Economic History of India 1860–1965.* 2nd ed. Bombay and New York: Asia, 1967.

1882. Comité Information Sahel. *Qui se Nourrit de la Famine en Afrique? Le Dossier Politique de la Faim au Sahel.* Paris: Maspero, 1974.

1883. Copans, Jean, ed. *Sécheresses et Famines du Sahel.* 2 vols. Paris: Maspero, 1975.

1884. de Castro, Josué. *The Black Book of Hunger.* Trans. Charles Markmann. New York: Funk & Wagnalls, 1967.

1885. ______. *The Geopolitics of Hunger.* rev. and enlarged ed. New York: Monthly Review, 1973. (Originally published as *The Geography of Hunger.* Boston: Little, Brown, 1952.)

1886. Dumont, René. *Lands Alive.* Trans. Suzanne and Gilbert Sale. London: Merlin Press, 1967.

1887. George, Susan. *How the Other Half Dies: The Real Reasons for World Hunger.* Montclair, N. J.: Allanheld, Osmun, 1977. (Also published as a paperback by Penguin, Harmondsworth, UK, 1976.)

1888. Hartmann, Betsy, and Boyce, Jim. *Bangladesh: Aid to the Needy?* International Policy Report. Washington, D. C.: Center for International Policy, 1978.

1889. ______. *Needless Hunger: Voices from a Bangladesh Village.* San Francisco, Calif.: Institute for Food and Development Policy, 1979.

1890. Lappé, Frances M., and Collins, Joseph. *Food First: Beyond the Myth of Scarcity.* rev. ed. New York: Ballantine, 1979.

1891. ______. *World Hunger, Ten Myths.* rev. ed. San Francisco. Calif.: Institute for Food and Development Policy, 1979.

1892. Morgan, Dan. *The Merchants of Grain: The Power and Profits of the Five Giant Companies at the Center of the World's Food Supply.* New York: Viking, 1979.

1893. Rama, Ruth, and Vigorito, Raul. *Transnacionales en el Sector de Frutas y Legumbres de Mexico.* DDE/R/13. Mexico City: ILET, April 1978.

1894. Robbins, Christopher, and Ansari, Javed. *The Profits of Doom: A War on Want Investigation into the "World Food Crisis."* London: War on Want, January 1976.

1895. Shepherd, Jack. *The Politics of Starvation.* New York and Washington, D. C.: The Carnegie Endowment for International Peace, 1975. (Chapters 1, 2, 10, and 11 are especially relevant.)

1896. Simon, Paul, and Simon, Arthur. *The Politics of World Hunger: Grass-Roots Politics and World Poverty.* New York: Harper's, 1973.

1897. Sinha, Radha. *Food and Poverty: The Political Economy of Confrontation.* New York: Holmes & Meier, 1976.

1898. Transnational Institute. *World Hunger: Causes and Remedies.* Washington, D. C.: Institute for Policy Studies, 1974.

1899. United Nations, Research Institute for Social Development. *Famine Risk and Famine Prevention in the Modern World: Studies in Food Systems Under Conditions of Recurrent Scarcity.* UNRISD/76/C.19. Geneva: June 1976.

1900. United States, Agency for International Development, Area Auditor General, Africa. *Report on Examination of the Title II Emergency Food Program in Ghana.* USAID Audit Report no. 3–641–78–1. Nairobi: 6 October 1977.

1901. Woodham-Smith, Cecil. *The Great Hunger.* New York: The New American Library/Signet, 1964.

Articles

Collins and Lappé summarize some of the more important hunger-related issues involved in the production of food crops for export by Western multinationals in third world countries. The article by George in *Africa* (entry 1912) summarizes very briefly the argument found in *How the Other Half Dies* (entry 1887) as it applies to Africa. The article by Omvedt is a short introduction to the political economy of starvation. The articles by Huessy and by Lappé and Collins should be read together (ideally in conjunction with *Food First,* entry 1890), as should the articles by Lofchie and Ball. Other recommended articles are Spitz and Almeida et al. *Feeding the Few* (entry 1605), also relevant here, discusses corporate control of food systems.

1902. Abdalla, Ismail-Sabri. "Depeasantization or Rural Development." *IFDA Dossier* no. 9 (1979).

1903. Almeida, S., et al. "Analysis of Traditional Strategies to Combat World Hunger and Their Results." *International Journal of Health Services* 5:1 (1975): 121–141.

1904. Baker, G. L. "Good Climate for Agribusiness." *The Nation* (5 November 1973): 456–462.

1905. Baker, Randall. "Famine: The Cost of Development?" *The Ecologist* 4 (June 1974): 170–175.

1906. Ball, Nicole. "Understanding the Causes of African Famine." *Journal of Modern African Studies* 14:3 (1976): 517–522.

1907. Cliffe, Lionel. "Capitalism or Feudalism? The Famine in Ethiopia." *Review of African Political Economy* no. 1 (August–November 1974): 34–40.

1908. Collins, Joseph, and Lappé, Frances M. "Still Hungry After All These Years." *Mother Jones* (August 1977): 27–33. (Also available in *Reprint Packet 1*. San Francisco, Calif.: Institute for Food and Development Policy, 1979.)

1909. Collins, Joseph; Lappé, Frances M.; and Kinley, David. "Puerto Rico: The 'Hunger Crop.'" *The Elements,* January 1977. (Also available in *Reprint Packet 1*. San Francisco, Calif.: Institute for Food and Development Policy, 1979.)

1910. Eberstadt, Nick. "Myths of the Food Crisis." *The New York Review of Books* (19 February 1976).

1911. Franke, Richard. "Solution to the Asian Food Crisis: 'Green Revolution' or Social Revolution?" *Bulletin of Concerned Asian Scholars* 6 (November–December 1974): 2–13.

1912. George, Susan. "How the Other Half Starves." *Africa* no. 67 (March 1977).

1913. ______. "Nestlé Alimentana SA: The Limits to Public Relations." *Economic and Political Weekly* 13 (16 September 1978): 1591–1602.

1914. Gibbon, Peter. "Colonialism and the Great Starvation in Ireland 1845–9." *Race and Class* 17 (Autumn 1975): 131–139.

1915. Gross, D. R. "The Great Sisal Scheme." *Natural History* (March 1971): 48–55.

1916. Huessy, Peter. "Population Control or Food First?" *Ag World* 4 (January 1978), and *Ag World* 4 (February 1978).

1917. Lappé, Frances M., and Collins, Joseph. "Food First Revisited." *Ag World* 4 (April 1978): A–H.

1918. Lappé, Frances M., and McCallie, Eleanor. "Banana Hunger." *Food Monitor,* March 1978. (Also available in *Reprint Packet 1*. San Francisco, Calif.: Institute for Food and Development Policy, March 1979, 7–9.)

1919. "Les Riches Mangent Trop" (Issue Title). *Croissance des Jeunes Nations* (November 1974).

1920. Lofchie, Michael F. "Political and Economic Origins of African Hunger." *Journal of Modern African Studies* 13:4 (1975).

1921. North American Congress on Latin America (NACLA). "US Grain Arsenal." *NACLA's Latin America & Empire Report* 9 (October 1975): 3–31.

1922. Omvedt, Gail. "The Political Economy of Starvation." *Race and Class* 17 (Autumn 1975): 111–130.

1923. Rothschild, Emma. "The Politics of Food." *The New York Review of Books* (16 May 1974): 16–18.

1924. Spitz, Pierre. "Silent Violence: Famine and Inequality." *International Social Science Journal* 30:4 (1978): 867–892.

1925. Taylor, Lance. "The Misconstrued Crisis: Lester Brown and World Food." *World Development* 3 (November–December 1975): 827–837.

1926. Warhaftig, Alan Matt. "Famine in Africa: No Act of God." *The Nation,* 22 February 1975, pp. 197–200.

Food Aid

The entries in this section cover a wide variety of food aid-related topics, ranging from simple descriptions of the workings of food aid programs to detailed case studies of the effects of food aid in individual countries.

Books and Monographs

To contrast the "radical" and the "liberal" point of view on food aid, Shenoy's book and the Isenman and Singer monograph should be read together. Both base their arguments on the Indian experience. Drawing on data from four countries, Stevens examines the arguments that food aid helps to sustain inefficient agricultural policies in developing countries, to encourage expensive food tastes, and to discourage agrarian reform. The study produced by the UN World Food Program concludes that few women benefit from food aid programs despite the potential of food aid to help improve women's status. The monograph by Zacher traces the political history of the US Food for Peace program while Goolsby, Kruer, and Santmyer describe the history, origin, payments arrangements, and effects of local currency on food aid transactions. All US General Accounting Office studies are also recommended.

1927. Adams, Dale W., et al. *Public Law 480 and Colombia's Economic Development.* Medellín, Colombia: Universidad Nacional de Colombia, March 1964.

1928. Bard, Robert. *Food Aid and International Agricultural Trade.* Lexington, Mass.: Lexington, 1972.

1929. Barlow, Frank D., and Libbin, Susan A. *Food Aid and Agricultural Development.* Foreign Agricultural Economic Report no. 51. Washington, D. C.: Economic Research Service, US Department of Agriculture, June 1969. (Focuses on India, Turkey, Colombia)

1930. Brown, Peter G., and Shue, Henry. *Food Policy.* New York: Free Press, 1977.

1931. Chakravarty, S., and Rosenstein-Rodan, P. N. *The Linking of Food Aid with Other Aid.* World Food Programme Studies no. 3. Rome: Food and Agriculture Organization, 1965.

1932. Dandekar, V. M. *The Demand for Food and Conditions Governing Food Aid During Development.* World Food Programme Studies no. 1. Rome: Food and Agriculture Organization, 1965.

1933. Dessau, Jan. *The Role of Multilateral Food Aid and Programs.* World Food Programme Studies no. 5. Rome: Food and Agriculture Organization, 1965.

1934. Food and Agriculture Organization. *Food Aid and Other Forms of Utilization of Agricultural Surpluses. A Review of Programs, Principles and Consultations.* FAO Commodity Policy Studies no. 15. Rome: 1964.

1935. ______. *Uses of Agricultural Surpluses to Finance Economic Development in Underdeveloped Countries.* Commodity Policy Studies no. 6. Rome: 1955.

1936. Goolsby, O. H.; Kruer, G. R.; and Santmyer, C. *P. L. 480 Concessional Sales.* Foreign Agricultural Economic Report no. 65. Washington, D. C.: Economic Research Service, US Department of Agriculture, September 1970.

1937. Isenman, Paul, and Singer, Hans W. *Food Aid: Disincentive Effects and Their Policy Implications.* A. I. D. Discussion Paper no. 31. Washington, D. C.: US Agency for International Development, 1975. (Also available in *Economic Development and Cultural Change* 25 [January 1977]: 205–237.)

1938. Maxwell, Simon. *Food Aid, Food for Work and Public Works.* IDS Discussion Paper D–127. Brighton, UK: Institute of Development Studies, University of Sussex, 1978.

1939. National Action/Research on the Military Industrial Complex (NARMIC). *Food as a Weapon—The Food for Peace Program.* Philadelphia: 1975. (Available from NARMIC, 112 South 16th Street, Philadelphia, Pa.)

1940. Organization for Economic Cooperation and Development. *Food Aid.* Paris: 1974.

1941. ______. *Food Aid for Development.* Report of an Expert Meeting on "Scope and Conditions for Improved Use of Food Aid for Development," Paris, March 1978. Paris: 1979.

1942. Poleman, Thomas T. *A Review of "A Review of the U. S. Food Aid Program."* Cornell Agricultural Economics Staff Paper no. 77–19. Ithaca, N. Y.: Cornell University, June 1977.

1943. ______. *Food Aid and Malnutrition: Comments.* Cornell Agricultural Economics Staff Paper no. 77–17. Ithaca, N. Y.: Cornell University, May 1977.

1944. Scott, Michael. *Aid to Bangladesh.* San Francisco, Calif.: Oxfam-America and Institute for Food and Development Policy, 1979.

1945. Shenoy, B. R. *PL 480 Aid and India's Food Problem.* New Delhi: East-West, 1974.

1946. Stevens, Christopher. *Food Aid and the Developing World.* London: Croom-Helm, 1979.

1947. Toma, Peter, with F. A. Schoenfeld. *The Politics of Food for Peace: Executive-Legislative Interaction.* Tucson: University of Arizona Press, 1967.

1948. United Nations, World Food Programme. *Multilateral Food Aid: Report of the Intergovernmental Committee of the World Food Programme.* Rome: 1967.

1949. ______. *Regional Seminar on the Use of Food Aid in Projects For Economic and Social Development in Latin America and the Caribbean.* Bogota: 1966.

1950. ______. *The Contribution of Food Aid to the Improvement of Women's Status.* Report by the Executive Director of the Intergovernmental Committee. Rome: March 1975, mimeo.

1951. United States, Congress, Senate, Committee on Agriculture and Forestry. Report: *Food and Fiber as a Force for Freedom.* Washington, D. C.: US Printing Office, 1958.

1952. ______. Hearing: *Foreign Food Assistance and Agricultural Development.* 94th Cong., 1st Sess. Washington, D. C.: US Printing Office, 1975.

1953. United States, General Accounting Office. *Disincentives to Agricultural Production in Developing Countries.* ID–76–2. Washington, D. C.: 26 November 1975.

1954. ______. *Examination of Funds Appropriated for Economic and Food Aid to Indochina.* ID–76–54. Washington, D. C.: 16 April 1976.

1955. ______. *Impact of U.S. Development and Food Aid in Selected Developing Countries.* ID–76–53. Washington, D. C.: 22 April 1976.

1956. ______. *U.S. Assistance for the Economic Development of Korea.* B–164264. Washington, D. C.: 12 July 1973.

1957. United States, President. *Food for Peace. 1977. Annual Report on Public Law 480.* Washington, D. C.: July 1978. (An annual publication.)

1958. Zachar, George. *A Political History of Food For Peace.* Cornell Agricultural Economics Staff Paper no. 77–18. Ithaca, N. Y.: Cornell University, May 1977.

Articles

The articles by Griffin, Goering, and Mann tend to stress the positive aspects of food aid programs. Mann finds that there was a decline in the domestic production of cereals in India which could be attributed to the PL–480 program. However, he concludes that since the decline in domestic production was less than the amount imported under PL–480, India in fact registered a net gain in cereal supplies through the operation of the PL–480 program. However, it seems that such a situation can succeed in the long term only if a country is financially able to import increasing amounts of food and if there is food available to import. Indeed, events in the 1970s have demonstrated that such conditions will not always hold.

The articles by McHenry and Bird, Scott, Burke, and Dudley and Sandilands are pessimistic about the effects of food aid in developing countries.

Somewhat in the middle of these two views is the article by Stevens which surveys the impact of food aid programs on four African countries—Lesotho, Tunisia, Botswana, and Upper Volta. Stevens considers some of the major criticisms of food aid (reduces domestic production, creates dependency on the government for food handouts, accustoms populations to inappropriate foods, and so on) and measures the programs in the four countries against them. He concludes that while food aid programs are not "ideal," they do fulfill many of the objectives set for them. Stevens cautions, however, that the programs in the four countries surveyed were relatively small and that the negative aspects of larger programs might simply be easier to quantify. In addition, although the negative aspects of food aid programs can, in theory, be minimized by proper governmental action, in practice this is not always possible. This article summarizes the argument in entry 1946.

The article by Maxwell and Singer surveys the literature on the impact of food aid. The authors find that the disincentive effect of food aid on domestic production has been exaggerated and can be avoided by the "proper mix of policy tools." At the same time, they identify other areas in which the beneficial effects of food aid are less clear: growth and distribution of income, storage and stabilization schemes, promotion of self-reliance. A helpful short bibliography is included.

The articles by Sen and Schultz should be read together. Other recommended articles are Rothschild and Wallensteen. In addition, chapter 1 of *The Aid Debate* (entry 1607), also available as chapter 42 in *Food First* (entry 1890), should be consulted.

1959. Burke, Melvin. Does 'Food for Peace' Assistance Damage the Bolivian Economy?" *Inter-American Economic Affairs* 25 (1971).

1960. Dudley, Leonard, and Sandilands, Roger. "The Side Effect of Foreign Aid: The Case of P. L. 480 Wheat in Colombia." *Economic Development and Cultural Change* 23 (January 1975): 325–336.

1961. Ezekiel, Mordecai. "Apparent Results in Using Surplus Food for Financing Economic Development." *Journal of Farm Economics* 40 (November 1958): 915–923.

1962. Goering, Theodore J. "Public Law 480 in Colombia." *Journal of Farm Economics* 44 (November 1962): 992–1004.

1963. Griffin, Philip. "The Impact of Food Aid—Peru, A Case Study." *Food Policy* 4 (February 1979): 46–52.

1964. Islam, Nasir. "New Ethics and Politics of World Food Scarcity." *International Perspectives* (November–December 1976): 18–22.

1965. McHenry, Donald F., and Bird, Kai. "Food Bungle in Bangladesh." *Foreign Policy* no. 27 (Summer 1977): 72–88.

1966. Mann, Jitendar S. "The Impact of Public Law 480 Imports on Prices and Domestic Supply of Cereals in India." *Journal of Farm Economics* 49 (February 1967): 131–146.

1967. Maxwell, S. J., and Singer, Hans W. "Food Aid to Developing Countries: A Survey." *World Development* 7 (March 1979): 225–247.

1968. Reuter, Richard W. "Food for Peace. A Positive Use for American Resources," pp. 36–42. In *Proceedings: Symposium on Food, People & Trade.* Seattle, Wash.: 17–18 January 1963.

1969. Rothschild, Emma. "Food Politics." *Foreign Affairs* 54 (January 1976): 285–307.

1970. ______ . "Is It Time to End Food For Peace?" *New York Times Magazine* (13 March 1977): 14, 43–48.

1971. Sarris, Alexander, and Taylor, Lance. "Cereal Stocks, Food Aid and Food Security for the Poor." *World Development* 4 (December 1976): 967–976.

1972. Schultz, Theodore W. "Value of US Farm Surpluses to Underdeveloped Countries." *Journal of Farm Economics* 42 (December 1960): 1019–1030.

1973. Sen, S. R. "Impact and Implication of Foreign Surplus Disposal on Underdeveloped Economies—The Indian Perspective." *Journal of Farm Economics* 42 (December 1960): 1031–1042.

1974. Stevens, Christopher. "Food Aid: Good, Bad, or Indifferent." *Journal of Modern African Studies* 16:4 (1978): 671–678.

1975. Sundaram, K. "P. L. 480 Transactions, Money Supply and Prices." *Indian Economic Review* 5 (New Series) (April 1970): 71–95.

1976. Wallensteen, Peter. "Scarce Goods as Political Weapons. The Case of Food," pp. 193–224. In *Industrialization, Development and the Demands for a New International Economic Order.* Ed. Kirsten Worm. Copenhagen: Samfundsvidenskabeligt Forlag, 1978.

US View

This section contains publications, by the US Government and others, that define the US position on food. Also included here are studies by people such as Lester Brown and Orville Freeman who have had influence in the policy planning system.

The USDA publication, *The World Food Situation and Prospects to 1985*, presents a review of the issues facing the US with regard to the world food situation. The three-volume report by the Panel on World Food Supply presents considerable material of interest to the reader of this bibliography.

The article by Rosenfeld discusses the political factors at work in the formulation of US food policy. Moyer outlines some of the domestic elements involved in US policy decisions relating to food stocks and food prices. The articles by George and Chatterjee critique US food policy, as does entry 1939. Chapters 4 and 5 of entry 197 are also of relevance here.

1977. American Enterprise Institute. *Farm Policy Proposals.* Legislative Analyses no. 6. Washington, D. C.: 30 June 1977. (Pages 33–49 are relevant.)

1978. Brandt, Karl. "Implications of the World Food Situation for Agricultural Policy," pp. 26–35. In *Proceedings: Symposium on Food, People & Trade.* Seattle, Wash.: 17–18 January 1963.

1979. Brown, Lester. *Increasing World Food Output: Problems and Prospects.* Foreign Agricultural Economics Report no. 25. Washington,

D. C.: Economic Research Service, US Department of Agriculture, April 1965.

1980. ______. "The Next Crisis? Food." *Foreign Policy* no. 13 (Winter 1973–74): 3–33.

1981. Chatterjee, R. "The CIA and the Politics of Food." *Economic and Political Weekly* 10 (12 April 1975): 617–618.

1982. Ford, Gerald. "Agriculture and Food Assistance," pp. 52–69. In *Development Issues: First Annual Report of the President on US Actions Affecting the Development of Low-Income Countries.* Washington, D. C.: US Development Coordination Committee, May 1975.

1983. Freeman, Orville L. *World Without Hunger.* New York: Praeger, 1968.

1984. George, Susan. "La Politique Agricole et Alimentaire Américaine Face au Reste du Monde." *Economie Rurale* (Revue de la Société Française d'Economie Rurale), September–October 1979.

1985. Hopkins, Raymond F. "How to Make Food Work." *Foreign Policy* no. 27 (Summer 1977): 89–108.

1986. Kissinger, Henry A. "Address to the World Food Conference." Washington, D. C.: US Department of State, 1974.

1987. Moyer, Wayne. "Iowa Dateline: A View from the Cornfields." *Foreign Policy* no. 19 (Summer 1975): 178–188.

1988. Organization for Economic Cooperation and Development. *Recent Developments in United States Agricultural Policies.* Agricultural Policy Reports. Paris: 1976.

1989. Rosenfeld, Stephen S. "The Politics of Food." *Foreign Policy* no. 14 (Spring 1974): 17–29.

1990. United States, Congress, Congressional Budget Office. *Food and Agriculture Policy Options.* Budget Issue Paper. Washington, D. C.: February 1977.

1991. United States, Department of Agriculture. *The World Food Situation and Prospects to 1985.* rev. ed. Foreign Agricultural Economic Report no. 98. Washington, D. C.: March 1975.

1992. United States, General Accounting Office. *Food and Agricultural Issues for Planning.* CED–77–61. Washington, D. C.: 22 April 1977. (Pages 25–33, 36–38 are relevant.)

1993. ______. *Grain Reserves: A Potential U.S. Food Policy Tool.* OSP–76–16. Washington, D. C.: 26 March 1976.

1994. ______. *U.S. Participation in International Food Organizations: Problems and Issues.* ID–76–66. Washington, D. C.: 6 August 1976.

1995. United States, House of Representatives, Committee on International Relations, Subcommittee on International Resources, Food and Energy. Hearings: *Food Problems of Developing Countries: Implications for U.S. Policy.* 94th Cong., 1st Sess. 21 May; 3,5 June 1975. Washington, D. C.: US Printing Office, 1975.

1996. United States, Panel on World Food Supply. *The World Food Problem. A Report.* 3 vols. Washington, D. C.: US Printing Office, 1967.

1997. West, Quentin. "The Developing Nations and U. S. Agricultural Trade." *Foreign Agriculture* 8 (5 April 1970): 2–6.

1998. _____. *World Food Needs.* Washington, D. C.: Foreign Regional Analysis Division, US Department of Agriculture, 16 February 1966.

The Population Connection

The views expressed in the studies below range from pessimistic (if world population growth is not controlled very soon, widespread famines are inevitable) to optimistic (even with the present state of technology, it is possible to feed the entire world for a long time to come). The need to control global population growth is increasingly accepted, although the leaders of many African countries might still dispute the necessity of doing so. There is also a growing acceptance of the notion that a major cause of overpopulation is poverty and that an attack on poverty must be made if the population problem is to be resolved.

Books and Monographs

Rich argues that economic growth by itself is not sufficient to reduce birth rates; rather, there must be a more equitable distribution of resources. Kocher concludes that increased participation by the rural population in development programs will lead to earlier and faster reductions in birth rates. Cépède, Houtart, and Grond consider the two most urgent requirements for solving the food crisis to be agrarian reform and the democratization of the political process. Berg discusses how agricultural development influences fertility by influencing nutrition. The King volume analyzes the impact of rising populations on efforts to reduce poverty and on the availability of food and other resources. In addition, the international and national policy implications of its findings are considered. The study by Moody is also recommended.

1999. Agrawal, Naresh Chandra. *The Food Problem of India: A Study in Agricultural Economics.* 1st ed. Bombay: Vora, 1961.

2000. Baldwin, Kenneth D. S. *Demography for Agricultural Planners.* Rome: Development Research and Training Service, Policy Analysis Division, Food and Agriculture Organization, 1975.

2001. Bansil, Puran Chand. *India's Food Resources and Population.* Bombay: Vora, 1958.

2002. Barbour, Kenneth Michael, and Prothero, R., eds. *Essays on African Population.* London: Routledge & Kegan Paul, 1961. (Chapters 9 and 10 are especially relevant.)

2003. Berg, Alan. *The Nutrition Factor: Its Role in Development.* Washington, D. C.: Brookings Institution, 1973.

2004. Borgstrom, Georg. *The Hungry Planet: The Modern World at the Edge of Famine.* 2nd rev. ed. New York: Collier, 1972.

2005. Brown, Lester R. *In the Human Interest: A Strategy to Stabilize World Population.* Washington, D. C.: Norton, 1974.

2006. ______. *Population and Affluence: Growing Pressures on World Food Resources.* Development Paper 15. Washington, D. C.: Overseas Development Council, September 1973.

2007. ______. *The Twenty-Ninth Day.* New York: Norton, 1978.

2008. ______. *World Population Trends: Signs of Hope. Signs of Stress.* Worldwatch Paper no. 8. Washington, D. C.: Worldwatch Institute, 1976.

2009. Brown, Lester R.; McGrath, P.; and Stokes, B. *Twenty-Two Dimensions of the Population Problem.* Worldwatch Paper no. 5. Washington, D. C.: Worldwatch Institute, 1976.

2010. Caldwell, John C., ed. *Population Growth and Socio-Economic Change in West Africa.* New York: The Population Council, 1975.

2011. Cantrelle, Pierre, ed. *Population in African Development.* Dolhain, Belgium: Ordina, 1974.

2012. Cépède, Michel; Houtart, Françoise; and Grond, Linus. *Population and Food.* New York: Sheed & Ward, 1964.

2013. Clark, Colin. *The Myth of Over-Population.* Melbourne: Advocate, 1973.

2014. ______. *Population Growth and Land Use.* 2nd ed. New York: St. Martin's, 1977.

2015. Food and Agriculture Organization. *Population and Agricultural Development.* F1337. Rome: 1977.

2016. Food and Agriculture Organization-United Nations Fund for Population Activities. *Seminar on Population Problems Related to Food and Agricultural Development in Asia and the Far East.* FAO/UN/TF 155. Rome: Food and Agriculture Organization, 1975.

2017. Frejka, Tomas. *The Future of Population Growth: Alternative Paths to Equilibrium.* New York: Wiley, Population Council Book, 1973.

2018. Gulhati, Ravi. *India's Population Policy: History and Future.* Working Paper 265. Washington, D. C.: World Bank, August 1977.

2019. Hutchinson, Sir Joseph, ed. *Population and Food Supply.* Cambridge, UK: Cambridge University Press, 1969.

2020. International Labour Organization. *World Employment Programme: Population and Development.* Geneva: 1977.

2021. International Union for the Scientific Study of Population, Committee on Economics and Demography. *Agrarian Change and Population Growth: An Interim Report.* Liège: c. 1976.

2022. King, Timothy, coord. *Population Policies and Economic Development.* Baltimore, Md.: Johns Hopkins University Press, 1974.

2023. Kocher, James E. *Rural Development, Income Distribution and Fertility Decline.* Occasional Paper. New York: The Population Council, 1973.

2024. McCormack, Arthur. *The Population Problem.* New York: Crowell, 1970.

2025. Madalgi, S. S. *Population and Food Supply in India.* Bombay: Lalvani, 1970.

2026. Moody, Tony. *Population Pressure and Agricultural Productivity in Nyanza, Kenya.* Research Project Paper, D.76.1. Copenhagen: Institute of Development Research, 1976.

2027. Ominde, Simeon H., and Ejiogu, C. N. *Population Growth and Economic Development in Africa.* London: Heinemann, 1972. (Chapters 15,18, and 22 deal directly with the food-population issue.)

2028. Penny, D. H., and Singarimbun, M. *Population and Poverty in Rural Java, A Case Study.* Ithaca, N. Y.: Department of Agricultural Economics, Cornell University, 1973.

2029. Rich, William. *Smaller Families Through Social and Economic Progress.* Monograph no. 7. Washington, D. C.: Overseas Development Council, 1973.

2030. Ridker, Ronald G., ed. *Population and Development: The Search for Selective Intervention.* Baltimore, Md.: Johns Hopkins University Press, 1976.

2031. Smith, T. Lynn. *The Race Between Population and Food Supply in Latin America.* Albuquerque: University of New Mexico Press, 1976. (Focuses on Brazil and Colombia.)

2032. Tabah, Léon, ed. *Population Growth and Economic Development in the Third World.* 2 vols. Liège, Belgium: Ordina Editions, 1976. (Chapters 7 and 8 are particularly relevant.)

2033. Thiesenhusen, William C. *Food and Population Growth.* Reprint no. 122. Madison: Land Tenure Center, University of Wisconsin, c. 1974.

2034. Thomlinson, Ralph. *Population Dynamics: Causes and Consequences of World Demographic Change.* New York: Random House, 1965. (Chapter 14 is relevant.)

2035. United Nations, Economic and Social Commission for Asia and the Pacific. *Comparative Study of Population Growth and Agricultural Change.* Asian Population Studies Series no. 23. 5 vols. Bangkok: 1975.

2036. United Nations, Economic and Social Council. *Population Growth and Social and Economic Development in Africa (A Review and Discussion of Country Case Studies).* Economic Commission for Africa, African Population Conference, Accra, Ghana, 9–18 December 1971. E/CN.14/POP/46. New York: 24 November 1971.

Articles

The articles by Ware and Germain deal with the relationship between women's roles and their fertility. Germain concludes that as a woman's status increases, her fertility decreases. But Ware argues that, at least in the African context, an improvement in a woman's subsistence and economic situation is more important for declining fertility than an increase in status. The Ware article is particularly useful in demonstrating the cultural limits of concepts and research evidence.

Orleans discusses the Chinese experience in population control. Other recommended articles include Cassen, Pathy, and Nadkarni.

2037. *Ambio* 3:3–4 (1974): 97–113. (The articles by Day, Adler-Karlsson, Thorsson, and Borgstrom are relevant.)

2038. Brown, Roy E., and Wray, Joe D. "The Starving Roots of Population Growth." *Natural History* (January 1974): 46–53.

2039. Cassen, Robert. "Development and Population." *Economic and Political Weekly* 11:31–33 (Special Number 1976): 1173–1186.

2040. ———. "Population and Development: A Survey." *World Development* 4 (October–November 1976): 785–830. (Section II.3, "Population and Food," is relevant.)

2041. Cook, Robert C. "Population and Food Supply," pp. 451–477. In *The Population Crisis and the Use of World Resources.* Ed. S. Mudd. The Hague: Junk, 1964.

2042. Durand, John D., ed. "World Population" (Issue Title). *The Annals of the American Academy of Political and Social Science* 369 (January 1967): 1–130. (The contributions by Täuber, Ackerman, Easterlin, and Sadie are particularly relevant.)

2043. Food and Agriculture Organization. "Population and Food Supply in Asia." *Economic Bulletin for Asia and the Far East* 24 (June 1973): 34–50.

2044. Germain, Adrienne. "Status and Roles of Women as Factors in Fertility Behavior: A Policy Analysis." *Studies in Family Planning* 6:7 (1975): 192–200.

2045. Johnson, D. G. "Food for the Future: A Perspective." *Population and Development Review* 2 (March 1976): 1–19.

2046. Marshall, Carter L. "Health, Nutrition, and the Roots of World Population Growth." *International Journal of Health Services* 4:4 (1974): 677–690.

2047. "Mead on Population and Food." *Front Lines* (14 September 1978): 1,6.

2048. Mueller, Eva. "The Impact of Agricultural Change on Demographic Development in the Third World," pp. 425–439. In *International Population Conference, Liège, Volume I. 1973.* Liège: International Union for the Scientific Study of Population, 1973.

2049. Nadkarni, M. V. "'Overpopulation' and the Rural Poor." *Economic and Political Weekly* 11:31–33 (Special Number 1976): 1163–1172.

2050. Orleans, Leo A. "China's Experience in Population Control: The Elusive Model." *World Development* 3 (July–August 1975): 497–525.

2051. Pathy, Jaganath. "Population and Development." *Economic and Political Weekly* 11 (24 July 1976): 1125–1130.

2052. "People and Population" (Special Issue). *New Internationalist* no. 15 (May 1974).

2053. Pimentel, David; Dritschile, W.; Kummel, J.; and Kutzman, J. "Energy and Land Constraints in Food-Protein Production." *Science* 190 (21 November 1975): 754–761.

2054. "Population Special" (Issue Title). *Ceres* no. 36 (November–December 1973).

2055. Revelle, Roger. "Food and Population." *Scientific Amerian* 231 (September 1974): 160–170.

2056. Schneider, Stephen H. "The Population Explosion: Can It Shake the Climate?" *Ambio* 3:3–4 (1974): 150–155.

2057. Sekhar, A. Chandra. "Population Growth and Agricultural Development in India." *Journal of the Indian Society of Agricultural Statistics* 25 (June 1973): 63–74.

2058. Tuma, Elias H. "Population, Food and Agriculture in the Arab Countries." *The Middle East Journal* 28 (Autumn 1974): 381–395.

2059. Ward, Richard J. "Part I: Food and Human Welfare," pp. 23–90. In his *Development Issues for the 1970s.* New York and London: Dunellen, 1973.

2060. Ware, Helen. "The Relevance of Changes in Women's Roles to Fertility Behavior: The African Evidence." Prepared for the Annual Meeting of the Population Association of America, Seattle, Washington, April 1975, mimeo.

2061. Yotopoulos, Pan A. "The Population Problem and the Development Solution." *Food Research Institute Studies* 16:1 (1977): 1–131.

World Food Conferences

All but three of the entries in this section (2063–2065) deal with the 1974 World Food Conference sponsored by the UN. Entries 2067–2071 are official documents relating to that conference. Entries 2062, 2066, and 2072 discuss the conference and its aftermath. Entry 2066 is a critique of the conference itself.

2062. "Aftermath of the World Food Conference" (Issue Title). *Ceres* no. 43 (February 1975).

2063. Food and Agriculture Organization. *Report of the World Food Congress.* (Washington, D. C., 4 to 18 June 1963). 2 vols. Rome: 1963.

2064. ______. *Report of the Second World Food Congress.* (The Hague, Netherlands, 16–30 June 1970). 2 vols. Rome: 1970.

2065. *Proceedings, The World Food Conference of 1976.* Ames: Iowa State University Press, 1977.

2066. Rondeau, Alain. "La Conférence Mondiale de l'Alimentation ou le Triomphe de la Rhétorique: Rome, 5–16 Novembre 1974." *Revue Tiers-Monde* 16 (July–September 1975): 671–684.

2067. United Nations. *Report of the World Food Conference.* (Rome, 5–16 November 1974). E/Conf.65/20. New York: 1975.

2068. United Nations, Economic and Social Council. *Assessment: Present Food Situation and Dimensions and Causes of Hunger and Malnutrition in the World.* E/Conf.65/PREP/6. New York: 8 May 1974.

2069. United Nations, World Food Conference. *Assessment of the World Food Situation: Present and Future.* E/Conf.65/3. Rome: 1974.

2070. ______. *Report of the Preparatory Committee for the World Food Conference on Its Third Session.* E/Conf.65/6. Rome: 1974.

2071. ______. *The World Food Problem: Proposals for National and International Action.* E/Conf.65/4. Rome: 1974.

2072. Weiss, Thomas G., and Jordan, Robert S. *The World Food Conference and Global Problem Solving.* Praeger Special Studies in International Economics and Development. New York: Praeger, 1976.

Food Security

Poor harvests in many parts of the world in the early 1970s underlined the degree to which global food reserves have shrunk in the last twenty years. Since then, and particularly after the World Food Conference of 1974, there has been a debate concerning the most appropriate mechanism to promote food security. Some proposals have focused on the creation of international grain reserves, for example Trezise, Josling, FAO (entry 2077), Johnson, Danin, Summer and Johnson, and Walker and Sharples. The latter three entries explore the possibility of reserves being held by the US or by the US and other industrialized countries. Entry 1993 also examines the feasibility of US-held reserves. The question of whether developing countries should attempt to maintain their own grain reserves is addressed by Reutlinger, Eaton, and Bigman. It is concluded that on traditional economic grounds (capacity to make profit and economic efficiency) reserves held by developing countries have only a limited justification. However, the authors point out that there are other reasons for a third world country to decide to hold grain reserves, chief among which is to increase the government's financial ability to ensure a minimally adequate level of grain consumption for the entire population at all times.

Another approach to food security which has been recommended is some sort of insurance scheme, possibly coupled with grain reserves. Insurance schemes are evaluated in Reutlinger (entries 2084 and 2085) and in Konandreas, Huddleston, and Ramangkura. McLaughlin surveys progress in reducing food insecurity during the first year following the 1974 World Food Conference. In fact, no food security scheme has yet been agreed upon, although some developing countries—notably India—were able to accumulate sizable national stocks at the end of the 1970s.

2073. Bigman, David, and Reutlinger, Shlomo. *National and International Policies Toward Food Security and Price Stabilization.* Washington, D. C.: World Bank, August 1978.

2074. Cochrane, Willard W. *Feast or Famine: The Uncertain World of Food and Its Policy Implications for the United States.* Report no. 36. Washington, D. C.: National Planning Association, February 1974.

2075. Danin, Yagil; Summer, Daniel; and Johnson, D. Gale. *Determination of Optimal Grain Carryovers.* Office of Agricultural Economic Research, Paper no. 74:12. Chicago, Ill.: University of Chicago, 1975.

2076. Food and Agriculture Organization. *National Food Reserve Policies in Underdeveloped Countries.* FAO Commodity Studies no. 11. Rome: 1958.

2077. ______. *Proposal by the Director General on International Action to Assume Adequate Basic Food Stocks.* Rome: FAO Council, 11–22 June 1973.

2078. Food and Agriculture Organization, Committee on Commodity Problems. *World Food Security: Draft Evaluation of World Cereals Stock Situation.* Rome: October 1974.

2079. Hazell, Peter B. R., and Scandizzo, Pasquale L. "Market Intervention Policies When Production is Risky." *American Journal of Agricultural Economics* 57 (1975): 641–649.

2080. Johnson, D. Gale. "Increased Stability of Grain Supplies in Developing Countries: Optimal Carryovers and Insurance." *World Development* 4 (December 1976): 977–987.

2081. Josling, Timothy. *An International Grain Reserve Policy.* London and Washington, D. C.: British-North American Committee, July 1973.

2082. Konandreas, Panos; Huddleston, Barbara; and Ramangkura, Virabongsa. *Food Security: An Insurance Approach.* Research Report 4. Washington, D. C.: International Food Policy Research Institute, September 1978.

2083. McLaughlin, Martin M. *World Food Insecurity: Has Anything Happened Since Rome?* Washington, D. C.: Overseas Development Council, 1975.

2084. Reutlinger, Shlomo. "Food Insecurity: Magnitude and Remedies." *World Development* 6 (June 1978): 797–811.

2085. ______. *Food Insecurity: Magnitude and Remedies.* Working Paper 267. Washington, D. C.: World Bank, July 1977.

2086. ______. *Simulation of World-Wide Buffer Stocks of Wheat.* Working Paper 219. Washington, D. C.: World Bank, November 1975.

2087. Reutlinger, Shlomo, and Bigman, David. *Food Price and Supply Stabilization: National Buffer Stocks and Trade Policies.* Washington, D. C.: World Bank, May 1978.

2088. Reutlinger, Shlomo; Eaton, David; and Bigman, David. *Should Developing Nations Carry Grain Reserves?* Working Paper 244. Washington, D. C.: World Bank, September 1976.

2089. Schnittker, John A. "Grain Reserves — Now." *Foreign Policy* no. 20 (Fall 1975): 225–231.

2090. Trezise, Philip H. *Rebuilding Grain Reserves: Toward An International System.* Washington, D. C.: The Brookings Institution, 1976.

2091. United States, Congress, Senate, Committee on Agriculture and Forestry. *U.S. and World Food Security.* 93rd Cong., 2nd Sess. Washington, D. C.: US Printing Office, 15 March 1974.

2092. Walker, R. L., and Sharples, J. S. *Reserve Stocks of Grain: A Review of Research.* Foreign Agricultural Economic Report no. 304. Washington, D. C.: US Department of Agriculture, August 1975.

Fisheries

While individual societies in the third world obtain much of their protein requirements from fish, the bulk of the fish caught each year is consumed in industrialized countries. Fleets from countries such as the USSR, Poland, or Japan can be found as far afield as West and South Africa. In the last decade or so, fishmeal exports from third world countries have become an increasingly important component in the diets of animals bred in industrialized nations. By the early 1970s, one-third of the total annual world fish catch was turned into fishmeal (Stamp, p. 8). Third world countries are expected to increase their exports of fish, particularly fishmeal, in the future, which, as Barlet argues, will only increase the dependence of the third world on food imports from the industrialized countries.

The four volumes edited by Borgstrom cover a wide variety of topics relating to "fish as food." Shorter essays on conditions in and potential of sea and freshwater fisheries can be found in entries 2004 (Chapter 18) and 1642 (Chapter 11), respectively. The articles by Glantz, Kent, and Kurien introduce a political element into the discussion of fisheries. Ecological aspects are considered by Johnson and Suckcharoen, Nuorteva and Häsänen, as well as in entry 1650 (Chapter 6) and entry 1645 (Chapter 9). The majority of the items in this section either survey the fishery resources of a particular third world country or region or analyze the possibilities of developing such resources.

2093. Allsop, W. H. L. "African Fisheries: Their Problems and Opportunities and Their Role in the Sahelian Famine." *Agricultural Economics Bulletin for Africa* no. 15 (June 1974): 1–12.

2094. Bah, Abdou. "Environnement Marin et Nutrition en Afrique de l'Ouest." *Revue Tiers-Monde* 19 (January–March 1978): 179–184.

2095. Barlet, Alain. "Productions Maritimes et Problèmes Alimentaires du Tiers Monde." *Revue Tiers-Monde* 12 (October–December 1971): 825–842.

2096. Borgstrom, Georg, ed. *Fish as Food.* 4 vols. New York: Academic, 1962–1965.

2097. Central Marine Fisheries Research Institute. *Proceedings of the Symposium on Living Resources of the Seas Around India.* Cochin: 1973.

2098. Crutchfield, James A., and Lawson, Rowena. *West African Marine Fisheries: Alternatives for Management.* RFF/PISFA Paper 3. Washington, D. C.: Resources for the Future, 1974.

2099. Food and Agriculture Organization. *Fisheries in the Food Economy.* FFHC Basic Studies no. 19. Rome: 1968.

2100. ______. "A Note on the Fisheries of Africa." *Agricultural Economics Bulletin for Africa* no. 6 (October 1964): 64–77.

2101. Gerking, Shelby D. "Freshwater Fish—A Global Food Potential." *Ambio* 6:1 (1977): 39–43.

2102. Glantz, Michael H. "The Science, Politics and Economics of the Peruvian Anchoveta Fishery." *Marine Policy,* July 1979.

2103. Gulland, J. A. "Fishery Management and the Needs of Developing Countries," pp. 175–188. In *World Fisheries Policy: Multidisciplinary Views.* Ed. Brian J. Rothschild. Seattle, Wash., and London: University of Washington Press, 1972.

2104. Holt, S. J. "The Food Resources of the Ocean." *Scientific American* 221 (September 1969): 178–194.

2105. ______. "Marine Fisheries and World Food Supplies." In *Man/Food Equation.* Ed. M. Rechcigl. New York: Academic, 1975.

2106. Horn, S. L., and Pillay, T. V. R. *Handbook on Fish Culture in the Indo-Pacific Region.* FAO Technical Paper no. 14. Rome: Food and Agriculture Organization, 1962.

2107. Jarrin, Edgardo Mercado. "Utilizing Sea Resources for Human and Social Welfare." *Pacific Community* 3 (January 1972): 302–312.

2108. Johnson, J. H. "Effects of Climate Change on Marine Food Production." In *Climate and Food-Climatic Fluctuation and U.S. Agricultural Production.* National Academy of Sciences. Washington, D. C.: 1976.

2109. Kasahara, Hiroshi. "State of Marine Fishery Resources—A General Review." *Agriculture and Environment* 2 (October 1975): 205–218.

2110. Kent, George. "The Political Economy of Fishing," pp. 284–293. In *Peace, Development, and New International Economic Order.*

Proceedings of the 7th IPRA General Conference. Eds. Luis Herrera and Raimo Väyrynen. Tampere, Finland: International Peace Research Association, 1979.

2111. Kollberg, Sven. *East African Marine Research and Marine Resources.* Sarec Report R1:1979. Stockholm: Swedish Agency for Research Cooperation with Developing Countries, 1979.

2112. Kurien, John. "Entry of Big Business into Fishing. Its Impact on Fish Economy." *Economic and Political Weekly* 13 (9 September 1978): 1557–1565.

2113. Lawson, Rowena. *Interim Report on Socio-Economic Aspects of the Development of Artisanal Fisheries on the East Coast of Malaysia.* Manila: South China Sea Fisheries Development and Coordinating Program, 1975.

2114. Lawson, Rowena, and Kwei, Eric A. *African Entrepreneurship and Economic Growth: A Case Study of the Fishing Industry in Ghana.* Accra: Ghana Universities Press, 1974.

2115. Linsenmeyer, Dean A. *Economic Analysis of Alternative Strategies for the Development of Sierra Leone Marine Fisheries.* Working Paper no. 18. East Lansing: African Rural Economics Program, Michigan State University, December 1976.

2116. Maar, A.; Mortimer, M. A. E.; and Van der Lingen, I. *Fish Culture in Central East Africa.* Rome: Food and Agriculture Organization, 1966.

2117. Marr, John C. *Fishery and Resource Management in Southeast Asia.* RFF/PISFA Paper no. 7. Washington, D. C.: Resources for the Future, February 1976.

2118. Oyeleye, D. A. "Fishery Resources of the Western State of Nigeria." *The Nigerian Geographical Journal* 16 (December 1973): 119–136.

2119. Roedel, Philip M. "Fishing for the Future." *Agenda* 1 (December 1978): 17–20.

2120. Stamp, Elizabeth. "The End of Cheap Food." *New Internationalist* (April 1973): 6, 8.

2121. Suckcharoen, S.; Nuorteva, P.; and Häsänen, E. "Alarming Signs of Mercury Pollution in a Freshwater Area of Thailand." *Ambio* 7:3 (1978): 113–116.

2122. Tussing, Arlon R., and Hiebert, Robin Ann, with Jon G. Sutinen. *Fisheries of the Indian Ocean: Issues of International Management and Law of the Sea.* RFF/PISFA Paper 5. Washington, D. C.: Resources for the Future, June 1974.

Commodities

Proposals set forward by third world countries in the early and mid-1970s for the establishment of a "new international economic order" (NIEO) (see pages 33–40) were rather quickly reduced to negotiations relating to the Integrated Commodity Program (ICP). The ICP essentially envisaged the creation of a common fund to support a series of (as yet largely unnegotiated) commodity agreements that would in theory act to stabilize commodity markets and thus the incomes of countries dependent on the export of these items. Eighteen commodities were originally included in the ICP, but only ten are being considered seriously. These have come to be called the "core commodities": coffee, tea, cocoa, sugar, jute, cotton, rubber, hard fibers, copper, and tin. The ICP also called for price indexing, linking prices received by (largely third world) producers of raw materials to prices of manufactured goods that they must import (largely from industrialized countries). Indexing has not been a popular topic with the developed countries and has not been a subject of negotiation.

In March 1979, the broad outlines of a common fund were agreed upon in Geneva. Going into the negotiations for this fund, developing countries proposed that the fund have $6 billion at its disposal to enable it to intervene actively in commodity markets and to offer assistance to the poorest third world countries who are most dependent economically on commodity exports. However, the power of the fund agreed upon in March 1979 will not be nearly as wide ranging as originally hoped and will have as its initial capital (derived from direct government contributions) only $750 million. Of this, $350 million is to be used to help the poorest commodity producers with activities such as marketing, improving productivity, research and development. The agreement of the industrialized countries to this portion of the fund (called the "second window") was considered a major concession on their part.

How much the fund will actually benefit the producers is debatable. The contributions to the "second window" are not mandatory and there is no guarantee that the full $350 million will be raised by the time the fund is expected to go into operation in 1981. The $400 million available to the "first window," which is to be used to maintain commodity stocks, is insufficient to allow the fund to intervene very actively in commodity markets and cause a long-term increase in prices. In negotiating commodity agreements, which must be done separately for each commodity that will be associated with the common fund, the US government has been particularly insistent on creating mechanisms that will prevent prices from rising too much over the long term.

General

The first two UNCTAD entries (2159 and 2160) are the initial documents that spelled out third world proposals on the issue of commodities. The third UNCTAD entry is the resolution for the Integrated Commodity Program passed by UNCTAD IV in 1976.

Part I of entry 1605, *Feeding the Few,* is a politically-oriented introduction to the commodity situation in third world countries and the recent NIEO-related attempts to improve that situation. Other entries discussing recent events relating to the commodity trade of third world countries are the issue of *Revue Tiers-Monde* (entry 2125) and the article by Maizels. The background paper from the US Congressional Budget Office evaluates the "costs" to the US of various responses to third world demands on commodity trade.

For a survey of the "commodity problem" and the various mechanisms that have been tried to alleviate that problem, readers should consult Singh and Singh and Staff. In the former, Singh argues that low prices and stagnant demand for commodities are more damaging to third world countries than price fluctuations. However, he concludes that the industrialized countries are unlikely to make the sort of concessions demanded by the third world that are necessary if the issue of commodity trade is to be resolved beneficially for developing nations.

Evans offers a critique of international commodity policy from a non-neoclassical perspective. He argues that the UNCTAD/NIEO proposals on commodities, even if they were fully implemented, would not be likely to result in the attainment of the desired ends. Evans concludes that the discussion of international commodity policy to date has failed to consider seriously the problems involved in making structural and/or institutional changes within the framework of the world capitalist system. Tims, on the other hand, does believe that it is possible to improve the situation of commodity exporting from third world countries within the present system. He argues that the removal of nontariff and tariff barriers would help increase the export earnings of developing nations. Tims estimates that the lower-income countries could be among the major beneficiaries of such a change.

Whether commodity price stabilization would benefit or hurt third world countries has been increasingly debated. The study by Brook, Grilli, and Waelbroeck finds that, as *exporters,* third world countries would benefit from price stabilization for cocoa, coffee, wool, jute, cotton, and sugar. However, as *importers,* they would benefit only from more stable wheat prices. This study also explains how to determine whether stable or unstable prices benefit importers or exporters. Valdés and Huddleston find that the potential of agricultural exports to finance increased food imports varies from country to country.

Austin provides considerable information on the involvement of agribusiness in Latin America by commodity. More politically oriented examinations of agribusiness in Latin America can be found in the sections entitled "Aid and Neocolonialism" (pages 178–181) and "Economic and Political Roots of Hunger" (pages 202–206). In specific, the operation of multinationals in the Mexican fruit and vegetable sector is discussed in entries 1603, 1628, and 1893. Other entries dealing with agribusiness in Latin America include entries 1606, 1609, 1616, 1630, and 1909.

Wood looks at the failure of a groundnut (peanut) scheme in colonial Tanganyika. Some of the shortcomings of the EEC Stabex scheme for stabilizing export earnings of Lomé Convention members are discussed by Rake.

2123. "Agriculture: Uneven Growth." *Economic and Political Weekly* 13 (28 October 1978): 1794.

2124. Austin, James E. *Agribusiness in Latin America.* New York: Praeger, 1974.

2125. "Avant la CNUCED–IV: Les Produits de Base et la Politique Internationale" (Issue Title). *Revue Tiers-Monde* 17 (April–June 1976): 235–560.

2126. Beshai, Adel Amin. *Export Performance and Economic Development in Sudan, 1960–67.* London: Ithaca Press, 1976.

2127. Blau, G., and Music, D. A. *Agricultural Commodity Trade and Development.* FAO Commodity Policy Studies no. 17. Rome: Food and Agriculture Organization, 1964.

2128. Brook, Ezriel M.; Grilli, Enzo R.; and Waelbroeck, Jean. *Commodity Price Stabilization and the Developing Countries: The Problem of Choice.* Working Paper 262. Washington, D. C.: World Bank, July 1977.

2129. Brown, C. P. *Primary Commodity Control.* Kuala Lumpur: Cambridge University Press, 1975.

2130. Chauhan, Brij Raj. "Rise and Decline of a Cash Crop in an Indian Village." *Journal of Farm Economics* 42 (August 1960): 663–666.

2131. Evans, David. *International Commodity Policy: UNCTAD and NIEO in Search of a Rationale.* IDS Discussion Paper D–132. Brighton, UK: Institute of Development Studies, University of Sussex, 1978. (Also available in *World Development* 7 (March 1979): 259–280.)

2132. Food and Agriculture Organization. *Commodity Bulletin Series.* no. 1–51. Rome: March 1947–1972.

2133. ———. *Commodity Policy Studies.* no. 1–22. Rome: 1952–1971.

2134. ______. *FAO Commodity Review. 1962. Special Supplement: Agricultural Commodities. Projections for 1970.* 2nd printing. Rome: 1963.

2135. ______. *FAO Commodity Review. 1964. Special Supplement: Trade in Agricultural Commodities in the United Nations Development Decade.* 2 vols. Rome: 1964.

2136. ______. *Synthetics and their Effects on Agricultural Trade.* Commodity Bulletin Series no. 38. Rome: 1964.

2137. Freivalds, J. "Agro-Industry in Africa." *World Crops* 25 (May–June 1973): 124–126.

2138. Green, Reginald H., and Singer, Hans W. "Toward a Rational and Equitable New International Economic Order: A Case for Negotiated Structural Change." *World Development* 3 (June 1975): 427–444.

2139. Hutchison, John E.; Naive, James J.; and Tsu, Sheldon K. *World Demand Prospects for Wheat in 1980. With Emphasis on Trade by Less Developed Countries.* Foreign Agricultural Economic Report no. 62. Washington, D. C.: Economic Research Service, US Department of Agriculture, July 1970.

2140. Instituto Centroamericano de Investigacion Agrícola y Technología Industrial (ICIATI). *La Producción y Exportación de Productos Agrícolas no Tradicionales en Centro América.* Guatemala: 1971.

2141. Kyesimira, Yoeri. *Agricultural Export Development.* Nairobi: East African Publishing House for Makerere Institute of Social Research, 1969.

2142. Maizels, Alf. "UNCTAD and the Commodity Problems of Developing Countries." *Institute of Development Studies Bulletin* 5:1 (January 1973): 42–53.

2143. Oroza, Gonzalo. "The Political Economy of the Commodity Agreements," pp. 124–135. In *Peace, Development, and New International Order. Proceedings of the 7th IPRA General Conference.* Eds. Luis Herrera and Raimo Väyrynen. Tampere, Finland: International Peace Research Association, 1979.

2144. Paige, Jeffry M. *Agrarian Revolution: Social Movements and Export Agriculture in the Underdeveloped World.* New York: Free Press, 1975.

2145. Payer, Cheryl, ed. *Commodity Trade of the Third World.* New York: Wiley, 1975.

2146. Pedroso, Iby A., and Freebairn, Donald K. *Food Crops vs. Monoculture Cane: The Case of Piracicaba, São Paulo, Brazil.* Cornell International Agricultural Development Bulletin 13. Ithaca, N. Y.: Cornell University, 1969.

2147. Powelson, John P. "Sugar and Cuba," pp. 99–108. In *Comparative Readings on Latin America.* Comp. and ed. Robert H. Terry. Berkeley, Calif.: McCutchan, 1969.

2148. Rake, Alan. "Stabex: How Effective Will it Really Be?" *African Development* 9 (June 1975): 23,25.

2149. Reddy, P. N. "The Role of Plantation Crops in India's Economy." *World Crops* 21 (November–December 1969): 352–353.

2150. Rojko, Anthony S., and Mackie, Arthur B. *World Demand Prospects for Agricultural Exports of Less Developed Countries in 1980.* Foreign Agricultural Economics Report no. 60. Washington, D. C.: Economic Research Service, US Department of Agriculture, June 1960.

2151. Singh, Shamsher. "The International Dialogue on Commodities." *Resources Policy* (June 1976): 87–96. (Also available as World Bank Reprint 39.)

2152. Singh, Shamsher, and Staff. *Commodity Trade and Price Trends.* EC–166/75. Washington, D. C.: World Bank, August 1975.

2153. Stanford Research Institute. *Middle Africa Transportation Survey (MATS). Agriculture Sector.* Supporting Document 2. SRI Project no. 6594. Contract no. AID/Afr–503. Menlo Park, Calif.: August 1968.

2154. Stein, Leslie. *The Growth of East African Exports.* London: Croom-Helm, 1979. (Discusses Tanzania, Kenya and Uganda.)

2155. Stewart, I. G., and Ord, H. W., eds. *African Primary Products & International Trade.* Edinburgh: University Press, 1965.

2156. Tay, T. H., and Wee, Y. C. "Success of a Malaysian Agro-Industry." *World Crops* 25 (March–April 1973): 84–86. (Deals with the pineapple industry.)

2157. Third World First/Haslemere. *Sugar: A Study of the Sell-Out over Commonwealth Sugar in the Common Market Negotiations.* London and Oxford: Haslemere Declaration Group and Third World First, 1971.

2158. Tims, Wouter. "Possible Effects of Trade Liberalization on Trade in Primary Commodities." Bank Staff Working Paper no. 193. Washington, D. C.: World Bank, January 1975, mimeo.

2159. United Nations, Conference on Trade and Development. *An Integrated Programme for Commodities; Reports by the Secretary General.* TD/B/C.1/166 and Supp. 1; Supp. 1/Add. 1; and Supp. 2–5. Geneva: 1974.

2160. ______ . *Indexation of Prices: Reports by the Secretary General.* TD/B/503/Supp. 1; Supp. 1/Add. 1. Geneva: 1974.

2161. ______ . *Resolution 93 IV.* TD/RES/43(IV). Nairobi: 30 May 1976.

2162. United Nations, Economic Commission for Africa. "Trade and Aid Prospects for Kenya, Tanzania and Uganda." *Economic Bulletin for Africa* 10 (June 1970): 41–61.

2163. United States. Agency for International Development. *Trade & Development: Trade Performance and Prospects of Developing Countries.* Washington, D. C.: October 1971.

2164. United States, Congress, Congressional Budget Office. *Commodity Initiatives of Less Developed Countries: U. S. Responses and Costs.* Background Paper. Washington, D. C.: US Printing Office, May 1977.

2165. Upton, Martin. "Development of Tree Crop Production in Southern Nigeria." *World Crops* 25 (May–June 1973): 152–156.

2166. Valdés, Alberto, and Huddleston, Barbara. *Potential of Agricultural Exports to Finance Increased Food Imports in Selected Developing Countries.* Occasional Paper 2. Washington, D. C.: International Food Policy Research Institute, August 1977.

2167. Williams, Gavin, and Tumusiime-Mutebile, Emmanuel. "Capitalist and Petty Commodity Production in Nigeria: A Note." *World Development* 6 (September–October 1978): 1103–1104.

2168. Wood, Alan. *The Groundnut Affair.* London: The Bodley Head, 1950.

Bananas

Latin American countries (particularly Colombia, Ecuador, Honduras, Guatemala, Costa Rica, and Panama) have been major banana producers for the past 50 years or so. In most cases, banana production and marketing have been controlled by US multinational corporations. In 1974, faced with fairly stable banana prices since the end of World War II, stagnant demand, and rising import bills, a number of Latin American producers attempted to increase their revenues by imposing a tax on each box of bananas exported. Partly because not all Latin American banana producers participated in the tax scheme but primarily because of actions on the part of the US government and US multinationals, this effort was not very successful. The two studies by Casey look at some of the problems facing the Latin American banana industry.

Clairmonte argues that simply to increase the price of bananas or the quantity consumed will not ensure significantly larger financial returns to banana-growing countries since a large proportion of the price of bananas goes toward financing marketing and distribution. These activities are largely in the hands of foreign agribusiness. The structure of agribusiness in the banana sector is examined by Arthur, Houck and Beckford. Entry 1637 looks specifically at United Fruit (now United Brands).

The report by McCallie and Lappé demonstrates that the situation of many banana industry workers (on plantations and at the docks) is deplorable. McCallie and Lappé look at the structure of the banana industry in the Philippines. They describe the relationship between the multinational corporations that market the fruit (largely in Japan) and the wealthy Filipino plantation owners who are responsible for banana production. Many of the banana workers were deprived of their land by the expansion of banana plantations (in southern Mindanao) and are now considerably poorer than they were before agribusiness began promoting banana production in the Philippines in the late 1960s. However, the banana workers are in a sense "lucky," since they have some means of support while many Filipinos who have lost their land to banana plantations have even less opportunity for earning a living. Entry 1918 summarizes this report. The book by Kepner also examines some of the social aspects of the banana industry.

The FAO monograph surveys the world banana economy at the beginning of the 1970s.

2169. Arthur, Henry B.; Houck, James P.; and Beckford, George L. *Tropical Agribusiness Structures and Adjustments—Bananas.* Boston, Mass.: Harvard University Press, 1968. (Chapters 4–6 are especially relevant.)

2170. Casey, Donald J. *The Latin American Banana Crisis.* Development Issue Paper 1. New York: UN Development Programme, c.1975.

2171. ———. *The Latin Amerian Banana Crisis.* Development Paper 1/Rev. 1. New York: UN Development Programme, c.1976.

2172. Clairmonte, Frederick F. "World Banana Economy: Problems and Prospects." *Economic and Political Weekly* 11:5–7 (Annual Number 1976): 277–292.

2173. Food and Agriculture Organization. *The World Banana Economy.* FAO Commodity Bulletin Series no. 50. Rome: 1971.

2174. Graham, Michael. "In Search of a Better Banana." *IDRC Reports* 7 (March 1978): 22–23.

2175. Kepner, Charles D., Jr. *Social Aspects of the Banana Industry.* New York: AMS, 1967.

2176. McCallie, Eleanor, and Lappé, Frances M., with assistance of Nicole Ballenger, Adele Beccar-Varela, Toby Stewart, and Terry McClain. *The Banana Industry in the Philippines.* San Francisco, Calif.: Institute for Food and Development Policy, 1977.

2177. Rodriquez, D. W. *Bananas: An Outline of the Economic History of Production and Trade with Special Reference to Jamaica.* Commodity Bulletin no. 1. Kingston, Jamaica: Department of Agriculture, 1955.

2178. Third World First/Haslemere. *Bananas: A Study of the Crisis in the Jamaican Banana Industry.* London and Oxford: Haslemere Declaration Group and Third World First, 1971.

2179. United States, Department of Agriculture, Economic Research Service. *World Prospects for Bananas in 1980 with Emphasis on Trade by Less Developed Countries.* Foreign Agricultural Economics Report no. 69. Washington, D. C.: c.1970.

Coffee

The structure of the world coffee economy is discussed in the report by the US Government Accounting Office and in the study by deVries. Watts examines the Diversification Fund set up by the International Coffee Organization to help countries produce other commodities. The North London Haslemere Group offers a politically-oriented critique of the world coffee market and the International Coffee Agreement. The article by Berryman discusses some of the environmental drawbacks of dependence on coffee production.

2180. Berryman, Phillip. "The Cost of Coffee." *Environment* 19 (August–September 1977): 12–15.

2181. "Brazil Feels Pressure to Drop Export Price; Calazans Explains Policy." *World Coffee & Tea* (November 1977): 30–31, 37.

2182. "High Cost of Labor, Threat of Rust Spread Have Producers Worried." *World Coffee & Tea* (January 1978): 68–71.

2183. North London Haslemere Group. *Coffee: The Rules of Neo-Colonialism. A Study of the International Coffee Trade and the International Coffee Agreement.* London and Oxford: Haslemere Declaration Group and Third World First, 1972.

2184. Singh, S.; Vries, J. de; Hulley, J. C. L.; and Yeung, P. *Coffee, Tea, and Cocoa: Prospects and Development Lending.* Baltimore, Md.: Johns Hopkins University Press, 1977.

2185. Timms, Daniel E. *World Demand Prospects for Coffee in 1980 with Emphasis on Trade by Less Developed Countries.* Foreign Agricultural Economics Report no. 86. Washington, D. C.: Economic Research Service, US Department of Agriculture, March 1973.

2186. United States, General Accounting Office. *Coffee: Production and Marketing Systems.* ID–77–54. Washington, D. C.: 28 October 1977.

2187. Vries, Jacob H. de. *Structure and Prospects of the World Coffee Economy.* Working Paper 208. Washington, D. C.: World Bank, June 1975.

2188. Watts, Ronald. "Diversification Away from Coffee." *World Crops* 25 (September–October 1973): 229–230.

Timber

A review of some recent literature dealing with the development of third world forestry resources is found in Cliff. Donaldson considers the importance of the forestry sector for economic development and some of the ecological problems involved. He concludes that the World Bank should become more involved in this sector.

The FAO study looks at the prospects for exploiting the forest resources of Africa while Gregersen and Contreras look at US investments in the forestry sector of Latin America. The timber resources of Asia are considered in Draper, Ewing, Burley, and Grayum, the special section of the *Far Eastern Economic Review* (entry 2193), and Takeuchi. The latter argues that remote areas of Asia can be industrialized and countries can triple their foreign exchange earnings by expanding wood processing operations. Unfortunately, considerable economic deprivation and ecological damage can also result, as entries 1624, 1632, and 1634 document. The latter, which discusses Nepal, is particularly recommended.

2189. Cliff, Edward P. *Utilization of Tropical Forests (A Review of the Forestry Literature in the Agency for International Development Reference Center).* PB–229–822. Washington, D. C.: US Agency for International Development, distributed by National Technical Information Service, US Department of Commerce, November 1973.

2190. Donaldson, Graham. *Forestry.* Sector Policy Paper. Washington, D. C.: World Bank, February 1978.

2191. Draper, S. A.; Ewing, A. J.; Burley, J.; and Grayum, G. *Pakistan: Forestry Sector Survey.* Working Paper 284. Washington, D. C.: World Bank, June 1978.

2192. Food and Agriculture Organization. *Timber Trends and Prospects in Africa.* Rome: 1967.

2193. "Forests: Save or Squander?" (Special Section). *Far Eastern Economic Review* (2 December 1977): 46–48, 53, 55–60, 63–66.

2194. Gregersen, Hans M., and Contreras, Arnoldo. *U. S. Investments in the Forest-Based Sector in Latin America: Problems and Potentials.* Baltimore, Md.: Johns Hopkins University Press, for Resources for the Future, 1975.

2195. Takeuchi, Kenji. *Tropical Hardwood Trade in the Asia-Pacific Region.* Baltimore, Md.: Johns Hopkins University Press, 1974. (Focuses on the Philippines, Malaysia, and Indonesia.)

Tea

The book by Sarkar is a useful survey of the world tea producing system. Entry 2184 is also relevant here.

2196. Avramovic, Dragoslav. *Stabilization, Adjustment and Diversification: A Study of the Weakest Commodities Produced by the Poorest Regions.* Working Paper 245. Washington, D. C.: World Bank, November 1976.

2197. Griffiths, Sir Percival. *The History of the Indian Tea Industry.* London: Weidenfeld and Nicolson, 1967.

2198. Habibullah, M. *Tea Industry of Pakistan.* Dacca: Bureau of Economic Research, University of Dacca, 1964.

2199. "Milking the British Cuppa." *Economic and Political Weekly* 13 (15 April 1978): 646–647.

2200. Sarkar, Goutam K. *The World Tea Economy.* London: Oxford University Press, 1972.

Fibers

Four of the entries here discuss jute — Stalker, Zondag, Grilli, and Morrison, and "Fleecing the Grower" (entry 2201). The latter shows once again how the actual producer of a commodity is often the one who receives the smallest remuneration for his or her activities. Entry 2196 is also relevant here.

Magleby and Missiaen and Kolawole discuss cotton. The article by Patel and Riordan deals with sisal. Entry 1915 also discusses sisal, specifically how a sisal scheme in Brazil has contributed to hunger.

2201. "Fleecing the Grower." *Economic and Political Weekly* 13 (20 May 1978): 835–836.

2202. Grilli, Enzo R., and Morrison, Ralph H. *Jute and the Synthetics.* Working Paper 171. Washington, D. C.: World Bank, January 1974.

2203. Kolawole, M. I. "Why Western Nigerian Farmers are Against Cotton Growing." *World Crops* 25 (July–August 1973): 179–181.

2204. Magleby, Richard S., and Missiaen, Edmond. *World Demand Prospects for Cotton in 1980: With Emphasis on Trade by Less Developed Countries.* Washington, D. C.: Economic Research Service, US Department of Agriculture, January 1971.

2205. Patel, H. D., and Riordan, E. B. "Making the Most of Sisal Exports: An Analysis of Prices Paid to Tanganyika and Kenya." *East African Journal of Rural Development* 1:1 (1968): 39–47.

2206. Stalker, Peter. "Lifeline to Bangladesh." *New Internationalist* no. 30 (August 1975): 13–15.

2207. Zondag, C. H. *Pakistan Jute. Its Problems and Promise.* Staff Study. Karachi [?]: Mission to Pakistan, US Agency for International Development, June 1967.

Nutrition

Books and Monographs

Although the book by Schofield is based on a very small sample, it is probably the most comprehensive survey of village nutrition in existence. Anyone interested in rural nutrition should certainly consult this work. The study by Berg is a useful introduction to the issue of nutrition in developing countries.

The study by Foster suggests that there are five ways of improving rural nutrition: changing the income of the rural poor, changing the distribution of income, changing demand patterns, changing the price of food, or changing fertility. Foster argues that Green Revolution technology can increase the incomes of semi-subsistence farmers and so improve their nutritional status. However, Palmer points out that the introduction of Green Revolution technology has both positive and negative effects for rural communities. If the technical improvements of the Green Revolution can be linked to social goals rather than to the pursuit of private profit, they are more likely to improve rural nutrition. Writing in 1972, Palmer finds no reason to believe that Green Revolution technology has done much to increase per capita food production in poor countries. In view of the many social inequities which researchers have found to be created or intensified through the introduction of Green Revolution technology (see the section entitled, "Green Revolution," pages 88–98), it is difficult to estimate the overall impact of the Green Revolution on nutrition.

Reutlinger and Selowsky argue that, in the normal course of development, malnutrition is unlikely simply to disappear. Policies designed to reallocate food to target groups and to help low-income farmers increase and stabilize food production for their own consumption are judged by the authors to be more cost-effective than redistribution of income. It is estimated that the costs, particularly the political costs, of income redistribution would outweigh the benefits for most third world countries and that most third world governments would not consider income redistribution as a policy option. The benefits in terms of improved nutrition that do occur when at least some income redistribution is effected are studied by Machicado. In Chile, income redistribution benefited the lowest income strata proportionately more than all other strata although, even after income redistribution, the lowest income group remained deficient in protein intake and all but the highest income group remained deficient in caloric intake.

Entries 2219 and 2222 look at the relationship between nutrition and working efficiency or energy production. Entries 2924, 2925, and 3072 provide a good deal of information on malnutrition in Latin America and the Caribbean.

2208. Austin, James E., ed. *Global Malnutrition and Cereal Fortification.* Cambridge, Mass.: Ballinger, 1978.

2209. Aykroyd, W. R., and Doughty, J. *Wheat in Human Nutrition.* 2nd printing. FAO Nutrition Studies no. 23. Rome: FAO, 1971.

2210. Bassir, Olumbe. *Biochemical Aspects of Human Malnutrition in the Tropics.* The Hague: Junk, 1962.

2211. Berg, Alan. *The Nutrition Factor: Its Role in Development.* Washington, D. C.: Brookings Institution, 1973.

2212. Berg, Alan; Scrimshaw, Nevin S.; and Call, David L. *Nutrition, National Development, and Planning.* Cambridge, Mass.: MIT Press, 1975.

2213. Darby, William J. *Nutrition Problems and the World's Food Supply.* International Agriculture Series 2. St. Paul: Institute of Agriculture, University of Minnesota, c. 1966.

2214. Diallo, Elise. *Malnutrition et Sous-Nutrition des Enfants en Haute-Volta: Pour la Recherche d'un Equilibre Vivrier dans les Zones Arides et Subarides.* Dakar: Institut de Développement Economique et de Planification, 1974.

2215. Eckholm, Erik P. *The Two Faces of Malnutrition.* Worldwatch Paper 9. Washington, D. C.: Worldwatch Institute, 1976.

2216. Ethiopian Government RRC (Relief and Rehabilitation Commission). *Harerghe under Drought: A Survey of the Effects of Drought upon Human Nutrition in Harerghe Province.* Report to the Ethiopian Government by the London Technical Group (J. Seaman, J. Holt, and J. Rivers). Addis Ababa: 1974.

2217. Food and Agriculture Organization. *Joint FAO/WHO Expert Committee on Nutrition: Seventh Report. Rome, 12–20 December 1966.* 2nd printing. FAO Nutrition Meetings Report Series no. 42. Rome: 1970.

2218. ______. *Manual on Food and Nutrition Policy.* 4th printing. FAO Nutritional Studies no. 22. FAO Food and Nutrition Series no. 15. Rome: 1978.

2219. ______. *Nutrition and Working Efficiency.* 3rd printing. FFHC Basic Studies no. 5. Rome: 1966.

2220. ______. *Report of the Fourth Conference on Nutrition Problems in Latin America. Guatemala City, 23 September–1 October 1957.* FAO Nutrition Meetings Report Series no. 18. Rome: 1959.

2221. ———. *Report of the Nutrition Committee for South and East Asia, Fourth Session, Tokyo, 25 September–2 October 1956*. FAO Nutrition Meetings Report Series no. 14. Rome: 1957.

2222. Food and Agriculture Organization-World Health Organization, Ad Hoc Expert Committee. *Energy and Protein Requirements.* Rome: Food and Agriculture Organization, 1973.

2223. Food and Agriculture Organization-World Health Organization, Joint Expert Committee on Nutrition. *Food and Nutrition Strategies in National Development.* FAO Food and Nutrition Series no. 5. WHO Technical Report Series no. 584. Rome: Food and Agriculture Organization, 1976.

2224. Foster, Phillips. *Agricultural Policies and Rural Malnutrition.* Occasional Paper no. 7. PN–AAF-296. Washington, D. C.: US Agency for International Development, 1978.

2225. Fox, Hazel M. *Protein Possibilities for a Hungry World.* International Agriculture Series 7. St. Paul: Institute of Agriculture, University of Minnesota, c. 1967.

2226. Hakim, Peter, and Solimano, Giorgio. *Development Reform and Malnutrition in Chile.* International Nutrition Policy Series. Cambridge, Mass.: MIT Press, 1978.

2227. Levinson, F. James. *Morinda: An Economic Analysis of Malnutrition Among Young Children in Rural India.* International Nutrition Policy Series. Cambridge, Mass.: MIT Press, 1974.

2228. *Lives in Peril: Protein and the Child.* Rome: Food and Agriculture Organization, on behalf of the Protein Advisory Group, 1970.

2229. Machicado, Flavio. *The Redistribution of Income in Chile and Its Impact on the Patterns of Consumption of Essential Foods.* Research Paper no. 62. Madison: Land Tenure Center, University of Wisconsin, September 1974.

2230. National Research Council, Commission on International Relations. *World Food and Nutrition Study. The Potential Contribution of Research. Volume IV.* Washington, D. C.: National Academy of Sciences, 1977.

2231. Palmer, Ingrid. *Food and the New Agricultural Technology.* Report no. 72.9. Geneva: UN Research Institute for Social Development, 1972.

2232. Pariser, E. R.; Wallerstein, M. B.; Corkery, C. J.; and Brown, N. L. *Fish Protein Concentrate: Panacea for Protein Malnutrition?* International Nutrition Policy Series. Cambridge, Mass.: MIT Press, 1978.

2233. Patwardhan, Vinayak N., and Darby, William J. *The State of Nutrition in the Arab Middle East.* Nashville, Tenn.: Vanderbilt University Press, 1972.

2234. Reutlinger, Shlomo, and Selowsky, Marcelo. *Malnutrition and Poverty: Magnitude and Policy Options.* Baltimore, Md.: Johns Hopkins University Press, 1976.

2235. Schofield, Sue. *Development and the Problems of Village Nutrition.* London: Croom-Helm, 1979.

2236. Simmons, Emmy Bartz, and Poleman, Thomas T. *The Food Balance Sheet as a Parameter of Tropical Food Economies: The Case of Mauritius.* Cornell International Agriculture Bulletin 29. Ithaca, N. Y.: Cornell University, June 1974.

2237. United Nations, Department of Economic and Social Affairs. *Strategy Statement on Action to Avert the Protein Crisis in the Developing Countries.* ST/ECA/144. E/5018/Rev. 1. New York: 1971.

2238. United Nations, Economic and Social Council, Advisory Committee on the Application of Science and Technology to Development. *Feeding the Expanding World Population: International Action to Avert the Impending Protein Crisis.* New York: 1968.

2239. United States, Agency for International Development. *An AID Nutrition Research Rationale and Program for the 70's.* Washington, D. C.: Office of Nutrition, Technical Assistance Bureau, USAID, February 1970.

2240. Vahlquist, Bo, ed. *Nutrition. A Priority in African Development.* Stockholm: Almqvist & Wiksell, 1972.

2241. Welbourne, N. *Nutrition in Tropical Countries.* New York: Oxford University Press, 1963.

2242. Whyte, Robert Orr. *Rural Nutrition in China.* Hong Kong and New York: Oxford University Press, 1972.

2243. ______. *Rural Nutrition in Monsoon Asia.* New York: Oxford University Press, 1974.

Articles

Berg (entry 2245) looks at the relationship between the growth of per capita income and the elimination of malnutrition. He gives four reasons why increased per capita income may not improve the nutrition of the poorest income groups, particularly pre-school children in the poorest groups. Berg also argues that a reliance on income growth is not necessarily the most effective way of improving the nutrition of the poor. Panikar (entry 2253) believes that household income and not wage rates should be the basis for studying living standards in third world countries. Panikar shows that in Kuttanad in Kerala state, agricultural laborers have low household incomes and consequently low food intake despite the fact that wage rates are relatively high. The discrepancy arises because the agricultural laborers are able to find work for only about four months of the year.

Both the article by Reutlinger and the one by Reutlinger and Selowsky question whether malnutrition arises from an insufficient supply of food or because people are too poor to be able to purchase food. They conclude, "malnutrition is a poverty problem." In the first article (entry 2254), a food stamp type program is suggested as the most cost-effective method of reducing malnutrition. Reutlinger and Selowsky conclude, as they do in their longer study above (entry 2234), that because redistribution of income is not likely to be "politically palatable," governments need more information on programs for increasing nutrition that "could be implemented realistically." This entry also surveys some of the problems involved in improving child nutrition.

The article by Jelliffe discusses the negative impact of the (multinational) "food industry" in third world countries. Kumar finds that increased foodgrain production in India has resulted from the increased production of cereals while the output of pulses, the cheapest source of protein in India, has actually declined.

2244. Bardhan, Pranab K. "On Life and Death Questions." *Economic and Political Weekly* 9:32–34 (Special Number 1974): 1293–1304.

2245. Berg, Alan. "Increased Income and Improved Nutrition: A Shibboleth Examined." *Economic and Political Weekly* 5 (26 September 1970): A125–A128.

2246. ______. "Malnutrition and National Development." *Foreign Affairs* 46 (October 1967): 126–136.

2247. Dupin, Henri, ed. "Nutrition Humaine et Développement Economique et Social" (Issue Title). *Revue Tiers-Monde* 16 (July–September 1975): 459–669.

2248. Greenstock, David W. "Food from the Locust Plant." *The New Ecologist* no. 2. (March–April 1978): 55–56.

2249. Jelliffe, D. B. "Commerciogenic Malnutrition?" *Nutrition Reviews* 30 (September 1972).

2250. Kaul, Avtar K. "Protein Resources and Production." *Ambio* 6:2–3 (1977): 141–145.

2251. Kumar, B. L. "Declining Trend in Production of Pulses and Factors Affecting It." *Economic and Political Weekly* 13 (8 July 1978): 1112–1114.

2252. Panikar, P. G. K. "Economics of Nutrition." *Economic and Political Weekly* 7:5–7 (Annual Number 1972): 413–430.

2253. ———. "Employment, Income and Food Intake among Selected Agricultural Labour Households." *Economic and Political Weekly* 13:31–33 (Special Number 1978): 1361–1372.

2254. Reutlinger, Shlomo. "Malnutrition: A Poverty or a Food Problem?" *World Development* 5:8 (1977): 715–724. (Also available as World Bank Reprint no. 47.)

2255. Reutlinger, Shlomo, and Selowsky, Marcelo. "The Economic Dimensions of Malnutrition in Young Children." *Finance & Development* 16 (June 1979): 20–24.

2256. Schofield, Sue. "Village Nutrition in Less Developed Countries." *Institute of Development Studies Bulletin* 5:4 (1974): 13–20.

2257. "Science and Food for Man." *Impact of Science on Society* 24 (April–June 1974). (The articles by Finot, Sai, Dupin, and Kracht are relevant.)

2258. Sukhatme, P. V. "Nitrogen in Malnutrition." *Ambio* 6:2–3 (1977): 137–140.

2259. Swaminathan, M. S. "Relating Research Expenditure to Nutrition Goals." *Ceres* no. 64 (July–September 1978): 45–47.

Part V: Country-Specific Studies

The entries in the following sections are primarily concerned with rural development and food issues in individual developing countries. A few items deal with more general development-related topics. Not all the entries dealing with individual countries are included in Part V. In a very few cases, sections in Parts I–IV are subdivided by geographical area: "Green Revolution," "Historical Studies," "Reaching the Small Farmer," and "Land Tenure and the Need for Agrarian Reform." In general, readers should consult the subject index in order to identify all the items dealing with individual countries.

Asia

Table 4 offers statistics on per capita food production and agricultural and population growth rates in the 1960s and the early 1970s for some twenty Asian countries.

General

Studies listed under "General" in this and other sections of Part V either focus on the region as a whole or deal with two or more countries within the region and are therefore difficult to place under a single country heading.

The first Asian agricultural survey by the Asian Development Bank (ADB) (entry 2261) reviews the state of Asian agriculture up to the mid-1960s. The second ADB survey (entry 2262) carries that review through another decade. The second survey is interesting because it documents both the failure of most Asian agricultural development strategies and the importance of agrarian reform. Readers who are unable to obtain a copy of the second ADB survey should at least read the review of it by Ho. Also recommended are the monograph by Rao, the article by Hainsworth, the four supplementary volumes to the second ADB survey (entry 2263), and the *Economic and Social Survey of Asia and the Pacific, 1975* (entry 2289).

TABLE 4

Per Capita Agricultural Production, Agricultural and Population Growth Rates, Selected Asian Countries, 1960s and 1970s

Country	Per capita food production (1965-67 = 100) Average 1974-76	Average Annual Rate of Growth of			
		Agri-culture 1960-70	Popula-tion 1960-70	Agri-culture 1970-76	Popula-tion 1970-75
	(1)	(2)	(3)	(4)	(5)
Singapore	208	5.0	2.3	0.3	1.7
Malaysia	146	6.8	2.9	6.4	2.7
Indonesia	117	2.7	2.2	4.0	2.4
Turkey	114	2.8	2.5	4.9	2.5
Pakistan	114	4.9	2.8	1.6	3.0
Sri Lanka	110	3.0	2.4	1.2	1.7
North Korea	110	—[a]	2.8	—	2.7
Iran	109	8.1	2.9	5.8	2.8
Philippines	108	4.3	3.0	4.6	2.8
People's Republic of China	108	—	1.6	—	1.7
India	107	1.9	2.3	1.4	2.1
Thailand	106	5.5	3.1	4.3	2.9
South Korea	104	4.5	2.6	4.8	1.8
Laos	103	—	2.4	—	2.5
Papua New Guinea	99	—	2.3	—	2.6
Nepal	98	—	2.1	1.9	2.1
Burma	98	4.1	2.2	2.5	2.2
Bangladesh	95	2.7	2.8	0.5	2.0
Afghanistan	94	—	2.2	—	2.2
Hong Kong	84	−3.4	2.5	−5.1	1.9
Democratic Kampuchea	53	2.3	2.7	—	2.8
Republic of China (Taiwan)	—	3.4	3.1	1.5	2.0
Average	109	3.7	2.5	2.5	2.3

a = — signifies information not available

Sources: Column 1: FAO as cited in World Bank, *Rapport sur le Développement dans le Monde, 1978,* Washington, D. C.: August 1978, Table 1, pp. 86–87.
Columns 2 + 4: World Bank, *Rapport sur le Développement dans le Monde, 1978,* Washington, D. C.: August 1978, Table 2, pp. 88–89.
Columns 3 + 5: World Bank, *Rapport sur le Développement dans le Monde, 1978,* Washington, D. C.: August 1978, Table 13, pp. 110–111.

2260. "Agro-Industries '75" (Section Title). *Far Eastern Economic Review,* 20 July 1975, pp. 3–18.

2261. Asian Development Bank. *Asian Agricultural Survey.* Manila: 1968. (Also published by the University of Washington Press, Seattle, 1969.)

2262. ______. *Rural Asia: Challenge and Opportunity.* New York: Praeger, 1978.

2263. ______. *Rural Asia: Challenge and Opportunity. Supplementary Papers.* 4 vols. Manila: 1978.

2264. Borton, Raymond E., ed. *Case Studies to Accompany Getting Agriculture Moving.* New York: The Agricultural Development Council, 1967. (Chapters 1–6 are relevant.)

2265. Bruneau, Michel, ed. *Types de Cultures Commerciales Paysannes en Asie du Sud-Est et Dans le Monde Insulindien.* Talence, France: Centre d'Etudes de Géographie Tropicale, 1975.

2266. Chang Chi-wen. *Rural Asia Marches Forward: Focus on Agriculture and Rural Development.* Los Baños: College of Agriculture, University of the Philippines, 1969.

2267. Chang Chi-wen, ed. *A Strategy for Agricultural and Rural Development in Asian Countries.* Laguna, Philippines: Southeast Asian Regional Center for Graduate Study and Research in Agriculture, 1974.

2268. Chattopadhyay, Boudhayan. *Water, Cereals and Economic Growth in South and East Asia in the Fifties and Sixties.* New Delhi: People's, 1977.

2269. *Comparative Experience of Agricultural Development in the Post-War Period in Asia and the South-East, Delhi, 1971.* Bombay: Indian Society of Agricultural Economics, distributed by Thacker, 1972.

2270. *Final Report: Seminar on Effective Partnership for Growth: Use and Abuse of Aid in Achieving Asian Rural Development Goals, December 12–18, 1971, Ramon Magsaysay Center.* Manila: Ramon Magsaysay Foundation, c. 1971.

2271. Food and Agriculture Organization. *Agriculture in Asia and the Far East: Development and Outlook.* Rome: 1953.

2272. ______. *Problems of Food and Agricultural Expansion in the Far East.* Rome: 1955.

2273. Gourou, Pierre. *Man and Land in the Far East.* Trans. S. H. Beaver. London and New York: Longman, 1975.

2274. Hainsworth, Geoffrey B. "Economic Growth and Poverty in Southeast Asia: Malaysia, Indonesia and the Philippines." *Pacific Affairs* 52 (Spring 1979): 5–41.

2275. Hayami, Yujiro, in association with M. Akino, M. Shintani, and S. Yamada. *A Century of Agricultural Growth in Japan: Its Relevance to Asian Development.* Minneapolis: University of Minnesota Press, 1975.

2276. Ho Kwon Ping. "Asian Agriculture's Decade in the Wrong Direction." *Far Eastern Economic Review* (15 September 1978): 47–50.

2277. International Labour Organization. *Human Resources Development in Rural Areas in Asia and the Role of Rural Institutions.* Geneva: 1975.

2278. International Rice Research Institute. *Interpretive Analysis of Selected Papers from Changes in Rice Farming in Selected Areas of Asia.* Los Baños, Philippines: 1978.

2279. Jacoby, Erich H. *Agrarian Unrest in Southeast Asia.* 2nd rev. ed. London: Asia, 1961.

2280. Klatt, Werner. "Agrarian Issues in Asia: I. Land as a Source of Conflict." *International Affairs* (UK) 48 (April 1972): 226–241.

2281. Osterrieth, M.; Verrydt, E.; and Waelbroeck, J. *The Impact of Agricultural Price Policies on Demand and Supply, Incomes and Imports: An Experimental Model for South Asia.* Working Paper 277. Washington, D. C.: World Bank, 1977.

2282. Rao, V. K. R. V. *Growth with Justice in Asian Agriculture: An Exercise in Policy Formulation.* Geneva: UN Research Institute for Social Development, 1974.

2283. Rosen, George. *Peasant Society in a Changing Economy: Comparative Development in Southeast Asia and India.* Urbana: University of Illinois Press, 1975.

2284. Shand, Richard Tregurtha, ed. *Agricultural Development in Asia.* Berkeley: University of California Press, 1969. (Surveys Taiwan, India, Thailand, Burma, Malaysia, Philippines, Indonesia, and Papua New Guinea.)

2285. ———. *Technical Change in Asian Agriculture.* Canberra: Australian National University Press, 1973.

2286. "South East Asia's Economy in the 1970's." *Journal of Contemporary Asia* 3:3 (1973): 357–362.

2287. Spencer, Joseph Earle. *Shifting Cultivation in South-East Asia.* Berkeley: University of California Press, 1966.

2288. Stevens, R. D.; Alavi, Hamza; and Bertocci, Peter, eds. *Rural Development in Bangladesh and Pakistan.* Honolulu: The University Press of Hawaii, 1976.

2289. United Nations. *Economic and Social Survey of Asia and the Pacific, 1975.* Bangkok: 1975.

2290. United Nations, Economic Commission for Asia and the Far East. "First Biennial Review of Social and Economic Development in ECAFE Developing Countries during the Second United Nations Development Decade," pp. 9–114. In *Economic Survey of Asia and the Far East.* Bangkok: 1973.

2291. United States, Department of Agriculture, Economic Research Service. *The Agricultural Situation in the People's Republic of China and Other Communist Asian Countries.* Foreign Agricultural Economic Report no. 111. Washington, D. C.: 1977.

2292. Wharton, Clifton R., Jr. *Research on Agricultural Development in Southeast Asia.* New York: Agricultural Development Council, 1965.

China

Since 1956, Chinese development strategies have given priority to agriculture and light industry over heavy industry. In 1978, two years after the death of Mao Zedong and the reemergence of Deng Xiaping, it was proposed to reorder these priorities under the "Four Modernizations" strategy. The Four Modernizations were industry (particularly steel), science and technology, agriculture (especially mechanization), and defense. The strategy called for "taking steel as the key link." Whereas Maoist development policy had been based on self-reliance, including as a principal tenet the avoidance of debt, the Four Modernizations strategy was based on large-scale technological, financial, and managerial imports from Western countries. Many foreign analysts were dubious about Beijing's ability to pay for its proposed imports and about the ability of the country as a whole to absorb the amount of new technology envisaged under the Four Modernizations.

By early 1979, it was clear that the Chinese leadership had its own doubts, for the new strategy was "readjusted" and priority was once again given to agriculture and light industry. In particular, the goals for mechanization of agriculture were severely curtailed, bringing them —some observers argued—more into line with reality.

Books and Monographs

The book by Tawney and the volume edited by Buck (entry 2293) discuss pre-revolutionary China. The studies by the FAO and IRRI consider what the Chinese experience can teach other Asian nations. *La Voie Chinoise* (entry 2301) gives considerable attention to questions pertaining to agricultural development but discusses other development-related topics as well. The compendium compiled for the Joint Economic Committee of the US Congress includes articles on general Chinese policy, manufacturing and extractive industries, population and labor utilization, agriculture, and foreign economic relations.

Other recommended entries include the three studies by Stavis, the two monographs edited by Etienne, the report by Jacoby, and the book edited by Perkins.

2293. Buck, John Lossing, ed. *Land Utilization in China.* Shanghai: Commercial, 1937.

2294. Buck, John Lossing; Dawson, Owen L.; and Wu Yuan-li. *Food and Agriculture in Communist China.* New York: Praeger, 1966.

2295. Chao, Kang. *Agricultural Production in Communist China, 1949–1965.* Madison: University of Wisconsin Press, 1970.

2296. Chao Kuo-chün. *Agrarian Policy of the Chinese Communist Party, 1921–1959.* New York: Asia, 1960.

2297. ———. *Agrarian Policies of Mainland China: A Documentary Study (1949–1956).* Cambridge, Mass.: Harvard University Press, 1957.

2298. China, People's Republic. *National Programme for Agricultural Development, 1956–1967.* Peking: Foreign Languages Press, 1960.

2299. Chung-kuo kang ch'an tang. *The Draft Programme for Agricultural Development in the People's Republic of China, 1956–1967.* Peking: Foreign Languages Press, 1956.

2300. Dutt, Gargi. *Rural Communes of China: Organizational Problems.* Bombay: Asia, 1967.

2301. Etienne, Gilbert. *La Voie Chinoise: La Longue Marche de l'Economie.* Paris: Presses Universitaires de France, 1974.

2302. Etienne, Gilbert, ed. *China: Men, Grain and Machines—Agricultural Growth and Prospects.* Studies and Documents, v. 11, nos. 3–4. Geneva: Asian Documentation and Research Centre, Graduate Institute of International Studies, 1977.

2303. ———. *China's Agricultural Development: Production, Inputs, External Trade, Research.* Studies and Documents, v. 1, nos. 3–4. Geneva: Asian Documentation and Research Centre, Graduate Institute of International Studies, 1974.

2304. Food and Agriculture Organization, Regional Office for Asia and the Far East. *Learning from China. A Report on Agriculture and the Chinese People's Communes by an FAO Study Mission.* Bangkok: 1977.

2305. Henle, H. V. *Report on China's Agriculture.* Rome: Food and Agriculture Organization, 1974.

2306. International Rice Research Institute. *Rice Research and Production in China: An IRRI Team's View.* PN–AAF–321. Washington, D. C.: US Agency for International Development, 1978.

2307. Jacoby, Erich. *The Green Revolution in China.* Geneva: UN Research Institute for Social Development, 18 December 1973.

2308. Johnson, Elizabeth and Graham. *Walking on Two Legs: Rural Development in South China.* IDRC–070e. Ottawa: International Development Research Centre, July 1976.

2309. Kapp, K. W. *Environmental Policies and Development Planning in Contemporary China and Other Essays.* The Hague: Mouton, 1974. (Chapter 1 is relevant.)

2310. Klatt, Werner. *The Chinese Model: A Political, Economic and Social Survey.* New Delhi: Eurasia, 1966.

2311. Kuitenbrouwer, Joost B. W. *Self-Reliance without Poverty.* Bangkok: UN Economic and Social Commission for Asia and the Pacific, 1976.

2312. Kuo, Leslie T. C. *The Technical Transformation of Agriculture in Communist China.* New York: Praeger, 1972.

2313. Liu Jung-chao. *China's Fertilizer Economy.* Chicago, Ill.: Aldine, 1970.

2314. National Council for US-China Trade. *China's Agriculture.* Washington, D. C.: 1976.

2315. Perkins, Dwight, ed. *China's Modern Economy in Historical Perspective.* Stanford, Calif.: Stanford University Press, 1975.

2316. Printz, Peggy, and Steinle, Paul. *Commune: Life in Rural China.* New York: Dodd, Mead, 1977.

2317. Schran, Peter. *The Development of Chinese Agriculture 1950–59.* Urbana: University of Illinois Press, 1969.

2318. Stavis, Benedict. *Ending Famines in China.* Report to the International Federation of Institutes for Advanced Study (IFIAS) for "The 1972 Case—Drought and Man: A Case History." Ithaca, N. Y.: Center for International Studies, Cornell University, c.1977, mimeo.

2319. ———. *Making Green Revolution: The Politics of Agricultural Development in China.* Rural Development Monograph no. 1. Ithaca, N. Y.: Rural Development Committee, Center for International Studies, Cornell University, 1974.

2320. ———. *People's Communes and Rural Development in China.* RLG no. 2. Ithaca, N. Y.: Rural Development Committee, Center for International Studies, Cornell University, 1974.

2321. Tawney, R. H. *Land and Labour in China.* New York: Octagon, 1964.

2322. United States, Congress, Joint Economic Committee. Compendium: *Chinese Economy Post-Mao. Volume 1: Policy and Performance.* 95th Cong., 2nd Sess. Washington, D. C.: US Printing Office, 9 November 1978. (Sections III and IV are particularly relevant.)

2323. United States, Department of Agriculture, Economic Research Service. *People's Republic of China: Agricultural Situation.* Washington, D. C.: May 1978.

2324. Walker, Kenneth R. *Planning in Chinese Agriculture: Socialization and the Private Sector, 1956–1962.* Chicago, Ill.: Aldine; and London: Cass, 1965.

Articles

The speech by Hua Guofeng at the Second Session of the Fifth People's Congress on June 18, 1979 (entry 2331) outlines the "readjustments" made to the Four Modernizations strategy. The reduced tempo of modernization and the renewed emphasis on agriculture is called "winning the first battle for the Four Modernizations" and is an admission that the Chinese economy is simply incapable of modernizing as quickly as at least some members of the Chinese leadership had anticipated. At the same time, it is clear that the interest in "catching up with the West" has not disappeared. The fact that the economy is too weak to move ahead rapidly is termed a result of "the grave effects of the sabotage by Lin Biao and the gang of four. . . ."

The two articles by Eberstadt survey the situation in post-Mao China concerning the provision of food and of health services (entry 2326) and the extent to which the goal of equality has been attained (entry 2327). Eberstadt points out that it is very difficult to ascertain per capita food production. For one thing, Chinese population estimates vary considerably. However, it seems that per capita food production has not risen as much as some analysts have suggested in the past. This conclusion would seem to be justified in view of the statement by Hua Guofeng, "The main problem now facing us is that our agricultural expansion . . . at times cannot even keep up with the demands of a growing population" (Hua, p. 11). Furthermore, Eberstadt says that the distribution of food between rural and urban areas is less equal than many have thought. Nonetheless, he concludes that China has provided a better standard of living for the "average" citizen than most third world countries. (A third article in this series on women and education can be found in the section entitled "Women in Development," pages 98–105.)

The article by Chiang Lei gives the official line on China's success in combating drought. Nolan compares the Chinese approach to collectivization with the Russian approach. The article by Wong and the issue of *World Development* edited by Unger discuss the relevance of the Chinese experience in agricultural development for other Asian countries.

Other recommended articles include Sinha, Stavis, the issue of *World Development* edited by Maxwell, Myers, Field and Kirkpatrick, Perkins (entry 2342), and Walker.

2325. Chiang Lei. "Three Years' Bad Drought, Three Years' Fine Crops." *China Reconstructs* 23 (February 1974): 2–5.

2326. Eberstadt, Nick. "Has China Failed?" *New York Review of Books* (5 April 1979): 33–40.

2327. ______. "China: How Much Success?" *New York Review of Books* (3 May 1979): 38–44.

2328. Etienne, Gilbert. "Some Trends in China's Agriculture." *Teaching Forum.* no. 37. New York: The Agricultural Development Council, March 1974.

2329. Field, Robert Michael, and Kilpatrick, James A. "Chinese Grain Production: An Interpretation of the Data." *The China Quarterly* no. 74 (June 1978): 385–400.

2330. Grey, Jack. "Mao Tse-Tung's Strategy for the Collectivization of Chinese Agriculture: An Important Phase in the Development of Maoism," pp. 39–65. In *Sociology and Development.* Eds. Emmanuel De Kadt and Gavin Williams. London: Tavistock, 1974.

2331. Hua Guofeng. "Report on the Work of the Government." *Beijing Review* no. 27 (6 July. 1979): 5–31.

2332. Khan, A. R. "Taxation, Procurement and Collective Incentives in Chinese Agriculture." *World Development* 6 (June 1978): 827–836.

2333. Khan, A. Z. M. Obaidullah. "The Three Great Struggles in the Chinese Countryside: A Case Study." *Bangladesh Development Studies* 4:2–3 (1976).

2334. Larsen, Marion R. "China's Crop Outlook Dims." *Foreign Agriculture* 19 (5 July 1976): 2–4.

2335. Maxwell, Neville. "The Fourth Mobilization: New Phase of the Tachai Movement." *World Development* 6 (April 1978): 499–518.

2336. Maxwell, Neville, ed. "China's Road to Development" (Issue Title). *World Development* 3 (July–August 1975): 453–608.

2337. Myers, Ramon H. "Wheat in China—Past, Present and Future." *The China Quarterly* no. 74 (June 1978): 297–333.

2338. Nolan, Peter. "Collectivization in China: Some Comparisons with the USSR." *Journal of Peasant Studies* 3 (January 1976): 192–220.

2339. Paine, S. "Balanced Development: Maoist Conception and Chinese Practice." *World Development* 4 (April 1976): 277–304.

2340. Perkins, Dwight. "Centralization and Decentralization in Mainland China's Agriculture: 1949–62." *Quarterly Journal of Economics* 78 (May 1964): 208–237.

2341. ______. "Chairman Mao's Foundation." *Far Eastern Economic Review* (1 October 1976): 50–53.

2342. ______. "Constraints Influencing China's Agricultural Performance." In *China: A Reassessment of the Economy.* US Congress, Joint Economic Committee. Washington, D. C.: US Printing Office, 10 July 1975.

2343. "Science in Agriculture," pp. 27–66. In *China: Science Walks on Two Legs. A Report from Science for the People.* New York: Discus/Avon, 1974.

2344. Sinha, Radha P. "Chinese Agriculture: A Quantitative Look." *The Journal of Development Studies* 11 (April 1975): 202–223.

2345. Stavis, Benedict. "How China is Solving its Food Problem." *Bulletin of Concerned Asian Scholars* 7 (July–September 1975): 22–38.

2346. Timmer, C. Peter. "Food Policy in China." *Food Research Institute Studies* 15:1 (1976):53–69.

2347. Unger, Jonathan, ed. "Chinese Rural Institutions and the Question of Transferability" (Issue Title). *World Development* 6 (May 1978): 559–717.

2348. Walker, Kenneth R. "Grain Self-Sufficiency in North China, 1953–1975." *The China Quarterly* no. 71. (September 1977): 555–590.

2349. Wertheim, Willem F. "The Communes Revisited." *Ceres* no. 29 (September–October 1972): 25–28.

2350. Wong, John. "Agricultural Production and Socialist Transformation in China: Two Decades After." *Malayan Economic Review* 18 (October 1973).

2351. ______. "An Economic Overview of Agriculture in the People's Republic of China." *Teaching Forum,* no. 26. New York: The Agricultural Development Council, January 1973.

2352. ______. "Some Aspects of China's Agricultural Development Experience: Implications for Developing Countries in Asia." *World Development* 4 (June 1976): 485–497.

2353. Wortman, Sterling. "Agriculture in China." *Scientific American* 232 (June 1975): 13–21.

India

After a period of poor harvests, food shortages, inflation, slow economic growth, and social unrest, India found itself in a relatively strong economic condition at the end of the 1970s, at least on paper. The economy grew at an annual rate of about 5 percent between 1975 and 1979. Grain reserves were above normal requirements and foreign exchange reserves reached a high of $7 billion in 1979. Nonetheless, about half the Indian population lives at or near subsistence level. There was virtually no increase in per capita food consumption during the 1970s. The poor, particularly the rural poor, have been unable to afford to increase their consumption rates in proportion to the growth of the food surplus. The expansion of land under irrigation was largely responsible for the increase in food production at the end of the 1970s. Some observers worry that further expansion of irrigated areas will lead to higher food surpluses in the coming years but that the ability of the poor to increase their food consumption will not grow correspondingly.

Books and Monographs

Bhowani Sen offers a critique of British colonial policy and of post-independence policies of the Indian government. Another excellent critique of British colonial policies is found in entry 1333. Srivastava and George evaluate the costs and benefits of four programs run by the Bharatiya Agro-Industries Foundation (set up by a disciple of Gandhi). The four programs were in the fields of irrigation, cattle raising, introduction of tractors, and construction of a cooperative society. While the level of analysis is not always satisfactory, this volume provides considerable information on the four programs.

Mencher argues that only a radical change in land tenure systems will allow a permanent increase in food production in Tamil Nadu. Other recommended items include Johl and Mudahar, Reddy, Mamoria, Hanumantha Rao, and Etienne.

2354. Bansil, Puran Chand. *Agricultural Problems of India.* 2nd rev. and enl. ed. Delhi: Vikas, 1975.

2355. Bharadwaj, Krishna. *Production Conditions in Indian Agriculture: A Study Based on Farm Management Surveys.* New York: Cambridge University Press, 1974.

2356. Bhatnagar, Kalka Prasad; Nigam, A. R.; and Srivastava, J. P. S. *Indian Rural Economy.* 5th rev. and enl. ed. Kanpur: Kishore, 1965.

2357. Broehl, Wayne G., Jr. *The Village Entrepreneur: Change Agents in India's Rural Development.* Cambridge, Mass.: Harvard University Press, 1978.

2358. Brown, Dorris D. *Agricultural Development in India's Districts.* Cambridge, Mass.: Harvard University Press, 1971.

2359. Chand, Shiv, and Kapoor, A. N. *Land and Agriculture of India. An Agronomic Study.* Delhi: Metropolitan, 1959.

2360. Dagli, Vadilal Jechand, ed. *A Regional Profile of Indian Agriculture.* 1st ed. Bombay: Vora on behalf of Commerce, 1975.

2361. Dasgupta, Sipra. *Agriculture: Producer's Rationality and Technical Change.* Bombay: Asia, 1970.

2362. Dayal, Rajeshwar. *India's New Food Strategy.* 1st ed. Delhi: Metropolitan, 1968.

2363. Duivedi, R. C. *New Strategy of Agricultural Development in India.* Meerut: Loyal, 1972.

2364. Etienne, Gilbert. *Studies in Indian Agriculture: The Art of the Possible.* Trans. Megan Mothersole. Berkeley: University of California Press, 1968.

2365. Farmer, Bertram H. *Agricultural Colonization in India Since Independence.* New York: Oxford University Press, 1974.

2366. Fliegel, Frederick C., et al. *Agricultural Innovations in Indian Villages.* Hyderabad: National Institute of Community Development, 1968.

2367. Franda, Marcus. *Dynamics of Indian Food Policy.* 1979/no. 1. Asia. Hanover, N. H.: American Universities Field Staff, 1979.

2368. Hanumantha Rao, C. H. *Technological Change and Distribution in Indian Agriculture.* Studies in Economic Growth, no. 17. Delhi: Macmillan Company of India, 1975.

2369. Hendrix, William E., and Giri, R. *India's Agricultural Progress in the 1950's and 1960's.* New Delhi: Directorate of Economics & Statistics, Government of India, 1970.

2370. Hopper, David. *Food Production in India: A Perspective.* IDRC–060e. Ottawa: International Development Research Centre, 1976.

2371. India (Republic), Department of Agriculture. *Agricultural Development, Problems and Perspectives.* New Delhi: 1965.

2372. Indian Council of Agricultural Research. *Developing Village India: Studies in Village Problems.* New Delhi: Imperial Council of Agricultural Research, 1946.

2373. Indian National Congress. *Report of the Congress Agrarian Reforms Committee.* 2nd ed. New Delhi: All-India Congress Committee, 1956.

2374. Jain, Sharad Chandra. *Indian Rural Economics.* Agra: L. N. Agarwal, 1965.

2375. Johl, S. S. and Mudahar, Mohinder S. *The Dynamics of Institutional Change and Rural Development in Punjab, India.* RLG 5. Ithaca, N. Y.: Rural Development Committee, Center for International Studies, Cornell University, c. 1974.

2376. Kivlin, Joseph; Fliegel, F. C.; Roy, P.; and Sen, L. K. *Innovation in Rural India.* Bowling Green, Ohio: Bowling Green State University Press, 1971.

2377. Kumar, Ladapuram S. S., and others. *Agriculture in India.* 3 vols. Bombay: Asia, 1963.

2378. Maheshwari, B. P. *Industrial and Agricultural Development of India Since 1914: A Study of Some Aspects of Economic History of India.* New Delhi: S. Chand, 1971.

2379. Mamoria, C. B. *Agricultural Problems in India.* 7th rev. and enl. ed. Allahabad: Kitab Mahal, 1972.

2380. Mathur, S. C., ed. *Agricultural Policy and Food Self-Sufficiency.* New Delhi: Associated, 1970.

2381. Mellor, John; Weaver, T.; Lele, U.; and Simon, S. *Developing Rural India: Plan and Practice.* Ithaca, N. Y.: Cornell University Press, 1968.

2382. Menamekat, Alexander. *Developmental Problems and the Role of Credit Cooperatives in Indian Agriculture.* Bern: Lang, 1975.

2383. Mencher, Joan P. *Agriculture and Social Structure in Tamil Nadu: Past Origins, Present Transformation, and Future Prospects.* New Delhi: Allied, 1978.

2384. Mitter, Swasti. *Peasant Movements in West Bengal.* Cambridge, UK: Department of Land Economy, Cambridge University, 1977.

2385. Mukhopadhyay, Sudhin K. *Sources of Variation in Agricultural Productivity.* Delhi: Macmillan Company of India, 1976.

2386. Nair, Kusum. *Blossoms in the Dust: The Human Factor in Indian Development.* New York: Praeger, 1962.

2387. Nanvati, Sir Manilal Balabhai, and Anjaria, J. J. *The Indian Rural Problem.* 7th rev. ed. Bombay: Indian Society of Agricultural Economics, 1970.

2388. Reddy, G. Ram. *Panchayati Raj and Rural Development in Andhra Pradesh, India.* RLG 4. Ithaca, N. Y.: Rural Development Committee, Center for International Studies, Cornell University, c. 1974.

2389. Sen, Bhowani. *Evolution of Agrarian Relations in India.* New Delhi: People's, 1962.

2390. Sen, Samar Ranjan. *Growth and Instability in Indian Agriculture.* Calcutta: Firma K. L. Mukhopadhyay, 1971.

2391. Shah, S. M. *Rural Development in India: Planning and Reforms.* Columbia, Mo.: South Asia, 1978.

2392. Shanmugasundaram, V., ed. *Agricultural Development in India: A Study of the Intensive Agricultural District Programme.* Economics Department Series no. 20. Madras: University of Madras, 1972.

2393. Shenoi, P. V. *Agricultural Development in India: A New Strategy in Management.* Delhi: Vikas, 1975.

2394. Sinha, Jasbir. *An Agricultural Atlas of India: A Geographical Analysis.* Kurukshetra: Vishal, 1974.

2395. Srivastava, Uma Kant, and George, P. S. *Rural Development in Action.* Bombay: Somaiya, 1977.

2396. Thirumalai, S. *Post-War Agricultural Problems and Policies in India.* Bombay: Vora, 1954. (This includes some discussion of agriculture in pre-independence India.)

Articles

Anyone interested in rural development in India should regularly survey *Economic and Political Weekly* (entry 3247). In particular, this journal publishes a special supplement entitled "Review of Agriculture" four times each year: in the last issue of March, June, September and December. The "Review" is composed of several articles on different aspects of agricultural development.

The two articles by Dandekar and Rath and the comments on them by Jayaraman, Madalgi, Medhora, and Sau (entry 2427) form an interesting debate on poverty in India. These articles do not deal solely with rural poverty, but should nonetheless be read by anyone interested in rural development in India. The article by Bardhan deals specifically with rural poverty. He computes an increase of approximately 65 percent in the number of people living below the rural poverty line between 1960/61 and 1968/69.

The development of capitalist farming is discussed in the articles by Patnaik and Pathy. Rudra and Swamy focus on social stratification. Ray looks at government food policies in entry 2424. He identifies three government objectives: to maintain a steady supply of food to consumers at a reasonable price, to provide adequate incentives to producers to increase food production, and to stabilize relative prices. Ray argues that the policies followed by the Indian government in the past have failed to balance the needs of consumers and those of producers. While food deficit States have obtained a proportionately larger share of government grain allocations, distribution to individuals has remained skewed. Furthermore, the policy has been more oriented toward the urban consumer than people in the rural sector.

Kothari discusses, in general terms, alternative rural development strategies. Other recommended articles include Shetty, Mencher, Narain, and Chandra. Also of relevance is entry 89 which offers a critique of the Draft Five Year Plan 1978–83.

2397. Achaya, K. T. "Tackling the Edible Oil Famine." *Economic and Political Weekly* 10 (10 May 1975): 758–769.

2398. Bardhan, Pranab K. "On the Incidence of Poverty in Rural India in the Sixties." *Economic and Political Weekly* 8:4–6 (Annual Number 1973): 245–254.

2399. Chandra, N. K. "Food Imports: Why and For Whom?" *Economic and Political Weekly* 10:5–7 (Annual Number 1975): 255–266.

2400. Dandekar, V. M., and Rath, Nilakantha. "Poverty in India—I: Dimensions and Trends." *Economic and Political Weekly* 6 (2 January 1971): 25–48.

2401. ______. "Poverty in India—II: Policies and Programmes." *Economic and Political Weekly* 6 (9 January 1971): 106–146.

2402. Dantwala, M. L. "Future of Institutional Reform and Technological Change in Indian Agricultural Development." *Economic and Political Weekly* 13: 31–33 (Special Number 1978): 1299–1306.

2403. Das, Purenendu Sekhar. "Growth and Instability in Crop Output in Eastern India." *Economic and Political Weekly* 13 (14 October 1978): 1741–1748.

2404. *The Ecologist.* Special Issue on Indian Agriculture. 5 (October 1975): 272–300.

2405. Engminger, Douglass. "Overcoming the Obstacles to Farm Economic Development in Less Developed Countries." *Journal of Farm Economics* 44 (December 1962): 1367–1387. (Discusses Ford Foundation-Government of India designed Intensive Agricultural District Program.)

2406. Gulati, I. S., and Krishnan, T. N. "Public Distribution and Procurement of Foodgrains: A Proposal." *Economic and Political Weekly* 10 (24 May 1975): 829–842.

2407. Hoskins, Martin. "The Kosi Project." *Institute of Development Studies Bulletin* 2:4 (July 1970): 32–39.

2408. Jayaraman, K. "Poverty in India—Policies and Programmes: A Comment." *Economic and Political Weekly* 6 (2 October 1971): 2109–2111.

2409. Kothari, Rajni. "India: An Alternative Framework for Rural Development," pp. 208–226. In *Another Development: Approaches and Strategies.* Ed. Marc Nerfin. Uppsala: Dag Hammarskjöld Foundation, 1977.

2410. Laxinarayan, H., and Tyagi, D. S. "Some Aspects of Size-Distribution of Agricultural Holdings." *Economic and Political Weekly* 11 (9 October 1976): 1637–1640.

2411. Lewis, John P. "Notes of a Rural Area Development Tourist." *Economic and Political Weekly* 9 (29 June 1974): A42–A54.

2412. Madalgi, S. S. "Poverty in India: A Comment." *Economic and Political Weekly* 6 (20 February 1971): 503–506.

2413. Medhora, Phiroze B. "Poverty in India: A Comment." *Economic and Political Weekly* 6 (27 February 1971): 543–546.

2414. Mencher, Joan P. "Socioeconomic Constraints to Development: The Case of South India." *Annals of the New York Academy of Sciences* (February 1973): 155–167.

2415. Millikan, Max F. "Economic Development: Performance and Prospects." *Foreign Affairs* 46:3 (1968): 531–547.

2416. Narain, Dharm. "Growth and Imbalances in Indian Agriculture." *Economic and Political Weekly* 7 (25 March 1972): A2–A6.

2417. Nath, V. "Progress of Rural Development Programmes. Regional Differences." *The Economic Weekly* 15:4–6 (Annual Number 1963): 175–177.

2418. Pathy, Jaganath. "Social Stratification in an Orissa Village." *Economic and Political Weekly* 10 (7 June 1975): 893–901.

2419. Patnaik, Utsa. "Capitalist Development in Agriculture." *Economic and Political Weekly* 6 (25 September 1971): A123–A130.

2420. ______. "Capitalist Development in Agriculture: Further Comment." *Economic and Political Weekly* 6 (25 December 1971): A190–A194.

2421. Ramanath, S. "The Bhakra-Nangal Project." *World Crops* 8 (February 1956): 74–77.

2422. Rao, G. V. K., and Thamarajakshi, R. "Some Aspects of Growth of Indian Agriculture." *Economic and Political Weekly* 13 (23–30 December 1978): A113–A118.

2423. Ray, S. K. "Foodgrains Demand and Supply: Projections of Regional Imbalances." *Economic and Political Weekly* 6 (26 June 1971): A59–A74.

2424. ______. "Imbalances, Instability and Government Operations in Foodgrains." *Economic and Political Weekly* 5 (26 September 1970): A115–A124.

2425. Rudra, Ashok. "Class Relations in Indian Agriculture—I." *Economic and Political Weekly* 13 (3 June 1978): 916–923; "II." 13 (10 June 1978): 963–968; and "III." 13 (17 June 1978): 998–1004.

2426. Rudra, Ashok; Majid, A.; and Tahib, B. D. "Big Farmers of Punjab." *Economic and Political Weekly* 4 (27 September 1969): A143–A146.

2427. Sau, Ranjit K. "Poverty in India: A Comment." *Economic and Political Weekly* 6 (20 March 1971): 679–680.

2428. ______. "Resource Allocation in Indian Agriculture." *Economic and Political Weekly* 6 (25 September 1971): A106–A116.

2429. Shetty, S. L. "Structural Retrogression in the Indian Economy Since the Mid-Sixties." *Economic and Political Weekly* 13:6–7 (Annual Number 1978): 185–244.

2430. Shivakumar, S. S. "Aspects of Agrarian Economy in Tamil Nadu: A Study of Two Villages. Part I: Class Structure." *Economic and Political Weekly* 13 (6 May 1978): 762–770; "Part II: Constraints on Production and Marketing." 13 (13 May 1978): 812–821; "Part III: Structure of Assets and Indebtedness." 13 (20 May 1978): 846–851.

2431. Shivamaggi, H. B. "Crucial Aspects of Agricultural Development: Problems of the Fourth Plan." *Economic and Political Weekly* 4 (27 September 1969): A133–A139.

2432. Sinha, Randhir, and Singh, D. K. "A Case for Boosting Bihar's Agriculture." *Economic and Political Weekly* 4 (10 May 1969): 817–821.

2433. Swamy, Dalip S. "Differentiation of Peasantry in India." *Economic and Political Weekly* 11 (11 December 1976): 1933–1939.

2434. Vyas, V. S., and Bandyopadhyay, S. C. "National Food Policy in the Framework of a National Food Budget." *Economic and Political Weekly* 10 (29 March 1975): A2–A13.

China and India Compared

The stagnation of the rural sector in India and the apparent success of rural development strategies followed by the Chinese government have led a number of analysts to compare the rural sector policies of the two largest countries in Asia. All of the studies in this section are recommended. As an introduction to the subject, readers might start with Sinha. Sinha finds that the consumption of food and the rate of growth in food production are roughly equivalent in China and India. However, because of institutional changes in China, which have no parallel in India, food and other resources are more equitably distributed in China and the Chinese have been more successful than the Indians in mobilizing resources for development purposes.

2435. Ahmad, Aqueil. "Science and Technology for Development: Policy Options for India and China." *Economic and Political Weekly* 13 (23–30 December 1978): 2079–2090.

2436. Bandyopadhyaya, Kalyani. *Agricultural Development in China and India: A Comparative Study.* New Delhi: Wiley Eastern, 1976.

2437. Bardhan, Pranab. "Chinese and Indian Agriculture: A Broad Comparison of Recent Policy and Performance." *Journal of Asian Studies* 29 (May 1970): 515–537.

2438. Bichl, Max. *Die Landwirtschaft in China und Indien: Vergleich Zweier Entwicklungswege.* Frankfurt/Main: M. Diesterweg, 1966.

2439. Byres, T. J., and Nolan, Peter. *Inequality Between Nations: India and China Compared.* Milton Keynes, UK: Open University Press, 1976.

2440. Jain, Netrapal. *Rural Reconstruction in India and China: A Comparative Study.* 1st ed. New Delhi: Writers and Publishers, distributed by Sterling, 1970.

2441. Marwah, O. S. "Change and Modernisation in India and China." *The Institute for Defence Studies and Analyses Journal* 7 (October–December 1974): 131–301.

2442. Sathyamurthy, T. V. "Patterns of Inequality." *Economic and Political Weekly* 13 (11 March 1978): 488–492.

2443. Sigurdson, Jon. "Development of Rural Areas in India and China." *Ambio* 5:3 (1976): 98–107.

2444. Sinha, Radha P. "Competing Ideology and Agricultural Strategy: Current Agricultural Development in India and China Compared with Meiji Strategy." *World Development* 1 (June 1973): 11–29.

2445. Stavis, Benedict. "Agricultural Performance and Policy: Contrasts with India." *Social Scientist* 5 (May–June 1977): 58–80.

2446. Swamy, Subramanian. "Economic Growth in China and India, 1952–1970: A Comparative Appraisal." *Economic Development and Cultural Change* 21 (July 1973): 1–83.

2447. Weisskopf, Thomas E. "China and India: A Comparative Survey of Performance in Economic Development." *Economic and Political Weekly* 10:5–7 (Annual Number 1975): 175–194.

Bangladesh

When the Pakistani civil war of 1971 resulted in the creation of Bangladesh, US Presidential advisor Henry Kissinger predicted that the new country would become "an international basket-case." While one cannot say that Kissinger's prediction was correct, Bangladesh has become a sort of "proving ground" for international agency development strategies. What is more, the government of General Ziaur Rahman has chosen to make dependence on large-scale imports of foreign aid a cornerstone of Bangladeshi development policy. (See Viratelle for a good summary of this policy.) Thus far, this strategy has done very little to improve the situation of Bangladesh's rural population, which is among the poorest in the world.

Barang reports it has been estimated that between 1963/64 and 1973/74 the number of people living on fewer than 1,935 calories per day had increased from 40.2 percent of the population to 78.5 percent. The article by Barang is largely a critique of the World Bank's study, *Bangladesh: Food Policy Review* (entry 2474). These entries should be read together. The misuse of food aid by the Bangladeshi government is well-known. It is discussed by Barang and also in entries 1888, 1889, 1944, and 1965.

Raper et al., Dupree, Khan (entry 2463), and Bose (entry 2453) all deal specifically with the Comilla program. This program has focused on smallholders and has been proposed as a model for diffusing Green Revolution technology throughout Bangladesh. However, Bose argues that the Comilla project has had only limited success in spreading this technology and that the costs of doing so have been high. Comilla is reportedly extremely dependent on government subsidies and outside assistance. The high concentration of administrative and financial resources lavished on Comilla, Bose argues, cannot be duplicated throughout Bangladesh. Furthermore, the landless and near-landless are not helped by the Comilla project any more than by most other development schemes. A large portion of the benefits have accrued to the largest farmers, with the middle farmers keeping the large farmers from completely dominating the scheme. The problem of large farmer domination of Comilla is also discussed in entry 1784.

The issue of landlessness and near-landlessness is discussed in entries 934, 1399, and 1407 (Appendix A).

2448. Ahmed, Manzoor. *BRAC: Building Human Infrastructure to Serve the Rural Poor.* Essex, Conn.: International Council for Educational Development, n.d. (Available from ICED, P.O. Box 217, Essex, Connecticut 06426.)

2449. Ahmed, Noazesh. "Bangladesh Agriculture Needs a New Strategy." *IDRC Reports* 7 (September 1978): 22–23.

2450. Ali, Qazi Azher. *Rural Development in Bangladesh.* Comilla: Bangladesh Academy for Rural Development, 1975.

2451. Barang, Marcel. "Latest Theories Tested Here." *Far Eastern Economic Review* (19 May 1978): 35–38.

2452. Bose, Swadesh R. "East-West Contrast in Pakistan's Agricultural Development," pp. 127–146. In *Economic Development in South Asia.* Ed. Edward A. G. Robinson and Michael Kidron. London: Macmillan; and New York: St. Martin's, 1970.

2453. ———. "The Comilla Cooperative Approach and the Prospects for Broad-based Green Revolution in Bangladesh." *World Development* 2 (August 1974).

2454. Dodge, Cole Patrick, and Wiebe, Paul D. "Famine Relief and Development in Rural Bangladesh." *Economic and Political Weekly* 11 (29 May 1976): 809–817.

2455. Dupree, Louis. *The Comilla Experiment: A Scheme for Village Development in East Pakistan.* Fieldstaff Report. South Asia Series. Hanover, N. H.: American Universities Field Staff, 1964.

2456. Etienne, Gilbert. "Du Bengale Britannique au Bangladesh: Comment Faire Reculer la Pauvreté Rurale?" *Revue Tiers-Monde* 18 (October–December 1977): 707–722.

2457. Faaland, Just, and Parkinson, J. R. "Bangladesh: Gradual Development or Deepening Misery?" *World Development* 4 (September 1976): 739–747.

2458. ———. *Bangladesh: The Test Case of Development.* Boulder, Colo.: Westview, 1976. (Chapters 7 and 8 are particularly relevant.)

2459. Farruk, Muhammad Osman. *Structure and Performance of the Rice Marketing System in East Pakistan.* Cornell International Agricultural Development Bulletin 23. Ithaca, N. Y.: Cornell University, May 1972.

2460. Griffin, Keith, and Robinson, Edward A. G., eds. *The Economic Development of Bangladesh within a Socialist Framework.* New York: Wiley/Halstead, 1974.

2461. Hossain, Mahabub. "Farm Size and Productivity in Bangladesh Agriculture: A Case Study of Phulpur Farms." *The Bangladesh Economic Review* 2 (January 1974).

2462. Katz, Robert. "The Will to Survive." *Ceres* no. 45 (May–June 1975): 33–36.

2463. Khan, Akhter Hameed. *Reflections on the Comilla Rural Development Projects.* OLC Paper no. 3. Washington, D. C.: Overseas Liaison Committee, American Council on Education, March 1974.

2464. Khan, Azizur Rahman. *The Economy of Bangladesh.* London: Macmillan, 1972. (Chapters 5 and 11 deal directly with the agricultural sector.)

2465. Ladejinsky, Wolf. "Food Shortage in West Bengal: Crisis or Chronic?" *World Development* 4 (February 1976): 102–110.

2466. National Academy of Sciences. *East Pakistan Land and Water Development as Related to Agriculture.* Washington, D. C.: January 1971.

2467. Rahman, M. A. "Farm Size, Efficiency and the Socio-economics of Land Distribution." *The Bangladesh Development Studies* 3 (July 1975).

2468. Rahman, M. M. *Rural Scene: A Socio-Economic Analysis.* Research Report no. 14. Mymensingh: Department of Agricultural Economics, Bangladesh Agricultural University, 1976.

2469. Raper, Arthur F., et al. *Rural Development in Action: The Comprehensive Experiment at Comilla, East Pakistan.* Ithaca, N. Y.: Cornell University Press, 1970.

2470. Sattar, Md. Ghulam. *Introductory Notes on Some Locally Initiated Projects in Bangladesh.* Comilla: Bangladesh Academy for Rural Development, 1975.

2471. Sobhan, Rahman. *Basic Democracies, Works Programme and Rural Development in East Pakistan.* Dacca: Bureau of Economic Research, University of Dacca, 1968.

2472. Thomas, Barbara, and Lavan, Spencer, eds. *West Bengal and Bangladesh: Perspectives from 1972.* Occasional Papers, no. 21. East Lansing: Asian Studies Center, Michigan State University, 1973. (The chapters by Morrison and J. W. Thomas are relevant.)

2473. Viratelle, Gérard. "Démocratisation au Bangladesh. II. L'Idéologie du 'Développement.'" *Le Monde,* 17 February 1979.

2474. World Bank. *Bangladesh: Food Policy Review.* Washington, D. C.: 1977.

Pakistan

In the 1960s, Pakistan was considered a development "success story." The stagnant economy of the 1950s had begun to grow quite rapidly in both the industrial and the agricultural sectors. However, the success was somewhat illusory. First of all, economic progress was not shared evenly throughout the country. Rather, the eastern wing was "squeezed" to the benefit of the western wing; foreign exchange earned by East Bengali exports, largely jute, was used to help finance expenditures for West Pakistan. This colonial-type relationship gave rise to the situation which led to the civil war of 1971 and the eventual break-up of the country.

Even within West Pakistan, the benefits of growth were not evenly distributed: the Punjab and Sind were favored over the Northwest Frontier Province and Baluchistan. Within the more favored provinces, increased agricultural output does not seem to have led to a reduction in the incidence of poverty (see article by Naseem in entry

1399), although the data on which such assessments must be based are not very detailed.

Recommended studies include Khan, Nicholson and Khan, Burki, and the volume edited by Griffin and Khan. The issues of landlessness and near-landlessness as they pertain to Pakistan are discussed in entries 934 and 1399. Political and bureaucratic constraints to agricultural development in Pakistan are surveyed in entries 1788 and 1806.

2475. Alavi, Hamza. "Elite Farmer Strategy and Regional Disparities in the Agricultural Development of Pakistan." *Economic and Political Weekly* 8 (31 March 1973): A31–A39.

2476. ______. "Structure of the Agrarian Economy in West Pakistan and Development Strategy." *Pakistan Administrative Staff College Quarterly* 7 (September–December 1968): 57–76.

2477. Bakhsh, Malik K. "Agricultural Progress in Pakistan." Paper presented to Symposium on Strategy for the Conquest of Hunger. New York: Rockefeller Foundation, April 1978, mimeo.

2478. Bose, Swadesh R., and Clark, Edwin H., III. "Some Basic Considerations on Agricultural Mechanization in West Pakistan." *The Pakistan Development Review* 9 (Autumn 1969): 273–308.

2479. Burki, Shahid Javed. *Agricultural Growth and Local Government in Punjab, Pakistan.* RLG 11. Ithaca, N. Y.: Rural Development Committee, Center for International Studies, Cornell University, c.1974.

2480. Colorado State University. *Water Management Research in Arid and Sub-Humid Lands of the Less Developed Countries.* AID/csd–2162. Fort Collins, Colorado: c.1974.

2481. Early, A. C.; Eckert, J. B.; Freeman, D. M.; Kemper, W. D.; Lowdermilk, M. K. M.; Radosevich, G. D.; and Skogerboe, G. V. *Institutional Framework for Improved On-Farm Water Management in Pakistan.* PN–AAF–270. Washington, D. C.: US Agency for International Development, 1976.

2482. Faculty of Agriculture. *Food Production and Consumption in Pakistan.* 2 vols. Vyallpur: West Pakistan Agriculture University, 1965.

2483. Falcon, W. P., and Gotsch, Carl H. "Lessons in Agricultural Development—Pakistan," pp. 269–315. In *Development Policy—Theory and Practice.* Ed. Gustav F. Papanek. Cambridge, Mass.: Harvard University Press, 1968.

2484. Falcon, Walter P., and Papanek, Gustav F., eds. *Development Policy II: The Pakistan Experience.* Cambridge, Mass.: Harvard University Press, 1971. (Chapters 2, 5–7 are especially relevant.)

2485. Finney, C. E. *Farm Power in West Pakistan.* Development Study no. 11. Reading, UK: Department of Agricultural Economics and Management, University of Reading, October 1972.

2486. Gill, Amjad H. *Pakistan's Agricultural Development and Trade.* ERS-Foreign 347. Washington, D. C.: Economic Research Service, US Department of Agriculture, February 1973.

2487. Government of Pakistan, Ministry of Food and Agriculture. *Report of the Food and Agriculture Commission.* Karachi: November 1960.

2488. Griffin, Keith, and Khan, Azizur Rahman, eds. *Growth and Inequality in Pakistan.* London: Macmillan, 1972. (Part II discusses agriculture.)

2489. Khan, Akhter Hameed. *Land Reform, Rural Works, and the Food Problem in Pakistan.* South Asia Series, Occasional Paper no. 20. East Lansing: Asian Studies Center, Michigan State University, 1973.

2490. Lieftinck, Pieter; Sadove, A. Robert; and Creyke, Thomas C. *Water and Power Resources of West Pakistan: A Study in Sector Planning. Volume 2: The Development of Irrigation and Agriculture.* Baltimore, Md.: Johns Hopkins University Press, 1969.

2491. Nicholson, Norman K., and Khan, Dilawar Ali. *Basic Rural Democracies and Rural Development in Pakistan.* RLG 10. Ithaca, N. Y.: Rural Development Committee, Center for International Studies, Cornell University, c.1974.

2492. Stubbings, B. J. J. "Integrated Rural Development in Pakistan." *Journal of Administration Overseas* 14 (April 1975): 91–104.

2493. Taylor, George C., Jr. "Water, History and the Indus Plain." *Natural History* (May 1965): 40–49.

2494. Thiesenhusen, William C. "A Brief Glimpse of Rural Punjab: Pakistan's Breadbasket." *LTC Newsletter* no. 45 (July–September 1974): 1–10.

2495. United States, Agency for International Development. *Pakistan Agriculture: Resources, Progress and Prospects.* Karachi: Food & Agriculture Division, 1966.

Philippines

The rural economy of the Philippines grew rapidly until at least the middle 1970s. Both per capita agricultural output and the value of agricultural production per worker have increased over the long term. Unfortunately, the living standards of the rural poor have declined over the past two decades; with the exception of 1966–1967, real wages declined steadily between 1957 and 1974 (see article by Khan in entry 1399). According to ILO figures, only the wealthiest 20 percent of rural Filipino households increased their share of rural income between the mid-1950s and the beginning of the 1970s. The fourth quintile maintained its share of rural income while each of the bottom three quintiles accounted for smaller portions of total rural income in 1970/71 than they had fifteen years earlier. For example, in 1956/57, the poorest 20 percent of rural Filipino households shared 7 percent of total rural income; in 1970/71, they shared 4.4 percent (see entry 295, p. 10).

According to Rosenberg and Rosenberg (entry 1407, Appendix D), there are four primary factors which have contributed to the impoverishment of the rural Philippines and to its increases in landlessness and near-landlessness. These are rapid population growth, government concentration on industrial expansion, failure to distribute the benefits of rural growth, and governmental policies that may have exacerbated post-1945 trends toward land concentration and the displacement of rural labor by mechanization.

Other recommended studies include Bowring, Contado and Jaime, Hayami, David, Flores and Kikuchi, Herrera, Kimpt Tan, Mears et al., Simpas, Carino and Pacho, Stewart and Arellano, and Wurfel.

2496. Bowring, Philip. "Rice: Manila's Facts and Fantasy." *Far Eastern Economic Review* (28 March 1975): 43–45.

2497. Cheetham, Russell J., and Hawkins, Edward K., coord. *The Philippines: Priorities and Prospects for Development.* World Bank Country Economic Report. Baltimore, Md.: Johns Hopkins University Press, 1976.

2498. Contado, T. E., and Jaime, R. C. *Changes in Rice Farming in Selected Areas of Asia: The Case of Leyte, Philippines.* Los Baños: College of Agriculture, University of the Philippines, 1973.

2499. Earle, John. "Luzon: A Strategic Choice." *Ceres* no. 2 (March–April 1968): 44–47.

2500. Grace, Brewster. *Food and Small Farm Strategies in the Philippines: Cooperatives and Credit.* no. 40. Hanover, N. H.: American Universities Field Staff, 1978.

2501. Haswell, Margaret R. "Economics of Agricultural Development in the Philippines." *Civilisations* 19:4 (1969): 437–450.

2502. Hayami, Yujiro; David, C. C.; Flores, P.; and Kikuchi, M. "Agricultural Growth Against a Land Resources Constraint: The Philippine Experience." *The Australian Journal of Agricultural Economics* 20 (December 1976): 144–159.

2503. Herrera, T. T. *Changes in Rice Farming in Selected Areas of Asia: Pigcawayan, Cotabato, the Philippines.* Los Baños, Philippines: Interna-

2504. Kimpt Tan, Eva. *Changes in Rice Farming in Selected Areas of Asia: The Case of Nueva Ecija, Philippines.* Los Baños, Philippines: International Rice Research Institute, 1974.

2505. Mears, L. A., et al. *Rice Economy of the Philippines.* Quezon City: University of Philippines Press, 1974.

2506. Reyes-Makil, Lorna Pena, and Fermin, Patria. *Landless Rural Workers in the Philippines.* Quezon City: Institute of Philippine Culture, Ateneo de Manila University, 1978.

2507. Rivera, Generoso F., and McMillan, Robert T. *The Rural Philippines.* Cooperative Project of the Philippine Council for US Aid and the US Mutual Security Agency. Manila: Office of Information, Mutual Security Agency, October 1952.

2508. Rocamora, Joel, and Panganiban, C. *Rural Development Strategies: The Philippine Case.* Quezon City: Institute of Philippine Culture, Ateneo de Manila University, 1975.

2509. Simpas, Santiago S.; Cariño, Ledvina; and Pacho, Arturo. *Local Government and Rural Development in the Philippines.* RLG 12. Ithaca, N. Y.: Rural Development Committee, Center for International Studies, Cornell University, c.1974.

2510. Spencer, Joseph Earle. *Land and People in the Philippines: Geographic Problems in Rural Economy.* Berkeley: University of California Press, 1952.

2511. Stewart, J. C., and Arellano, A. B. *Changes in Rice Farming in Selected Areas of Asia: Davos Del Sur, Philippines.* Los Baños, Philippines: International Rice Research Institute, 1974.

2512. Takahashi, Akira. *Land and Peasants in Central Luzon: Socio-Economic Structure of a Philippine Village.* Honolulu: East-West Center Press, 1970.

2513. Wurfel, David. *Philippine Agrarian Policy Today: Implementation and Political Impact.* Occasional Paper no. 46. Singapore: Institute of Southeast Asian Studies, May 1977.

Taiwan

Taiwan is increasingly portrayed as a (non-communist) model whose experiences are of considerable importance for the poor nations of Asia (see, for example, Christensen and Yeh). Griffin concludes, "... when viewed in historical perspective the growth performance is not quite as impressive as the government would have us believe, but in terms of allocative efficiency and income equality, Taiwan's record is superior to virtually all other poor Asian countries" (p. 31).

Griffin discusses the agricultural and industrial sectors in terms of growth performance, development financing, links between the two sectors, and income distribution. As an introduction to the topic, this article is highly recommended. The contribution of agriculture to Taiwan's economic growth is also discussed in entry 546. Agriculture in Taiwan under the Japanese colonial administration is the topic of entries 1324 and 1327. The Japanese built up the Taiwanese agricultural sector so that it could provide food for Japanese industrial workers. The role played by rural institutions in promoting rural development in Taiwan is considered by Stavis.

2514. Chang Te-tsui. *Long-Term Projections of Supply, Demand and Trade for Selected Products in Taiwan.* Taipei: Research Institute of Agricultural Economics, National Taiwan University, October 1970.

2515. Christensen, Raymond P. *Taiwan's Agricultural Development: Its Relevance for Developing Countries Today.* Foreign Agricultural Economic Report no. 39. Washington, D. C.: Economic Research Service, US Department of Agriculture, 1968.

2516. Griffin, Keith. "An Assessment of Development in Taiwan." *World Development* 1 (June 1973): 31–42.

2517. Ho, M. S., and Chen, J. "Farm Management Extension in Taiwan." In *Some Notes on Farm Management Extension in Six Asian Countries.* Extension Bulletin no. 84. Taiwan: Food and Fertilizer Technology Center, 1977.

2518. Ho Yhi-min. *Agricultural Development of Taiwan, 1903–1960.* Nashville, Tenn.: Vanderbilt University Press, 1966.

2519. Kwoh Min-hioh. *Farmers' Associations and their Contributions Toward Agricultural and Rural Development in Taiwan.* Bangkok: Food and Agriculture Organization, 1964.

2520. Lee Teng-hui. *Agricultural Diversification and Development.* New York: Asia Society, 1971.

2521. Lee Teng-hui, and Chen Yueh-eh. *Growth Rates of Taiwan Agriculture 1911–1972.* Taipei: Joint Commission on Rural Reconstruction, 1975.

2522. Lionberger, Herbert, and Chang, H. *Farm Information for Modernizing Agriculture: The Taiwan Case.* New York: Praeger, 1970.

2523. Shên, Tsung-han. *Agricultural Development on Taiwan Since World War II.* Ithaca, N. Y.: Comstock, 1964.

2524. Stavis, Benedict. *Rural Local Governance and Agricultural Development in Taiwan.* RLG 15. Ithaca, N. Y.: Rural Development Committee, Center for International Studies, Cornell University, 1974.

2525. Tsui Young-chi. "Land-Use Improvement: A Key to the Economic Development of Taiwan." *Journal of Farm Economics* 44 (May 1962): 363–372.

2526. Wang Sung-hsing, and Apthorpe, Raymond J. *Rice Farming in Taiwan: Three Village Studies.* Nankang, Taipai: Institute of Technology, Academia Sinica, 1974.

2527. Yeh, Sing-min. "Learning from Taiwan's Agricultural Development Experience." *Teaching Forum.* no. 23. New York: The Agricultural Development Council, December 1972.

South Korea

Rao argues that in general South Korea has had a good record in combining rapid economic growth with a reasonably wide distribution of the benefits of that growth. He discusses some of the ways in which the government has sought to reduce rural-urban income disparities, primarily by controlling the price of grain and, to a lesser extent, by subsidizing inputs. While official government statistics show a decline in rural-urban income disparities over the last ten or fifteen years, Rao estimates that the gap has remained approximately the same. He also identifies a number of conditions that are leading to growing inequity, both between urban and rural sectors and within them.

Reed reaches a similar conclusion in entry 2536. His analysis suggests that "income inequity among farm households has increased substantially since 1970" (p. 24). Both Reed and Rao cite the slow growth of non-farm employment opportunities as an important element in the exacerbation of rural-urban and intra-rural income gaps.

Ho is somewhat more critical of the policies followed by the South Korean government. He argues that rural-urban income gaps widened even in the 1960s. Ho outlines the government strategy devised in 1971 for reducing these income gaps and discusses how it has failed to alleviate the problem. The strategy was based on increasing rural productivity and expanding non-farm employment opportunities in rural areas. However, the agricultural sector received only 10% of investment resources in the early and mid-1970s while most companies have not ventured far into the rural areas, preferring to remain close to Seoul and Pusan.

2528. Aqua, Ronald. *Local Institutions and Rural Development in South Korea.* RLG 13. Ithaca, N. Y.: Rural Development Committee, Center for International Studies, Cornell University, c.1974.

2529. Ban, Sung Hwan. *Growth and Sources of Agricultural Production and Productivity in Korea 1945–1974.* Korean Modernization Study Series, 3. Seoul: Korean Development Institute, April 1977.

2530. Bong, Kyun Suh. *The Strategy for Agricultural Development in Korea.* Seoul: Samhwa Corporation, 1971.

2531. Brandt, Vincent. "Rural Development and the New Community Movement in South Korea." *Korean Studies Forum* no. 1 (Autumn–Winter 1976/77): 33–39.

2532. Government of the Republic of Korea. *National Land Development Plan, 1972–1981.* Seoul: 1971.

2533. Ho, Samuel P. S. "Rural-Urban Imbalance in South Korea in the 1970s." *Asian Survey* 19 (July 1979): 645–659.

2534. Moon, Pal Yong. "The Evolution of Rice Policy in Korea," pp. 3–41. In *Essays on the Korean Economy. Volume II: Industrial and Social Development Issues.* Ed. Chuk Kyo Kim. Seoul: Korean Development Institute, 1977.

2535. Rao, D. C. "Economic Growth and Equity in the Republic of Korea." *World Development* 6 (March 1978): 383–396.

2536. Reed, Edward P. "Analysis of Farm Household Income Trends and Structure in South Korea." *Land Tenure Center Newsletter* no. 58 (October–December 1977): 12–26.

2537. ______. *Organizational Issues in Group Farming in South Korea.* LTC no. 119. Madison: Land Tenure Center, University of Wisconsin, December 1978.

2538. Republic of Korea Ministry of Contruction, Korea Water Resources Development Corporation, in cooperation with the United States Department of Interior, Bureau of Reclamation and Geological Survey. *Han River Basin. Appendix I: Agricultural Economics.* Seoul [?]: 1971.

Iran

Among the many purported achievements of his rule, Shah Mohammed Reza Pahlavi liked to point to the land reforms instituted by his government in the 1960s as evidence of his concern for the Iranian peasantry. In fact, the land reform program was little more than an attempt to shift control over the countryside from the large landlords to the State. An important part of the Shah's agricultural "modernization" program was the introduction of agribusiness to Iran. At the same time, the real emphasis was on rapid industrialization and many men were drawn from the countryside to the rapidly expanding urban centers to take advantage of relatively well paying jobs in construction and other urban activities. As one result of this migration, food production in Iran failed to keep pace with demand and by 1977 the Iranian food import bill had risen to $2 billion.

All of the entries in this section deal with Iran prior to the downfall of the Shah. Recommended studies include Richards, Keddie, and Brun and Dumont. Readers will also want to consult the chapter by Schulz in entry 465.

2539. Ajami, Ismail. "Agrarian Reform, Modernization of Peasants, and Agricultural Development." In *Iran: Past, Present and Future.* Ed. Jane W. Jacqz. New York: The Aspen Institute for Humanistic Studies, 1976.

2540. Aresvik, Oddvar. *The Agricultural Development of Iran.* New York: Praeger, 1976.

2541. Brun, Thierry, and Dumont, René. "Iran: Imperial Pretensions and Agricultural Dependence." *MERIP Reports* no. 71 (October 1978): 15–20.

2542. Field, Michael. "Agrobusiness and Agricultural Planning in Iran." *World Crops* 24 (March–April 1972): 68–72.

2543. Freivalds, J. "Farm Corporations in Iran: An Alternative to Traditional Agriculture." *The Middle East Journal* 26 (Spring 1972): 185–193.

2544. Keddie, Nikki R. *Historical Obstacles to Agrarian Change in Iran.* Claremont Asian Studies, no. 8. Claremont, Calif.: Society for Oriental Studies, Claremont Graduate School, 1960.

2545. Lambton, A. K. S. *Landlord and Peasant in Persia.* 2nd ed. London: Oxford University Press, 1969.

2546. Noori, H. M. "Examination of Economic and Social Conditions in Rural Cooperative Communes in Iran." In *Modern Cooperatives and Traditional Societies.* Tel Aviv: International Center on Rural Cooperatives, 1968.

2547. Okazaki, Shoko. *The Development of Large-Scale Farming in Iran: The Case of the Province of Gorgan.* Occasional Papers 3. Tokyo: The Institute of Asian Economic Affairs, 1968.

2548. Richards, Helmut. "Land Reform and Agribusiness in Iran." *MERIP Reports* no. 43 (December 1975): 3–18, 24.

2549. Sadrolachrafi, M. "Les Nouvelles Méthodes d'Exploitation Agricole dans les Villages Iraniens." *Revue Tiers-Monde* 15 (April–June 1974): 397–406.

2550. Weinbaum, Marvin G. "Agricultural Policy and Development Politics in Iran." *The Middle East Journal* 31 (Autumn 1977): 434–450.

2551. World Bank. *Etude de l'Economie Agricole de l'Iran.* Prepared for the Iranian Agricultural Development Bank. Tehran [?]: 1974.

Thailand

The report by the Agribusiness Council is interesting as an example of the sort of evaluation which is made to recommend "large-scale, profitable, programmed farming" projects. The report by Ingersoll concentrates on identifying the human dimension of river basin projects and argues that these elements should be evaluated prior to the initiation of such projects. The monographs by Ingle and Janlekha are recommended.

2552. The Agribusiness Council, Inc. *Report of Northeast Thailand Agribusiness Survey Team.* New York: October 1968, mimeo.

2553. Greene, Brook A. *Rate of Adoption of New Farm Practices in the Central Plains, Thailand.* Cornell International Agriculture Bulletin 24. Ithaca, N. Y.: Cornell University, 1973.

2554. Ingersoll, Jasper. *Human Dimensions of Mekong River Basin Development. A Case Study of the Nam Pong Project. Northeast Thailand 1967–1968.* Washington, D. C.: US Agency for International Development, October 1968.

2555. Ingle, Marcus. *Local Governance and Rural Development in Thailand.* RLG 16. Ithaca, N. Y.: Rural Development Committee, Center for International Studies, Cornell University, 1974.

2556. Janlekha, Kamol. *Sapaphi. A Survey of Socio-Economic Conditions in a Rural Community in North-East Thailand.* The World Land Use Survey, Occasional Paper, no. 8. Bude, UK: Geographical Publications, Ltd, 1968.

2557. Kunstadter, Peter; Chapman, E. C.; and Sabhasri, Sanga. *Farmers in the Forest. Economic Development and Marginal Agriculture in Northern Thailand.* Honolulu: The University Press of Hawaii, 1978.

2558. Motooka, Takeshi. *Agricultural Development in Thailand.* Kyoto: Center for Southeast Asian Studies, Kyoto University, 1971.

2559. Nuttonson, M. Y. *The Physical Environment and Agriculture in Thailand.* Washington, D. C.: American Institute of Crop Ecology, 1963.

2560. Stirling, John. "Thailand Breaks the Monocrop Barrier." *Ceres* no. 5 (September–October 1968): 43–46.

2561. Sylvester, Anthony. "Helping the Thailand Smallholder: F. A. O. Blazes the Trail." *Civilisations* 20:2 (1970): 212–226.

2562. Tinker, Jon. "How the Brown Wereng Did a Red Khmer on the Green Revolution." *New Scientist* 67 (7 August 1975): 316–317.

2563. Wilcock, T. H. *The Economic Development of Thai Agriculture.* Ithaca, N. Y.: Cornell University Press, 1970.

Sri Lanka

The report by Richards and Stoutjesdijk is a good introduction to Sri Lankan agriculture to the mid-1970s. It surveys past and present conditions in the agricultural sector and offers projections for the future. It also provides a fair amount of statistical data. The monographs by Blackton and by Jogaratnam and Poleman are also recommended. Landlessness and near-landlessness are discussed in the chapter by Lee in entry 1399 and in Appendix E of entry 1407.

2564. Appaduri, R. R. "Prospects for Grassland Farming in Ceylon." *World Crops* 21 (November–December 1969): 347–349.

2565. Bansil, Puran Chand. *Ceylon Agriculture: A Perspective.* Delhi: Dhanpat Rai, 1971.

2566. Blackton, John S. *Local Government and Rural Development in Sri Lanka.* RLG 14. Ithaca, N. Y.: Rural Development Committee, Center for International Studies, Cornell University, 1974.

2567. Jogaratnam, Thambapillai, and Poleman, Thomas T. *Food in the Economy of Ceylon.* Cornell International Agricultural Development Bulletin 11. Ithaca, N. Y.: Cornell University, October 1969.

2568. Richards, P., and Stoutjesdijk, E. *Agriculture in Ceylon Until 1975.* Development Centre Studies. Paris: Organization for Economic Cooperation and Development, 1970.

2569. Rodrigo, Dervin M. "Ceylon Aims at Rice Self-Sufficiency." *World Crops* 21 (September–October 1969): 297–298.

2570. Stanley, Bob. "Sri Lanka the Living Laboratory." *IDRC Reports* 7 (June 1978): 8–9.

Indonesia

Over half the studies in this section deal uniquely with Java. Sinaga and Collier argue that because of relatively rapid technical, economic, and social change, there has been an increase in unemployment and inequitable distribution of income in rural Java in recent years. A similar argument is offered by Rosenberg and Rosenberg (entry 1407, Appendix C) in their study of landlessness and near-landlessness. The chapter by Palmer in entry 1399 is also relevant.

Other recommended studies include Prabowo and Prabowo, Sajogyo, Collier, Crouch, and the study of Bimas by Hansen (entry 2575). Entry 734, which discusses the side effects of the Green Revolution in Java, is also recommended.

2571. Asian Development Bank, Technical Assistance Mission to Indonesia. *The Production and Availability of Foodstuffs in Indonesia.* 2 vols. Rizal, Philippines, 1967.

2572. Collier, William L. *Agricultural Evolution in Java: Decline of Shared Poverty.* Bogor: Indonesian Agro-Economic Survey, 1976.

2573. Crouch, Harold. "Generals and Business in Indonesia." *Pacific Affairs* no. 4 (Winter 1975–76): 519–540.

2574. Geertz, Clifford. *Agricultural Involution: The Processes of Ecological Change in Indonesia.* Berkeley: University of California Press, 1963.

2575. Hansen, Gary E. *Regional Administration for Rural Development in Indonesia: The Bimas Case.* Working Paper Series no. 26. Honolulu: East-West Center, 1972.

2576. ———. *Rural Local Government and Agricultural Development in Java, Indonesia.* RLG 7. Ithaca, N. Y.: Rural Development Committee, Center for International Studies, Cornell University, 1974.

2577. Palmer, Ingrid. "To Be Poor in Java." *Ceres* no. 58 (July–August 1977).

2578. Prabowo, Dibyo, and Prabowo, Sajogyo. *Changes in Rice Farming in Selected Areas of Asia: East and West Java, Indonesia.* Los Baños, Philippines: International Rice Research Institute, 1974.

2579. Sajogyo. *Modernization Without Development in Rural Java.* UN/FAO Agrarian Conference. Bogor: Indonesian Agricultural Institute (IPB), 1972.

2580. Sinaga, Rudolf, and Collier, William L. "Social and Regional Implications of Agricultural Development Policy." *Prisma, Indonesian Journal of Social and Economic Affairs* 84 (December 1975): 24–35.

2581. Vries, Egbert de. *The Agro-Economic Survey in Indonesia, 1965–1968: A Summary Report of Activities.* Bogor: Indonesian Agro-Economic Survey, 1968.

Nepal

In addition to the article by Feldman and Fournier, entry 1634 is recommended.

2582. Feldman, David, and Fournier, Alain. "Social Relations and Agricultural Production in Nepal's Terai." *The Journal of Peasant Studies* 3 (July 1976): 447–464. (Also available as Reprint 17. Norwich, UK: School of Development Studies, University of East Anglia, c.1976.)

2583. Regmi, Mahesh C. *Landownership in Nepal.* Berkeley: University of California Press, 1976.

2584. Schroeder, Mark C. W., and Sisler, Daniel G. *The Impact of the Sonauli-Pokhara Highway on the Regional Income and Agricultural Production of Pokhara Valley, Nepal.* Occasional Paper no. 32. Ithaca, N. Y.: Department of Agricultural Economics, Cornell University, June 1970.

2585. United States, Agency for International Development. *Hydrology and Water Resources Development in Nepal.* Washington, D. C.: US Geological Survey under the auspices of USAID, June 1969.

Malaysia

The monographs by Bhati and by Chee are recommended.

2586. Beau, K. W. "Muda River Project." *World Crops* 21 (March–April 1969): 13–16.

2587. Bhati, U. N. *Some Social and Economic Aspects of the Introduction of New Varieties of Paddy in Malaysia: A Village Case Study.* Report no. 76.8. Geneva: UN Research Institute for Social Development, 1976.

2588. Chee, Stephen. *Local Institutions and Rural Development in Malaysia.* RLG 9. Ithaca, N. Y.: Rural Development Committee, Center for International Studies, Cornell University, c.1974.

2589. Gripstra, B. G. *Common Efforts in the Development of Rural Sarawak, Malaysia.* Assen, Netherlands: Royal Vangorcum, 1976.

Oceania

The monographs by Mitchell and Shand and Straatmans are recommended.

2590. Mitchell, Donald Dean. *Land and Agriculture in Nagovisi, Papua New Guinea.* Monograph 3. Boroko, Papua New Guinea: Institute of Applied Social and Economic Research, 1976.

2591. Payne, W. J. A., and Mason, R. R. "Agricultural Developments in Fiji." *World Crops* 8 (May 1956): 187–191.

2592. Shand, Richard Tregurtha, and Straatmans, W. *Transition from Subsistence: Cash Crop Development in Papua New Guinea.* Port Moresby: New Guinea Research Unit, Australian National University, 1974.

2593. Ward, Ralph Gerard. *Land Use and Population in Fiji: A Geographical Study.* London: Her Majesty's Stationery Office, 1965.

2594. "Working for the Village: An Interview with Raphael Oraka." *Development Dialogue* no. 1 (1977): 50–63.

Other Asia

2595. Kubicka, Louis and Eryl. "Channelling Long-Term Aims." *Far Eastern Economic Review,* 8 September 1978, pp. 34–35. (About Laos)

2596. Lefebvre, René. *Rapport sur l'Economie Agricole du Royaume du Cambodge Année 1968.* Paris [?]: Institut National de la Statistique et des Recherches Economiques, c.1969.

Africa and the Middle East

Table 5 offers statistics on per capita food production and on agricultural and population growth rates in the 1960s and early 1970s for 45 countries in Africa and the Middle East.

TABLE 5

Per Capita Agricultural Production, Agricultural and Population Growth Rates, Selected African and Middle Eastern Countries, 1960s and 1970s

Country	Per capita food production (1965-67 = 100) Average 1974-76	Average Annual Rate of Growth of			
		Agriculture 1960-70	Population 1960-70	Agriculture 1970-76	Population 1970-75
	(1)	(2)	(3)	(4)	(5)
NORTH AFRICA & MIDDLE EAST					
Tunisia	134	2.0	2.1	9.2	2.3
Syria	113	4.4	3.7	6.4	3.3
Egypt	104	2.9	2.6	3.0	2.2
Morocco	103	4.2	2.4	0.6	2.4
Saudi Arabia	102	—[a]	1.7	3.6[b]	2.4
Yemen Arab Republic	101	—	2.3	—	1.9
Algeria	100	−1.6	3.2	−8.7[b]	3.2
Yemen People's Democratic Republic	97	—	3.4	6.2[b]	2.7
Libya	96	2.2	4.0	23.5[b]	4.2
Lebanon	95	6.3	2.5	—	3.0
Iraq	89	5.7	3.2	−2.0[b]	3.3
Jordan	47	5.0	3.3	2.6	3.2
Average	98	3.4	2.9	4.4	2.8
SUB-SAHARAN AFRICA					
Ivory Coast	124	4.2	3.4	3.5	4.2
Sudan	117	3.3	2.2	8.8[b]	2.1
Rwanda	114	—	3.6	3.3	2.3
Tanzania	113	3.7	3.0	2.5	2.7
Cameroon	108	6.5	2.1	3.4	1.9
Liberia	108	6.3	3.3	4.9	3.3
Southern Rhodesia (Zimbabwe)	107	—	3.3	—	3.5

Country	Per capita food production (1965-67 = 100) Average (1974-76)	Average Annual Rate of Growth of			
		Agriculture 1960-70	Population 1960-70	Agriculture 1970-76	Population 1970-75
	(1)	(2)	(3)	(4)	(5)
Malawi	107	2.9	2.6	5.5[b]	2.3
Zambia	104	2.0	2.9	3.2	2.9
Central African Republic	103	0.8	2.2	1.9	2.2
Lesotho	102	—	2.2	—	2.2
Burundi	101	—	2.0	1.0	2.1
Sierra Leone	97	1.4	2.2	2.0	2.5
Senegal	96	1.9	2.6	3.4	2.7
Mozambique	95	2.1	1.9	2.1[b]	2.4
Guinea	94	2.1	2.8	10.2	2.8
Zaire	93	3.9	2.7	1.9[b]	2.7
Republic of the Congo	93	4.6	2.6	−7.2	2.2
Ghana	93	3.7	2.6	1.3	2.7
Angola	92	4.0	1.3	−0.7[b]	0.1
Somalia	91	−1.5	2.4	−1.2[b]	2.4
Madagascar	90	—	2.6	1.2	3.1
Nigeria	89	−0.5	2.5	−0.2	2.5
Uganda	89	2.8	2.7	1.3	3.3
Kenya	88	5.9	3.1	1.6	3.5
Upper Volta	84	0.0	2.1	3.2	2.3
Ethiopia	83	2.2	2.0	0.9	2.6
Benin	83	—	2.7	−0.3	2.7
Chad	76	1.8	1.7	−1.3	2.1
Mali	71	1.3	2.1	0.8	2.5
Mauritania	68	2.4	1.8	−2.1[b]	2.7
Niger	67	3.3	2.7	−4.0[b]	2.7
Togo	59	4.3	2.7	3.0[b]	2.6
Average	94	2.8	2.5	1.7	2.6

a = — signifies information not available
b = 1970–75

Sources: Column 1: FAO as cited in World Bank, *Rapport sur le Développement dans le Monde, 1978,* Washington, D. C.: August 1978, Table 1, pp. 86–87.

Columns 2 + 4: World Bank, *Rapport sur le Développement dans le Monde, 1978,* Washington, D. C.: August 1978, Table 2, pp. 88–89.

Columns 3 + 5: World Bank, *Rapport sur le Développement dans le Monde, 1978,* Washington, D. C.: August 1978, Table 13, pp. 110–111.

General

Books and Monographs

There are several books which can be recommended as introductions to agricultural development in Africa. The study by Makings should be of particular interest to those who want to understand the institutional factors involved in rural development in Africa. Of the two books by Dumont, entry 2606 is a good survey of the situation up to the mid-1960s, while entry 2607 discusses the failure of agricultural development strategies in sub-Saharan Africa. A good deal of information is available in the two volumes by de Wilde et al.

The volume by Comte discusses the contribution of peasant farmer cooperatives to African rural development. It contains a large bibliography on this topic. The report by the Arizona Agrochemical Corporation and Early California Foods Inc. is of interest as an example of the kind of survey that is made to encourage US agribusiness to invest in developing countries.

The environmental aspect of African development is considered by Harrison Church. The report by Weaving summarizes the book by Lele. The book by Amin is also recommended. Chapters 19–27 in entry 2264 discuss Africa.

2597. *L'Agriculture Africaine 1976.* Paris: Ediafric-La Documentation Africaine, 1977.

2598. Allan, W. *The African Husbandman.* Edinburgh and London: Oliver & Boyd, 1965.

2599. Amin, Samir, ed. *L'Agriculture Africaine et le Capitalisme.* Paris: Anthropos, 1975.

2600. Anthony, Kenneth R. M.; Johnston, B. F.; Jones, W. O.; and Uchendu, V. C. *Agricultural Change in Tropical Africa.* Ithaca, N. Y.: Cornell University Press, 1979.

2601. Arizona Agrochemical Corporation-Early California Foods, Inc. *Phase I Study for Potential Investment in the Agribusiness Sectors of Ethiopia, Kenya and Morocco.* Washington, D. C.: US Agency for International Development, June 1968, mimeo.

2602. Arrighi, Giovanni, and Saul, John S. *Essays on the Political Economy of Africa.* New York and London: Monthly Review, 1973.

2603. Comte, Bernard. *Développement Rural et Coopération Agricole en Afrique Tropicale.* Cahiers de l'Institut des Sciences Economique et Sociales de l'Université de Fribourg. Fribourg: Editions Universitaires, 1968.

2604. Damachi, Ukandi G.; Routh, Guy; and Ali Taha, Abdel-Rahman. *Development Paths in Africa and China.* Boulder, Colo.: Westview, 1976.

2605. De Schlippe, Pierre. *Shifting Cultivation in Africa.* London: Routledge & Paul, 1956.

2606. Dumont, René. *African Agricultural Development. Reflections on the Major Lines of Advance and the Barriers to Progress.* New York: Food and Agriculture Organization, 1966.

2607. ______. *False Start in Africa.* Trans. Phyllis Ott. New York and Washington, D. C.: Praeger, 1966.

2608. Gutkind, Peter C. W., and Wallerstein, Immanuel M., eds. *The Political Economy of Contemporary Africa.* Beverly Hills, Calif.: Sage, 1976.

2609. Harrison Church, R. J. *West Africa: A Study of the Environment and of Man's Use of It.* 6th ed. London: Longmans, Green, 1968.

2610. International Labour Organization. *The Promotion of Balanced Rural and Urban Development.* Geneva: 1973.

2611. Jain, Sharad Chandra. *Agricultural Development of African Nations.* 2 vols. Bombay: Vora, 1965 and 1967.

2612. Lappé, Frances M., and Beccar-Varela, Adele. *Tanzania and Mozambique: Asking the Big Questions,* San Francisco, Calif.: Institute for Food and Development Policy, 1980.

2613. Lele, Uma. *The Design of Rural Development: Lessons from Africa.* Baltimore, Md.: Johns Hopkins University Press, 1975.

2614. McLoughlin, Peter F. M. *African Food Production Systems: Cases and Theory.* Baltimore, Md.: Johns Hopkins University Press, 1970.

2615. Makings, S. M. *Agricultural Problems of Developing Countries in Africa.* Lusaka: Oxford University Press, 1967.

2616. Mann, R. D. *An Approach to Identification of the Factors Which Limit Crop Production in African Farming Communities.* NCAE Silsoe Project Report no. 1. Bedford, UK: National College of Agricultural Engineering, March 1971.

2617. Markovitz, Irving Leonard. *Power and Class in Africa.* Englewood Cliffs, N. J.: Prentice-Hall, 1977.

2618. Moncure, Robert Clarke. *Agricultural Developments in Angola, British East Africa, Rhodesia and Nyasaland, and Zanzibar. Their Effects on U. S. Farm Exports.* Washington, D. C.: Foreign Agricultural Service, US Department of Agriculture, 1958.

2619. Mountjoy, Alan B., and Embleton, Clifford. *Africa. A New Geographical Survey.* New York: Praeger, 1967.

2620. National Academy of Sciences, Committee on African Agricultural Research Capabilities. *African Agricultural Research Capabilities.* Washington, D. C.: 1974.

2621. Okwuosa, Emanuel A. *New Directions for Economic Development in Africa.* London: Africa, 1976.

2622. Société d'Etudes pour le Développement Economique et Social. *Le Développement Rural Dans les Pays d'Afrique Noire d'Expression Française (Synthèse).* Paris: 1967.

2623. ______. *Le Développement Rural dans les Pays d'Afrique Noire d'Expression Française. Les Perspectives Alimentaires en Afrique Occidentale et Centrale en 1985.* Paris: 1967.

2624. ______. *Principes et Propositions Pour Une Analyse et Une Relance des Opérations de Développement Rural (Afrique Noire-Madagascar).* Paris: 1972.

2625. ______. *Propositions Pour Une Réorientation des Actions de Développement Rural (Afrique Noire et Madagascar).* Paris: 1968.

2626. United Nations. *Africa's Strategy for Development in the 1970s.* E/CN.14/RES/218(X) and E/CN.14/RES/238(XI). New York: 1973.

2627. Weaving, Rachel. *African Experiences with Rural Development: A Digest Report on the Africa Rural Development Study.* Bank Staff Working Paper no. 195. Washington, D. C.: World Bank, January 1975.

2628. Whetham, Edith H. *Agricultural Marketing in Africa.* London: Oxford University Press, 1972.

2629. White, Henry Patrick. *Commercial Agriculture in Tropical Africa.* Wellington, NZ: Hicks Smith, 1971.

2630. Wilde, John C. de, et al. *Experiences with Agricultural Development in Tropical Africa.* 2 vols. Baltimore, Md.: Johns Hopkins University Press, 1967. (*Volume I: The Synthesis;* and *Volume II: The Case Studies (Kenya, Mali, Chad, Upper Volta, Ivory Coast, Tanzania).*)

Articles

The role played by cooperatives in promoting rural development in Africa is discussed by Goussault, Apthorpe, and Dumont. The articles by Hunter and Bernstein and the issue of *Rural Africana* edited by Hayward and Ingle are recommended.

2631. Acharya, Shankar N. "Perspectives and Problems of Development in Low Income, Sub-Saharan Africa," pp. 1–64. In *Two Studies of Development in Sub-Saharan Africa.* Shankar N. Acharya and Bruce

Johnston. Working Paper 300. Washington, D. C.: World Bank, October 1978.

2632. Apthorpe, Raymond. "Cooperatives in Rural Africa." *Journal of Administration Overseas* 11 (July 1972): 150–161.

2633. Belloncle, Guy. "L'Animation Rurale: Facteur Crucial du Développement Agricole." *Afrique* no. 67 (1967): 11–17. (Discusses Madagascar, Upper Volta, Cameroon, Senegal, and Niger.)

2634. Bernstein, Henry. "Notes on Capital and Peasantry." *Review of African Political Economy* no. 10 (September–December 1977): 60–73.

2635. Bessis, Sophie. "Les Cultures Vivrières, Ces Mal-Aimées des Planificateurs." *Jeune Afrique* nos. 938–939 (27 December 1978–3 January 1979): 61–64.

2636. Dumont, René. "Le Mouvement Coopératif Africain: Plus d'Echecs Que de Réussites." *Revue Africaine d'Etudes Politiques Africaines* no. 59 (November 1970): 37–54.

2637. Ergas, Zeki. "Réflexions sur la Question de la Productivité Agricole en Afrique Tropicale." *Revue Tiers-Monde* 13 (July–September 1972): 591–602.

2638. "Food Situation in Africa: Towards an African Food Development Plan." *Agricultural Economics Bulletin for Africa* no. 15 (June 1974): 13–54.

2639. Goussault, Yves. "La Participation des Collectivités Rurales au Développement." *Revue Tiers-Monde* 2:5 (1961): 27–40.

2640. Hayward, Fred M., and Ingle, Clyde R., eds. "African Rural Development: The Political Dimension." *Rural Africana* no. 18 (Fall 1972).

2641. Hill, F. "Agricultural Scheme and Class Formation in Africa." *African Studies Review* 20:3 (1977): 25–42.

2642. Hunter, Guy. "Employment Policy in Tropical Africa: The Need for Radical Revision." *International Labour Review* 105 (January 1972): 35–57.

2643. Kofi, T. A. "Peasants and Economic Development: Populist Lessons from Africa." *African Studies Review* 20:3 (1977): 91–120.

2644. Lele, Uma. "Designing Rural Development Programs: Lessons from Past Experience in Africa." *Economic Development and Cultural Change* 24 (January 1976): 287–308.

2645. Obeng, A. "Money, Underdevelopment, and Rural Development in Africa." *African Administrative Studies* 17 (1977): 31–43.

2646. Silberfein, M. "The African Cultivator: A Geographic Overview." *African Studies Review* 20:3 (1977): 7–24.

2647. "Systèmes Agraires Africaines" (Issue Title). *Cahiers d'Etudes Africaines* no. 47 (1972): 333–511.

2648. United Nations, Economic Commission for Africa. "Food Demand, Prospects and Policies in Africa South of the Sahara." *Economic Bulletin for Africa* 10 (June 1970): 15–39.

East Africa

GENERAL

For an overview of the state of agriculture in East Africa up to the beginning of the 1970s, the two articles by Stoces and the one by the UN Economic Commission for Africa are recommended. The articles by Walker and by Neumark should be read together. The volume edited by Widstrand on the role of cooperatives in rural development in East Africa is also recommended.

2649. McLoughlin, Peter F. *Agriculture in East and Central Africa: An Overview.* London: Longmans, 1970.

2650. ———. *Research on Agricultural Development in East Africa.* New York: The Agricultural Development Council, 1967.

2651. Miller, Norman N. *Journey in a Forgotten Land, Part I: Food and Drought in the Ethiopia-Kenya Border Lands.* Northeast Africa Series, Vol. 19, no. 4. Hanover, N. H.: American Universities Field Staff, 1974.

2652. Neumark, S. D. "Some Economic Development Problems of African Agriculture." *Journal of Farm Economics* 41 (February 1959): 43–50.

2653. Ominde, Simeon H., ed. *Studies in East African Geography and Development.* Berkeley: University of California Press, 1971.

2654. Rigby, Peter. "Society and Social Change in Eastern Africa." *Nkanga* no. 4 (c.1971).

2655. Stoces, Ferdinand. "Notes on Current Plans for Development of African Agriculture in East Africa." *Agricultural Economics Bulletin for Africa* no. 10 (July 1968): 1–26.

2656. ———. "Place of Agriculture in the East African Economy." *Agricultural Economics Bulletin for Africa* no. 9 (October 1967): 79–104.

2657. United Nations, Economic Commission for Africa. "Part I. Agriculture in the East African Sub-Region." *Economic Bulletin for Africa* 9:2 (1969): 1–49.

2658. Walker, David. "A Note on the Economic Development of East African Agriculture." *Journal of Farm Economics* 42 (November 1960): 871–878.

2659. Watts, E. Ronald. "Reaching East Africa's Farmers—A Survey of Recent Efforts to Increase the Effectiveness of Agricultural Extension in Kenya, Uganda, and Tanzania." *Journal of Administration Overseas* 12 (April 1973): 112–124.

2660. Widstrand, Carl Gösta, ed. *Co-operatives and Rural Development in East Africa.* Uppsala: Scandinavian Institute of African Studies; and New York: Africana, 1970.

ETHIOPIA

Most of the entries in this section deal with pre-revolutionary Ethiopia. The principal work on pre-revolutionary Ethiopian agriculture is Huffnagel. The book by Cohen and Weintraub is also recommended. Most of the post-revolution studies have concentrated on the effect of land reform on rural development in Ethiopia, for example Cohen, Goldsmith and Mellor, Holmberg, and entries 1533, 1535, and 1548.

Prior to the 1960s, the agricultural sector in Ethiopia was largely neglected by the central government except as a source of revenue. Partly as a result of this, the Ethiopian highlands have suffered considerable ecological damage, which has in turn worsened the plight of the traditional sector. In the early 1960s, the government of Haile Sellassie, at the behest of international aid agencies such as the World Bank and USAID, began to promote the development of large-scale agriculture, often in collaboration with foreign corporations, sometimes with local landlords in charge. The ecological and social ramifications of such projects were in some cases disastrous for the small farmers, landless laborers, and pastoralists of Ethiopia. Bondestam and entry 1620 provide good descriptions of the impact of agribusiness in the Awash Valley.

The Chilalo Agricultural Development Unit (CADU), financed by Swedish aid, attempted to reach the small farmer in southern Ethiopia. While "CADU was successful in promoting the adoption of Green Revolution inputs and in increasing farmers' yields . . . it has caused substantial social hardships in that the adoption of modern techniques and resulting increases in harvests led to higher tenancy rents, dramatic rises in land values, great interest in increased production by landowners, and resulting tenant eviction by those who wanted to consolidate their lands and cash in on the innovations" (entry 774, pp. 356–357). CADU is also discussed by Nekby and Ståhl.

The post-revolution government has attempted to improve the situation of smallholders, but its efforts have been hampered by population growth rates of about 2.5 percent annually, the wars with Somali and Eritrea and related expenditures on arms (perhaps as much as $1 billion in 1978–1979), declining export revenues, and political factionalism.

2661. Bondestam, Lars. "People and Capitalism in the North-Eastern Lowlands of Ethiopia." *Journal of Modern African Studies* 12:3 (1974): 423–439.

2662. Chilalo Agricultural Development Unit, Extension and Education Department. *General Agricultural Survey of the Project Area.* CADU Publication no. 14. Addis Ababa: July 1968.

2663. Cohen, John M.; Goldsmith, Arthur A.; and Mellor, John W. *Revolution and Land Reform in Ethiopia: Peasant Associations, Local Government and Rural Development.* Occasional Paper no. 6. Ithaca, N. Y.: Rural Development Committee, Center for International Studies, Cornell University, January 1976.

2664. Cohen, John M., and Weintraub, Dov. *Land and Peasants in Imperial Ethiopia: The Social Background to a Revolution.* Assen: Van Gorcum, 1975.

2665. Green, David A. G. *Ethiopia: An Economic Analysis of Technological Change in Four Agricultural Production Systems.* East Lansing: African Studies Center, Michigan State University, 1974.

2666. Harbeson, John W., and Brietzke, Paul H., eds. "Rural Development in Ethiopia." *Rural Africana* no. 28 (Fall 1975).

2667. Holmberg, Johan. *Grain Marketing and Land Reform in Ethiopia.* Research Report 41. Uppsala: Scandinavian Institute of African Studies, 1977.

2668. Huffnagel, H. P. *Agriculture in Ethiopia.* Rome: Food and Agriculture Organization, 1961.

2669. Karlock, Merlin, and Fitzgerald, Harry. *A Technical and Economic Feasibility Study Pertaining to the Production and Marketability of Crops and Livestock.* Washington, D. C.: US Agency for International Development, June 1969.

2670. Miller, Clarence J.; Shaner, Willis W.; and Borton, Raymond E. *Development in Agriculture and Agro-Industry in Ethiopia. Strategy and Programs.* SRI Project 6350. Menlo Park, Calif.: Stanford Research Institute, December 1969.

2671. Nekby, B. *CADU: An Ethiopian Experiment in Developing Peasant Farming.* Stockholm: Prisma, 1971.

2672. Ståhl, Michael. *Ethiopia: Political Contradictions in Agricultural Development.* Stockholm: Raben & Sjögren, 1974.

2673. Wolde-Mariam, Mesfin, et al. *Welen Komi. A Socio-Economic and Nutritional Survey of a Rural Community in the Central Highlands of*

Ethiopia. The World Land Use Survey, Occasional Papers, no. 11. Bude, UK: Geographical Publications, 1971.

2674. Yeates. Maureen. "A Pattern of Agricultural Change in Ethiopia." *World Crops* 25 (May–June 1973): 141–144.

SOMALIA

The six volumes of the FAO agricultural and water survey of Somalia contain considerable information of interest to readers of this bibliography. Also recommended are the report from the ILO Jobs and Skills Programme for Africa and the chapter by Swift in entry 1650. In addition, entry 859 discusses "pastoral democracy" among Somalian herders.

2675. Barre, Siad. "We Intend to Base Our Development on Agriculture and Animal Husbandry." *Ceres* no. 45 (May–June 1975): 42–43.

2676. Davis, Bruce G., and Haworth, Howard F. *Review of USAID Water Resources Development Project: Somali Republic.* Mogadiscio: November 1963.

2677. Di Giorgi, Umberto. "Learning from Disaster." *Ceres* no. 45 (May–June 1975): 41–45.

2678. Food and Agriculture Organization. *FAO Agricultural and Water Surveys. Somalia.* 6 vols. Rome: 1967.

2679. International Labour Office, Jobs and Skills Programme for Africa. *Economic Transformation in a Socialist Framework: An Employment and Basic Needs Development Strategy for Somalia.* Addis Ababa: 1976.

2680. International Labour Organization. *Report to the Government of the Somali Democratic Republic on the Integrated Development of the Nomadic Zones,* ILO/OTA/Somalia/R.6. Geneva: 1972.

2681. Konczacki, Z. A. "Nomadism and Economic Development of Somalia." *Canadian Journal of African Studies* 1:2 (1967): 163–176.

2682. Laquian, A. A. "Somalia. Nomads no More." *IDRC Reports* 7 (September 1978): 6–7.

2683. Mahamed, O. O., and Wehrmann, M. "The Rural Development Campaign in Somalia (1974–75)." *Vierteljahresberichte: Problem der Entwicklungsländer* 72 (1978): 135–145.

SUDAN

Until quite recently, it was hoped that the combination of Sudanese land and labor and Arab financing would turn Sudan into a major food exporter. Since Sudan imported a large portion of its food requirements at the beginning of the 1970s, a considerable effort was clearly needed if Sudan were to become the "breadbasket" of the Arab world by the mid-1980s as envisaged by government officials and their Arab financeers.

The monograph by Kiss surveys the situation in Sudan's agricultural sector in the mid-1970s and considers the potential for increasing output and the obstacles to the realization of that potential. Kiss asks if the hope of turning Sudan into an Arab "breadbasket" is not unrealistic; in particular, it is suggested that Sudan could be exchanging one form of dependence (on cotton monoculture) for another (on food exports). By mid-1978, it was evident that the partnership between Sudan and its major Arab backers—Kuwait, Saudi Arabia, and Iraq—was not working out well and that Sudan had vastly overestimated its ability to set up large-scale agricultural projects. In addition, the Sudanese government was reportedly beginning to understand that emphasizing food exports would leave the country dependent on imports for just about everything else and government officials were said to be rethinking the whole "breadbasket" notion.

A good introduction to the Gezira Scheme is found in Barnett. El Jack Taha examines the Managil extension of the Gezira Scheme while Von Blanckenburg and Hubert discuss the Khashm el Girba Agricultural Scheme. Entries 1780 and 1799 look at some of the bureaucratic problems facing the Gezira Scheme. Entry 1723 discusses some ecological problems confronting Sudanese farmers. Entry 2126 examines the export orientation of the Sudanese economy and concludes that this has not hindered economic development. Rather, the problem is seen as one of ensuring the more equitable distribution of export earnings. Entry 292 presents the ILO strategy for increasing employment in Sudan by focusing investment on the small-scale agricultural producer as well as on small-scale industries and the poorer regions of the country. The chapter by Hoyle in entry 990 discusses the attempt to settle nomads on the Khashm el Girba Agricultural Scheme.

2684. Barnett, Tony. *The Gezira Scheme: An Illusion of Development.* London: Cass, 1977.

2685. El Jack Taha, Taha. "The Development of Managil South-Western Extension to the Gezira Scheme—A Case Study." *Journal of Administration Overseas* 14 (October 1975): 240–250.

2686. Food and Agriculture Organization. *Land and Water Resources Survey in the Jebel Marra Area: The Sudan.* FAO/SF:48/SUD–17. Rome: 1968.

2687. Hendry, Peter. "Choosing Among Awkward Options." *Ceres* no. 64 (July–August 1978): 16–22.

2688. Kiss, Judit. *Will Sudan Be an Agricultural Power?* Studies on Developing Countries no. 94. Budapest: Institute for World Economics of the Hungarian Academy of Sciences, 1977.

2689. Lebon, J. H. G. *Land Use in Sudan.* The World Land Use Survey, Monograph 4. Bude, UK: Geographical Publications, 1965.

2690. O'Hagan, J. P., ed. *Growth and Adjustment in National Agriculture: Four Case Studies and an Overview.* London: Macmillan, 1978. (Chapter 4 is relevant.)

2691. Saleh, Aziz. "Food Consumption and Nutrition in the Sudan—Projections for 1985." *Agricultural Economics Bulletin for Africa* no. 16 (December 1974): 1–9.

2692. Tothill, John Douglas, ed. *Agriculture in the Sudan.* London: Oxford University Press, 1948.

2693. Von Blanckenburg, P., and Hubert, K. "The Khashm el Girba Settlement Scheme in Sudan." *Zeitschrift für Ausländische Landwirtschaft* 4 (December 1969).

KENYA

The book by Odingo and the volume edited by Cone and Lipscomb focus on agriculture in the colonial period in Kenya. While Odingo deals primarily with European agriculture in the last phase of colonialism, the articles in Cone and Lipscomb are largely concerned with the impact of the Europeans on African agriculture. Recommended studies include Ruthenberg, the two Institute for Development Studies reports, and the study edited by Heyer, Maitha, and Senga. Entries 40 and 1594 are also relevant. The latter is an excellent summary of governmental bias in favor of the "progressive" farmer in the Million Acre Settlement Scheme. The failure of the "progressive" farmer to outperform the poorer members of the scheme is analyzed.

2694. Chambers, Robert, and Moris, Jon, eds. *Mwea: An Irrigated Rice Settlement Scheme in Kenya.* Munich: Weltforum Verlag, 1973.

2695. Clayton, Eric. *Agrarian Development in Peasant Economies: Some Lessons from Kenya.* New York: Macmillan, 1964.

2696. Cone, L. Winston, and Lipscomb, J. F., eds. *The History of Kenya Agriculture.* Nairobi: University Press of Africa, 1972.

2697. Heyer, Judith; Maitha, J. K.; and Senga, S. M., eds. *Agricultural Development in Kenya.* Nairobi: Oxford University Press, 1976.

2698. Institute for Development Studies. *An Overall Evaluation of the Special Rural Development Programme 1973.* Occasional Paper no. 8. Nairobi: University of Nairobi, 1973.

2699. ———. *Second Overall Evaluation of the Special Rural Development Programme 1975.* Occasional Paper no. 12. Nairobi: University of Nairobi, 1975.

2700. Lamb, Geoff B. *Peasant Politics: Conflict and Development in Muranga (Kenya).* New York: St. Martin's, 1974.

2701. Livingstone, I. "Rural Development in Kenya." *Journal of Administration Overseas* 15 (July 1976): 132–140.

2702. Odingo, Richard S. *The Kenya Highlands: Land Use and Development.* Nairobi: East African Publishing House, 1971.

2703. Ruthenberg, Hans. *African Agricultural Production Development Policy in Kenya, 1952–1965.* Afrika Studien no. 10. Berlin and New York: Springer-Verlag, 1966.

2704. Trapman, Christopher. *Change in Administrative Structures: A Case Study of Kenyan Agricultural Development.* London: Overseas Development Institute, 1974.

2705. Witucki, Lawrence A. *Agricultural Development in Kenya Since 1967.* Foreign Agricultural Economic Report no. 123. Washington, D. C.: Economic Research Service, US Department of Agriculture, July 1976.

UGANDA

All of the entries in this section were written prior to the Amin period which greatly weakened the Ugandan economy. According to FAO figures, the rate of growth of the agricultural sector in Uganda declined by over 50 percent from 1960–70 to 1970–76 and per capita food production in the mid-1970s was only 89 percent of what it had been in 1965–67 (see Table 5).

The book edited by Jameson is rather technical but is nonetheless recommended to readers seeking an explicit description of tropical agriculture.

2706. Jameson, J. D., ed. Completed by David Stephens. *Agriculture in Uganda.* 2nd ed. New York: Oxford University Press, 1970.

2707. Masefield, Geoffrey B. "Agricultural Change in Uganda, 1945–60," pp. 38–57. In *Readings in the Applied Economics of Africa. Volume I.* Cambridge, UK: Cambridge University Press, 1967. (This is also available in *Food Research Institute Studies* 3:2 (1962): 87–124.)

2708. Richards, Audrey I.; Sturrock, Ford; and Fortt, Jean M., eds. *Subsistence to Commercial Farming in Present Day Buganda.* Cambridge, UK: Cambridge University Press, 1973.

2709. Vail, David Jeremiah. *A History of Agricultural Innovation and Development in Teso District, Uganda.* Eastern African Studies VI. Syracuse, N. Y.: Program of Eastern African Studies, Maxwell School, Syracuse University, 1972.

TANZANIA

Tanzania is perhaps the most widely studied African country. It has been of interest because of its attempts to develop its own form of socialism. Central to this attempt has been the ujamaa strategy which sought to transform rural Tanzania into socialist communities. However, by the mid-1970s, this approach had run into serious problems and Tanzania's food imports rose significantly. While the decline in domestic production can be partly attributed to drought conditions, the failure of the ujamaa strategy—due to bureaucratic and administrative problems as well as to peasant resistance—has been cited as a major cause of shortfalls in agricultural production.

Books and Monographs

The study by Boesen, Madsen and Moody looks at the development of the ujamaa strategy from 1968 to 1973. In 1973, the policy shifted to compulsory mass villagization (moving farmers into villages) with socialization relegated to a secondary role. This study is recommended as an introduction to the topic of ujamaa. The volume edited by Coulson includes chapters on villagization and ujamaa villages. Other recommended books are those by Knight and Ruthenberg. Also of relevance is entry 2612.

2710. Anthony, K. R. M., and Uchendu, V. C. *Agricultural Change in Geita District: Tanzania.* Nairobi: East Africa Literature Bureau, 1974.

2711. Boesen, Jannik. *Tanzania: From Ujamaa to Villagisation.* A76.7. Copenhagen: Institute of Development Research, 1976.

2712. Boesen, Jannik; Madsen, Birgit Storgård; and Moody, Tony. *Ujamaa—Socialism from Above.* Uppsala: Scandinavian Institute of African Studies, 1977.

2713. Cliffe, Lionel, ed. *Rural Cooperation in Tanzania.* Dar es Salaam: Tanzania Publishing House, 1975.

2714. Connell, John. *The Evolution of Tanzanian Rural Development.* IDS Communication 110. Brighton, UK: Institute of Development Studies, University of Sussex, 1973.

2715. Coulson, Andrew, ed. *Socialism in Africa—Lessons from Tanzania.* Sheffield, UK: Review of African Political Economy with Spokesman, 1979.

2716. Finucane, James R. *Rural Development and Bureaucracy in Tanzania. The Case of Mwanza Region.* Uppsala: Scandinavian Institute of African Studies, 1974.

2717. Green, Reginald H. *Toward Socialism for Self Reliance. Tanzania's Striving for Sustained Transition Period.* Research Report no. 38. Uppsala: Scandinavian Institute of African Studies, 1977.

2718. Hekken, P. M. van, and Thoden van Velzen, H. U. E. *Land Scarcity and Rural Inequality in Tanzania.* The Hague: Mouton, 1972.

2719. Kjekshus, Helge. *Tanzania Year 15: Crisis and Development.* NUPI Notat no. 129. Oslo: Norsk Utenrikspolitisk Institutt, September 1976.

2720. Knight, C. Gregory. *Ecology and Change. Rural Modernization in an African Community.* New York: Academic, 1974.

2721. Newman, James L. *The Ecological Basis for Subsistence Change Among the Sandawe of Tanzania.* Washington, D. C.: National Academy of Sciences, 1970.

2722. Pritchard, Brian J. *Tanzania's Agricultural Economy in Brief.* ERS–Foreign 366. Washington, D. C.: Economic Research Service, US Department of Agriculture, September 1974.

2723. Rald, Jørgen and Karen. *Rural Organization in Bukoba District, Tanzania.* Uppsala: Scandinavian Institute of African Studies, 1975.

2724. Ruthenberg, Hans. *Agricultural Development in Tanganyika.* Afrika-Studien no. 2. Berlin and New York: Springer-Verlag, 1964.

2725. Ruthenberg, Hans, ed. *Smallholder Farming and Smallholder Development in Tanzania.* London: Hurst, 1968. (Also published as Afrika-Studien no. 24. Berlin and New York: Springer-Verlag, 1968.)

2726. Smith, Hadley E. *Agricultural Development in Tanzania.* London and Nairobi: Oxford University Press, 1965.

Articles

Nellis discusses how the ujamaa strategy evolved. Lofchie (entry 2734) looks at some of the problems which have faced Tanzania in its attempt to socialize agriculture. The article by Raikes in the *Review of African Political Economy* (entry 2740) also surveys the problems that have arisen in the course of implementing the ujamaa policy. Raikes argues that these problems have resulted in part from "the absence of a concerted strategy for the transformation of the economy" and in part from the control exerted by the bureaucratic bourgeoisie over the ujamaa program. This article should be read in conjunction with the one by Coulson in the same issue of the *Review of African Political Economy* (entry 2729).

The second article by Coulson (entry 2728) examines conflicts that have occurred because bureaucrats have attempted to force peasants to act in accordance with bureaucratic conceptions of appropriate peasant activities. The second article by Lofchie (entry 2733) examines the breakdown of attempts to promote village socialism in Tanzania.

The second article by Raikes (entry 2739) is also recommended.

2727. Brooke, C. "Types of Food Shortages in Tanzania." *Geographical Review* 57 (July 1967): 333–357.

2728. Coulson, Andrew. "Agricultural Policies in Mainland Tanzania." *Review of African Political Economy* no. 10 (September–December 1977): 74–100.

2729. ______. "Peasants and Bureaucrats." *Review of African Political Economy* no. 3 (May–October 1975): 53–58.

2730. Feldman, D. "The Economics of Ideology: Some Problems of Achieving Rural Socialism in Tanzania," pp. 85–111. In *Politics and Change in Developing Countries.* Ed. Colin Leys. London: Cambridge University Press, 1969.

2731. Helleiner, Gerald K. "Agricultural Export Pricing Strategy in Tanzania." *East African Journal of Rural Development* 1:1 (1968): 1–17.

2732. Kjekshus, Helge. "The Tanzanian Villagization Policy: Implementational Lessons and Ecological Dimensions." *Canadian Journal of African Studies* 11:2 (1977): 269–282.

2733. Lofchie, Michael F. "Agrarian Crisis and Economic Liberalisation in Tanzania." *Journal of Modern African Studies* 16 (September 1978): 451–475.

2734. ______. "Agrarian Socialism in the Third World" (Review Article). *Comparative Politics* 8 (April 1976).

2735. Mapolu, H., and Philippeson, G. "Agricultural Co-Operation and the Development of the Productive Forces: Some Lessons from Tanzania." *Africa Development* 1 (May 1976): 42–58.

2736. Mwapacha, Juma Volter. "Operation Planned Villages in Rural Tanzania: A Revolutionary Strategy for Development." *The African Review* 6:1 (1976): 1–16.

2737. Nellis, J. R. "Prelude to Arusha: A Study of Productivity Problems on a Rural Development Scheme in Tanzania." *Journal of Administration Overseas* 11 (July 1972): 169–181.

2738. Omari, C. K. "The Emerging Rural Development Policy in Tanzania." *Africa Today* 21 (Summer 1974): 9–14.

2739. Raikes, Philip. "Rural Differentiation and Class-Formation in Tanzania." *The Journal of Peasant Studies* 5 (April 1978): 285–325.

2740. ______. "Ujamaa and Rural Socialism." *Review of African Political Economy* no. 3 (May–October 1975): 33–52.

MADAGASCAR

2741. Heseltine, Nigel. "The Ecological Basis of Agriculture in Madagascar." *World Crops* 25 (January–February 1973): 34–40.

2742. Latremolière, Jacques. "Les Contradictions de l'Agriculture Malgache." *Afrique Contemporaine* no. 79 (1975): 1–6.

North Africa and the Middle East

GENERAL

2743. Antoun, Richard, and Harik, Iliya F., ed. *Rural Politics and Social Change in the Middle East.* Bloomington: Indiana University Press, 1972.

2744. Food and Agriculture Organization. *Agriculture in the Near East: Development and Outlook.* Rome: 1953.

2745. Goussault, Yves; Marthelot, Pierre; and Meister, Albert. "Associationnismes Ruraux et Participation des Masses Rurales aux Programmes de Développement dans les Pays Méditerranéens." *International Review of Commodity Development* no. 15–16 (1966): 89–116. (Focuses on Morocco, Algeria, Libya, and Tunisia.)

2746. Pallas, Philippe. "Water Resources in the Northern Sahara." *Nature and Resources* 8 (July–September 1972): 9–17.

2747. United Nations, Economic Commission for Africa. "Part II. Agriculture in the North African Sub-Region." *Economic Bulletin for Africa* 9:2 (1969): 51–77.

EGYPT

During the last two decades, overall agricultural productivity and the per capita production of food have stagnated in Egypt. In part, this is due to the enormous expansion of the Egyptian population, which was 3 million in the early nineteenth century, 27 million in the early 1960s, and 37 million in 1975. In part, the problem results from the export of food crops to earn foreign exchange and the diversion of Egypt's resources toward the military sector due to the decades-long conflict with Israel. In addition, much of the land in Egypt has been farmed intensively for a very long period of time, causing soil depletion, salinity, and water-logging. It has been suggested, "It is at the price of the long-term degradation of the soil that levels of production have been maintained or marginally increased over the last 15 years" (entry 2760, p. 4).

Attempts to reclaim land have met with varying degrees of success; 18 percent of the 900,000 acres reclaimed between 1953 and 1975 have reverted to waste land. Urban sprawl accounts for additional reductions in agricultural land. It has been estimated that the 6 million acres under cultivation in the mid-1970s might decline by one-third (to 4 million acres) by the year 2000.

Some of the problems associated with the reclamation of land are discussed in the report co-authored by the US Department of Agriculture, the US Agency for International Development, and the Egyptian Ministry of Agriculture. It is concluded that up to the year 2000 the problem will be one of water management and after the year 2000 one of water supply. The study by Fried and Edlund looks at the economic potential for desalinization in Egypt. The book by Mabro contains considerable information on agricultural development. Also recommended are Harik, Elkington, Mayfield, and Megalli.

2748. Abdallah, Hassan. *U. A. R. Agriculture.* Cairo [?]: Foreign Relations Department, Ministry of Agriculture, March 1965.

2749. Elkington, John. "Beware of the Wrath of Osiris." *New Scientist* 68 (11 December 1975).

2750. Field, Michael. "Developing the Nile." *World Crops* 25 (January–February 1973): 11–15.

2751. Fried, Jerome J., and Edlund, Milton C. *Desalting Technology for Middle Eastern Agriculture. An Economic Case.* Praeger Special Studies in International Economics and Development. New York: Praeger, 1971.

2752. Harik, Iliya F. *The Political Mobilization of Peasants: A Study of an Egyptian Community.* Bloomington: Indiana University Press, 1974.

2753. Mabro, Robert. *The Egyptian Economy, 1952–1972.* Oxford: Clarendon, 1974.

2754. Mayfield, J. B. *Local Institutions and Egyptian Rural Development.* PN–AAB–193. Washington, D. C.: US Agency for International Development, 1974. (Also available as RLG 3. Ithaca, N. Y.: Rural Development Committee, Center for International Studies, Cornell University, c.1974.)

2755. Megalli, Nabil. "Agriculture: Suffering from Plunders of the Past." *African Development* 9 (October 1975): E23–E24.

2756. O'Brien, Patrick. "The Long-Term Growth of Agricultural Production in Egypt," pp. 162–195. In *Political and Social Change in Modern Egypt.* Ed. P. M. Hold. Oxford: Oxford University Press, 1968.

2757. Oweis, Jiryis S. *The Impact of Land Reform on Egyptian Agriculture: 1952–1965.* LTC Reprint no. 78. Madison: Land Tenure Center, University of Wisconsin, c.1971.

2758. Parker, Christopher. "Irrigation: Priority for a Desert Land." *African Development* 9 (October 1975): E27–E28.

2759. United States Department of Agriculture, United States Agency for International Development, and the Egyptian Ministry of Agriculture. *Egypt: Major Constraints to Increasing Agricultural Productivity.* Foreign Agricultural Economic Report no. 120. Washington, D. C.: US Department of Agriculture, June 1976.

2760. Waterbury, John. *'Aish: Egypt's Growing Food Crisis.* Northeast Africa Series. Hanover, N. H.: American Universities Field Staff, December 1974.

2761. ———. *The Balance of People, Land, and Water in Modern Egypt.* Northeast Africa Series. Hanover, N. H.: American Universities Field Staff, January 1974.

2762. ———. *The Nile Stops at Aswan.* 3 parts. Northeast Africa Series. Hanover, N. H.: American Universities Field Staff, March 1977.

TUNISIA

The report by Hauri is recommended.

2763. Apthorpe, Raymond J. *Peasants and Planistrators: Cooperatives in Rural Tunisia.* Discussion Paper 8. Norwich, UK: School of Development Studies, University of East Anglia, 1975.

2764. Ashford, Douglas. "Organization of Cooperatives and the Structure of Power in Tunisia." *Journal of Developing Areas* 1 (April 1967): 317–332.

2765. Bale, M. D., and St. Andre, Jerry. *Feedgrain Production and Potential in Tunisia.* PN–AAC–691. Washington, D. C.: US Agency for International Development, 1977.

2766. Ben Salah, Ahmed. "Tunisia: Endogenous Development and Structural Transformation," pp. 242–262. In *Another Development: Approaches and Strategies.* Ed. Marc Nerfin. Uppsala: Dag Hammarskjöld Foundation, 1977.

2767. Hauri, Irene. *Le Projet Céréalier en Tunisie: Etudes aux Nivaux National et Local.* Report no. 74.4. Geneva: UN Research Institute for Social Development, 1975.

2768. Makhlouf, Ezzedine. *Structures Agraires et Modernisation de l'Agriculture dans les Plaines de Kef.* Cahiers du CERES. Série Géographique, no. 1. Tunis: Centre d'Etudes et de Recherches Economiques et Sociales, Université, 1968.

2769. Simmons, John L. "Agricultural Cooperatives and Tunisian Development. Part I." *The Middle East Journal* 24 (Autumn 1970): 455–465.

2770. ———. "Agricultural Cooperatives and Tunisian Development, Part II." 25 (Winter 1971): 45–57.

2771. Zghal, Abdelkader. *Modernisation de l'Agriculture et Populations Semi-Nomades.* The Hague: Mouton, 1967.

MOROCCO

The report by van de Kloet and the article by van Wersch are recommended.

2772. Bull, Mary R. "Morocco's Agricultural Policy." *World Crops* 24 (September–October 1972): 243–244.

2773. Moati, P., and Rainaut, P. *La Réforme Agricole: Clé Pour le Développement du Maghreb.* Paris: Dunod, 1970.

2774. Schmidt, Monique. "Problèmes de Développement Agricole dans le Périmètre des Abda-Doukkala (Maroc)." *Revue Tiers-Monde* 11 (October–December 1970): 793–814.

2775. van der Kloet, Hendrik. *Inégalités dans les Milieux Ruraux: Possibilités et Problèmes de la Modernisation Agricole au Maroc.* Report no. 75.1. Geneva: UN Research Institute for Social Development, 1975.

2776. van Wersch, H. J. "Rural Development in Morocco: Operation Labor (Operation Plow)." *Economic Development and Cultural Change* 17 (October 1968): 33–49.

ALGERIA

Tidafi discusses why worker-managed farms are not a success in Algeria. The attitudes of officials and landowners, the impoverishment of the traditional sector, and the growth of "parasitical" occupations are the focus of this examination. Three other recommended studies, Leucate, Krieger, and Jönsson, all discuss the Algerian agrarian reform.

2777. Abdi, Nourredine. "Réforme Agraire et Voie Algérienne de Développement." *Revue Tiers-Monde* 17 (July–September 1976): 663–674.

2778. Foster, Phillips W., and Steiner, Herbert. *The Structure of Algerian Socialized Agriculture.* Miscellaneous Publication no. 527. College Park: Department of Agricultural Economics, College of Agriculture, University of Maryland, 1964.

2779. Guichaoua, André. "La Réforme Agraire Algérienne. Portée et Limites: Politique Agricole et Transformation Sociales." *Revue Tiers-Monde* 18 (July–September 1977): 581–601.

2780. Jönsson, Lars. *La Révolution Agraire en Algérie: Historique, Contenu et Problèmes.* Research Report no. 47. Uppsala: Scandinavian Institute of African Studies, 1978.

2781. Krieger, Annie. "Les Prémices d'une Réforme Agraire en Algérie," pp. 97–165. In *Essais sur l'Economie de l'Algérie Nouvelle.* Françoise d'Arcy, Annie Krieger, and Alain Marill. Paris: Presses Universitaires de France, 1965.

2782. Leucate, Christian. "Révolution Agraire en Algérie?" *Critique de l'Economie Politique* no. 15 (January–March 1974): 67–88.

2783. Ollivier, Marc. "The Decolonization of Agriculture." *Ceres* no. 31 (January–February 1973): 24–28.

2784. Tidafi, Tami. *L'Agriculture Algérienne et Ses Perspectives de Développement.* Paris: Maspero, 1969.

MIDDLE EAST

For an introduction to agriculture in the Middle East, readers should consult the volume edited by Stickley, Asmar, Saghir, Atallah, and Pellett. The articles included in this book cover a wide variety of topics relating to agricultural economics, soil and irrigation, animal production, nutrition, and crop production in the region.

2785. Aresvik, Oddvar. *The Agricultural Development of Jordan.* New York: Praeger, 1976.

2786. Birch, B. P. "Recent Developments in Agriculture, Land and Water Use in Jordan." *World Crops* 25 (March–April 1973): 67–74.

2787. Clawson, Marion; Landsberg, Hans H.; and Alexander, Lyle T. *The Agricultural Potential of the Middle East.* New York: American Elsevier, 1971.

2788. Dorozynski, Alexander. "Change Comes Again to the Fertile Crescent." *IDRC Reports* 6:4 (1977): 3–6.

2789. Food and Agriculture Organization. *FAO Mediterranean Development Project. Lebanon: Country Report.* Rome: 1959.

2790. ———. *FAO Mediterranean Development Project. Iraq: Country Report.* Rome: 1959.

2791. ———. *FAO Mediterranean Development Project. United Arab Republic/Syria Region: Country Report.* Rome: 1959.

2792. ———. *FAO Mediterranean Development Project. Jordan: Country Report.* Rome: 1967.

2793. Gabby, Rony. *Communism and Agrarian Reform in Iraq.* London: Croom-Helm, 1978.

2794. Hassan, M. F. "Agricultural Development in a Petroleum-based Economy: Qatar." *Economic Development and Cultural Change* 27 (October 1978): 145–167.

2795. Kaul, R. N. "An Integrated Natural Resources Survey in Northern Iraq." *Nature and Resources* 9 (April–June 1973): 13–18.

2796. Stickley, Thomas S.; Asmar, J. A.; Saghir, A.-R.; Atallah, N.; and Pellett, R. L., eds. *Man, Food and Agriculture in the Middle East.* Beirut: American University of Beirut, 1969.

2797. Taylor, Donald C. *Research on Agricultural Development in Selected Middle Eastern Countries.* New York: The Agricultural Development Council, 1968.

2798. Yudelman, Montague. "Some Issues in Agricultural Development in Iraq." *Journal of Farm Economics* 40 (February 1958): 78–88.

West Africa

GENERAL

The volume by Dumont is recommended.

2799. Dumont, René. *Afrique Noire, Développement Agricole. Reconversion de l'Economie Agricole: Guinée, Côte d'Ivoire, Mali.* Paris: Presses Universitaires de France, 1962.

2800. Eicher, Carl K. *Research on Agricultural Development in Five English Speaking Countries in West Africa.* New York: The Agricultural Development Council, 1970.

2801. Food and Agriculture Organization. *West African Pilot Study of Agricultural Development, 1960–1975.* 3 vols. WIPA/W.AFR.65/1–2. Rome: 1965.

2802. Irvine, Frederick R., ed. *West African Agriculture.* 3rd ed. London: Oxford University Press, 1970.

2803. Johnston, Bruce F. *The Staple Food Economies of Western Tropical Africa.* Stanford, Calif.: Stanford University Press, 1958.

2804. Joint ECA/FAO Agricultural Division. "Agricultural Development Through Multilateral Co-operation and Trade Expansion: Possibilities for Dahomey, Niger and Nigeria." *Economic Bulletin for Africa* 11:1 (1975): 12–56.

2805. Ofori, I. M., ed. *Factors of Agricultural Growth in West Africa: Proceedings of an International Conference held at Legon, April 1971.* Legon: Institute of Statistical, Social and Economic Research, University of Ghana, 1973.

2806. Viguier, Pierre. *L'Afrique de l'Ouest Vue par un Agriculteur: Problème de Base en Afrique Tropicale.* no. 60. Paris: La Maison Rustique, 1961.

NIGERIA

The article by Joseph discusses how the response of the Nigerian government and people to the country's oil wealth has been antithetical to economic development. By 1976, total annual government expenditure had reached the level of annual income derived from the sale of oil and Nigeria was forced to draw on its reserves to finance some of its commitments. This article is a good introduction to many of the problems currently facing the Nigerian economy.

The report by Tiffen traces the transformation of agriculture in Gombe from small-scale subsistence herding and farming to larger farms producing for the market. The book by Smock and Smock is already somewhat of a classic and should be read by anyone interested in rural development in Nigeria. Other recommended studies include Ọlatunbọsun, Helleiner, and Oluwasanmi, Dema et al.

2807. Adeyoju, S. Kolade. "The Forest Resources of Nigeria." *The Nigerian Geographical Journal* 8 (December 1965): 115–126.

2808. Ajaebu, Hyacinth I. *Urban and Rural Development in Nigeria.* London: Heinemann, 1976.

2809. Alao, J. A. "The Dilemma of Modernizing Peasant Agriculture in Nigeria." *Journal of Rural Cooperation* 5:2 (1977): 141–153.

2810. Coppock, J. T. "Agricultural Developments in Nigeria." *Journal of Tropical Geography* 23 (December 1966): 1–18.

2811. Floyd, Barry. "Terrace Agriculture in Eastern Nigeria: The Case of Maku." *The Nigerian Geographical Journal* 7 (December 1964): 91–108.

2812. Food and Agriculture Organization. *Agricultural Development in Nigeria, 1965–1980.* Rome: 1966.

2813. Güsten, Rolf. *Studies in the Staple Food Economy of Western Nigeria.* Afrika-Studien no. 30. Munich: Weltforum Verlag, 1968.

2814. Hartoungh, Ir J. C. C. "Problems of Development in Ogoni." *World Crops* 21 (July–August 1969): 182–185.

2815. Helleiner, Gerald K. *Peasant Agriculture, Government, and Economic Growth in Nigeria.* Homewood, Ill.: Irwin, 1966.

2816. Joseph, Richard. "Affluence and Underdevelopment: The Nigerian Experience." *Journal of Modern African Studies* 16:2 (1978): 221–239.

2817. Norman, David W. *An Economic Study of Three Villages in Zaria Province, Part I. Land and Labour Relationships.* Samaru Miscellaneous Paper no. 19. Zaria, Nigeria: Institute of Agricultural Research, Ahmadu Bello University, 1967.

2818. ______. *An Economic Study of Three Villages in Zaria Province. Volume i. Text.* Samaru Miscellaneous Paper no. 37. Zaria, Nigeria: Institute of Agricultural Research, Ahmadu Bello University, 1972.

2819. Ọlatunbọsun, 'Dupẹ. *Nigeria's Neglected Rural Majority.* Ibadan: Oxford University Press, for the Nigerian Institute of Social and Economic Research, 1975.

2820. Olayide, S. O.; Ọlatunbọsun, 'D.; Idusogie, E. O.; and Abiagom, J. D. *A Quantitative Analysis of Food Requirements, Supplies and Demand in Nigeria, 1968–1985.* Lagos: Federal Department of Agriculture, 1972.

2821. Oluwasanmi, H. A.; Dema, I. S. and others. *A Socio-Economic and Nutritional Survey of a Rural Community in Eastern Nigeria.* The World Land Use Survey, Occasional Papers, no. 6. Bude, UK: Geographical Publications, 1966.

2822. Oyenuga, Victor A. *Agriculture in Nigeria: An Introduction.* Rome: Food and Agriculture Organization—World Health Organization—UNICEF, 1967.

2823. Pickstock, Michael. "Filling Nigeria's Larder." *New Scientist* 63 (22 August 1974): 452–456.

2824. Smock, David R., and Smock, Audrey C. *Cultural and Political Aspects of Rural Transformation: A Case Study of Eastern Nigeria.* New York: Praeger, 1972.

2825. Tiffen, Mary. *The Enterprising Peasant: Economic Development in Gombe Emirate in North Eastern State, 1900–1968.* Overseas Research Publication no. 21. London: Her Majesty's Stationery Office, 1976.

2826. Upton, Martin. *Agriculture in South-Western Nigeria.* Development Studies no. 3. Reading, UK: Department of Agricultural Economics, University of Reading, December 1967.

GHANA

Lawson and Miracle and Seidman are recommended.

2827. Benneh, G. "Decentralisation and Rural Development." *African Administrative Studies* 17 (1977): 45–50.

2828. Darkoh, M. B. X. "An Outline of Post–1966 Regional Planning and Rural Development in Ghana." *Pan-Africa Journal* 9:2 (1976): 153–167.

2829. Gurnah, A. M. "Large Scale Maize Production in Ghana." *World Crops* 25 (November–December 1973): 308–311.

2830. Lawson, Rowena. *The Changing Economy of the Lower Volta. 1954–67: A Study in the Dynamics of Rural Economic Growth.* London and New York: Oxford University Press, 1972.

2831. Miracle, Marvin, and Seidman, Ann. *State Farmers in Ghana.* LTC no. 43. Madison: Land Tenure Center, University of Wisconsin, 1968.

2832. Poleman, Thomas T. *The Food Economies of Urban Middle Africa: The Case of Ghana.* Cornell International Agricultural Development Reprint 14. Ithaca, N. Y.: Cornell University, n.d. (Also available in *Food Research Institute Studies* 2 (May 1961).)

2833. Thornton, D. S. *Agriculture in South East Ghana: Volume I. Summary Report.* Development Study no. 12. Reading, UK: Department of Agricultural Economics and Management, University of Reading, June 1973.

SAHEL ZONE

For probably the first time since they became independent of France in the early 1960s, the countries of the Sahel zone were the focus of international attention when famine threatened in 1973. However, by the time the Sahel drought/famine was "discovered," the crisis was half a decade old for many of the region's inhabitants. Even prior to the onset of drought in 1968, Sahelian countries had had to import considerable amounts of their food requirements. The primary reasons for this are the orientation of agriculture toward cash crop production, the decline of soil productivity due to reduced fallowing or reduced manuring, and the extension of food crop production into more marginal agricultural lands with poorer soils and less regular rainfall.

Books and Monographs

The Ivory Coast is increasingly being held up as an "economic showcase," not only for the Sahel zone but for all of Africa. The Ivory Coast has the highest per capita income in sub-Saharan Africa and its economy is built on agricultural production for export. It is also highly dependent on foreign capital and manpower, particularly from France. The books by Vaurs, Goreux, and Condos, den Tuinder et al., Maldant et al., and Amin look at various aspects of economic activity in the Ivory Coast. Amin argues that the sort of strategy pursued by the Ivory Coast cannot lead to self-centered development. As long as the dependence on foreign capital is maintained, the bulk of the benefits derived from economic growth will be exported to the owners of that capital and the Ivory Coast will be unable to accumulate sufficient domestic capital to enable it to direct its own economic destiny.

The monograph by Berg provides considerable statistical information on Sahelian economies. The monograph by Sircoulon presents data on climatic and hydrological conditions in Sahelian West Africa from the early 1900s, with the emphasis on the most recent drought period. The SIDA/FAO report contains much information on conditions in the Sahel zone both before and as a result of the 1968–1973 drought/famine. Caldwell's monograph also offers useful information on the region during and after the 1968–1973 drought.

In addition, readers should consult the following sections in which there are a number of books and monographs pertaining to the Sahel zone: "Pastoralism," "Aid and Neocolonialism," "Ecology and Resources," and "Economic and Political Roots of Hunger." In particular, readers interested in the relationship between economic development and ecological degradation and famine are recommended to look at at least one of the following: entries 1604, 1882, and 1883. Entry 6 is also recommended.

2834. Amin, Samir. *Le Développement du Capitalisme en Côte d'Ivoire.* Paris: Editions de Minuit, 1967. (Chapters 1–3 are relevant.)

2835. Becker, J. A. *An Analysis and Forecast of Cereals Availability in the Sahelian Entente States of West Africa.* PN–AAE–504. Washington, D. C.: US Agency for International Development, 1974. (Discusses Upper Volta and Niger.)

2836. Berg, Elliot. *The Recent Economic Evolution of the Sahel.* Ann Arbor, Mich.: Center for Research in Economic Development, 1 June 1975.

2837. Caldwell, John C. *The Sahelian Drought and Its Demographic Implications.* Washington, D. C.: Overseas Liaison Committee, American Council on Education, 1975.

2838. Diarassouba, Valy Charles. *L'Evolution des Structures Agricoles du Sénégal. Destruction et Restructuration de l'Economie Rurale.* Paris: Editions Cujas, 1968.

2839. Ernst, Klaus. *Tradition and Progress in the African Village: Non-Capitalist Transformation of Rural Communities in Mali.* Trans. Salomea Genin. New York: St. Martin's, 1976.

2840. Food and Agriculture Organization. *Chad: Problems and Prospects of Rural Development. FAO Africa Survey, Country Study.* Rome: 1963.

2841. ———. *Mali: Problems and Prospects of Rural Development. FAO Africa Survey, Country Study.* Rome: 1962.

2842. Maldant, Boris, with C. Frelin, S. Alonso, Y. Breton, G. Coutsinas, and C. Paix. *Les Facteurs de la Production Agricole en Côte d'Ivoire.* Paris: Institut d'Etude du Développement Economique et Social, 1977.

2843. Michigan University, Center for Research on Economic Development. *Marketing, Price Policy and Storage of Food Grains in the Sahel,*

A Survey; Volume I: Synthesis with Statistical Compilation and Annotated Bibliography. PN–AAF–398. Washington, D. C.: US Agency for International Development, 1977.

2844. ______. *Marketing, Price Policy and Storage of Food Grains in the Sahel, A Survey; Volume II: Country Studies.* PN–AAF–399. Washington, D. C.: US Agency for International Development, 1977. (Contains studies of Upper Volta, Senegal, Niger, Mauritania, Mali, the Gambia, and Chad.)

2845. Rockefeller Foundation. *Conference on International Development Strategies for the Sahel.* Working Papers. New York: May 1975.

2846. Sircoulon, J. *Les Données Climatiques et Hydrologiques de la Sécheresse en Afrique de l'Ouest Sahélienne.* Stockholm: Secretariat for International Ecology, Sweden (SIES), 1974.

2847. Swedish International Development Authority-Food and Agriculture Organization. *Report on the Sahelian Zone: A Survey of the Problems of the Sahelian Zone with a View to Drawing Up a Long-Term Strategy and a Programme for Protection, Restoration, and Development.* Rome: FAO, 1974.

2848. Thomas, M. E. R., and des Bouvrie, M. C. *Enquête sur les Conséquences de la Sécheresse en Zone Sahélienne (Mali, Niger, Haute-Volta).* Accra: Food and Agriculture Organization Regional Bureau, 1973.

2849. den Tuinder, Bastiaan, et al. *Ivory Coast: The Challenge of Success.* Baltimore, Md.: Johns Hopkins University Press, 1978.

2850. United Nations, Economic Commission for Africa/Food and Agriculture Organization Joint Division. *Report of a Mission for the Study of Problems and Prospects in Rural Development of Mali, Niger and Upper Volta.* RU–E/CN.14/SWCD/29. New York: Economic and Social Council, UN, 1966.

2851. Vaurs, R.; Goreux, Louis M.; and Condos, Apostolos. *An Agricultural Model from the Ivory Coast Programming Study.* Working Paper 125. Washington, D. C.: World Bank, March 1972.

2852. Wilcock, D. C. *The Political Economy of Grain Marketing and Storage in the Sahel.* PN–AAF–071. Washington, D. C.: US Agency for International Development, 1978.

Articles

A brief introduction to agriculture in the Sahel zone can be found in the FAO/UNECA article. Marcussen and Torp look at the Ivory Coast and argue that, contrary to the position adopted by Amin (entry 2834), a country need not isolate itself from the world market to create self-centered development. This article should be read in conjunction with *Le Développement du Capitalisme en Côte d'Ivoire.*

The article by Hubert discusses a successful program to increase groundnut production in Mali. It is suggested that this project's success is in part due to the complete involvement of the peasantry. The article by Glantz (along with entry 872) demonstrates that the problems afflicting the Sahelian pastoral sector have less to do with the inability to predict climatic conditions accurately than with interventions made in the pastoral zones in the name of "progress." The article by Adams is also recommended.

Once again, the sections on "Pastoralism," "Aid and Neocolonialism," "Ecology and Resources," and "Economic and Political Roots of Hunger" contain a number of articles that readers interested in the Sahel zone will wish to consult. In particular, readers interested in the relationship between economic development and environmental degradation should consult entries 1614 and 1714. Those interested in the relationship between economic development and famine should consult entries 1614 and 1625. Chapter 5 of entry 1650 discusses the question of what constitutes "normal" rainfall in a region such as the Sahel in which variations can be quite great from place to place and from year to year. Since many development projects for the Sahel zone have been based on the expectation that the level of rainfall in the middle and late 1950s was "normal"—whereas it seems to have been unusually high—this question is of considerable importance.

2853. Adams, Adrian. "The Senegal River Valley: What Kind of Change?" *Review of African Political Economy* no. 10 (September–December 1977): 33–59.

2854. Bennoune, Mahfoud. "The Political Economy of Mauritania: Imperialism and Class Struggle." *Review of African Political Economy* no. 12 (May–August 1978): 31–51.

2855. Braun, Armelle. "The Art of Gentle Tutelege." *Ceres* no. 63 (May–June 1978): 42–45.

2856. Cherel, Jacques. "Secteur Traditionnel et Développement Rural en Mauritanie." *Revue Tiers-Monde* 8 (July–September 1967): 631–677.

2857. Esseks, John D. "The Food Outlook for the Sahel: Regaining Self-Sufficiency or Continuing Dependence on International Aid?" *Africa Today* 22 (April–June 1975): 45–56.

2858. Food and Agriculture Organization–United Nations, Economic Commission for Africa. "General Characteristics of the Economy and Agriculture in the Sub-Region," pp. 4–22. In *Intra-Sub-Regional Co-Operation and Trade in West Africa in the Field of Agriculture, Phase 1.* Rome: Food and Agriculture Organization, 1971.

2859. Geylat. "Le Président de la Famine." *Afrique-Asie* no. 167 (7 August–3 September 1978): 19–20. (Concerns food shortages in Senegal.)

2860. Glantz, Michael H. "The Social Value of a Reliable Long-Range Weather Forecast." *Ekistics* 43 (May 1977): 305–313.

2861. Haig, E. F. G. "Famine in the Sahel." *Nigerian Field* 40 (March 1975): 23–40.

2862. Hopkins, Elizabeth. "'Operation Groundnuts': Lessons from an Agricultural Extension Scheme." *Institute of Development Studies Bulletin* 5:4 (May 1974): 59–66.

2863. Hubert, J. "Une Opération de Développement Rural au Mali: L'Opération 'Arachide.'" *Coopération et Développement* no. 43 (September 1972): 16–27.

2864. Laya, D. "Interviews with Farmers and Livestock Owners in the Sahel." *African Environment* 1:2 (1974): 49–93.

2865. Maiga, Mahamadou. "The Policy of Rice Import Substitution: The Case of the Senegal River Valley and Delta." *Africa Development* 1 (September 1976): 9–22.

2866. Marcussen, Henrik Secher, and Torp, Jens Erik. "The Ivory Coast: Towards Self-Centered Development?" pp. 155–191. In *Industrialization, Development and the Demands for a New International Economic Order.* Ed. Kirsten Worm. Copenhagen: Samfundsvidenskabeligt Forlag, 1978.

2867. Matin, Guy. "A Policy for Irrigation Dam Construction." *Actuel Développement* no. 3 (September–October 1974): 7–11.

2868. Matlock, W. Gerald, and Cockrum, E. Lendell. "Agricultural Production Systems in the Sahel," pp. 232–255. In *The Politics of Natural Disaster: The Case of the Sahel Drought.* Ed. Michael H. Glantz. Praeger Special Studies in Economics and Development. New York: Praeger, 1976.

2869. Morabito, V. "L'Office du Niger au Mali, d'Hier à Aujourd'hui." *Journal des Africanistes* 47:1 (1977): 53–82.

2870. Morel, A. "Expériences de Développement Agricole dans le Massif de l'Air-Niger." *Culture et Développement* 8:2 (1976): 266–286.

2871. Reboul, Claude. "Economie Marchande et Systèmes de Culture dans les Campagnes Sénégalaises." *Revue Tiers-Monde* 18 (October–December 1977): 779–796.

2872. Sow, A. "Evolution du Système de Production Agricole dans la Région du Cap Vert." *African Administrative Studies* 17 (1977): 59–65.

THE GAMBIA

The Nature of Poverty (entry 2875) is recommended as an introduction to rural Gambia.

2873. Haswell, Margaret R. *Economics of Agriculture in a Savannah Village. Report on Three Years' Study in Genieri Village and Its Lands, The Gambia.* London: Her Majesty's Stationery Office, 1953.

2874. ———. *The Changing Pattern of Economic Activity in a Gambian Village.* London: Her Majesty's Stationery Office, 1963.

2875. ———. *The Nature of Poverty.* London: Macmillan, 1975.

2876. Surndell, Ken. "Family Farms and Migrant Labour: The Strange Farmers of the Gambia." *Canadian Journal of African Studies* 12:1 (1978): 3–17.

OTHER WEST AFRICA

2877. Darpoh, Rufus. "On the Road to Self-Sufficiency in Rice Production." *African Development* (July 1975): L17–L18. (About Liberia)

2878. Heseltine, Nigel. "Mining and Agriculture. Development or Disappearance? The Case of Liberia." *World Crops* 25 (May–June 1973): 128–131.

2879. Marticou, Henri. *Les Structures Agricoles du Centre Cameroun.* Yaoundé[?]: Cameroun Oriental, Secretariat d'Etat au Développement Rural, Direction de l'Agriculture, c.1962.

2880. Ongla, Jean. *An Economic Survey of Food Production Variables in the Zone of Intervention: Yemossoa.* Research Report no. 1. Yaoundé: Department of Rural Economy, National Advanced School of Agriculture, University of Cameroon, March 1973.

2881. Sargent, Merritt. *The Use of Animal Traction in the Kouande and Kerou Districts, Province de l'Atakora, Rèpublique du Bénin; A Preliminary Report.* PN–AAE–510. Washington, D. C.: US Agency for International Development, 1977.

Southern Africa

BOTSWANA

For an overview of rural development in Botswana, the report by Chambers and Feldman and the monograph by Hjort and Östberg are recommended. The latter is probably more accessible. Considerable information is also available in the papers contained in *Botswana Notes and Records* (entry 2890). Of these, the paper by Campbell and Child that discusses man's impact on Botswana's environment is especially recommended.

2882. Ansell, D. J. *Cattle Marketing in Botswana.* Development Study no. 8. Reading, UK: Department of Agricultural Economics and Management, University of Reading, January 1971.

2883. Chambers, Robert, and Feldman, D. *Report on Rural Development.* Gaborone, Botswana: Ministry of Finance and Development, 1973.

2884. Cooke, H. J. *The Problem of Drought in Botswana.* Working Paper 17. Gaborone: NIRDAS, 1978.

2885. Epstein, G. A. *A Framework for U. S. Assistance in Southern Africa; Country Resource Paper: Botswana.* PN–AAF–096. Washington, D. C.: US Agency for International Development, 1977.

2886. Hjort, Anders, and Östberg, Wilhelm. *Farming and Herding in Botswana.* Sarec Report R:1/1978. Stockholm: Swedish Agency for Research Cooperation with Developing Countries, 1978.

2887. Kowet, Donald Kalinde. *Land, Labour Migration and Politics in Southern Africa: Botswana, Lesotho, and Swaziland.* Uppsala: Scandinavian Institute of African Studies, 1978.

2888. Lever, B. G. *Agricultural Extension in Botswana.* Development Study no. 7. Reading, UK: Department of Agricultural Economics, University of Reading, February 1970.

2889. Reynolds, N. *Rural Development in Botswana.* Working Paper 13. Cape Town: SALDRU, 1977.

2890. "Section II: Rural Development Conference Papers." *Botswana Notes and Records* 3 (1971): 73–215.

2891. Zumer-Linder, M.; Devitt, P.; and Wik, M. *Report of the Development of the Village Areas of the Western States Lands of Botswana.* Stockholm: Swedish International Development Authority, 1973.

ZAMBIA

In the past, the Zambian government has allocated very few of its budgetary resources to agriculture and that sector shows the results of such neglect. According to Christie and Scott, 54 percent of all rural households do not produce any marketable surplus. FAO figures show that the growth of the agricultural sector has only recently exceeded the growth rate of the population. Per capita food production in the mid-1970s was only 4 percent greater than it had been in the mid-1960s.

To overcome the stagnant condition of traditional agriculture, Christie and Scott suggest in their report to the World Bank that resources should be concentrated on the larger commerical farmers. However, the World Bank itself has concluded that some way must be found to increase the output of the traditional sector if Zambia's food needs are to be met and if incomes of the poorest Zambians are to be raised (Christie and Scott, Preface).

A useful introductory work is the monograph by Ollawa. Also of relevance is entry 107.

2892. Bates, Robert H. *Rural Responses to Industrialization: A Study of Village Zambia.* New Haven: Yale University Press, 1976.

2893. Christie, Malcolm, and Scott, Guy. *Zambia: An Agricultural Development Strategy for the Next Twenty-Five Years.* EDI Sem 14. Washington, D. C.: World Bank, 1977.

2894. Dodge, Doris Jansen. *Agricultural Policy and Performance in Zambia.* Berkeley: Institute of International Studies, University of California, 1977.

2895. Kinsey, B. H. *Agricultural Technology, Staple Food Crop Production and Rural Development in Zambia.* Monograph 6. Norwich, UK: School of Development Studies, University of East Anglia, 1979.

2896. Nadeau, E. G. "Prospects for Agricultural Cooperatives in Zambia." *Land Tenure Center Newsletter* no. 51 (January–March 1976): 25–30.

2897. Ollawa, Patrick. *Rural Development Policies and Performance in Zambia: A Critical Inventory.* ISS Occasional Paper no. 59. The Hague: Institute for Social Studies, 1977.

2898. Schultz, Jürgen. *Land Use in Zambia. Part I: The Basically Traditional Land Use Systems and their Regions.* Munich: Weltforum-Verlag, 1976.

2899. Sedjo, R. A. *A Framework for U. S. Assistance in Southern Africa; Country Resource Paper: Zambia.* PN–AAF–097. Washington, D. C.: US Agency for International Development, 1977.

2900. Vanzetti, N. R., and Bessell, J. E. "Education and the Development of Farming in Two Areas of Zambia." *The Journal of Development Studies* 11 (October 1974): 41–54.

MALAWI

The two issues of *Rural Africana* edited by Page provide an overview of rural conditions in Malawi. Chilvumbo argues that the material situation of the peasantry has not improved to any significant extent since Malawi achieved its independence in 1964. Rather, he points out, the benefits of development have gone to the elites, particularly the bosses of the party-political machinery.

2901. Chilvumbo, Alifeyo. "On Rural Development: A Note on Malawi's Programmes of Development for Exploitation." *Africa Development* 3 (April–June 1978): 41–54.

2902. Dequin, Horst. *Agricultural Development in Malawi.* 2nd unch. ed. Munich: Ifo-Institut für Wissenschaftsforschung, Afrika-Studienstelle, 1970.

2903. Farrington, J. *Farm Surveys in Malawi: The Collection and Analyses of Labour Data.* Development Study no. 16. Reading, UK: Department of Agricultural Economics and Management, University of Reading, 1975.

2904. Moeller, P. W. *A Framework for U. S. Assistance in Southern Africa; Country Resource Paper: Malawi.* PN–AAF–093. Washington, D. C.: US Agency for International Development, 1977.

2905. Page, Melvin E., ed. "Land and Labor in Malawi. Part I." *Rural Africana* no. 20 (Spring 1973).

2906. ______. "Land and Labor in Rural Malawi, Part II." *Rural Africana* no. 21 (Summer 1973).

OTHER SOUTHERN AFRICA

Entries 2612 and 2887 are also relevant here.

2907. Lumumba, T. C. *Le Rôle de l'Agriculture dans les Pays du Tiers Monde, Particulièrement au Zaire.* Etudes sur les Pays en Voie de Développement, no. 89. Budapest: Institut d'Economie Mondiale de l'Académie des Sciences de Hongrie, 1976.

2908. Maane, Willem, and van der Wigt, Robert. *Lesotho: A Development Challenge.* Washington, D. C.: World Bank, 1975.

2909. Miracle, Marvin P. *Agriculture in the Congo Basin.* Madison: University of Wisconsin Press, 1967.

2910. Palmer, R., and Parsons, N., eds. *The Roots of Rural Poverty in Central-Southern Africa.* London: Heinemann, 1977.

2911. Steiner, Herbert. *Mozambique's Agricultural Economy in Brief.* Foreign Agricultural Economic Report no. 116. Washington, D. C.: Economic Research Service, US Department of Agriculture, March 1976.

2912. Weinrich, A. K. H. *African Farmers in Rhodesia. Old and New Peasant Communities in Karangaland.* London: Oxford University Press, 1975.

2913. Wuyts, M. *Peasants and Rural Economy in Mozambique.* Maputo: Centre of African Studies, 1978.

Latin America

Table 6 offers statistics on per capita food production and on agricultural and population growth rates in the 1960s and early 1970s for some twenty countries in Latin America and the Caribbean.

TABLE 6

Per Capita Agricultural Production, Agricultural and Population Growth Rates, Selected Latin American and Caribbean Countries, 1960s and 1970s

Country	Per capita food production (1965-67 = 100) Average 1974-76	Average Annual Rate of Growth of			
		Agri-culture 1960-70	Popula-tion 1960-70	Agri-culture 1970-76	Popula-tion 1970-75
	(1)	(2)	(3)	(4)	(5)
Costa Rica	130	5.7	3.5	3.8[a]	2.5
Bolivia	119	3.0	2.6	5.6	2.7
Brazil	114	1.9	2.9	5.5	2.9
Panama	114	5.7	3.1	—[b]	3.1
Guatemala	114	—	3.2	—	3.2
Venezuela	113	5.7	3.4	3.1	3.1
Dominican Republic	111	2.2	2.9	3.0[a]	2.9
Uruguay	110	1.9	0.6	−0.7[a]	0.4
El Salvador	108	3.0	3.5	4.2	3.1
Colombia	106	3.5	2.9	4.5	2.8
Argentina	104	2.3	1.4	2.4	1.3
Nicaragua	103	6.7	2.9	5.7	3.3
Haiti	103	0.8	1.6	1.6[a]	1.6
Honduras	102	5.7	2.7	−0.6	2.7
Peru	99	1.9	2.9	0.6	2.9
Mexico	98	3.9	3.4	1.4	3.5
Ecuador	97	4.0	3.3	5.7	3.5
Cuba	95	—	2.1	—	1.8
Paraguay	94	2.1	2.6	5.9	2.7
Chili	92	2.6	2.1	0.5	1.8
Trinidad & Tobago	92	3.5	2.1	—	1.1
Jamaica	89	1.4	1.7	1.3	1.8
Average	105	3.4	2.6	2.97	2.48

a = 1970–75
b = — signifies information not available

Sources: Column 1: FAO as cited in World Bank, *Rapport sur le Développement dans le Monde, 1978,* Washington, D. C.: August 1978, Table 1, pp. 86–87.

Columns 2 +4: World Bank, *Rapport sur le Développement dans le Monde, 1978,* Washington, D. C.: August 1978, Table 2, pp. 88–89.

Columns 3 +5: World Bank, *Rapport sur le Développement dans le Monde, 1978,* Washington, D. C.: August 1978, Table 13, pp. 110–111.

General

Birou argues that the evolution of Latin American agrarian structures can be understood only in the context of the general underdevelopment and dependence of the region. The experiences of a number of Latin American countries with regard to agrarian reform are surveyed. Murcia looks at the operation of various rural community enterprise programs and suggests that this model can significantly change social structures and help the production process in rural Latin America to become more democratic. Other articles discussing the rural community enterprise model can be found in the section entitled "Agrarian Change and Land Reform: Latin America," pages 166–171.

Economic Development of Latin America by Furtado is a useful survey of the history and current state of economic development in the region. The two books by May and McLellan offer a good deal of information on malnutrition in South America. A review of the state of agriculture in Latin America in the mid-1960s is found in the ECLA article in entry 2934. A survey of the state of food supplies within the region is found in the ECLA article in the *ECLA Bulletin* (entry 2935).

Also recommended are the studies by Fals Borda and Pugh et al. and the volume edited by deVries and Gonzales Casanova. In addition, chapters 7–18 in entry 2264 and annexes G–L in entry 886 are relevant.

2914. Barraclough, Solon. "Dynamics of Government-Cooperative Relationships in Rural Latin America." *Journal of Rural Cooperation* 2:2 (1974): 123–139.

2915. Birou, Alain. *Forces Paysannes et Politiques Agraires en Amérique Latine.* Paris: Editions Economie et Humanisme, Les Editions Ouvrière, 1970.

2916. Domike, Arthur L., and Tokman, Victor E. "The Role of Agricultural Taxation in Financing Agricultural Development in Latin America," pp. 113–151. In *Financing Development in Latin America.* Ed. Keith Griffin. London: Macmillan, 1971.

2917. Dozier, Craig L. *Land Development and Colonization in Latin America. Case Studies of Peru, Bolivia and Mexico.* New York: Praeger, 1969.

2918. Fals Borda, Orlando. *Cooperatives and Rural Development in Latin America.* Geneva: UN Research Institute for Social Development, 1971.

2919. Food and Agriculture Organization. *Prospects for Agricultural Development in Latin America.* Rome: 1953.

2920. Furtado, Celso. *Economic Development of Latin America: Historical Background and Contemporary Problems.* Trans. Suzette Macedo. Cambridge, UK and New York: Cambridge University Press, 1976.

2921. ______. *Les Etats-Unis et le Sous-Développement de l'Amérique Latine.* Paris: Calmann-Lévy, 1970.

2922. Garcia, Antonio. *Reforma Agraria y Economía Empresarial en Ameríca Latina.* Santiago de Chile: Editorial Universitaria, 1967.

2923. Inter-American Committee for Agricultural Development. *Inventory of Information Basic to the Planning of Agricultural Development in Latin America.* Washington, D. C.: Organization of American States, c. 1963.

2924. May, Jacques M., and McLellan, Donna L. *The Ecology of Malnutrition in Eastern South America: Venezuela, Surinam (and the Netherlands Antilles), French Guiana, Brazil, Uruguay, Paraguay, Argentina.* New York: Hafner, 1974.

2925. ______. *The Ecology of Malnutrition in Western South America: Colombia, Ecuador, Peru, Bolivia and Chile.* New York: Hafner, 1974.

2926. Murcia, Héctor. "Analisis Sobre Modelos de Desarrollo Rural en Ameríca Latina." *Desarrollo Rural en las Américas* 8:2 (1976): 137–152.

2927. Nelson, Michael. *The Development of Tropical Lands: Policy Issues in Latin America.* Baltimore, Md.: Johns Hopkins University Press, 1973.

2928. Padis, Pedro Calil. "Agriculture et Sous-Développement." *Revue Tiers-Monde* 17 (October–December 1976): 987–1010.

2929. Pugh, Ramón, et al. *Estudios de la Realidad Campesina: Cooperacíon y Cambio.* Geneva: UN Research Institute for Social Development, 1970. (Focuses on Venezuela, Ecuador, and Colombia.)

2930. Ross, James E. *Cooperative Rural Electrification: Case Studies of Pilot Projects in Latin America.* New York: Praeger, 1972. (Discusses Colombia, Costa Rica, Ecuador, Nicaragua.)

2931. "South America: Continent of Enormous Agricultural Potential." *World Crops* 9 (September 1957): 363–370.

2932. Thiesenhusen, William C. *Current Development Patterns in Latin America with Special Reference to Agrarian Policy.* LTC no. 111. Madison: Land Tenure Center, University of Wisconsin, January 1977.

2933. United Nations, Department of Economic Affairs. *Agricultural Requisites in Latin America. Report of the Joint ECLA/FAO Working Party.* Lake Success, N. Y.: 1950.

2934. United Nations, Economic Commission for Latin America. "Agriculture in Latin America," pp. 311–369. In *Economic Survey of Latin America,* 1966. New York: 1968.

2935. ______. "Situation and Evolution of Food Supplies in Latin America." *ECLA Bulletin* 19:1–2 (1974).

2936. Vries, Egbert de, ed. in cooperation with P. Gonzales Casanova. *Social Research and Rural Life in Central America, Mexico, and the Caribbean.* Paris: UN Educational, Scientific and Cultural Organization, 1966.

Mexico

According to the FAO, in the mid-1970s, per capita food production in Mexico was only 98 percent of what it had been in the mid-1960s (see Table 6). In 1970, as many as 40 percent of all Mexican families may have been eating nutritionally deficient diets. The decline in nutritional standards that has occurred since 1945 has resulted from a variety of conditions. The more important of these are population growth, the monetarization of the rural economy, the increased availability of processed foods, and the growth in the numbers of landless laborers and urban slum-dwellers. Preliminary figures from the 1970 Mexican agricultural census suggest that 3.3 percent of all Mexican farms produced 81 percent of the agricultural output of the country in 1970 while 81 percent of the agricultural holdings produced 3.6 percent of total output.

The problems currently facing the rural sector in Mexico can be traced to the failure of post-Cárdenas governments to continue the agricultural development strategy initiated by Cárdenas. This strategy was based on the participation of small rural producers and on the creation of collective *ejidos* and was abandoned in favor of a program of rapid industrialization. One requirement of this industrialization program was the production of a considerable "marketable surplus" which post-Cárdenas governments judged could be provided more easily by large private farms than by small family farms or by the collective *ejidos.* Thus, after 1940, public investment in agriculture focused on developing a few large, irrigated, commercial farms. One result of this strategy was that Mexican agricultural output grew at 4.6 percent per year between 1935 and 1967, a record rate of growth for Latin America during that period. Another result has been the increased impoverishment of rural (and subsequently urban) Mexico as the benefits of agricultural growth have been shared by fewer and fewer people.

As an introduction to the rural strategies of post-1940 Mexican governments, the monograph by de Alcantara is recommended. A summary of these strategies can also be found in entry 145. Other good summaries of the conditions in rural Mexico are found in Centro de Investigaciones Agraria and in Gutelman. Various alternative policies which governments might follow to reduce underemployment and unemployment in the rural sector are outlined in Martinez. The situation of agricultural laborers is examined by Stavenhagen. The volume edited by Flores and the article by Dozier are also recommended.

2937. Alcantara, Cynthia Hewitt de. *Modernizing Mexican Agriculture. Socioeconomic Implications of Technical Change 1940–1970.* Report no. 76.5. Geneva: UN Research Institute for Social Development, 1976.

2938. Carlos, Manuel L. *Politics and Development in Rural Mexico: A Study of Socio-Economic Modernization.* New York: Praeger, 1974.

2939. Centro de Investigaciones Agraria. *Estructura Agraria y Desarrollo Agricola en Mexico.* rev. ed. Mexico: Fondo de Cultura Economica, 1974.

2940. Cummings, Ronald. *Water Resource Management in Northern Mexico.* Baltimore, Md.: Johns Hopkins University Press, 1972.

2941. Dozier, Craig L. "Mexico's Transformed Northwest." *The Geographical Review* 53 (October 1963): 548–571.

2942. Dumont, René. *Réforme Agraire et Modernisation de l'Agriculture au Mexico.* Paris: Presses Universitaires de France, IEDES, 1969.

2943. Flores, Edmundo, ed. *Desarrollo Agrícola.* Mexico City: 1972.

2944. Freebairn, Donald. "The Dichotomy of Prosperity and Poverty in Mexican Agriculture." *Land Economics* 45 (February 1969): 31–42.

2945. Gomez-Pompa, Arturo. "An Old Answer to the Future." *Mazingira* no. 5 (1978): 50–55.

2946. Gutelman, Michel. *Réforme et Mystification Agraire en Amérique Latine: Le Cas du Mexique.* Paris: Maspero, 1971.

2947. Hansen, Roger D. *The Politics of Mexican Development.* Baltimore, Md.: Johns Hopkins University Press, 1971.

2948. Hicks, W. Whitney. "Agricultural Development in Northern Mexico, 1940–1960." *Land Economics* 43 (November 1967): 393–402.

2949. Martinez, Jorge. "Las Alternativas de la Reforma Agraria Mexicana Frente al Proceso de Marginalizacíon." *Desarrollo Rural en las Américas* 5:3 (1973): 243–261.

2950. School, John. "Mexico's Grain Problem: A Production Boom that Won't Turn Off." *Foreign Agriculture,* 3 July 1970.

2951. Stavenhagen, Rodolfo. "Los Jornaleras Agrícolas." *Revista del México Agrario* 1:1 (1967).

2952. Venezian, Edward, and Gamble, William. *The Agricultural Development of Mexico: Its Structure and Growth Since 1950.* New York: Praeger, 1969.

2953. Wellhausen, E. J. "Rockefeller Foundation Collaboration in Agricultural Research in Mexico." *Agronomy Journal* 42 (1950): 167–175.

Central America

Ashcraft is suggested as an introduction to Belize. The report by Ashe argues that Costa Rica's rural development policies must focus on employment generation, crop production, natural resource protection, rural industry creation, and improvements in basic services and infrastructure. The rural development plan of the Costa Rican government is found in entry 2957. The study by the Centro Agronomico Tropical de Investigacion y Ensénanza is recommended.

2954. Ashcraft, Norman. *Colonialism and Underdevelopment: Process of Political Economic Change in British Honduras.* New York: Columbia University Press, 1973.

2955. Ashe, Jeffrey. *Rural Development in Costa Rica.* PN–AAF–225. Washington, D. C.: US Agency for International Development, 1978.

2956. Centro Agronomico Tropical de Investigacion y Ensénanza. *A Farming System Research Approach for Small Farms of Central America.* Turrialba, Costa Rica: CATIE, 1978.

2957. Costa Rica, Presidencia de la Republica, Oficina de Planificacion. *Plan Nacional de Desarrollo. Sectores Productivos.* San Jose: January 1974.

2958. Food and Agriculture Organization. *Survey of Agricultural and Forest Resources: Nicaragua. Final Report.* FAO/SF: 49/NIC–2. Rome: 1969.

2959. Harrison, Kelly; Shaffer, James D.; and Weber, Michael T. *Fomenting Improvements in Food Marketing in Costa Rica.* Marketing in Developing Communities Series, Research Report no. 10. East Lansing: Latin American Studies Center, Michigan State University, n.d.

2960. Kreisberg, M.; Bullard, M.; and Becraft, W. *Crop Priorities and Country Policies: Suggestions for USAID Support of the Agricultural Sector in Costa Rica.* San Jose: US Agency for International Development, 1970.

2961. Norton, R.; Cappi, C.; Fletcher, L.; Pomareda, C.; and Wainer, M. *A Model of Agricultural Production and Trade in Central America.* Working Paper 276. Washington, D. C.: World Bank, c.1977.

2962. Nunes, Frederick. "Administration and Culture: Subsistence and Modernization in Crique Sarco, Belize." *Caribbean Quarterly* 23 (December 1977): 17–45.

2963. Romney, D. H.; Wright, A. C. S.; Arbuckle, R. J.; and Vial, V. E. *Land Use in British Honduras: A Report of the British Honduras Land Use Survey Team.* Colonial Research Publication no. 24. London: Her Majesty's Stationery Office, 1959.

2964. United States Army, Inter-American Geodetic Survey, Natural Resources Division. *Recommendations on Natural Resources Studies for Development of Nicoya-Tempisque Region, Costa Rica.* Fort Clayton, Canal Zone: June 1965.

Colombia

Land ownership and wealth are highly skewed in Colombia. Some 70 percent of the land is controlled by less than 20,000 people while one million peasants farm 7 percent of the land. Large areas of the most fertile land are given over to cattle production for export. Another major export of Colombia is coffee, and the rise in coffee prices between 1975 and 1977 increased government reserves significantly but led to serious inflation. The Federation of Coffee Growers is reported to have invested much of its profits in US Treasury bonds, banks, industries, and real estate speculation—in short, in just about everything *but* agriculture.

An overview of Colombian agricultural production and trade in the early 1970s can be found in Bennett. The two monographs by Atkinson show that most of the increases in agricultural production in Colombia in the 1950s and 1960s occurred on the larger mechanized farms, with crops destined for export such as cotton, rice, and sugarcane. Furthermore, most production increases resulted from the expansion of cropped area rather than from the increased productivity of land already under cultivation. Atkinson stresses the need for special measures to help small farmers; but as long as the social organization of Colombia remains as it is today, such special measures seem unlikely to be implemented.

The book by Fals Borda (entry 2970) is recommended (to Spanish readers) as an introduction to rural development in Colombia.

2965. Atkinson, L. Jay. *Agricultural Productivity in Colombia.* Foreign Agricultural Economic Report no. 66. Washington, D. C.: Economic Research Service, US Department of Agriculture, 1970.

2966. ______. *Changes in Agricultural Production and Technology in Colombia.* Foreign Agricultural Economic Report no. 52. Washington, D. C.: Economic Research Service, US Department of Agriculture, 1969.

2967. Bennett, Gae A. *Agricultural Production and Trade of Colombia.* ERS-Foreign 343. Washington, D. C.: Economic Research Service, US Department of Agriculture, February 1973.

2968. Berry, L. Albert. "Land Distribution, Income Distribution, and the Productive Efficiency of Colombian Agriculture." *Food Research Institute Studies in Agricultural Economics, Trade, and Development* 12:3 (1973): 199–232.

2969. Colombian Agropecuarian Institute. "Analysis of the Technical Problems that Colombia Faces in the Development of its Crops and Livestock Sector," pp. 35–46. In *Colombia–U.S. Workshop on Science and Technology in Development. Volume II: Contributed Papers.* National Academy of Sciences in Cooperation with the Colombian Ministry of Education. Fusagasuga, Colombia: 26 February–1 March 1968.

2970. Fals Borda, Orlando. *Historia de la Cuestión Agraria en Colombia.* Bogotá: Fundación Rosca de Investigación y Acción Social, Distribuidora Colombiana, 1975.

2971. ______. *The Importance of Research in Rural Development in Colombia.* Bogotá: Fundación Para el Analisis de la Realidad Colombiana (FUNDARCO), September 1978.

2972. International Bank for Reconstruction and Development. *The Agricultural Development of Colombia.* Washington, D. C.: 1956.

2973. Riley, Harold M.; Harrison, Kelly; Suarez, Nelson et al. *Market Conditions in the Development of the Cauca Valley Region of Colombia.* Marketing in Developing Communities Series, Research Report no. 5. East Lansing: Latin American Studies Center, Michigan State University, 1970.

2974. Rochin, Refugio, and Londoño R., Diego. "Integrated Rural Development: Lessons from the Colombian Experience." *Land Tenure Center Newsletter* no. 48 (April–June 1975): 18–28.

2975. Rockefeller Foundation. *Colombian Agricultural Program. Director's Annual Report.* New York: 1954–1959. (Superseded by entry 462.)

2976. Rosenstiel, Annette. "Rural Development and Directed Social Change in Colombia." *Civilisations* 21:2–3 (1971): 178–184.

2977. Smith, Thomas Lynn. *Colombia: Social Stucture and the Process of Development.* Gainesville: University of Florida Press, 1967.

2978. Survey Team from United States Department of Agriculture, United States Department of Interior, and Land Grant Universities. *Rural Development in Colombia—Evaluation and Recommendations.* Rural Development Series no. 4. Washington, D. C.: Department of State, October–November 1963.

2979. Velez, Ernesto, and Feder, Ernest. *The Lagging Growth of the Cooperative Movement in Colombia.* Bogotá: Ministerio de Agricultura, August 1961.

2980. Velloso, José-Miguel. "Las Gaviotas. The Centre for Integrated Development Where Everything is Tried Out in the Field." *Ceres* no. 63 (May–June 1978): 24–27.

Peru

According to FAO figures, per capita food production in Peru has been stagnant since the mid-1960s. According to the World Bank, the growth of the agricultural sector as a whole has been very slow, declining from an average annual rate of increase of 1.9 percent between 1960 and 1970 to 0.6 percent annually between 1970 and 1976 (see Table 6). A combination of falling copper prices, declining anchovy yields, governmental mismanagement, and large arms purchases produced a foreign debt that was estimated to have reached $4.1 billion at the end of 1977. The price paid for debt rescheduling was the acceptance of IMF austerity measures which inevitably will hit the poorer sections of the Peruvian population the hardest.

The articles by Whyte and by Long and Winder and the longer study by Van der Berghe and Primov are recommended. Entries 1001 and 1002 are also recommended.

2981. Coutu, Arthur J., and King, Richard A. *The Agricultural Development of Peru.* Praeger Special Studies in International Economics and Development. New York: Praeger, 1969.

2982. Cuche, Denys. "Pouvoir et Participation dans les Coopératives Agraires de Production au Pérou." *Communauté: Archives Internationales de Sociologie de la Coopération et du Développement.* no. 40 (July–December 1976): 125–146.

2983. Ferroni, Marco A. *Toward a Food Policy for Latin America's Urban Areas: Lima as a Case Study.* Ithaca, N. Y.: Center for International Studies, Cornell University, March 1976.

2984. Ford, Thomas R. *Man and Land in Peru.* Gainesville: University of Florida Press, 1955.

2985. International Bank for Reconstruction and Development. *The Agricultural Development of Peru.* Washington, D. C.: 1959.

2986. Long, Norman, and Winder, David. "From Peasant Community to Production Co-Operative: An Analysis of Recent Government Policy in Peru." *The Journal of Development Studies* 12 (October 1975): 75–94.

2987. Stein, William W. *Changing Vicos Agriculture.* Special Studies no. 15. Buffalo: Council on International Studies, State University of New York at Buffalo, April 1972.

2988. Van der Berghe, Pierre L., and Primov, George P. *Inequality in the Peruvian Andes.* Columbia: University of Missouri Press, 1977.

2989. Whyte, William Foote. "Potatoes, Peasants and Professors: A Development Strategy for Peru." *Sociological Practice* 2 (Spring 1977): 7–23.

Bolivia

Despite rather little post-reform governmental assistance, the Bolivian land reform of 1952 seems to have benefited smallholders significantly, particularly those in northern Bolivia. The benefits have included more equitable patterns of land ownership and tenure, income distribution, and social structures (notably the liberation of the campesino). Although two-thirds of the country's agricultural land is still held in parcels exceeding 1,000 hectares, the largest holdings are primarily in the livestock sector and the division of cropland is much more equal. As a result, agricultural production has increased substantially since about 1955. FAO figures show nearly a 20 percent increase in per capita food production in Bolivia between the mid-1960s and the mid-1970s (see Table 6).

Two fairly successful peasant-led reforms are examined by Dorsey (entries 2990 and 2991). An overview of the agricultural sector is found in Wennergren and Whitaker.

2990. Dorsey, Joseph F. *A Case Study of Ex-Hacienda Toralapa in the Tiraque Region of the Upper Cochabamba Valley.* Research Paper no. 65. Madison: Land Tenure Center, University of Wisconsin, June 1975.

2991. ______. *A Case Study of the Lower Cochabamba Valley: Ex-Haciendas Parotani and Caramarca.* Research Paper no. 64. Madison: Land Tenure Center, University of Wisconsin, June 1975.

2992. Patch, Richard W. "Bolivia: US Assistance in a Revolutionary Setting." In *Social Change in Latin America Today.* Ed. Richard N. Adams et al. New York: Vintage/Random House, 1960.

2993. Slater, C. C., et al. *Marketing Processes in La Paz, Bolivia.* Marketing in Developing Communities Series, Research Report no. 3. East Lansing: Latin American Studies Center, Michigan State University, 1969.

2994. Wennergren, E. Boyd, and Whitaker, Morris D. *The Status of Bolivian Agriculture.* Praeger Special Studies in International Economics and Development. New York: Praeger, 1975.

Brazil

In terms of production, Brazil's agricultural sector has been highly successful. Output has risen by about 100 percent since the 1960s and World Bank figures show the agricultural sector growing at an average annual rate of 5.5 percent between 1970 and 1976 (see Table 6). Agricultural exports accounted for some 60 percent of all exports in the mid-1970s.

However, in terms of equity, Brazilian agriculture is much less of a success. Since the mid-1950s, development strategies have focused on economic growth at the expense of the equitable distribution of the benefits of that growth. This strategy, primarily as it relates to the industrial sector, is succinctly outlined by Singer and Lamounier. In the agricultural sector, government assistance—high food prices, subsidies and cheap credit—has benefited the already wealthy farmers in the already wealthy regions of Brazil. Agricultural development in São Paulo state and Paraná state are discussed in Missiaen and Ruff, Strachan, and Brazil (Instituto de Economia Agrícola). The latter covers a wide variety of topics dealing with agricultural progress in Brazil's most "advanced" region.

At the same time, some 45 percent of Brazil's population (50 million people) live in rural areas, many of them as agricultural laborers or subsistence farmers. The poorest of them live in the Nordeste. While per capita income in Brazil as a whole is put at about $1,100, rural income in the Nordeste has been estimated to be as little as 15 percent of that. The studies by Goodman, Martins Dias, Patrick, and Hall deal with various aspects of rural development in this region. The book by Hall surveys the effects of the introduction of irrigated farming based on the construction of large dams and makes suggestions for alternative uses of resources beneficial to subsistence farmers. However, this book lacks the political dimension since it does not come to terms with the fact that such alternatives are likely to be ignored as long as the current distribution of economic and political power is maintained. Entry 73 discusses class structure in the Nordeste.

One of the most controversial elements of Brazilian development strategy has been the opening up of the Amazon jungle to exploitation by impoverished peasants and (largely foreign-funded) mining, ranching, and plantation operations. The ecology of the Amazon region is deceptively fragile and there has been considerable concern (in just about every circle except the Brazilian government) that the attempt to exploit the mineral and agricultural potential of the region will end in ecological disaster. The study by Goodland and Irwin provides an excellent discussion of the dangers involved in developing the Amazon. The impact of this development on the indigenous inhabitants of the region is discussed in Davis. The entries by Johnson, Meggers, and Moran also deal with Amazonia.

Chapter 15 of entry 2004 is also relevant here.

2995. Brazil, Instituto de Economia Agrícola. *Modernization of Agriculture in the State of São Paulo.* São Paulo: 1973.

2996. Davis, Shelton H. *Victims of the Miracle. Development and the Indians of Brazil.* New York: Cambridge University Press, 1977.

2997. Goodland, Roberto J. A., and Irwin, Howard S. *Green Hell to Red Desert? An Ecological Discussion of the Environmental Impact of the Highway Construction Program in the Amazon Basin.* Amsterdam and New York: Elsevier, 1975.

2998. Goodman, D. E. "Rural Structure, Surplus Mobilisation, and Modes of Production in a Peripheral Region: The Brazilian Northeast." *The Journal of Peasant Studies* 5 (October 1977): 3–32.

2999. Gross, Daniel R. "Factionalism and Local Level Politics in Rural Brazil." *Journal of Anthropological Research* 29 (Summer 1973): 123–144.

3000. Hall, Anthony L. *Drought and Irrigation in North-East Brazil.* Cambridge, UK: Cambridge University Press, 1978.

3001. Herrmann, Louis F. *Changes in Agricultural Production in Brazil, 1947–65.* Foreign Agricultural Economic Report no. 79. Washington, D. C.: Economic Research Service, US Department of Agriculture, June 1972.

3002. Johnson, Peyton. "Fighting the Frontier Fever." *Ceres* no. 64 (July–August 1978): 22–30.

3003. Knight, Peter T. *Brazilian Agricultural Technology and Trade: A Study of Five Commodities.* Praeger Special Studies in International Economics and Development. New York: Praeger, 1971.

3004. Lopez, J. R. B. *Rural Development in Brazil: Some Trends, Research, Policies and Programs.* Amsterdam: Centro Brasiliero de Análise e Planejamento (CEBRAP), 1979.

3005. Margolis, Maxine. *The Moving Frontier: Social and Economic Change in a Southern Brazilian Community.* Gainesville: University of Florida Press, 1973.

3006. Martins Dias, Gentil. "New Patterns of Domination in Rural Brazil: A Case Study of Agriculture in the Brazilian Northeast." *Economic Development and Cultural Change* 27 (October 1978): 169–182.

3007. Meggers, Betty Jane. *Amazonia: Man and Culture in a Counterfeit Paradise.* Chicago, Ill.: Aldine-Atherton, 1971.

3008. Missiaen, Edmond, and Ruff, Samuel O. *Agricultural Development in Brazil: A Case Study of São Paulo.* Foreign Agricultural Economic Report no. 109. Washington, D. C.: Economic Research Service, US Department of Agriculture, June 1975.

3009. Moran, Emilio F. *Agricultural Development in the Transamazon Highway.* Bloomington: Indiana University, 1976.

3010. National Academy of Sciences. *Science and Brazilian Development.* Report of the Second Workshop on Contributions of Science and Technology to Development. Washington, D. C.: 5–9 February 1968. (Progress Reports III and IV are relevant.)

3011. ———. *Study for Agricultural Engineering Development in Brazil.* Report of the Joint Study Group on Agricultural Engineering, US-Brazil Science Cooperation Program. Rio de Janeiro: 24 July–12 August 1972.

3012. Nicholls, William H. "The Brazilian Food Supply: Problems and Prospects." *Economic Development and Cultural Change* 19 (April 1971): 378–390.

3013. Paiva, Ruy Miller; Schattan, Salamão; and Trench de Freitas, Claus F. *Brazil's Agricultural Sector: Economic Behavior, Problems and Possibilities.* São Paulo: XV International Conference of Agricultural Economists, 1973.

3014. Patrick, George F. *Desenvolvimento Agricola do Nordeste.* Rio de Janeiro: IPEA/INPES, 1972.

3015. Prado, Caio, Jr. "The Development of Plantations." In his *The Colonial Background of Modern Brazil.* Trans. Suzette Macedo. Berkeley: University of California Press, 1971.

3016. Sanders, John H., and Bein, Frederick L. "Agricultural Development on the Brazilian Frontier: Southern Mato Grosso." *Economic Development and Cultural Change* 24 (April 1976): 593–610.

3017. Schuh, George Edward with Eliseu R. Alves. *The Agricultural Development of Brazil.* New York: Praeger, 1970.

3018. Shorrocks, V. M. "Recent Agricultural Developments in Brazil." *World Crops* 29 (March–April 1977): 56–60.

3019. Singer, Paul. "More is Sometimes Less." *Ceres* no. 45 (May–June 1975): 46–48.

3020. Singer, Paul, and Lamounier, Bolivar. "Brazil: Growth Through Inequality," pp. 125–151. In *Another Development. Approaches and Strategies.* Ed. Marc Nerfin. Uppsala: Dag Hammarskjöld Foundation, 1977.

3021. Slater, C. C.; Riley, Harold M.; and Farace, V. *Market Processes in the Recife Area of Northeast Brazil.* Marketing Developing Communities Series, Research Report no. 2. East Lansing: Latin American Studies Center, Michigan State University, 1969.

3022. Strachan, Lloyd W. "A Survey of Recent Agricultural Trends in Northwestern Paraná." *LTC Newsletter* no. 40 (April–June 1973): 19–29.

3023. Viégas, G. P. "Contribution of Science and Technology to the Development of Brazilian Agriculture," pp. 1–49. In *Science and Brazilian Development. Report of a Workshop on Contribution of Science and Technology to Development. Volume II: Contributed Papers by Brazilians.* Brazilian National Research Council and National Academy of Sciences-National Research Council (US). Itatiaia, Brazil: 11–16 April 1966.

3024. Wheeler, Richard G. *Production and Export of Corn and Rice in Brazil—Prospects for the 1970s.* Foreign Agricultural Economic Report no. 54. Washington, D. C.: Economic Research Service, US Department of Agriculture, September 1969.

Chile

Compared with other Latin American countries, the percentage of the Chilean population engaged in agriculture is quite low. Even in 1955, only 26 percent of the population was employed in the agricultural sector (entry 1483, p. 31). However, this has not prevented inequality in the rural sector. Many of the large estates occupied the best land and were used extensively to grow wheat or graze cattle, while the smaller holdings were constantly divided and were increasingly plagued by soil degradation and low yields. According to the 1965 Agricultural Census of Chile, 61 percent of all farms were smaller than the minimum area considered necessary to provide subsistence (10 hectares) and nearly 50 percent were half that size (Gall, p. 5). While some 47 percent of Chile's farm land had been redistributed by 1973 as a result of the 1967 land reform act, only 13 percent of all agricultural families had benefited from the redistributions (entry 1483, p. 11). Since the military coup in 1973, even this small amount of progress has been reversed. Collins looks at the agrarian policies of the military junta and concludes that the beneficiaries of these policies have been the "capitalist entrepreneur farmers in the rich central zone." The post-coup production of basic food crops has declined while agricultural exports rose in value from $26 million in 1973 to $159 million in 1977. Food imports—destined largely for urban dwellers—have risen substantially as well.

The agrarian situation in Chile during the Allende period is discussed by Barraclough and by Varela. The sorts of development strategies followed by Chilean governments since the 1950s are briefly outlined by Bitar who also proposes alternative strategies that would be consistent with creating greater economic and political equality among Chileans. Information on nutrition can be found in Bucher et al. Collarte is also recommended.

3025. Barraclough, Solon. "The State of Chilean Agriculture Before the Coup." *LTC Newsletter* no. 43 (January–March 1974): 11–13.

3026. Bitar, Sergio. "Chile: Elements of a Strategy for Another Development," pp. 227–241. In *Another Development. Approaches and Strategies.* Ed. Marc Nerfin. Uppsala: Dag Hammarskjöld Foundation, 1977.

3027. Bray, James O. "Demand, and the Supply of Food in Chile." *Journal of Farm Economics* 44 (November 1962): 1005–1020.

3028. Bucher, L., et al. *Estudios de Alimentos Esenciales por Estrato de Ingresos.* Santiago: Food and Agriculture Organization, 1973.

3029. Chile, Oficina de Planificación Agrícola. *Plan de Desarrollo Agropecuario, 1965–1980.* 3 vols. Santiago de Chile: La Oficina, 1970.

3030. Collarte, Juan Carlos. "New Agricultural Policies in Chile." *LTC Newsletter* no. 46 (October–December 1974): 1–5.

3031. Collins, Joseph. *Agrarian Reform and Counter-Reform in Chile.* San Francisco, Calif.: Institute for Food and Development Policy, 1979.

3032. Crosson, Pierre R. *Agricultural Development and Productivity: Lessons from the Chilean Experience.* Baltimore, Md.: Johns Hopkins University Press, 1970.

3033. Gall, Norman. *The Agrarian Revolt in Cautín. Part I: Chile's Mapuches.* West Coast South America Series. Hanover, N. H.: American Universities Field Staff, July 1972.

3034. Kay, Cristóbal. "Agrarian Reform and the Class Struggle in Chile." *Latin American Perspectives* 5 (Summer 1978): 117–140.

3035. Mamalakis, Markos. "Public Policy and Sectoral Development: A Case Study of Chile 1940–1958." In *Essays on the Chilean Economy.* Eds. Markos Mamalakis and Clark W. Reynolds. Homewood, Ill.: Irwin, 1965.

3036. Rockefeller Foundation. *Chilean Agricultural Program, Director's Annual Report.* New York: 1955–1959. (Superseded by entry 462.)

3037. Silva Hernandez, V. "Le Développement Capitaliste de la Campagne Chilienne." *Critique de l'Economie Politique* no. 15 (January–March 1974): 19–65.

3038. Smith, Stephen M.; Stanfield, David; and Brown, Marion. "Some Consequences for Production and Factor Use of the Chilean Agrarian Reform." *LTC Newsletter* no. 46 (October–December 1976): 6–18.

3039. Smole, William J. *Owner-Cultivatorship in Middle Chile.* Research Paper no. 89. Chicago, Ill.: Department of Geography, University of Chicago, 1963.

3040. Varela, Luis Quiros. "Chile: Agrarian Reform and Political Processes." In *Allende's Chile.* Ed. Kenneth Medhurst. London: Hart-Davis MacGibbon, 1972.

3041. World Bank-Food and Agriculture Organization. *Joint Report: The Agricultural Economy of Chile.* Washington, D. C.: World Bank, 1952.

Argentina

3042. Fienup, Darrell F. *Changes in Argentinian Agricultural Production and Productivity Over the Past 25 Years.* International Agriculture Series 5. St. Paul: Institute of Agriculture, University of Minnesota, c. 1966.

3043. Hutchison, John E.; Urban, Francis S.; and Dunmore, John C. *Argentina: Growth Potential of the Grain and Livestock Sectors.* Foreign Agricultural Economic Report no. 78. Washington, D. C.: Economic Research Service, US Department of Agriculture, 1972.

3044. Morris, A. S. "Factors in Changes of the Argentine Pampas Farm Economy." *Oxford Agrarian Studies* 3:1 (New Series) (1974): 50–67.

3045. Taylor, Carl. *Rural Life in Argentina.* Baton Rouge: Louisiana State University Press, 1948.

Cuba

For an introduction to the state of agriculture in post-revolution Cuba, readers should consult the two works by Ritter and the book by Dominguez. The latter covers social, political, and cultural aspects of the Castro regime as well as purely economic ones and is therefore recommended to anyone wanting a balanced assessment of the changes which have occurred in Cuba over the last twenty years. Entry 1805 is also relevant here.

3046. Aranda, Sergio. *La Revolucíon Agraria en Cuba.* Mexico: Siglo Veintiuno, 1968.

3047. Auroi, Claude. "L'Agriculture Cubaine." *Civilisations* 23–24:3–4 (1973–1974): 213–231.

3048. ______. *La Nouvelle Agriculture Cubaine.* Paris: Editions Anthropos, 1975.

3049. Barkin, David. "L'Agriculture, Pivot du Développement à Cuba." *Revue Tiers-Monde* 11 (October–December 1970): 643–673.

3050. Boorstein, Edward. *The Economic Transformation of Cuba: A First-Hand Account.* New York: Monthly Review, 1968.

3051. Dominguez, Jorge I. *Cuba: Order and Revolution.* Cambridge, Mass.: Belknap/Harvard University Press, 1978.

3052. Dumont, René. *Cuba, Socialisme et Développement.* Paris: Editions du Seuil, 1964.

3053. Edel, Matthew. "An Experiment in Growth with Social Justice. Thoughts on the 1970 Cuban Harvest." *Economic and Political Weekly* 5:29–31 (Special Number 1970): 1227–1230.

3054. Gagnon, Gabriel. "II. Cuba." In his *Coopératives ou Autogestion: Sénégal, Cuba, Tunisie.* Montreal: Les Presses de l'Université de Montréal, 1976.

3055. Gutelman, Michel. *L'Agriculture Socialisée à Cuba.* Paris: Maspero, 1967.

3056. Jacoby, Erich. "Cuba: The Real Winner is the Agricultural Worker." *Ceres* no. 10 (July–August 1969): 29–33.

3057. Ritter, Archibald R. *The Economic Development of Revolutionary Cuba.* New York: Praeger, 1974.

3058. ———. "Growth Strategy and Economic Performance in Revolutionary Cuba: Past, Present and Prospective." *Social and Economic Studies* 21 (September 1972): 313–337.

3059. Seers, Dudley, ed. *Cuba: The Economic and Social Revolution.* Chapel Hill: University of North Carolina Press, 1964.

The Caribbean

The article entitled "Caribbean Rural Economy" by Beckford (entry 3063) is a good introduction to the topic. Considerable information about agriculture in the region is also found in the issue of *Caribbean Quarterly* entitled "Agriculture" (entry 3061), the section of *Social and Economic Studies* edited by Beckford (entry 3064), and in the report edited by Alleyne. The latter results from a conference which has been held annually since 1966 and readers may wish to consult other volumes in this series.

May and McLellan provide a good deal of information concerning malnutrition in the region. However, their study does not supply much political analysis of the problem. Richardson concludes that plantation agriculture is so deeply embedded in the Caribbean that diversification will be difficult to achieve. Enochian identifies a number of impediments to agricultural development in the Caribbean: limited natural resources, the small size of nations in the region, the lack of complementarity among Caribbean countries, and high rates of population growth.

3060. Adams, Nassau A. "An Analysis of Food Consumption and Food Import Trends in Jamaica, 1950–1963." *Social and Economic Studies* 17 (March 1968): 1–22.

3061. "Agriculture" (Issue Title). *Caribbean Quarterly* 18 (March 1972): 5–99.

3062. Alleyne, Garth O'G., ed. *Proceedings of the Twelfth West Indies Agricultural Economic Conference.* St. Augustine, Trinidad: University of the West Indies, 1978.

3063. Beckford, George L. "Caribbean Rural Economy," pp. 77–91. In *Caribbean Economy: Dependence and Backwardness.* Ed. George L. Beckford. Kingston, Jamaica: Institute of Social and Economic Research, 1975.

3064. Beckford, George L., ed. "Agricultural Development and Planning in the Caribbean." *Social and Economic Studies* 17 (September 1968): 233–364.

3065. Buckmire, George E. "Land Use and Agricultural Development." *The Farmer* 77:3 (1972): 69–95.

3066. Davis, Darlton G. "Agricultural Research and Agricultural Development in Small Plantation Economies: The Case of the West Indies." *Social and Economic Studies* 24 (March 1975): 117–152.

3067. De Young, Maurice. *Man and Land in the Haitian Economy.* Latin American Monographs, 8. Gainesville: University of Florida Press, 1958.

3068. Duclos, B. Havard. *Rapport sur le Développement Agricole de la Région des Caraïbes.* FAO Report no. 629. Rome: Food and Agriculture Organization, 1957.

3069. Enochian, Robert V. *Prospects for Agriculture in the Caribbean.* Foreign Agricultural Economic Report, no. 58. Washington, D. C.: Economic Research Service, US Department of Agriculture, 1970.

3070. Foster, Phillips W., and Creyke, Peter. *The Structure of Plantation Agriculture in Jamaica.* Miscellaneous Publication 623. College Park: Agricultural Experiment Station, University of Maryland, 1968.

3071. Gooding, E. Graham. "Progress of Agricultural Diversification in Barbados." *World Crops* 23 (July–August 1971): 186–189.

3072. May, Jacques M., and McLellan, Donna L. *The Ecology of Malnutrition in the Caribbean.* New York: Hafner, 1973.

3073. Miller, H. C., ed. *Report on the Caribbean Conference in Agricultural Extension.* Jamaica: Ministry of Agriculture and Lands, 1966.

3074. Moral, Paul. *Le Paysan Haitien (Etude sur la Vie Rurale en Haiti).* Paris: Maisonneuve & Larose, 1961.

3075. Niddrie, David L. *Land Use and Population in Tobago.* The World Land Use Survey, Monograph 3. Bude, UK: Geographical Publications, 1961.

3076. Richardson, Bonham C. "The Agricultural Dilemma of the Post-Plantation Caribbean." *Inter-American Economic Affairs* 26:1 (1972): 59–70.

3077. Riley, Harold M.; Slater, C. C.; Harrison, Kelly et al. *Food Marketing in the Economic Development of Puerto Rico.* Marketing in Developing Communities Series, Research Report no. 4. East Lansing: Latin American Studies Center, Michigan State University, 1970.

3078. Roux, Bernard. "Aspects de la Dépendance aux Caraïbes: Agriculture et Déficit Alimentaire à la Barbade." *Revue Tiers-Monde* 19 (October–December 1978): 845–866.

3079. Sanderson, Agnes. *The Agricultural Trade of the West Indies.* FAS M–103. Washington, D. C.: Foreign Agricultural Service, US Department of Agriculture, 1961.

3080. Shillingford, John D. *A Survey of the Institutions Serving Agriculture on the Island of Dominica, W.I.* Cornell International Agricultural Development Mimeograph 35. Ithaca, N. Y.: Cornell University, 1972.

3081. United States, Department of Agriculture, Economic Research Service. *Summary and Evaluation of Jamaica, Trinidad and Tobago, Windward Islands, Barbados, and British Guiana: Projected Levels of Demand, Supply and Imports of Agricultural Products to 1975.* Washington, D. C.: 1966.

3082. Wilgus, A. Curtis, ed. *The Caribbean: Natural Resources.* Gainesville: University of Florida Press, 1961.

3083. Young, Ruth C. "The Structural Context of Caribbean Agriculture: A Comparative Study." *The Journal of Developing Areas* 10 (July 1976): 425–444.

Other Latin America

3084. Brannon, Russell H. *The Agricultural Development of Uruguay: Problems of Government.* Praeger Special Studies in International Economics and Development. New York: Praeger, 1967.

3085. Gutierrez, Alfredo; Zea-Barriga, H.; Wipplinger, W.; and Lu, M. *Paraguay: Regional Development in Eastern Paraguay.* World Bank Country Study. Washington, D. C.: Latin America and the Caribbean Regional Office, World Bank, August 1978.

3086. Heaton, Louis E. *The Agricultural Development of Venezuela.* Praeger Special Studies in International Economics and Development. New York: Praeger, 1969.

3087. Redclift, M. R. *Agrarian Reform and Peasant Organization in the Ecuadorian Coast.* London: Athlone Press, University of London, 1978.

3088. United States, Agency for International Development. *Rural Development in Venezuela. Evaluation and Recommendations.* Rural Development Series no. 2. Washington, D. C.: August 1963.

3089. Vining, James W. "The Rice Economy of Government Settlement Schemes in Guyana." *Inter-American Economic Affairs* 29 (Summer 1975): 3–20.

Part VI: Resources

Statistical Sources

Since the FAO collects so much of the data on world agriculture, it is suggested that the two monographs by Zarkovich be consulted as well as the statistics themselves. In addition, entry 3098 discusses the methods used by different countries in collecting their own statistics. This should be of particular interest to readers working with data acquired directly from developing countries. The volume produced by the US Arms Control and Disarmament Agency is included for readers who wish to compare development aid or budgetary allocations for the agricultural sector with military expenditures.

3090. Atkinson, L. Jay. *World Population Growth: Analysis and New Projections of the United Nations.* Foreign Agricultural Economic Report no. 129. Washington, D. C.: Economic Research Service, US Department of Agriculture, February 1977.

3091. Bansil, Puran Chand. *Agricultural Statistics in India.* 2nd rev. ed. New Delhi: Heinemann (India), 1974.

3092. Chrisler, Donald. *The World Agricultural Situation: Review of 1969 and Outlook for 1970.* Foreign Agricultural Economic Report no. 57. Washington, D. C.: Economic Research Service, US Department of Agriculture, February 1970.

3093. Food and Agriculture Organization. *Annual Fertilizer Review.* Rome: 1951–.

3094. ______. *Food Balance Sheets, 1964–66.* Rome: 1971.

3095. ______. *Monthly Bulletin. Food and Agricultural Statistics.* Volumes 1–5. Washington, D. C.: 1948–1952.

3096. ______. *Monthly Bulletin of Agricultural Economics and Statistics.* Vols. 1–26. Rome: 1952–1977.

3097. ______. *Monthly Bulletin of Statistics.* Vols. 1–. Rome: 1978–.

3098. ______. *National Methods of Collecting Agricultural Statistics.* 2 vols. Rome: 1974–1975.

3099. ______. *1946 Handbook of Agricultural Statistics.* Washington, D. C.: 27 July 1946.

3100. ______. *Production Yearbook.* Vols. 1–. Rome: 1951–.

3101. ______. *Report on the 1950 World Census of Agriculture.* 2 vols. Rome: 1955, 1958.

3102. ______. *Report on the 1960 World Census of Agriculture.* 5 vols. Rome: 1966–1971.

3103. ______. *Statistics of Crop Responses to Fertilizers.* Rome: 1966.

3104. ______. *Trade Yearbook.* Rome: 1958–. (Annually). (Previously Part 2 of *Yearbook of Food and Agricultural Statistics,* entry 3112.)

3105. ______. *World Crop Statistics: Area, Production, and Yield, 1948–1964.* Rome: 1966.

3106. ______. *World Forest Inventory, 1963.* Rome: 1968.

3107. ______. *World Forest Products Statistics: A Ten-Year Summary 1954–63.* Rome: 1965.

3108. ______. *World Grain Trade Statistics.* Rome: 1951–. (Annually)

3109. ______. *The World Rice Economy in Figures 1909–1963.* Commodity Reference Series no. 3. Rome: 1966.

3110. ______. *Yearbook of Fishery Statistics.* Rome: 1947–. (Beginning with 1964, two volumes are published annually: *Catches and Landings,* and *Fishery Commodities.)*

3111. ______. *Yearbook of Food and Agricultural Statistics—1947.* Washington, D. C.: 1947.

3112. ______. *Yearbook of Food and Agricultural Statistics.* Volumes 1–3. Washington, D. C.: 1948–1950.

3113. ______. *Yearbook of Forest Products Statistics.* Rome: 1947–1966.

3114. ______. *Yearbook of Forest Products.* Rome: 1967–.

3115. India (Republic), Directorate of Economics and Statistics. *Growth Rates in Agriculture: 1949–50 to 1964–65.* New Delhi: Economic and Statistical Adviser, Ministry of Food and Agriculture, Government of India, 1968.

3116. Institut National de la Recherche Agronomique, Groupe d'Etude de Relations Economiques Internationales. *Les Exportations des Etat-Unis de l'Aide Alimentaire: Bilan Chiffré 1955–1973.* Paris: INRA, 6 Passage Tenaille, n.d.

3117. International Labour Office. *Household Income and Expenditure Statistics, 1968–1976. No. 3.* Geneva: 1979.

3118. Kirby, Riley H. *Agricultural Trade of the People's Republic of China, 1935–69.* Foreign Agricultural Economic Report no. 83. Washington, D. C.: Economic Research Service, US Department of Agriculture, August 1972.

3119. Majumdar, Ashutosh Ghosh. *Distribution of Agricultural Income Arising from Crop Production in India, 1960–61 & 1970–71.* ESRF Monograph, 4. New Delhi: Economic and Scientific Research Foundation, 1973.

3120. Organization for Economic Cooperation and Development. *Aid to Agriculture in Developing Countries.* Paris: 1968.

3121. People's Republic of China, State Statistical Bureau. "Communiqué on Fulfilment of China's 1978 National Economic Plan." *Bejing Review* no. 27 (6 July 1979): 37–41. (These are the first official Chinese statistics published since entry 3122.)

3122. ———. *Ten Great Years.* Peking: 1960.

3123. Regier, Donald W. *Livestock and Derived Feed Demand in the World GOL Model.* Foreign Agricultural Economic Report no. 152. Washington, D. C.: Economic Research Service, US Department of Agriculture, September 1978.

3124. Reidinger, Richard B. *World Fertilizer Review and Prospects to 1980/81.* Foreign Agricultural Economic Report no. 115. Washington, D. C.: Economic Research Service, US Department of Agriculture, February 1976.

3125. Republic of Korea, Ministry of Agriculture and Fisheries. *Report on Results of Farm Household Economic Survey.* Seoul: various years.

3126. Salamat, M. *La Statistique Agricole dans les Pays Africains.* Rome: Regional Bureau for Africa, Food and Agriculture Organization, August 1968.

3127. United States, Arms Control and Disarmament Agency. *World Military Expenditures and Arms Transfers, 1968–1977.* Publication 100. Washington, D. C.: October 1979. (This is the most recent volume in a series that is updated every few years.)

3128. United States. Department of Agriculture. *Foreign Crops and Markets.* Weekly Bulletin. Volumes 1–85. Washington, D. C.: 1919–1962. (Incorporated into entry 3136 in 1962.)

3129. United States, Department of Agriculture, Economic Research Service. *The Agricultural Situation in Africa and West Asia. Review of 1974 and Outlook for 1975.* Foreign Agricultural Economic Report no. 108. Washington, D. C.: May 1975.

3130. ———. *The Agricultural Situation in the People's Republic of China and Other Communist Asian Countries: Review of 1974 and Outlook for 1975.* Foreign Agricultural Economic Report no. 111. Washington, D. C.: September 1975.

3131. ———. *The Agricultural Situation in the Western Hemisphere: Review of 1975 and Outlook for 1976.* Foreign Agricultural Economic Report no. 122. Washington, D. C.: July 1976.

3132. ______. *The 1966 Agricultural Data Book for the Far East and Oceania.* Washington, D. C.: 1966. (Annually)

3133. ______. *U. S. Agricultural Exports under Public Law 480.* ERS-Foreign 395. Washington, D. C.: October 1974.

3134. ______. *Western Hemisphere Agricultural Situation: Review of 1976 and Outlook for 1977.* Foreign Agricultural Economic Report no. 136. Washington, D. C.: May 1977.

3135. ______. *World Agricultural Situation.* Washington, D. C.: three times per year in June, September and December.

3136. United States, Department of Agriculture, Economics, Statistics, and Cooperatives Service. *Alternative Futures for World Food in 1985. Volume 2, World GOL Model Supply-Distribution and Related Tables.* Foreign Agricultural Economic Report no. 149. Washington, D. C.: May 1978.

3137. United States, Department of Agriculture, Foreign Agricultural Service. *Foreign Agricultural Circulars.* (Various series covering various years for different commodities.)

3138. ______. *Foreign Agricultural Trade of the United States.* Washington, D. C.: 1946–. (Monthly)

3139. Zarkovich, S. S. *The Quality of Statistical Data.* 2nd printing. Rome: Food and Agriculture Organization, 1976.

3140. ______. *Sampling Methods and Censuses.* 3rd printing. Rome: Food and Agriculture Organization, 1975.

Additional Bibliographies

A number of the entries cited here are bibliographies that are updated regularly, on a monthly or a quarterly basis. These include entries 3146, 3155, 3159, 3163, 3166, 3174, and 3220. The FAO publishes a list of its own books and reports in print annually (entry 3165). The Land Tenure Center at the University of Wisconsin-Madison publishes the Training and Methods Series of bibliographies, individual items in which are published and updated periodically (for example, entry 3183).

The resource guide published by the Institute for Food and Development Policy (entry 3173) is really a bibliographic essay rather than an annotated bibliography. It is highly recommended, particularly for activist groups and college students. The annotated bibliography by Lock, Wulf, Kalyadin, and Väyrynen (entry 3204) is included for readers who are interested in reading more on the relationship between the use of resources for military purposes and underdevelopment.

3141. Adams, Dale W.; Nehman, Gerald; and Reichert, Alan. *An Annotated Bibliography on Rural Credit & Savings in LDC's.* Occasional Paper no 84. Columbus: Ohio State University, June 1972.

3142. Anderson, Teresa J., comp. *Bolivia: Agricultura, Economía y Política: A Bibliography.* Training & Methods Series no. 7. Madison: Land Tenure Center, University of Wisconsin, December 1968. (*Supplement,* April 1970). (Largely Spanish-language sources.)

3143. Barrès, Jean-François. *Analytical Bibliography on the Sahel.* Rome: FFHC Action for Development, Food and Agriculture Organization with the support of the World Council of Churches, 1974.

3144. Bellamy, Margot A., ed. *Aspects of Agricultural Policy and Rural Development in Africa: An Annotated Bibliography.* Oxford: Commonwealth Agricultural Bureaux, 1971.

3145. Beudot, François. *Elements for a Bibliography of the Sahel Drought.* Updating nos. 1 & 2. Paris: Development Centre, Organization for Economic Cooperation and Development, November 1977 and August 1978.

3146. *Bibliography of Agriculture.* Phoenix, Ariz.: The Orynx Press, 1942–. (Monthly. Index to holdings of the US National Agricultural Library.)

3147. Blair, Patricia, comp. *Development in the People's Republic of China: A Selected Bibliography.* ODC Occasional Paper no. 8. Washington, D. C.: Overseas Development Council, 1977.

3148. Broadbent, Kieran Patrick, ed. *Chinese Agriculture and Rural Society.* Annotated Bibliography no. 30. Oxford: Commonwealth Agricultural Bureaux, 1974.

3149. ———. *The Development of Chinese Agriculture: 1949–1970: An Annotated Bibliography.* Oxford: Commonwealth Bureau of Agricultural Economics, 1971.

3150. Bush, E. A. R. *Agriculture: A Bibliographical Guide.* 2 vols. London: MacDonald, 1974.

3151. Buvinić, Mayra. *Women and World Development: An Annotated Bibliography.* Washington, D. C.: Overseas Development Council, 1976.

3152. Caldwell, John C. *African Drought Bibliography: Documents Held by the Department of Demography, Australian National University.* Canberra: Australian National University, 1974.

3153. ———. *African Drought Bibliography. First Supplement, 1974: Documents Held by the Department of Demography, Australian National University.* Canberra: Australian National University, 1974.

3154. Calvo, Manuel. *Connaissance du Système de l'Alimentation des Peuples.* 2 vols. Paris: IEDES Recherche, Université de Paris, c.1975.

3155. Centro Interamericano de Documentacíon e Informacíon Agrícola. *Indice Agrícola de América Latina y el Caribe.* Turrialba, Costa Rica: 1975–. (Quarterly. Supersedes *Bibliografia Agrícola Latinoamericana y del Caribe,* 1974, which in turn superseded *Bibliografia Agrícola Latinoamericana,* 1966–1973.)

3156. Chapman, Cynthia B. *Agricultural Policy, Food Policy, Nutrition Policy, World Food Problems: A Select Bibliography, 1969–1975.* HD 9002 Gen./75–120 SP. Washington, D. C.: Congressional Research Service, Library of Congress, 30 April 1975.

3157. Cohen, John M.; Culagovski, G. A.; Uphoff, N. T.; and Wolf, D. L. *Participation at the Local Level: A Working Bibliography.* Bibliography Series no. 1. Ithaca, N. Y.: Rural Development Committee, Center for International Studies, Cornell University, June 1978.

3158. Commonwealth Bureau of Agricultural Economics. *Chinese Agriculture and Rural Society: Annotated Bibliography.* Oxford: 1971.

3159. ———. *World Agricultural Economics and Rural Sociology Abstracts.* Oxford: 1959–. (Monthly. Covers topics such as cooperatives, extension and research, rural sociology, credit, marketing, distribution, and so on.)

3160. Conklin, H. C. "The Study of Shifting Cultivation." *Current Anthropology* 2 (February 1961): 27–61.

3161. Dean, Genevieve C. *Science and Technology in the Development of Modern China: An Annotated Bibliography.* London: Mansell, 1974.

3162. Dejene, Tekola, and Smith, Scott E. *Experiences in Rural Development: A Selected, Annotated Bibliography of Planning, Implementing and Evaluating Rural Development in Africa.* OLC Paper no. 1. Washington, D. C.: Overseas Liaison Committee, American Council on Education, August 1973.

3163. Food and Agriculture Organization. *Agrindex.* Rome: 1975. (Monthly. "International Information System for the Agricultural Sciences and Technology.")

3164. ———. *Contribution à Une Bibliographie des Phénomènes de Désertisation, de l'Ecologie Végétale, des Pâturages et du Nomadisme dans les Régions Arides de l'Afrique et de l'Asie du Sud-Ouest.* Rome: 30 October 1973.

3165. ———. *FAO Books in Print 1979.* New York: UNIPUB, 1979.

3166. ———. *FAO Documentation: Current Bibliography.* Rome: 1972–. (Monthly. Supersedes *FAO Documentation: Current Index,* 1967–1971, which in turn superseded *FAO Quarterly List of Publications and Main Documents,* February 1961–1967.)

3167. ______. *The Sahelian Zone. A Selected Bibliography for the Study of its Problems.* WI/E5460. FAO Library Occasional Bibliographies no. 9. Rome: December 1973.

3168. Food and Agriculture Organization, Rural Institutions Division. *Bibliography on Land Tenure.* Rome: 1972.

3169. Gittings, John. "Bibliography: Some Recent Writings on Development in China." *World Development* 3 (July–August 1975): 607–608.

3170. Henderson, E. *Food Aid: A Selective Annotated Bibliography on Food Utilization for Economic Development.* Rome: Food and Agriculture Organization, 1964.

3171. Imaoka, Hideki, comp. *A Selected Bibliography on Agricultural Products, With Emphasis on International Trade.* Tokyo: Institute of Developing Economies, March 1977.

3172. Institut de Recherches d'Application des Méthodes de Développement. "Bibliographie sur l'Animation en Afrique Noire." *Archives Internationales de Sociologie de la Coopération* no. 20 (July–December 1966): 200–217.

3173. Institute for Food and Development Policy Staff and Fellows. *Food First Resource Guide. Documentation on the Roots of World Hunger and Rural Poverty.* San Francisco, Calif.: Institute for Food and Development Policy, 1979.

3174. Instituut voor de Tropen. *Abstracts on Tropical Agriculture.* Amsterdam: 1975–. (Monthly. Supersedes *Tropical Abstracts,* vols. 1–29, 1946–1974.)

3175. Inter Documentation Company Ag. Catalogues on Rare Books and Serials available on Microfiche. (Includes catalogues on Africa, Asia, East Asia, Indonesia, Latin America, Middle East/North Africa, South Asia, South East Asia, social and economic development plans of LDCs. Available from IDC, Poststrasse 14, Zug, Switzerland. Catalogues free-of-charge.)

3176. International Labour Office. *Bibliography of Published Research of the World Employment Programme.* Geneva: 1975.

3177. International Rice Research Institute. *Bibliography on Socio-Economic Aspects of Asian Irrigation.* Manila: 1976.

3178. Joyce, Stephen J., and Beudot, François. *Elements for a Bibliography of the Sahel Drought.* 2 vols. Paris: Development Centre, Organization for Economic Cooperation and Development, 1976 and 1977.

3179. Katz, Saul M., and McGowan, Frank, comps. *A Selected List of U.S. Readings on Development.* Washington, D. C.: US Agency for International Development, n.d. (Annotated)

3180. Kflu, Tesfai. *A Bibliography on the Economic and Social Aspects of Agriculture in Ethiopia, Kenya, Tanzania and Uganda.* Ithaca, N. Y.: Cornell University, 1972.

3181. Lambert, Claire, ed. *Village Studies: Data Analysis and Bibliography. Volume 2: Africa, Middle East and North Africa, Asia (Excluding India), Pacific Islands, Latin America, West Indies, and the Caribbean, 1950–75.* London: Mansell, 1978.

3182. Lambert, Claire, ed., and Connell, John, comp. *Labour Utilization: An Annotated Bibliography of Village Studies.* Brighton, UK: Institute of Development Studies, University of Sussex, 1975.

3183. Land Tenure Center Library Staff. *Agrarian Reform in Brazil: A Bibliography.* 2 vols. Training & Methods Series nos. 18 and 19. Madison: Land Tenure Center, University of Wisconsin, January 1972 and April 1972. (*Supplement,* January 1977 and July 1978.) (Largely Spanish-language sources.)

3184. ———. *Agrarian Reform and Land Tenure: A List of Source Materials.* Training & Methods Series no. 4. Madison: Land Tenure Center, University of Wisconsin, August 1965.

3185. ———. *Agrarian Reform in Latin America: An Annotated Bibliography.* Land Economics Monograph no. 5. Madison: Land Tenure Center, University of Wisconsin, 1974.

3186. ———. *Agriculture in the Economy of the Caribbean: A Bibliography.* Training & Methods Series no. 24. Madison: Land Tenure Center, University of Wisconsin, June 1974.

3187. ———. *The Central American Agrarian Economy. A Bibliography. (Part I: Regional, Belize, Costa Rica, El Salvador.)* Training & Methods Series no. 26. Madison: Land Tenure Center, University of Wisconsin, September 1975.

3188. ———. *The Central American Agrarian Economy: A Bibliography. (Part II: Guatemala, Honduras, Nicaragua, Panama.)* Training & Methods Series no. 27. Madison: Land Tenure Center, University of Wisconsin, November 1978.

3189. ———. *Chile's Agricultural Economy: A Bibliography.* Training & Methods Series no. 12. Madison: Land Tenure Center, University of Wisconsin, July 1970. (*Supplement,* December 1971 and January 1974.) (Largely Spanish-language sources.)

3190. ———. *Colonization and Settlement: An Annotated Bibliography.* Training & Methods Series no. 8. Madison: Land Tenure Center, University of Wisconsin, March 1969. (*Supplement,* April 1972 and January 1977.)

3191. ———. *Colombia: Background and Trends. A Bibliography.* Training & Methods Series no. 9. Madison: Land Tenure Center, Uni-

versity of Wisconsin, May 1969. (*Supplement,* February 1971 and October 1973.) (Largely Spanish-language sources.)

3192. ______. *Cuban Agrarian Economy: A Bibliography.* Training & Methods Series no. 23. Madison: Land Tenure Center, University of Wisconsin, May 1974.

3193. ______. *East & Southeast Asia: A Bibliography.* Training & Methods Series no. 14. Madison: Land Tenure Center, University of Wisconsin, March 1971. (*Supplement,* October 1972.)

3194. ______. *Economic Aspects of Agricultural Development in Ecuador: A Bibliography.* Training & Methods Series no. 21. Madison: Land Tenure Center, University of Wisconsin, December 1972.

3195. ______. *Land Tenure and Agrarian Reform in Mexico—A Bibliography.* Training & Methods Series no. 10. Madison: Land Tenure Center, University of Wisconsin, October 1969. (*Supplement,* September 1971 and March 1976.) (Largely Spanish-language sources.)

3196. ______. *Near East & South Asia: A Bibliography.* Training & Methods Series no. 13. Madison: Land Tenure Center, University of Wisconsin, January 1971. (*Supplement,* July 1976 and October 1976.)

3197. ______. *Peru; Land and People: A Bibliography.* Training & Methods Series no. 15. Madison: Land Tenure Center, University of Wisconsin, June 1971. (*Supplement,* December 1972.) (Largely Spanish-language sources.)

3198. ______. *Rural Development in Africa: A Bibliography (Part I: General, Central, East).* Training & Methods Series no. 16. Madison: Land Tenure Center, University of Wisconsin, July 1971. (*Supplement,* March 1973 and September 1974.) (Some French-language sources.)

3199. ______. *Rural Development in Africa: A Bibliography (Part II: North, South, West).* Training & Methods Series no. 17. Madison: Land Tenure Center, University of Wisconsin, December 1971. (*Supplement,* April 1973 and December 1974.) (Some French- and German-language sources.)

3200. ______. *Rural Development in Venezuela: A Bibliography.* Training & Methods Series no. 20. Madison: Land Tenure Center, University of Wisconsin, July 1972.

3201. Lebrun, Jean. *Fertilité des Sols et Eléments de Sociologie Rurale en Afrique au Sud du Sahara.* Enquêtes Bibliographiques 10. Brussels: Centre de Documentation Economique et Sociale Africaine, 1964.

3202. Lefevre, P. C. *Alimentation des Populations Africaines au Sud du Sahara.* Enquêtes Bibliographiques 13. Brussels: Centre de Documentation Economique et Sociale Africaine, 1965.

3203. ______. *Les Paysannats en Afrique au Sud du Sahara.* Enquêtes Bibliographiques 12. Brussels: Centre de Documentation Economique et Sociale Africaine, c.1965.

3204. Lock, Peter; Wulf, H.; Kalyadin, A.; and Väyrynen, R. *Review of Research Trends and an Annotated Bibliography: Social and Economic Consequences of the Arms Race and of Disarmament.* no. 39. Paris: UN Educational, Scientific and Cultural Organization, 1978.

3205. Lott, Charlotte, comp. *Sources for Development Statistics: A Bibliography.* Training & Methods Series no. 25. Madison: Land Tenure Center, University of Wisconsin, November 1974.

3206. Lundeen, Glen, and Lundeen, Barbara. *World Food Problems Bibliography.* Fresno, Calif.: Food Science Research Center, 1969.

3207. Marks, Kenneth, comp. *World Food Problems: An Interdisciplinary View.* Ames: Iowa State University Library, 1976.

3208. Meister, Marcie, comp. *Serials for Development Studies.* Training & Methods Series no. 22. Madison: Land Tenure Center, University of Wisconsin, March 1973.

3209. Neville-Rolfe, Edmund. *Economic Aspects of Agricultural Development in Africa: A Selected Annotated Reading List of Reports and Studies Concerning 40 African Countries During the Period 1960–1969.* Oxford: University of Oxford Agricultural Economics Research Institute, 1969.

3210. Newman, Mark D. *Changing Patterns of Food Consumption in Tropical Africa: A Working Bibliography.* Working Paper no. 23. East Lansing: African Rural Economy Program, Michigan State University, January 1978.

3211. Newman, Mark D., and Wilcock, David C. *Food Self-Sufficiency, Marketing and Reserves in the Sahel: A Working Bibliography.* Working Paper no. 16. East Lansing: African Rural Economy Program, Michigan State University, September 1976.

3212. Oi Committee International. *International Development and the Human Environment: An Annotated Bibliography.* New York: Macmillan Information, 1974.

3213. Oxby, Claire. *Pastoral Nomads and Development. A Select Annotated Bibliography with Special Reference to the Sahel.* London: International African Institute, 1975.

3214. Rhett, Anita, comp. *Rural Development in Africa.* Current Reading List Series, vol. 9, no. 2. Washington, D. C.: African Bibliographic Center, 1972.

3215. Sanchez, Pedro A., ed. *A Review of Soils Research in Tropical Latin America.* Technical Bulletin no. 219. Raleigh: North Carolina Agricultural Experiment Station, in Cooperation with US Agency for International Development, July 1973. (Includes short introductory essays on the topics surveyed.)

3216. Saulniers, S. S. *Women in the Development Process: A Select Bibliography.* Austin: University of Texas Press, 1977.

3217. Sherbrooke, Wade, and Paylore, Patricia. *World Desertification: Cause and Effect. A Literature Review and Annotated Bibliography.* Tucson: Office of Arid Land Studies, University of Arizona, 1973.

3218. Talukder, Aluddin. *Bangladesh Agricultural Economics: A Select Bibliography.* Dacca: Bangladesh Institute of Development Studies, 1975.

3219. United Nations, Environment Programme, Secretariat of the United Nations Conference on Desertification. *UNEP Working Bibliography on Desertification.* Nairobi: Microfilm, 1976.

3220. United States, Agency for International Development. *A. I. D. Research and Development Abstracts.* Washington, D. C.: April 1974–. (Monthly. Announces AID-sponsored research and development studies once completed; explains how to obtain them.)

3221. United States, Agency for International Development, Bureau for Technical Assistance. *Catalogue of Research Literature for Development. Volume I: Food Production and Nutrition.* Washington, D. C.: December 1976.

3222. ______. *Catalogue of Research Literature for Development. Volume II: Food Production and Nutrition, Development and Economics, Education and Human Resources, Health, Selected Development Areas.* Washington, D. C.: December 1977.

3223. Vaptistis, M., and Patrikios, T. *Development. A Bibliography.* MI/A0572. Rome: Freedom from Hunger Campaign, Food and Agriculture Organization, 1970. (Annotated)

3224. Vasiliades, Kanella C., and Shannon, Cecille. *Bibliography for Programming for Agriculture.* EDI Sem 6. Washington, D. C.: World Bank, 1973.

3225. VITA. *Appropriate Technology in Social Context: An Annotated Bibliography.* Mt. Ranier, Md.: c.1978.

3226. Vries, C. A. de. *Agricultural Extension in the Developing Countries: A Bibliography.* Wageningen: International Institute of Land Reclamation and Improvement, 1968.

3227. Walsh, Gretchen. *Access to Sources of Information on Agricultural Development in the Sahel.* Working Paper no. 17. East Lansing: African Rural Economy Program, Michigan State University, December 1976.

3228. West, H. W., and Sawyer, O. H. M. *Land Administration.* London: Cambridge University Library, 1975.

Journals and Monograph Series of Particular Relevance

3229. *Actuel Développement.* Paris. Bimonthly.

3230. *Africa Today.* Center on International Race Relations, University of Denver, and Graduate School of International Studies, University of Denver. Quarterly.

3231. *Africa Development.* Council for the Development of Economic and Social Research in Africa. Dakar, Senegal. Quarterly.

3232. *The African Review.* Department of Political Science, University of Dar-es-Salaam. Quarterly.

3233. *Ag World.* Ag World, Inc. St. Paul, Minnesota. Monthly (except June–July).

3234. *Agricultural Mechanization in Asia.* Farm Machinery Industrial Research Group. Tokyo. Quarterly.

3235. *Agriculture and Environment.* "A Journal for Scientific Research into the Relationship Between Agriculture, Food Production, and the Management of the Biosphere." Amsterdam. Quarterly.

3236. *Ambio.* Royal Swedish Academy of Sciences. Stockholm. Bimonthly.

3237. *Appropriate Technology Journal.* Intermediate Technology Development Group. London. Quarterly.

3238. *The Bangladesh Development Studies.* The Bangladesh Institute of Development Studies. Dacca. Quarterly.

3239. *The China Quarterly.* Contemporary China Institute, School of Oriental and African Studies. London. Quarterly.

3240. *Civilisations.* The International Institute of Different Civilizations. Brussels. Quarterly.

3241. *Community Development Journal.* London. Three times per year.

3242. *Desarrollo Rural en las Américas.* Instituto Interamericano de Ciencias Agricolas de la OEA. San Jose, Costa Rica. Quarterly.

3243. *The Developing Economies.* Institute of Developing Economies. Tokyo. Quarterly.

3244. *Development and Change.* Institute of Social Studies. The Hague. Quarterly.

3245. *Development Forum.* United Nations, Division of Economic and Social Information/DPI. New York. Monthly.

3246. *Eastern Africa Journal of Rural Development.* Eastern Africa Agricultural Economics Society and Department of Rural Economy and Extension, Makerere University. Kampala, Uganda. Biannually.

3247. *Economic and Political Weekly.* Bombay, India. Weekly.

3248. *Economic Bulletin for Asia and the Pacific.* United Nations, Economic Commission for Asia and the Far East. Bangkok, Thailand. Three times per year.

3249. *Economic Development and Cultural Change.* Research Center in Economic Development and Cultural Change, University of Chicago. Chicago, Illinois. Quarterly.

3250. *Environment.* Scientists' Institute for Public Information. St. Louis, Missouri. Monthly (except January–February and July–August).

3251. *FAO Commodity Review and Outlook.* Food and Agriculture Organization. Rome. Annually.

3252. *Food and Nutrition.* Food and Agriculture Organization. Rome. Biannually.

3253. *Food Policy.* Guildford, Surrey, UK. Quarterly.

3254. *Food Research Institute Studies.* Food Research Institute, Stanford University. Stanford, California.

3255. Foreign Agricultural Economic Reports. Economic Research Service, United States Department of Agriculture. Washington, D. C. Occasional monograph series.

3256. *Foreign Agriculture.* Foreign Agricultural Service, United States Department of Agriculture. Washington, D. C. Monthly.

3257. *IDS Bulletin.* Institute of Development Studies, University of Sussex. Brighton, Sussex, UK. Quarterly.

3258. *Indian Farming.* Indian Council of Agricultural Research. Monthly.

3259. *International Labour Review.* International Labour Office. Geneva. Monthly. (Each issue contains a useful bibliography which surveys new books related to employment.)

3260. *Journal of Administration Overseas.* Social Affairs Department, Ministry of Overseas Development. London. Quarterly.

3261. *Journal of Contemporary Asia.* Stockholm and London. Quarterly.

3262. *The Journal of Developing Areas.* Western Illinois University. Quarterly.

3263. *The Journal of Development Studies.* London. Quarterly.

3264. *Journal of Modern African Studies.* London. Quarterly.

3265. *The Journal of Peasant Studies.* London. Quarterly.

3266. *Journal of Rural Cooperatives.* International Research Center on Rural Cooperative Communities. Tel Aviv.

3267. *The Journal of Tropical Geography.* Department of Geography, University of Singapore, and Department of Geography, University of Malaya. Biannually.

3268. *Land Reform.* Rural Institutions Division, Food and Agriculture Organization. Rome. Biannually.

3269. *Land Tenure Center Newsletter.* Land Tenure Center, University of Wisconsin. Madison, Wisconsin. Quarterly.

3270. Land Tenure Center Research Papers. Land Tenure Center, University of Wisconsin. Madison, Wisconsin. Occasional paper series.

3271. Land Tenure Center Papers, LTC Series. Land Tenure Center, University of Wisconsin. Madison, Wisconsin. Occasional paper series.

3272. Land Tenure Center Training & Methods Series. Land Tenure Center. University of Wisconsin. Madison, Wisconsin. Occasional bibliography series.

3273. *Nature and Resources.* United Nations Educational, Scientific and Cultural Organization. Paris. Quarterly.

3274. *The New Ecologist.* Wadebridge, Cornwall, UK. Bimonthly.

3275. *The Nigerian Geographical Journal.* The Nigerian Geographical Association. Ibadan. Biannually.

3276. *ODI Review.* Overseas Development Institute. London. Biannually.

3277. *Pacific Affairs.* University of British Columbia. Vancouver. Quarterly.

3278. *Problemas del Desarrollo.* Instituto de Investigaciones Económica. Mexico City. Quarterly.

3279. *Review of African Political Economy.* Sheffield, UK. Three times per year. (Each issue contains a section entitled "Current Africana" in which some 300–400 recent books and articles relating to all aspects of African development are listed.)

3280. *Revue Tiers-Monde.* L'Institut d'Etude du Développement Economique et Social, Université de Paris. Quarterly.

3281. *Rural Africana.* African Studies Center, Michigan State University. East Lansing. Occasional.

3282. *Third World Quarterly.* Third World Foundation for Social and Economic Studies. London. Quarterly.

3283. *World Agriculture.* International Federation of Agricultural Producers. Paris. Quarterly. (Available in French also.)

3284. *World Crops.* London. Monthly.

3285. *World Development.* Oxford, UK. Monthly.

3286. Worldwatch Papers. Worldwatch Institute. Washington, D. C. Occasional paper series.

Glossary of Terms

capital intensive development: . . . development requiring heavy use of capital rather than heavy use of labor power

factor endowments: . . . . (usually) land, labor, and capital

Green Revolution: . . . . agricultural development strategy based on the use of high-yielding varieties of seeds plus such inputs as fertilizer and water, developed initially by the Centro Internacional de Mejoramiento de Maiz y Trigo (CIMMYT) and the International Rice Research Institute (IRRI) which, it was hoped, would cause substantial increases in third world food production

import-substitution development strategies: . . . . strategies that promote the domestic production of goods otherwise imported

inputs: . . . . water, fertilizer, pesticides, improved seeds

labor intensive development: . . . . the reverse of capital intensive—development requiring heavy use of labor power

land ceilings: . . . . legal restrictions on the amount of land that any one person may own

marginalization: . . . . impoverishment plus the closing of options available to people being driven to the margins of existence

marginal savings behavior: . . . . . . degree to which an individual or a group (for example, landlords or smallholders) saves an increase in income rather than consumes it minimum-needs program: ...... a program that provides, or helps provide, the poor to obtain the minimum needs of food, health care, housing, and clothing

monetarization: .... spreading the use of money to segments of an economy that previously did not use money

productive resources: .... land and capital labor

villagization: .... a policy followed by the Tanzanian government which involved the mandatory resettlement of farmers (living in scattered groups) in villages

Author Index

Author Index Errata

The following entries were omitted from page 365.

World Hunger: A Guide to the Economic and Political Dimensions
by NICOLE BALL

ABC-Clio

SANTA BARBARA OXFORD

Subject Index

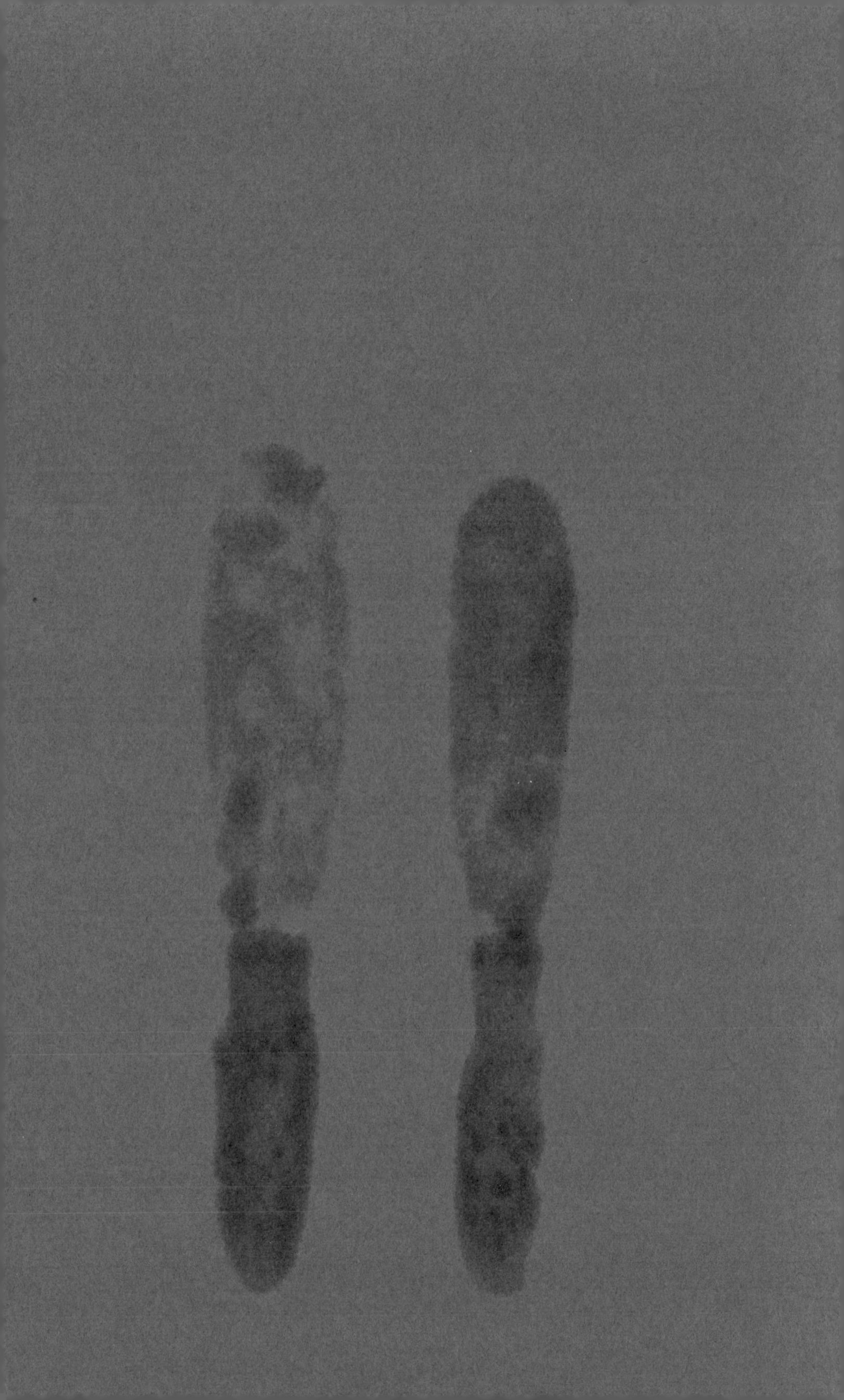

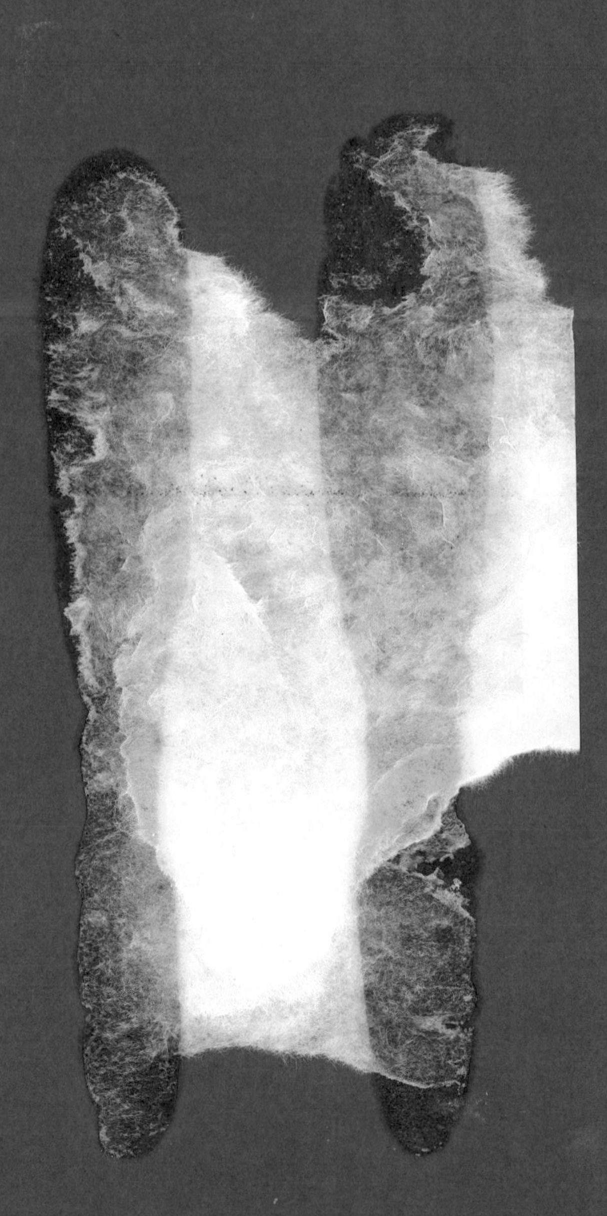